# Piano Music
## of
# Six Great Composers

# Piano Music
## of
# Six Great Composers

## Donald N. Ferguson

*Essay Index Reprint Series*

 BOOKS FOR LIBRARIES PRESS
FREEPORT, NEW YORK

STANDARD BOOK NUMBER:

8369-1652-2


LIBRARY OF CONGRESS CATALOG CARD NUMBER:

73-111830


PRINTED IN THE UNITED STATES OF AMERICA

To

CELIUS DOUGHERTY

*An echo of our distant Wednesdays*

# FOREWORD

~~~~~~~~~~~~~~~~~~~~~~~~~~~~~~~~~~~~~~~~~~~~~~~~~~~~~~~~~

THIS BOOK is frankly an experiment. It is an attempt to present, in comparatively compact space but with reference to a large number of musical problems, that word to the wise which the proverb says is sufficient.

It assumes on the part of the reader no profound musical knowledge, but nevertheless a certain musical wisdom. The ability—or perhaps one should rather say, the disposition—to read music accurately is presupposed, including that decent respect for time values which does not always accompany precise observation of the pitch values of notes. It assumes also some familiarity with the ordinary terminology of music. But this being taken for granted, the book is addressed to the reader's common sense, a faculty indispensable to wisdom; and it is thus addressed because of the author's belief—often disappointed, yet in the main substantiated by long practical experience—that the true musical instinct, which is a species of common sense, is not rare, and that that faculty, properly oriented, is capable of illuminated vision.

The experiment has been set up with care. The orienting facts have been set forth with every effort toward clarity, and the more general appeals to the reader's intuition have been made in the hope that they will be seen to rest upon or derive from a basis of knowable fact. The most indisputable of these facts—and for many readers doubtless the most unwelcome—is that the piano is a mechanism, whose operation is in no way miraculous. Good piano playing does indeed disguise this fact successfully and might almost be said to be good in proportion as it is successful. The highly gifted pianist may often achieve the most flawless results without ever being aware of the mechanical fact; but even he cannot produce those results in defiance of it. And his intuitive discovery of the possibilities of his instrument is almost inevitably slower than it might have been if the nature and the limitations of the mechanism had been recognized from the beginning.

These limitations have therefore been discussed at the outset. What follows is an attempt to shorten the reader's path to an interpretative understanding of a fairly large portion of the great literature of the piano—and to shorten it by recognizing and invoking the elemental facts. Appeal to the intuition is often made. In many instances, indeed, it is the only offered comment; for it is evident that minute discussion of the technical problems presented by all the compositions mentioned would fill innumerable pages. It is believed, however, that enough detailed analysis of technical and interpretative questions has been offered so that the reader, having studied in this light a number of works of a given grade, may interpret similar pieces for himself with a growing confidence in his own judgment.

In the selection of certain compositions for detailed study, and in the consequent rejection of others, it may appear that the author's personal preference, rather than the individual reader's need or desire, has been consulted. Against this plea, the only defense that can be offered is that the selection has been made rather out of the writer's experience of his pupils' interest than out of his own, and that he had no better guide than the preference of those pupils to show him what would probably be the most interesting pieces for his readers.

It may also be objected that the book is confined almost wholly to music of the nineteenth century. But for such an experiment as this, it was natural to deal with the period in which the pianoforte had emerged as the world's most favored solo instrument and in which the most significant literature for that instrument was written. Keyboard music before the end of the eighteenth century was composed not for the piano but for the harpsichord or the clavichord, and the transfer to the piano of music in this older idiom is a special problem, best solved when the literature here explored is familiar. The author can imagine no pleasanter task than to attempt another experiment in that field. But he would need, for such an effort, to know in what ways this present experiment has been at fault. Criticism in this direction will be most gratefully received.

The following is a list of the easier compositions for which more or less explicit directions for study are given in the text. They are divided into two grades, the second being the more difficult. It should be understood that all the comments presuppose the approach suggested in Chapter 1.

## I

## II

The student who has mastered a fair number of these pieces may browse at will among the more difficult numbers. It would serve no purpose to attempt to grade these according to their difficulty.

# CONTENTS

# Piano Music
## of
# Six Great Composers

# 1
# THE PIANO
# AND ITS POSSIBILITIES

A̲LL of us, either in our own homes or at public concerts, have occasionally had the experience of hearing the same piano played by two or more performers; and we have all remarked (whether audibly or not) the extraordinary differences in the sounds they evoked. Under the fingers of the one, the piano sounded like the mechanical contraption of wood and wire which it obviously is; but when the other played, fiddles and flutes and horns seemed to be hidden in the long black box, and we almost believed that he was playing these instruments instead of his own. We felt that this performer had a beautiful touch. The one, perhaps more skilful, was nevertheless hard and brittle—lacking that "musicalness" and that beauty of tone which was apparent in the other's every phrase.

The beautiful touch, therefore, must be that which produces beautiful quality in tones. And since the act of touch is unquestionably a kind of contact between fingers and keys, we are moved to explore both the act of the finger and the behavior of that mechanism inside the piano which produces the tone. The ultimate origin of the finger's act is the imagination—a region so difficult to explore that we shall avoid that effort as long as we can. We may, however, explore the piano, which is the

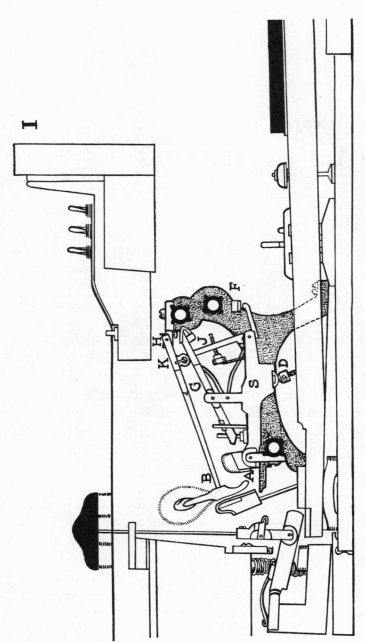

I. The Hammer at Rest. When the key is depressed, the "capstan," D, will lift the whole "support," S, which is pivoted at A. The "jack," J, will thus be driven against the "Knuckle," K (the round knob on the hammer-shank, B). This shank is pivoted at H. The jack, which is pivoted at its lower end (at the extremity of the support), has a projecting arm which, as the jack rises, is tripped by the "button," F. The upper end of the jack, therefore, which rises through a slot in the "balancier," G, to strike the knuckle, moves also to the right, thus giving a glancing stroke on the knuckle. It is this glancing stroke which makes it impossible for the jack to remain in contact with the knuckle until the hammer reaches the string. (If you depress the key very slowly, you can feel the slip of the jack off the knuckle.) The damper is now in contact with the string. When the key is struck, it will obviously be lifted clear of the string.

II. The Hammer in Action. The hammer at the instant of its contact with the string. The jack is shown, shifted to the right, and out of contact with the knuckle—as it must be, if the hammer reaches the string.

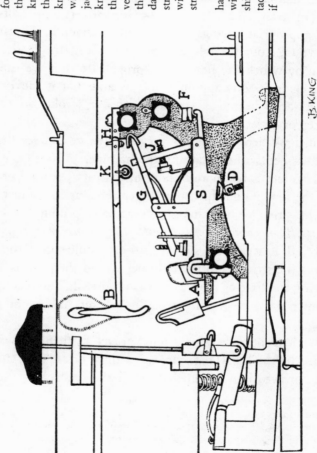

physical source of the music. Let us therefore look inside the instrument and see what happens when it responds—as it obediently does—either to the hard or the beautiful touch; for everything obviously depends on what happens here.

What we find, when we lift the lid, does not immediately suggest imaginative music. We see a great array of strings—enough so that there are for the most part three to every note. And beneath them (or in front, in uprights) is the "action"—a row of felt hammers on sticks, which, when the keys are depressed, rise (in grand pianos) or move forward (in uprights), strike their appropriate strings, and instantly rebound. We cannot, unless we take out the whole action, see all of the intricate mechanism by which the hammer is propelled; [1] but we can see that it travels in its one appointed plane, and that it moves faster or slower, accordingly as the force of our stroke on the key is greater or lesser.

But if we depress the key very slowly, we can see that it may reach its bed without causing the hammer to touch the string at all. This fact is far more important than it appears. For it means that the key, with which our finger remains in contact throughout the stroke, when that stroke actually produces a tone, *does not itself maintain contact with the hammer throughout the stroke*. If it were not so, our stroke would press the hammer against the string, and the hammer would then act as a damper, choking the tone as soon as it was produced. The rebound of the hammer must be instantaneous to permit full vibration of the string.

The hammer, therefore, must travel farther than it can be pushed by the key. That is to say, it must be *thrown;* and having been thrown, it is as much beyond the control of the striking

[1] Most of it is designed to catch the hammer as it rebounds, without its having to return to its original point of rest. From this position a quicker repetition of the hammer-stroke is possible than if the hammer had to return all the way. But nothing in the elaborate mechanism alters the essential facts of the hammer's behavior, which are described in the text.

finger as if it were a ball thrown from the hand. The hammer is actually propelled by a little stick called a "jack," or sometimes a "hopper," which strikes the hammer-shank near its joint. As a matter of fact, the shank loses contact with the jack instantaneously—as you can see from the simplified diagram of the action, on pages 2 and 3.

The beautiful touch is thus no more than an instantaneous contact between the jack and the hammer-shank. The speed of the hammer is determined by the speed with which the key descends. Once that speed has been imparted the player has no further control over the resultant tone. Either he can let it continue until the energy imparted to the string is exhausted, or he can silence it by releasing the key; but he can do nothing whatever to the vibrating string to change its quality.

However unpromising for the imagination, these are obvious and unalterable facts; and those which remain to be described are no more inspiring. You can see quite clearly the dampers by which the tone of the string may be silenced. They are little felt pads that lie in contact with the strings unless they are lifted. There are two means for lifting them: the individual key, which, when it propels the hammer, at the same time lifts the damper from its string; and the "damper" (the right-hand) pedal, which, depressed, lifts all the dampers at once, leaving all the strings free to vibrate. The release of the key, or of the pedal, causes the dampers to fall back onto the strings.

The "soft" (the left-hand) pedal, in grand pianos, shifts the whole keyboard slightly to the right, and thus causes the hammers to strike only two of the three unison strings that are provided for most of the notes. The volume of the tone is thus lessened. Its quality is also (to an undetermined degree) affected by the sympathetic vibration of the unstruck string. In uprights, the whole row of hammers is moved slightly forward, thus lessening the distance the hammer must travel to the string, and so its acceleration or imparted energy. But neither pedal has any effect on the essential behavior of the hammer, nor—in consequence—upon the act of touch.[2]

The tone of the piano, however, with the damper pedal depressed, is perceptibly different from its tone without the pedal. Strike any key (say, the C an octave above middle C) without the pedal, and listen attentively to its tone. Depress the pedal and strike the same key, with the same force. The tone is now decidedly richer—because a considerable number of strings have added a part of their own vibration to that of the tone coming from the string you struck. These strings are vibrating "sympathetically" with the one originally activated string.[3] You may

[2] All American grands, and some uprights, have a third pedal between the damper (in popular jargon, the "loud") and the soft pedals. This is a "sostenuto" or selective pedal which, depressed while any keys are held down, will hold up the dampers *of those keys only* until the pedal is released. It is useful for sustaining notes which cannot be held by the fingers; but its operation is somewhat tricky, and its effect is the same as if the dampers were lifted by any other means. It has no influence on the tone.

[3] Since the phenomenon of sympathetic vibration is familiar to many, we may confine its explanation to a footnote. Such vibrations occur when a body (not only a string, but a vase, a metal plate, or any other object) which is so constituted as to vibrate at a given pitch is acted upon by sound waves from another source which are of that same frequency (or pitch). The energy transmitted through the air from the source of sound is sufficient to set up vibration in that sympathetic object. Hold down the pedal, sing loudly a single note, and you will hear the piano sing that note after you are silent.

But strings and other sources of musical tone do not vibrate merely at that "fundamental" pitch which you hear them give out. They vibrate also in fractions of their length; and every fractional vibration produces a tone, much fainter than the fundamental, but often loud enough to be heard clearly if the fundamental is silenced. Any sounding string vibrates, not only as a whole, but in halves, thirds, quarters, fifths, sixths, and so on, of its whole length. The tones thus produced are called the "harmonic series"—"harmonic" being another name for a fractional or "partial" vibration of a string, a column of air in an organ pipe, or any other source of tone. Here is the harmonic series of C':

1 2 3 4 5 6 7 8 9 10 11 12 13 14 15 16
The notes in parentheses are out of tune with our scale.

The proportional length of the fraction that produces the given partial will be indicated by placing 1 as the numerator of a fraction of which the partial's num-

easily discover the presence of their vibration by this simple experiment:

Depress *silently* C' (No. 1 in the series illustrated in the footnote) and hold down the key. Strike sharply middle C (No. 4), perhaps two or three times; hold it for a second, and release it. You will still hear middle C; and to prove that it comes from the low C string, release that key. The sound—which was produced by the vibration of the low string in quarters of its length—will stop. Now depress middle C silently and strike the low C. Middle C will prove to be vibrating. Now hold the low C and strike the whole chord of middle C—Nos. 4, 5, and 6. You can hear the whole chord from the one low string.

Since all the strings are free to vibrate when the damper pedal is depressed, it is obvious that a great complex of sympathetic vibrations must arise when a chord, or even a note, is struck. Thus the enrichment of the single tone you struck was an inevitable result of that stroke with the pedal depressed. The various qualities of tone producible by the use of the pedals are thus readily at the pianist's command. They are not strictly effects of touch, however, for the pedals operate quite independently of the hammers.

There is one other factor inevitable in the operation of the keys which is generally (and for the most part rightly) ignored: the factor of noise. The impact of the hammer on the string, and of the key on its bed, produces a kind of thud, generally proportionate to the force of the blow on the key, which is ordinarily inaudible—or at least unobserved—since it is drowned in the tone of the string, and is of no apparent musical interest. If you

---

ber is the denominator: i.e., g (No. 6) is produced by the vibration of $1/6$ of the whole string; d' (No. 9), by $1/9$, and so on. The frequencies of the partials are in the proportion of the numbers in the series, and any two stand to each other in the ratio of their respective numbers: *i.e.*, C' : G :: 1: 3; c : e :: 4 : 5; d' : e' :: 9 : 10. The actual frequencies of any partial may be found by multiplying the frequency of the fundamental by the series number of the partial: for example, if C' = 64, then G (No. 3) = 64 × 3 = 192; e' (No. 10) = 640, and so on.

damp a string with a firm pressure of your finger, and then strike its key, you can get a fair idea of the amount of noise that is added to the tone of the piano by the action. It is doubtless true that incisive strokes on notes or chords produce more noise than gentle, "relaxed" strokes; and the bite of a vigorous rhythm can in this way be sharpened, just as the fluidity of a legato melody may be increased by avoiding this noise as far as possible.[4]

You will look in vain for any other means of producing or coloring the tone of the piano than those we have described. What they add up to is the fact that the pianist can produce, *with his fingers only,* nothing more than tones of any desired volume, from the softest to the loudest of which his fingers are capable. He can color that tone with one or both of the pedals; but neither you nor I nor the greatest pianist in the world has more at his disposal than these simple resources.

"And do you mean to say," you will ask, "that the secret of the beautiful touch is explained by these commonplace and even disagreeable facts?"

The answer is, of course, that as yet we have not even attempted to explain the beautiful touch. We have only set forth facts about the operation of the piano. But if these are facts (and they have been amply demonstrated in the physical laboratory [5]), they provide us with a framework of physical law within which alone the explanation can be found. You would never pretend to judge the beauty of a pianist's touch from hearing him strike a single note, or a single common chord. You have forgotten that when you decided that one of those pianists whom we mentioned at the beginning did possess such a touch, you were hearing not merely tones and chords, but *music;* and the question is not one of the beauty of an isolated tone, but of the appropriateness of a given tone to the musical idea you were hearing.

---

[4] For a stimulating discussion of this point, see the article by W. G. Hill, "Noise in Piano Tone," *Musical Quarterly,* Vol. 26 (1940), 244.

[5] See *The Physical Basis of Piano Touch,* by Otto Ortmann, Dutton, 1925.

The problem of the beautiful touch is the problem of producing, out of no more than the resources we have described, such sequences and complexes of tone as will yield a vivid musical idea. These resources are but few; yet they are far less meager than those at the disposal of the half-tone engraver, for example, who illustrates our daily newspapers. Look closely at one of those pictures—if convenient, with a magnifying glass. What you find, in detail, is a distribution of diamond-shaped black specks, some larger and some smaller, on white paper. But what you see, when you look at the whole picture, is a very tolerable representation of a burning building, or a river in flood, or Miss America. Your eye, aided by your intelligence, makes an image of reality out of a collection of small black specks. Is it any more impossible that your ear—aided also by your intelligence—can make an image of musical beauty out of louder and softer tones (which are like the larger and smaller specks), especially when these tones are colored, as they can be, by the pedals?

Our study of the resources of the instrument has now made it possible for us to formulate a theoretical statement of the essentials of the beautiful touch. We can say that the act of touch, at its highest perfection, consists in the application of exactly the right forces to the right keys at the right moment. (The addition of appropriate color through the pedals, although highly significant, is not in the strict sense an act of touch.) The judgment, however, of what is the right force can be made only when the act of touch is devoted to the utterance of a musical idea.

Let us turn, then, to a fairly simple example of music, and try to see all that the fingers (together with the indispensable feet) must do to "realize" a musical idea. Take the Chopin *Prélude in D-flat, Op. 28, No. 15*. We shall have to study its melody, its harmony, and its rhythm, so that our analysis will be considerably extended. We shall begin with the melody.

If you play the first eight bars of this melody (without any accompaniment) you will feel that you have uttered a clear, well-rounded musical sentence. But you will also feel that for any proper utterance this sentence must be more definitely punctuated than Chopin, with his one long slur, cared to indicate.[6] You will feel that something like a comma should be placed after the C, in bar 2; that a semicolon—or perhaps a colon—should follow the quarter note, D-flat, in bar 4; that there should be another comma after the C in bar 6, and a period after the last note of the sentence—D-flat. Each of these smaller divisions is analogous to a phrase of words, just as the whole eight-bar section is analogous to the sentence.

Commas, semicolons, and periods, however, indicate only the gross divisions of the thought which is expressed in a sentence. Whether in words or in music, each phrase demands *inflection*— a "bending" of the voice to suit not only the literal sense but also the implication of the words or the tones. In every well-uttered phrase, whether of words or music, there will be a point of highest intensity or stress, which is determined by no rule of syntax, but by the particular meaning intended to be conveyed. The phrase, "I am going to New York," without any change in its syntax, may have many shades of meaning. I may say, *"I* am going to New York," or "I *am* going to New York," or "I am *going* to New York," or "I am going to *New York";* and each inflection represents a considerably different feeling of expectation. Unless a predominant emphasis appears somewhere, the whole utterance will be insignificant. "I AM GOING TO NEW YORK" may look very threatening, but its loud noise smacks of violence, rather than of any purpose; and its equivalent in music—a phrase in which every note receives heavy and equal emphasis—is similarly pointless and fatiguing.

A first rule of musical expression is thus revealed. *In any melodic phrase, some one note must be predominant.* In phrases

---

[6] The slur, as a mark of punctuation, was very carelessly treated by all composers until the last half of the nineteenth century. Chopin was by no means the only offender.

of some length, also, points of secondary emphasis will appear. And not only must the gradations between these points be so managed as to show the continuity (the musical syntax) of the whole phrase: the successive phrases and sentences must themselves be similarly weighted, according to their relative significance in the whole discourse.

No more than in language is there any rule that will tell us where this emphasis is to fall. A certain rhythmic stress will usually fall on the first beat of any measure, but there is no certainty that the *rhetorical* stress will also fall on this note. Indeed, it may fall almost anywhere, just as it did in the verbal phrase, above. It is not the purpose of the good interpreter, however, to devise an unusual meaning for his phrase. It is his problem to utter the meaning the composer intended; and with well-written music this question is probably not more difficult than with well-written words. Chopin seems to have given no more than the very general direction, *Sostenuto,* for the whole first sentence. (Even the *p,* appearing in many editions, seems to be an editorial addition.) We must therefore find these points of emphasis from the "context"—that is, by the exercise of our musical common sense.

Three notes, the initial F, the A-flat, and the C, will each bear some stress. Which should predominate?

The F is the highest note of all, and it falls on a strong beat. But if we put our major stress here, the rest of the phrase seems to trail off into indifference; and no good writer begins with such a phrase. The A-flat makes sense in the strong position; but with the weight here, the two preceding notes sound like an "up-beat," and A-flat sounds as if it were "one" in the measure. Chopin, however, put it on "two," and we have no right to contradict him.

The final C, then, remains. It also is a "one," and, although it is not so high as the F, it is longer. It is, moreover, the seventh note of the scale of our D-flat key: the "leading tone," and an

"active" note.[7] Its intrinsic interest is thus greater than that of F.
Emphasized predominantly, it creates expectancy (and loses this
quality with lessened stress). And its greater length almost automatically accomplishes the sense of punctuation which we felt
to be unmistakable after this note.

The initial F, then, will have only secondary emphasis. Even
so, it is hard to manage. Played in strict time, it seems either too
weak (if subordinated to the C) or too strong (if it compels us
to exceed the dynamic range of *piano* for the final C). The solution will be found in a resource which we have as yet ignored—
that of elasticity in rhythm.

This elasticity is again an inflection—a bending of the normally
precise timing of those successions of accent and nonaccent which
give us the patterns of rhythm. Musical rhythm, however, is more
than a pattern of accents and nonaccents. It is *motion*—patterned,
to be sure, else it would be neither interesting nor intelligible—
but motion of a body without its equal for fluidity, grace, or
energy: the body of tone. Because it is so fluid, this tonal body seldom needs to depart perceptibly from the path of regularity in
time. Sometimes, nevertheless, it must do so, if it is not to appear
cramped and rigid. Just when to depart from strict time is a
question that cannot be answered by rule. Good musicians, however, all follow a practice in this matter which can be stated in
this way: Keep to strict time as far as you can, gaining your effects through dynamic variety only, together with such variations
of quality as are available. Use *Tempo rubato* ("Stolen time"—
the conventional name for controlled departures from strict time)
only when the desired effect can be gained by no other means;

---

[7] "Leading" in the sense of "drawing toward," not in the sense of "leader" or
"most important" note. "Active" needs to be more fully explained.

Musical common sense agrees that the keynote or tonic is the firmest note of
the scale. The common chord or "triad" of this note (here, the chord D-flat–F–
A-flat) is a similarly firm harmony. This is so generally perceived that even when
the notes of the scale appear merely in succession, as in melody, the notes of the
tonic chord are felt as "rest" tones. All the other notes, diatonic or chromatic, are
"active," and tend, ultimately, to progress to the nearest rest tone in the scale.

and be sure that the underlying pattern of the rhythm is always perceptible. (That is to say, hastened or retarded eighth, quarter, or half notes must always be intelligible as such, so that the *proportions* of the rhythm are inviolate.)

This resource we shall have to apply, if we are to realize fully the meaning of our phrase. If we lengthen, ever so little, the time of this first note, we can now feel that its emphasis is sufficient, while at the same time the C may now have its proper dynamic stress. Such a time stress, applied to a single note, is often called an *agogic*[8] accent. You will find, as your discrimination of musical values increases, that it is often hard to tell whether a note is really a little louder, or is a little longer, than normal. This fact makes possible the substitution of agogic for dynamic accent; but if you make the note *perceptibly* too long, you will have no substitution, but only a distortion.[9]

The next melodic phrase will evoke no argument. The high G-flat, although on a weak beat of the bar, is unmistakable as the point of greatest stress; and of the two following F's, the second (on the "one" of the next bar) is obviously louder than the first, though decidedly less loud than the G-flat. Note also that there must be no retardation in the approach to the final note of the phrase (D-flat); for the sense at this point is still that of going on, and a *rit.* would bring about the full stop that must not be felt until the real end of the sentence, four bars later. (There, indeed, a slight retardation will be found altogether suitable.)

Having determined the contour of our melodic phrases, we may now turn to the accompaniment. We shall see at once that a similar discrimination in dynamic values is necessary here; and

[8] From a Greek word, *agōgē,* meaning a leading toward, and also a drawing out. It was apparently first used as a musical term by Dr. Hugo Riemann.

[9] The importance of this dynamic shading for the conveyance of melodic meaning will be more clearly seen if we deliberately put our stress in the wrong place. If we make the B-flat the predominant note, the phrase becomes sentimental; and if we thus exaggerate the sixteenth-note, D-flat, the effect is almost hysterical. Sentimentality, indeed, may be not inaccurately defined as a great fuss about things that do not really matter.

there will also be the problem of relating the accompaniment to the melody.

The first note, the low D-flat, is the essential bass of the harmony for the whole bar, even though it is written as an eighth note. It must have body, therefore, and more length than is indicated. (This, of course, can be given by the pedal.) It must support and enrich the F and the following notes of the melody. You will find that if it is too soft, the F will sound harsh; if it is too loud, the F will lose its significance as a point of secondary stress in the melody.

The next left-hand note, A-flat, weak in both rhythm and harmonic interest, will be much softer; but the following notes $\frac{\text{F}}{\text{D-flat}}$, have the higher importance that is indicated by their notation as half notes. These two, however, are not alike. F is harmonically the more valuable, and must be a little louder than the D-flat. The next three A-flat's would be inconspicuous if it were not that they initiate one of the principal features of this piece—the incessant beating on this one note. A slight increase in their intensity will not only signalize their coming high significance, but will also be assimilated into our valuation of the melody itself.

With this approach, the B-flat of the melody may be a little more fully supported by the repeated third in the accompaniment, so that the whole substance will seem to press forward (in tone, but not in hastened speed) toward the dissonant third, $\frac{\text{G-flat}}{\text{E-flat}}$, which harmonizes the climactic note of the phrase. Thereafter, the reiterated A-flat's undergo an undulation (A-flat–B-flat–A-flat) that will again be absorbed into our sense of the melodic tone. This undulation is another inflection that helps to convey the sense of the comma at the phrase end.

We have used an alarming number of words to describe five melodic notes and their accompaniment; but the subtle and ever-changing values we have discussed will prove, if the reader will translate them into finger acts, no more than that which is the constant endeavor of any sensitive pianist to realize. It should be noted that save for one point of agogic emphasis, every comment on the first phrase has been concerned with dynamic gradations. And if these have been now satisfactorily mastered, the reader will already have proved for himself that the beautiful touch is indeed a high sensitivity to dynamic values, and a subtle control of their execution.

In our concentration on the working of the fingers, we have omitted any minute consideration of the pedal. This omission must now be remedied. We have seen what the pedal does; we must now see how it is to be operated.

Its chief function is to aid in the playing of *legato*. This word means "bound together"—that is, connected without break. The notes of melody ordinarily can be so played without the pedal. Note that to produce this continuity, the finger that has struck the first note must hold down its key until the next note is sounded. In other words, the damper of the first note will fall upon its string at the instant when the next note is sounded. (If it is released too early, there will be silence between the two notes; if it is released too late, the two will sound together, perhaps making a disagreeable harmony, as with A–B-flat). Now, the function of the pedal is also to operate the dampers. We can play a scale legato with the fingers alone, manipulating the dampers in the manner just described. But we can also manage this effect with the pedal; and to do so will give us a fundamental process for the use of that device.

Strike C. Immediately thereafter, depress the pedal. You may now release the C key without silencing the tone. After the C, thus sustained, has been clearly heard, strike D, and, *at the instant of that stroke,* release the pedal. You will have done to the C damper, with your foot, exactly what you did with the finger before you began to use the pedal. Observe that the motion of your foot, when the new note is struck, is *upward,* just as was the motion *of the finger that released the key.* If you are not already habituated to this motion, it may take a little practice to make it automatic; but it will soon become so. Observe that the pedal is depressed *after* the stroke of the finger on the note which it is desired to hold. The depression may occur at any time, so long as the finger is holding the key; but since the pedal greatly enriches the tone, it is best to depress it immediately after the finger stroke.[10]

The soft pedal requires no especial skill. It may be used at the player's discretion; but it is easy to fall into the habit of using it whenever the general intensity falls as low as *piano*—certainly a bad habit. Your fingers need to learn the command of wide dynamic gradations, and to use the soft pedal for the whole lower register of dynamics is to leave the fingers insensitive just where sensitivity is most needed. For it is important to note that gradations of loudness within the range of piano are far more perceptible to the ear than are such gradations in forte. (All our senses are alike in this regard. To turn on all the lamps in the room makes little difference if the sun is shining in at the window; but the merest match flare, in a dark room, seems almost a glare of light.)

The three following phrases of our musical sentence will now hardly require comment. Although we shall make no retardation at the end of the second phrase, in bar 4, the ornamental approach to the third phrase may be slightly lengthened in time.

---

[10] The Chopin *Prélude in C minor, Op. 28, No. 20,* is an excellent study in what is often called "syncopated" pedaling. Each chord must be "caught" with the pedal *before* the hands are released to prepare the attack of the next chord; the pedal must be released *with* each new chord. Do not release the pedal with the sixteenth notes in the third beat of each bar. Although dissonant, they are so short that their collision with the existing harmony is not perceptible. You will find it possible to pedal right over many such dissonances; but only your ear can tell you whether to sustain or to release the pedal. In fact, the experienced pianist almost never thinks consciously of his foot, but only of the effect his pedal is making. He learns, that is, to pedal "by ear": there is no other guide so good.

Although the third and fourth phrases are almost identical with the first two, they will not be played with identical shading. The third phrase might be made a little louder than the first; but the reader will probably agree with us that it is more meaningful when played still softer, though with about the same general gradations. The final phrase, on the other hand, may be just a little louder than the second, and with a very slight *rit.* for the last three notes.

We have attempted to embody the gist of our long description in the notation of this sentence given below. The figures above or below the notes are not fingerings, but signs for tone gradation. They range from 1 to 6; yet all are assumed to be contained within the general range of piano. You will perhaps find it hard to keep within this range. The gradations are the principal problem, however, and if you get them too wide at first, you will learn by practice how to contain them within the desired range, and still make them perceptible.

The foregoing is a fairly accurate sketch of the operation of

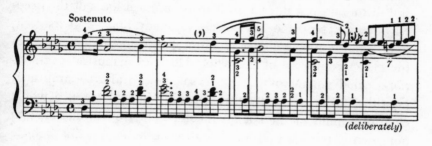

the hands, the feet, and the mind of the performing pianist. But it describes the product of his thinking and action, rather than his thought itself. No skilled performer thinks as slowly as this, nor does he calculate, consciously, his effects. Skill is an acquired power of unconscious action toward a desired end; and when the skill has been acquired, conscious thinking will be directed wholly toward the end. That end is here the impressive utterance of a musical idea, through the medium of an instrument that is capable of little else than an infinite gradation of dynamics. The required skill, therefore, is chiefly a command of dynamic gradations. "Command," however, does not mean, or even imply, laborious calculation. It means the use of these powers, just as you use the possible flexibilities and gradations of your voice in speaking English, as the immediate resources through which you express a thought.

To those of us who have musical common sense—and there are many such—a musical thought is no mystery. We lack only the skill to utter it. And it is not necessary to acquire inordinate skill before we can utter a great many musical ideas of the deepest interest. The piano still possesses the advantage that made it, long ago, the most popular of musical instruments. For it gives the player command of the whole fabric of a musical composition: melody and accompaniment; solo voice and orchestral tutti; even the interweaving of what is readily imaginable as a whole choir of human voices. The great composers, from Bach's time to our own, have realized the inestimable value of this vehicle through which one may make music for oneself; and the literature of the piano, accordingly, is incomparably richer than the literature of any other instrument.

Virtuosi, of course, play in a fashion that makes us very discontented with our own efforts. It is also true, however, that many brilliant performances are presented less with the purpose of making the hearer love music than with the desire of making him love the performer. And the significant literature of music was written, not for those who love virtuosity, but for those who love music. The word *amateur* really means "one who loves"; and there is perhaps no heavier charge to be laid against the virtuosi and the musically learned than that they have made us suppose the word to mean "a hopelessly unskilled person" or "a dilettante." If you are a true amateur, you may feel sure that music was written *for you*. There is no doubt that your own attempts to play the music you love will hasten and deepen your understanding of it as no other contact can do.

The studies of musical compositions which follow have been written to help you to a quicker perception of those qualities which have endeared the pieces to the world. The foregoing sketch of the act of touch has been presented in the hope that it will also aid you in realizing those values. The order in which the compositions are presented, however, is not that of progressive difficulty; it is rather an order that reveals the growth of great musical minds. If your technical powers are unequal to the performance of some of them, you should seek out only those that are within your scope, perhaps using the discussions of the harder pieces as guides to the understanding of better performances than you can give.

Something of the history of these compositions, where that is important; something of their style, and of the thought or emotion they express, where that can be put into words; and something by way of help in passages that are technically or interpretatively troublesome—these are what you will find. Not much of the matter can be cursorily read apart from the study of the actual scores to which it refers. Some little knowledge of musical terms has been taken for granted, but for the most part there has been every effort to make the discussions as simple and clear as possible. If you are a teacher, you will find much that you know already—but you may find help in the presentation of various points to your pupils. If you are an accomplished pianist, you will find little help with technique, but perhaps a good deal with interpretation. Primarily, however, this book is addressed to you, whatever your technical powers may be, as an amateur—a lover of music.

# 2
# BEETHOVEN —
# THE SONATA FORM

LET US begin with Beethoven. No other composer's works are so consistently played, and no others will better repay consistent study.

His earlier works, although they reflect the eighteenth century and all its traditions, are nevertheless flushed with a youthful, energetic color which that century hardly knew. Those of the middle period are a vivid presentment of enthusiasm for that new social order which produced our own revolution and our democracy. And the last sonatas, far head of their time—and perhaps of ours—burn with a clear flame of idealism far removed from sentimentality: a flame barely visible in the glare of our present conflagrations, but, to those who can perceive it, as commanding as a pillar of fire by night.

The structure of this music is generally beyond criticism. From it, many of the "laws" of musical form not only are illustrated, but are directly derived. These laws are important, and we shall study the most elemental of them. But the excellence of its structure still does not explain the greatness of Beethoven's music. For like the great monuments of our literature, this music is more than a supreme example of form. It is a presentment of the human spirit in action—a setting forth of the very substance of woe and triumph and other impulses between these two extremes, which drive men to do and exult and suffer and pray. Common sense accepts music as a vehicle for such expression.

Of late years the notion has been much bruited about that music has nothing to do with these things, that its excellence lies wholly in its perfection of design, and that the ideal of perfect form in art is higher and nobler than that profound expressiveness which has always been supposed to be the glory of music. That is a notion which not only Beethoven but every great artist of the past would have laughed to scorn. Great art speaks of human things, not of abstractions. The form of great art must indeed be perfect; but that perfection reveals only a part of the artist's effort. He is moved to utterance by spiritual realities, and his forms are not the forms of idle dreams but are designs which embody the meaning of realities.

These meanings can be but lamely suggested in words, but they are not on that account either unfamiliar or unintelligible. They are grasped by people of sensitivity everywhere, and take the mental form of a sense of character. Your friends have also character, which is for you a kind of summary, partly of their knowledge and their ability, but mostly of their emotional disposition. What you know about your friends is too complex to be fully described; but you will hardly admit that you do not *know* their character. Every act of theirs either fits into the "picture" you have formed of them as persons, or compels you, if it seems unaccountable, to enlarge that picture. The character of your friend is, indeed, his "meaning" for you. The character of a musical composition is likewise its meaning; and, as with persons, it is a meaning largely revealed through indicated emotional impulses.

The medium or vehicle through which these impulses are made intelligible is the structure of the music. The facts of musical form are really the common sense of musical structure. They are like the facts of sound sentence structure and orderly exposition in language—indispensable for the ready intelligibility

of what is said. We must therefore preface our study of Beethoven's music by an account of the form which he found most
congenial—that of the sonata. That preface will not long delay our
approach to the music itself, since we shall illustrate our study
of the form (after a brief glance at its origins) by reference to one
of his sonatas.

The word *sonata* is much older than the form which Hayden
and Mozart called by that name, and which Beethoven filled with
meaning beyond the dreams of his predecessors. In the fifteenth
century, when instrumental music was in its infancy, the word
*sonata* meant merely "something played" in contrast to *cantata,*
which meant "something sung." Two types of sonata were presently distinguished: the Church Sonata (*Sonata da Chiesa*[1]) and
the Chamber Sonata (*Sonata da Camera*). The Church Sonata,
although it was sometimes played in church, was rather a piece
of sober and dignified character than a specifically religious composition. It had four movements—slow, fast, slow, fast—the slow
movements being lyrical and the fast largely fugal. It did not
survive beyond Bach's time, but some of its details contributed to
the later sonata form which we are to study.

The *Sonata da Camera* was much less aristocratic, but far more
vital. As its name suggests, it was music for the home, and its
popular character is seen in the fact that it was a sequence or
*suite* of dance tunes. (The name *suite* is often used, instead of the
longer title.) It was not expected that these pieces would always
be used for dancing; hence we find that the tunes were often
idealized, much as the waltz was later idealized by Chopin. Still
higher idealization, entailing great enlargement of the form,
resulted in the *Viennese Classical Sonata*—Beethoven's form.
(Bach and Handel, Domenico Scarlatti, Philipp Emanuel Bach,
Mozart, and Haydn all contributed to the evolution of the form.)
A simple diagram will show the general pattern of the suite

[1] *Chiesa* (pronounced kyāzà) is from a Greek word whose Latin form, *ecclesia,*
is familiar in our word "ecclesiastic."

dance, and comparison of this with the diagram of the sonata form (p. 28), will reveal their close relationship:

| Subject | Cadential Figures | Modulations | Partial Cadence | Final Cadence |
|---|---|---|---|---|
| Tonic | Dominant or Relative Key | | Relative or Dominant | Tonic |

The "subject" is the principal thought or main melodic idea of the piece. In the dance tunes, this was a characteristic strain in the conventional rhythm of the dance, rather than a concise, epigrammatic phrase such as usually forms the "principal subject" of the later sonata form. No striking contrasts appear, but the "cadential figures" usually depart from the melodic pattern announced at the beginning. The main feature of the structure is seen in the key relations: the clear statement of the tonic key at the outset, with the close of the first section in a closely related key (dominant, if the original key was major, but either relative major or dominant if the piece began in minor). The second section begins in the key in which the first part closed, but it becomes at once far more adventurous. It does this by modulating to keys more remote than any that appeared in the first section. The modulatory part usually ends with a not very emphatic cadence in that one of the alternative keys (dominant or relative major or minor) which was *not* used at the end of the first section. Thereafter, you will soon feel the approach of the final cadence, which will of course be in the original tonic, and usually with the same cadential figures that closed the first section.

If you will examine any single movement from the French Suites of Bach, you will find that it is in the form we have just described. This is a useful exercise in analysis, and will greatly clarify your vision of the larger sonata structure that grew out of this one. You may also find larger examples of the same general form in others of Bach's pieces (the *Fantasia in C minor,* and ten of the Preludes in Book II of the *Well-tempered Clavichord,* for example), and in the Sonatas of Domenico Scarlatti.

In both cases you will see that the change from the tonic to the related key is signalized by a change in the character of the musical idea—that, in fact, a step is being taken toward the "second subject" of the sonata form,[2] whose significance we shall soon see. The fifth Prelude in the *Well-tempered Clavichord*, Book II, is remarkably advanced toward the later sonata form.

If you will open your volume of the Beethoven Sonatas at the first page (the *Sonata Op. 2, No. 1*), you will find a perfect specimen of the classical sonata form. You will also see that most of its features are related to something in the earlier dance form. About a third of the way through, there is a double bar with a sign for repetition. This is a descendant of the double bar in the suite dance; and we shall find many other survivals. In both forms, the tonic key is firmly established at the outset. (Here, of course, it is the key of F minor.) But where the "subject" in the dance was a figurated pattern merely, Beethoven's principal subject is succinct, epigrammatic, and clearly defined. Its weightiest element is obviously the high A-flat with its attendant figure, to which the upward-marching quarter notes are only an approach, for this element is presently repeated without the preparation. This thought being too important to be dropped, the bass takes it up, and the upper voices dwell on its chief figure in dissonant harmonies that gradually effect a modulation away from F minor. The syncopated descent (bars 15–19) relaxes the sternness of the main subject, and leads us into the dominant of A-flat, the relative key to F minor.

We find here, however, much more than a mere contrast of key. There is also a *contrast of subject:* no mere cadential figure, as at the close of the first part of the dance, but a new melody,

---

[2] The first of the two, three, or four movements of the Classical Sonata is usually in the so-called *sonata form*. Other movements, especially the last, may have the same form. The word *sonata,* that is, will be used to designate not only the first movement's pattern, but also, more loosely, the group of movements as a whole. This ambiguous terminology is unfortunate, but it is so deeply rooted in our technical language that we cannot hope to remedy it.

very different in feeling from the principal subject, yet altogether equal to it in interest.[3] This contrast or antithesis of co-ordinate subject matter is the most important feature of the sonata form. It makes possible both a great expansion of the form (far beyond the limit of interest in the simple dance piece), and also a range and a variety of expression•which we shall find to be almost limitless.

There is no fixed rule as to the character of the subjects. Mostly, however, the first or "principal" subject (as here) is the bolder and more energetic, with the second gentler and more "feminine." But precisely on this account the second subject is not a desirable thought with which to close a whole section. Mere cadential figures sufficed, in the dance, for this purpose; but here they would sound dwarfed and perfunctory. Thus, although the second subject breaks off at bar 26, seven more bars ensue on an agitated figure still in character with the second subject; and these, in turn, are followed by eight more bars of scale passage which are evidently a transition to some new thought. This new idea is the "closing subject," unmistakably conclusive, not merely in design but in character.[4] How much more comprehensive is the discussion here than in the demure little dance need hardly be pointed out. (Some theorists speak of all that follows the entrance of the primary key contrast as the "second-subject group," including in that group what we have called the "closing subject." This question is largely academic, and need not be argued here.)

The whole section now ended is called the "Exposition" of the

[3] This particular theme, with its two F-flats, is almost in A-flat minor, though the C-natural in the harmony finally determines the key as A-flat major. Its rhythmic pattern, also, is almost the same as that of the principal subject. Both these details make the second subject seem very much in character with the first; and you will note that the closing subject, with its C-flat, is again similar in feeling-tone to the second. Such rhythmic similarity between the subjects of a sonata is not infrequent (see, for example, the *Appassionata*), though it is in no sense obligatory. Its value of expression is thus at least equal to its value of form.

[4] Note that its first phrase has the rhythm ♩. ♪♩ essentially that of the main phrase of the principal subject, and the close of the second.

sonata form. The next section (following the double bar) is called the "Development." (The terms "Working-out," or "Free Fantasia" are sometimes employed.) This is an expansion of that part of the dance form which we marked as "Modulations"; and one of its chief features is still the fact of energetic modulation. In the dance, however, the only material for modulation was the one predominating pattern of the opening subject. But in the sonata, the composer has for material all that variety of subject matter we have just described. With the horizon thus widened, we shall expect to find a further departure from the two principal keys, and a correspondingly great intensification of the subject matter itself.

In the development of this Sonata, the antithesis of the two subjects is sharpened by omitting all transition from the one to the other. Figures from the subsidiary of Subject II then effect a swift modulation, after which that subject is more insistently sounded than ever. Eventually, after a long passage of syncopation on heavy harmonies that are not suggested in the exposition, but are clearly in character,[5] we reach the dominant of F minor. Detached figures, derived from the first two notes of Subject II —at first ejaculatory and forceful, then dwindling to pianissimo— and two bars of hesitant reiteration of the obviously preparatory note, C, bring us to a resumption of Subject I in its original form and key.

We have now reached a point analogous to that of the cadence in the middle of the second section of the suite dance; but the excursion into foreign keys has been so long that to announce the end of our modulations merely by the assertion of the dominant or the relative key would seem inconclusive. The original

[5] Analytically, such passages as this look somewhat irrelevant. Actually, they are not so. For they serve, without actual repetition of the subject matter (which would now likely seem redundant) to keep up the mood that has been attained, and which we should be loth to abandon. Such passages are frequent, both in Beethoven and in other composers, and are by no means an evidence of loose thinking.

tonic, therefore, appears with a force which we feel to be distinctly gratifying.

What ensues is called the "Recapitulation." It is a restatement of the whole Exposition, but with the transitions now so rearranged or altered that both the second and the closing subjects appear in the tonic key (F minor or major). It will be seen that these alterations are quite sufficient to keep the tonic from becoming monotonous.

This form, like that of the suite dance, may be compactly presented in a diagram. In that which follows, the part marked "Exposition" corresponds to the first section, and that marked "Development" and "Recapitulation" to the second, of our diagram of the Dance:

EXPOSITION

| · S.I (Tonic maj.) | Trans. | S.II (Dominant) | Trans. | Closing S. · |
|---|---|---|---|---|
| · S.I (Tonic min.) | Trans. | S.II (Rel. maj.) | Trans. | Closing S. · |

DEVELOPMENT                    RECAPULATION

| · Subject matter from | S.I (Tonic maj.) | Trans. | S.II (Tonic) | Trans. | Cl. S. · |
|---|---|---|---|---|---|
| · Expo. in remote keys | S.I (Tonic min.) | Trans. | S.II (Tonic major) | Trans. | Cl. S. · |

In more expanded forms, the transitions often contain subsidiary themes which may play a large part in the development. Such a theme, in the first transition, may be mistaken for the Second Subject. The true S.II, however, will usually be distinguishable, both by its more distinctive character and by its appearance in the prescribed key.

Although Op. 2, No. 1 is one of the shortest of Beethoven's sonata forms, it is much larger than the dance form. But this is itself a tiny piece by comparison with many of the later works. The first movement is three or four times as long as one of the dances; but the *Waldstein* and the *Appassionata* sonatas have first movements—essentially in the same form—which are five times as large as this. And what one might call the coefficient of expressive interest in these larger works is even higher. The pages we have devoted to the description of this form are thus devoted to a topic of the highest musical importance.

The other movements of the sonata can be described in less space; but their study is equally desirable.

In a great majority of cases, the second movement of the sonata is a slow movement. Its character is generally lyrical. Lyric expression arises from highly individual feeling, which conforms reluctantly to rules; hence the form of slow movements is less exactly prescribed (but is not in itself less logical) than the first movement form. Some slow movements, indeed, are in sonata form; but our emotional interest is usually sufficiently aroused by shorter pieces. Mostly, however, that contrast of subject matter which gives such vitality to the sonata form appears also in slow movements. The same key relations, also, are often observed; but more latitude in this matter may be expected in slow movements than in fast.

Using the letters A, B, and so on, to designate the first and later subjects, we may briefly indicate as follows the patterns of a few slow movements:

I. A-B‖A-B′. (B is in the dominant or relative key; B′ is in the tonic.) The second half will often be highly ornamented. Example: the slow movement of Op. 2, No. 1—the sonata we are studying.

II. A-b, A-c, A-b*, A*-b**, A**. (Here b and c indicate such brief and obviously subordinate thematic material that A stands out as the one main theme of the movement. The * indicates an altered form of the subject affected.) Example, Beethoven, Op. 2, No. 2.

III. A-a-B-b-C-c-A*-a-B-A*. (Here a, b, and c are immediate pendants of A, B, and C. This approximates the Rondo form, to be described in a moment.) Example, Op. 10, No. 3.

IV. The Theme and Variations—probably requiring no general description. Examples, Op. 14, No. 2, and the first movement of Op. 26.

If there are four movements in a sonata, the third is usually either a Minuet or a Scherzo. The Minuet is the survival of the old dance form, and has exactly the pattern already described. It may, however, present in the modulation section a new theme, thus acquiring that interest which thematic contrast gives to the larger movements. Also, the Minuet proper is usually followed by a Trio, which is another Minuet, with wholly different, lighter subjects, and somewhat shorter. After the Trio, the first Minuet is played *da capo* (from the beginning), but without the repeats. The Scherzo is identical with the Minuet in form, but its speed is much faster and its character more humorous. Occasionally the form is expanded or otherwise altered; and rarely we find a kind of Minuet, with a character somewhere between that of the dance and that of the slow movement, appearing as the slow movement itself.

The last movement of the sonata, if it is not in sonata form, will usually be a Rondo. This name is borrowed from a poetic form, the *Rondeau,* in which the opening line or couplet is made to recur (in the simplest examples, merely at the end; in more elaborate examples, several times) always with new or added meaning. In the older musical Rondos there is no second or third subject, but only excursions away from the theme in order that its return may be refreshing. This type of Rondo is rare in Beethoven and later writers. Even Haydn, as well as Mozart and Beethoven, employed the true contrasting subject, and the form was finally established as A-B-A-C-A-B′-A (Coda), where B′ again indicates the return of that subject in the tonic. The key of theme C is not exactly prescribed. The recurrences of A, also, although they are conventionally in the tonic, are often varied or ornamented. For a Coda, the main theme is sometimes put through a series of modulations, or is made more lively in tempo.

All this gives but a bare outline of the sonata's various movement forms. It will pave the way, however, for our more minute examination of details of form and character in the actual music.

Let us see, then, what is to be our problem in interpreting this sonata. To interpret is to reveal meaning. There is a certain meaning in a formal design; but if we do no more than make clear that design, we shall hardly fulfil all the desire either of the composer or of ourselves. These themes have character, as well as their formal function; and we shall probably feel certain, once that character is revealed, that the form itself was governed, as to most of its details, by the desire to realize a persistent image of character in the composer's mind.

Our principal subject has two motives: the rising arpeggio of five quarter notes, and the figure in bar 2, beginning with A-flat. Obviously, A-flat is the crisis note; obviously, the arpeggio must be felt as approaching this crisis; and we can hardly do this without a slight crescendo (within the limit of piano) together with just enough stress on the first beat of bar 1 so that the march of the rhythm in 4-4 time is unmistakable. Too rapid a speed will spoil this approach. (Liszt gave the metronome mark $\downarrow = 112$. Schnabel gives 126–138—too fast, surely, to yield the full sense of this by no means flippant theme.) Each recurrence of the crisis figure will be more insistent, with full observance of the *ff* in bar 7. Note that bars 7–8 are a kind of expansion of the crisis figure. The *fermata,* or "hold" $\curvearrowright$ justifies a slight *rit.* as it is approached. Resume the tempo, and study well the dynamic differences that will bring out the dissonances in bars 11–14.[6] In bars 15, 17, and 19, make the stress note, B-flat, pull downward to

---

[6] Dissonances or discords (the terms are virtually synonyms) are the most vital tone elements of music. If timidly attacked, they will lose their point, and may even sound like wrong notes. In a dissonant chord, therefore, the notes must be of different intensity, corresponding to the musical importance of the notes. In bar 11, for example, the bass, C, must be strong enough so that when the D-flat appears above it the dissonance of these two notes will be clearly heard, and so that the tendency of the C to move to B-flat in the next bar will be definitely felt. In bar 12, the A-flat which was consonant in bar 11 becomes dissonant, and must be played so that this value can be realized.

Verbal description of all the discords in these four bars alone would fill pages. From the few we have noted, however, the careful student may gain a hint of the extreme sensitivity that is required for artistic playing. Note particularly that, although this is ultimately a sensitivity to musical values, it is elementally a sensibility to fine gradations of loudness.

A-flat by giving the D-natural such volume as will make clear its values of rhythm and dissonance. Do not diminish the rocking E-flat's in bar 20. The entrance of the second subject (on F-flat in this bar) will be much more significant if it appears in a sudden piano, as the composer directed.

Since the crisis in this new phrase is on the low F-flat (*sf*), this first note may gain its proper darkened color (implied by its chromatic lowering) through a slight hesitation in the time of its attack. A considerable swell is needed as you approach the low F-flat, and a relatively gentle release of the last two notes will give a satisfying phrase end. Accentuate slightly the middle of the three-note figures, following; and do not ignore the values of melody and dissonance in the bass. The abrupt contrasts of *p* and *f* in the ensuing passage are distinctive traits of Beethoven's style, and must be exactly observed. Play the C-flat in the closing subject so that its feeling quality recalls that of the F-flat in the second theme. Approach the *ff* in bar 47 so that without harshness it may yet have almost explosive intensity—i.e., with but little crescendo. Pianists, as a rule, do not nowadays repeat the exposition sections of sonatas; but both the brevity and the character of this piece will amply justify the repetition.

The development, if the exposition has been carefully studied, should present few difficulties.[7] Darken, by appropriate diminuendo, the descending repetitions of Subject II in bars 68–72, and make the sforzandi in the following passage maintain this brooding character. Although there is little thematic matter in the music, it serves admirably to maintain the mood already engendered. Thus, if the tone colors are sensitively and progressively

[7] At bar 14 of the development, beat 4, the original edition gives D-flat, which is followed by Schnabel and Casella. Most older editions, Liszt, D'Albert, and Klindworth among them, give D-natural. D-flat accords with the similar figure at bar 27; but it produces, against the A-flat and F-sharp of the harmony, a form of the augmented sixth chord which was certainly unusual in Beethoven's day. D-natural gives a more fitting culmination of the modulatory passage, though the D-flat is also in accord with the minor ninth of the subject. The author, somewhat hesitantly, votes for D-natural.

darkened, in accord with the dwindling power of the last phrases of the subject, the hesitant C's in bars 91–92, with the ensuing hints of the return of the main subject in the tonic key, may form a dramatic approach to the recapitulation.

The slight differences between recapitulation and exposition call for no comment. The brief Coda intensifies the last bars of the closing subject; and the sforzandi in the final chords must clinch the sense of bitter decision which, for the most part (though in various degrees), has imbued the whole movement.

Simple and reticent as it is, this has been the utterance of one who looks forward to the nineteenth century. The *Adagio,* on the other hand, reverts to the eighteenth. This movement, indeed, was first conceived as part of a quartet for piano and strings, written at Bonn in 1785. It thus exhibits much of the suave and finely drawn filigree that was expected in those days. Even so, you may detect beneath the quiet surface of the opening strain a hint of nostalgia—a quality of feeling hardly to be expected of a fifteen-year-old boy in a time when romanticism was hardly budded. (Do not overdo this suggestion. It is beneath, not on, the surface!)

The essential calmness of the opening theme will be gained by taking Liszt's tempo $\flat = 88$; but you can ensure a legato curve only through the most exquisite care for dynamic shading. Be careful, also, that the tenor (a sixth below the soprano) enriches the upper voice. Take the turn in the time of the last sixteenth, subtracting the grace note, C, from the time of the B-flat, which is the stress note of the phrase. Put slight secondary emphasis on F in bar 2. Bar 3, with legato beneath the gently detached sixteenths, is hard to play, since it must also grow toward the A in bar 4. In bar 5, diminish the eighth notes less than in bar 1, so that the crisis of the whole sentence may fall on the high G, in bar 6. The high register of bars 9–12 gives this subordinate clause grace and lightness; but the $\prec sf$ in bars 9–10 warns us against treating it too lightly. (Remember, however, that sforzando does not necessarily mean forte, but is only a heavy stress within the existing dynamic range. The sign *sf* applies only to the note against which it stands.) Beethoven gave no dynamic mark for the B subject (bar 17). But the internal stress is here much higher. Schnabel suggests *f;* Casella, *più f;* D'Albert, *poco f,* and so forth, any of which is natural. The main melodic line is firm and even stern; the accompanying thirds (of which the stressed middle notes are always dissonant) are strained and swerving; and the climax (bar 23) by no means timid. Hold the tied B-natural a shade too long against the *sf* A-flat, with a compensating accelerando of the thirty-seconds; and do not ignore the melody of the alto voice. Play the thirty-seconds softly, increasing with the four sixteenths to the reiterated *sf,* bar 24. Begin the three-note grace *on the beat,* maintaining *f* to the high E. Lessen the excitement with each beat of bar 25, and try to give a kind of smiling quality to the fade-out in bar 26. Thus the intensity of bars 27–28 ('cello phrases, surely) and their ensuing parallel will have full value. The rest is figurated variation of the first part, save that the intenser strain of the B subject is omitted. The figurations should give little trouble if the delicate dynamic fluctuations are well mastered.[8]

The next movement is a real Menuetto, not a Scherzo. There is

---

[8] The eight thirty-seconds against six sixteenths in bars 37–38 *are* troublesome. There is no practical way of counting (as with three notes against two); so that the left hand must learn to do its part unconsciously, while the musical attention is given to the melody in the right. To do this, set the left hand going, at the proper tempo, giving a somewhat exaggerated accent to the first note of each triplet. Repeat these two beats, over and over, until you can ignore your left hand, save at the accent. Now, while the left hand goes on, begin to *think* the notes of the right hand (or sing them, if you can). When you can do this, begin to play the two hands together. You will doubtless fail, at the first attempt; but do not despair. The trick will soon become so easy that you will wonder that you had any difficulty.

We may add here a note on the easier problem of two notes against three. Whatever may be the basic rhythm, count out the groups of three as "one, two, *and* three," being careful not to shorten the "three." Play the first of the two-note group on the "one," and the second on the *"and"* between two and three. (Two notes against five may similarly be counted as "one, two, three *and* four, five," with the second of the two notes against the "and.")

a faint sadness about it, akin to that which we found in the theme of the Adagio. Make the staccato of the phrase ends (bars 1 and 2) very delicate, with the second phrase a little softer than the first. Then, extreme legato for the ensuing phrase, with a definite swell to the crisis note, B-flat. The next six bars are analogous. The appoggiaturas in bars 11 and 13 are long—that is, they have the value of eighth notes. (Casella expressly denies this. See footnote 3 on p. 42 below.) The Trio, although in the brighter major key, maintains the note of tranquillity, and, in the author's opinion, should be in the same tempo as the Menuetto. Beethoven fingered the fourths in section II in a way that hardly seems to us to solve the problem.[9] Although this little piece is seen at its best when played in its place with the other movements, it may be played separately, and is a delightful study for those who are diffident of their technical powers.

The Finale is the most difficult of the four movements. It is also probably the least interesting. The eighteenth-century tradition which demanded a happy ending, even for tragic opera, seems also to have governed in what we might call the "last act" of a four-movement sonata. It will be some time before Beethoven escapes that tradition. Even here, however, the interest of character considerably predominates over the lure of brilliancy.

The movement is in sonata form, modified to the extent that the development section consists largely of new material. The principal subject appears at once, above the swift and excited triplets of the left hand. It is the mere three-note phrase, F-E-F. Make it sound nervous and purposive, in spite of the *p*, with the crisis clearly on the down-beat. Note that the real melody, F-E-F, is in the bass, in the next bar. The rhythmic germ here set forth

[9] Beethoven's fingering is given above the notes. Liszt's fingering, which we find the most convenient, is given below.

is embodied in a gentler phrase at bar 5. The main thought returns at bar 13, essentially in the dominant of C minor, in which key the second subject will appear. Here (bar 22) the dark minor key (instead of the orthodox relative major) and the persistent *ff*,[10] are proof that character is more desired than brilliancy. The closing subject, which is still pregnant with the opening three-note motive, begins in bar 34. Persistent modulation somewhat heightens its faintly renunciatory tone. Perhaps because the principal subject will not recur until the end of the development, that subject is forcefully presented as the actual close of the exposition.

Almost as if this were a rondo instead of a sonata form, the major part of the development consists of a wholly new melody, songful in contrast to the ejaculatory exposition, but also in accord with it in feeling-tone.[11] There is appropriate bitterness in the sudden outcry of bars 53–54 of the development, after the long-delayed pianissimo reappearance of the principal subject; and the expansion of this outcry, beginning at bar 61, is a part of the very effective transition to the recapitulation. This section differs but slightly from the exposition. There is no extended Coda—only an appropriate insistence on the principal motive.

We have attempted, in this chapter, to introduce the reader both to the sonata and to its greatest master. If you cultivate the acquaintance further, you will find both the form and the man to be of immeasurable significance. The form will prove flexible and expansible enough to contain an endless variety of thought.

[10] Beethoven wrote no contradiction of the *ff* at this point. Many editors feel that the intensity should be lessened (Schnabel suggests *p*, and Casella *mf*), but D'Albert reinforces Beethoven's implied intention by repeating the *ff*. Sufficient dynamic fluctuation is possible within the range of *ff* so that the passionate quality of the phrase may be maintained without loss of character. The *p* of the ensuing octave melody will then be far more significant.

[11] Observe that the first four notes of this melody still set forth the essential rhythm of the main motive: the whole note, E-flat, representing the opening half bar, the two half notes, A-flat–C, corresponding to the quarter notes F–E-flat, and the high E-flat to the final F of the motive. This and the earlier instances we have noted will suggest a fact to be more fully established as we go on: that rhythm was the most powerful "drive" in Beethoven's musical imagination.

The man, as Dr. Tovey has said, is not only one of the greatest musicians, but one of the greatest artists in any medium, who ever lived. And in studying his music we are in fact making his personal acquaintance; for no one can write vivid music without revealing himself. In the sonatas, as we follow them, we shall find, then, a kind of autobiography of Beethoven.

He was of course unconscious of this revelation. But this only makes it the more truthful. Studied narration in music, such as that in Berlioz's *Symphonie Fantastique,* yields a most untrustworthy story. Music almost always speaks foolishly about things or events as such. But what it tells of the inner workings of a composer's mind—of the things that lure him, of his energies, his obsessions, his tendernesses, his fears—these are perhaps the truest things that can be said; for music is a swifter metaphor of the soul that any but the most inspired language of poesy. You cannot tell lies about yourself in music, though you may readily prove yourself to be a liar. Feeling that is false or feigned is as unstable under the scrutiny of the musical instinct as is the shifty eye of the reprobate child before a stern father. Musical common sense, once cured of its induced timidity, is an almost infallible lie detector. And the best cure for that timidity is your own actual effort to make music sound as you feel it must sound, to be true.

It is the musical common sense of the million, rather than the analytical demonstrations of the learned, that has raised Beethoven to his enduring position among the artists; for he speaks what the million know to be true. No theory can "prove" the greatness of Beethoven, or of any other great man. Such proof would amount to a formula for greatness; and to propose such a formula (which criticism sometimes feebly attempts) would be merely to prove one's own stupidity. Greatness demonstrates itself by departing from formula; but this departure is always in obedience to compulsions beyond the understanding of rule makers, and the compulsions themselves—the composer's own rules of musical common sense—are obeyed with the most ineluctable logic. Having been taught to recognize these compulsions, we recognize a new dimension of greatness.

In this one sonata, we have found Beethoven a young man not merely earnest, but fearless; suspicious of convention; disdainful of the pretty; aware of new meanings which even to himself are not yet quite lucid. But he pursues his thought to the end. He has the boldness of the revolutionary, though he is no mere rebel; he is earnest to the point of obsession, yet he is no fanatic; he is gentle, but he can seldom be lured into over-ready sentimentalism.

The form of his music is the vehicle through which these characteristics are made manifest; but they are only incidentally characteristic of that form. They are attributes of the music contained within the form, and that music is the metaphor of a man. How that man grew, until he understood things which we can but dimly perceive—things which perhaps no other art than music can reveal—will be told in the further chapters of his unconscious autobiography.

# 3
# BEETHOVEN'S FIRST PERIOD

REGRETFULLY, we forego detailed study of the two remaining sonatas in Op. 2. Each of them is more brilliant, more impressive to the ear, and more difficult to play, than No. 1. But both are nevertheless lacking in the structural logic and the conciseness of expression which we found in the first Sonata. They were written, no doubt, as pieces for the display of the composer's powers as a pianist; for it was his remarkable playing, rather than the somewhat bizarre style of his compositions, which first won for him the affection of the Viennese public.

There are, to be sure, many striking passages. The second subject of the first movement of No. 2 is an extraordinary adventure (for that day) into the realm of chromatic progression. The slow movement—much of it a literal transcription for piano of music that might well have been given to a string quartet—is somber in color and is rhythmed with the tread of death: already a convincing foretaste of the sense of tragedy that will one day produce the *Funeral March* in the *Eroica* Symphony. The *Scherzo* (so called by the composer, though the pace of it is still Allegretto) has a delicate sparkle, halfway between the dignity of the old Minuet and the boisterousness of the later Scherzi. But the last movement is almost wholly a virtuoso piece.

Almost the same incongruity between passages of meaningless euphony and others of distinctive expression is to be found in Op.

2, No. 3, in C major. The first and last movements are extremely difficult to play, and are musically the least interesting. Both the second subject of the first movement (bar 47) and the earlier episodic theme in G minor are expressively significant; but they cannot lift the rest of the material to their level. This is in some measure proved in the development section, where the real subject matter is almost ignored for the sake of brilliant figurations and sonorous arpeggiations. The last movement, an extended Rondo, is much less diffuse. But both the slow movement and the Scherzo are "real Beethoven." The *Adagio* presents one perplexity that seems to us not fully admitted in either the original or later editions. Liszt's suggested metronome mark $\flat = 54$ is certainly not too slow for the opening subject. The ensuing long section in thirty-second-note figurations, however, if continued at this tempo, is simply unendurable. Even the *pochettino* (or *poco*) *più animato,* which various editors suggest, gives so little relief that—in apparent defiance not only of the usual caution of an interpreter but of Beethoven himself—the writer can find no other solution than a precise *doppio movimento* (a tempo exactly twice as fast as the former) for this and the similar passage just before the Coda. To say this is of course to assert that Beethoven meant to write sixty-fourth notes instead of the thirty-seconds—a sufficiently bold assertion. Yet, so played, the passage in question not only has the turbulence which the agitated figures seem to imply, but has also complete rhythmic unity with the actual Adagio; for when the principal subject recurs, the original tempo can be taken without any apparent break in the rhythm. "If this be heresy, make the most of it!"

Although the next sonata (Op. 7) is still somewhat diffuse, it reveals more of the originality of Beethoven's musical imagination than any of the three in Op. 2. The terse ejaculation of two notes with which its principal subject begins hints at that impatience with triviality which will increase with the years. This phrase makes several dramatic entrances. It has also a kind of complement in the extraordinarily colorful excitement of the arpeggiated closing subject (bar 111). The slow movement is more remarkable than that of Op. 2, No. 2, as an example of somber music in a major key. Its tone is already definitely romantic, as is that of the Trio of the third movement, where again the arpeggio figures yield an obscure and threatening murmur. But the too-ingratiating Rondo somewhat defeats the more serious purpose of the earlier parts.

The two very interesting and relatively easy sonatas, Op. 10, Nos. 1 and 2, would yield, if we had space to study them, many interesting traits of budding humor—a type of expression not very freely exploited in music before Beethoven. The first, in C minor, has little of this quality (you will generally expect something ra'.er stern, when Beethoven chooses the key of C minor), but the second has much of it. The middle movement is an Allegretto which develops what might have been a Minuet into a more diversified movement, although the general form of the dance with its Trio is still apparent. And the last movement has a kind of plebeian impudence for which you will hunt in vain in earlier music.

Op. 10, No. 3, however, is so important that we must look into it in some detail. The principal subject—a stark line, staccato save for the up-beat, presenting in scale or arpeggio the unadorned fact of the key of D—is hardly ingratiating. Taken at its proper, breakneck speed, however, and in the hushed piano prescribed,[1] we find in it a sense of urgency and determination—a kind of repressed excitement—which, as it expands, becomes of compelling interest. The first four (descending) notes of the theme, harmonized with gentle chords of the sixth, present an unexpected antithesis of feeling. But the original excitement, even

[1] Many editors (even Casella) follow Liszt in inserting a ◁ in bar 2, leading to the *sf* A. Beethoven wrote no such mark here, though he did use it later. In our opinion, the whole character of the theme is obscured if the sudden explosion of the A is even faintly anticipated. (But it is very difficult to execute the high contrast.) The added octaves in themselves sufficiently thicken the texture.

intensified, reappears at once as the four-note figure is ejaculated in broken sixths, and is vigorously pursued with the whole theme, in octaves, extended to the limit of the keyboard as it was in 1796.[2]

No mere transition, but a subtheme that is a pertinent commentary on the main theme, follows the fermata. Though it is confined to the intensity of piano, the half notes, D–F-sharp–D are uneasy, and within the descending continuation the four-note figure of the main theme is conspicuous. Only with bar 38 does a true transition appear, and even this is motivated by the impetuosity that has ruled from the beginning.

The second theme enters in bar 53. The appoggiatura is "long" —i.e., it has the value of an eighth-note, on the beat, so that the half bar has again the pattern of four descending notes.[3] This theme gives a moment of engaging naïveté, in grateful but not incongruous contrast to all that has preceded. In the ensuing figure of leaping octaves, keep the weak beats (although they are doubled by the left hand) weak and the strong beats strong (of course, all in piano). In bar 67, the lightness begins to wane. The syncopated *sf* is again urgent, and the four-note figure now forms the bass of the music. It soon becomes, with its inversion (four notes ascending) the core of the thought. (The *sf* on the fourth beat intensifies the value of the slur over the first two

---

[2] The limit was five octaves, from low F. The final F-sharp of this passage had therefore to be written as a single note, on the fifth line of the staff. Many instances of Beethoven's difficulties with this narrow compass appear in the earlier sonatas. Usually—and certainly here—the sensible thing is to play the higher notes. Sometimes, however, Beethoven makes a great virtue out of his necessity, and no one would make substitutions in such cases.

[3] Casella insists that Beethoven wrote *no* "long" appoggiaturas. The tradition as to the time value of these notes was changing, in Beethoven's day, and Casella is able to support his contention by a few fairly convincing instances. Even these, however, seem to us debatable, and in the present case the short appoggiatura gives a result which is jerky and unpleasant in itself, and which obliterates all reference to the figure of four descending notes that has already been found highly important. Many editions print the figure as four eighth notes. Schnabel and others, printing the appoggiatura, yet interpret it as having the value of an eighth. We vote emphatically for the long appoggiatura.

notes of the sonata.) The determined octave descent leads to the closing subject, whose parallel we shall find in the next sonata to be studied. At bar 104, the figure had to be foreshortened because of the limit of the keyboard. Most editors agree (and we heartily concur) that the figure should be continued at the octave up to the high A. Schnabel objects; but his conservatism here seems extreme.

The development is almost wholly concerned with the principal subject, and will thus require little comment. Pedal the B-flat and the continuing line of melody in the bass at bars 13–16 after the change of signature. (The B-flat may well be struck with the right thumb.) A similar use of the pedal seems implied (though it is not expressly indicated) at the final bars of the development. The recapitulation will need no discussion. The four-note figure is the basis of the whole Coda. The author emphasizes with the pedal the A-flat which, in the unaccompanied successions of the four-note figure, modulates from G minor to the dominant seventh of E-flat. Make the enharmonic change from this chord to the augmented sixth (B-flat–D–E-natural–G-sharp) conspicuous by giving clarity to the E-natural which contradicts the E-flat in the previous bar. Note that the four-note figure, augmented (i.e., in the equivalent of half notes), appears in the B, A, G, F-sharp, and so on, in the bass, twelve bars from the end.

The slow movement of this sonata is an important chapter in the autobiography we are discovering. All men know grief, and most of us, under its impact, are bewildered and silent, even ascribing it to the malignity of fate. But he who can express it with the solemnity and dignity which belong to tragedy not only alleviates our pain; he gives us a kind of understanding to which, unaided, our misery could never attain. He is a humanist. This movement is a great human document.

Although the notes are easy to strike, the first two bars are the most difficult in the whole piece to *play*. *Lento e mesto*—slow and measured—is the composer's direction; and before you play, you must first *think* the melody in that manner. Even so, the tone line offers a precarious problem. Each bar is obviously a phrase, and in each the crisis falls on the fourth beat—that in the second bar being the more intense. Each note, however, dynamically, must merge into the next, else we shall have no legato, but only a succession of thumps. Any rubato is unthinkable: it would yield only querulousness and sentimentality.[4] The loudness of the sustained harmonies must naturally be appropriate to that of the melodic tones. The subdominant harmony of bar 2 is itself more tense than the tonic harmony of bar 1, so that the general dynamic level of bar 2 is slightly higher.

With the fingers alone, you will hardly be able to realize these values. Both pedals, however, are available, and will give much help. A dark and somewhat muffled color, from the soft pedal, is certainly appropriate. The damper pedal may be used anew with each melodic note; but since D and F in bar 1, and D and G in bar 2 are each in the supporting harmony, the pedal may hold through both notes, thus smoothing the dynamic path up to the crisis. Doubtless, there should be *dim.* from F down to C-sharp in bar 3. This will enhance the composers' ⟋ in bar 4. But observe that he has also prescribed, over the bar line, a diminution from A to B-flat. Pedal the *portamento* B-flat's in bar 5, so that the entrance of the diminished seventh in bar 6 may be tenuous enough to permit the stress (marked by the composer) on the D-sharp's. The *cresc.* at bar 7 must be considerable, reaching *f* with the arpeggiated chord. (Many editions give *sf* for this chord, though it is not in the original editions. Casella omits the second *cresc.* in this bar.) This second *cresc.* implies that the dotted sixteenth, E, must be much weaker than the preceding F. Similarly, the A (on "three" of bar 8) must be up-beat to the *pp* A on "four"; even though this contradicts the second *cresc.* for this one note. Nor must the *pp* be allowed to impair the simple strength of the cadence.

[4] If we use the numerical indications of shading that we employed in the Chopin *Prélude,* the twelve melody notes of the first two bars will be something like this:

| D | C-sharp | D | F | C-sharp | D | D | C-sharp | D | G | C-sharp | D |
|---|---|---|---|---|---|---|---|---|---|---|---|
| 3 | 1 | 2 | 4 | 2 | 1 | 3 | 2 | 3 | 5 | 2 | 1 |

all, of course, within the range of piano.

More poignant, but less depressed, is the subtheme which enters in bar 9. Study carefully the dynamics of the undulant accompanying figure. Wherever the melody pauses (as in bars 11 and 13), this 'cello-like figure should emerge as an answering phrase. The melody itself will be imagined without effort, save for the arpeggio descent (*f* to *p*) in bar 16, which is difficult to shape against the continued legato of the left hand. This is really a return of the darker tragic mood, which is tensely expressed in the phrases on the chord of the augmented sixth which follow. The melody is transferred to the tenor in bars 21–23, and is there even more embittered by the octave ejaculations above it. Be sure that the highest note of the right hand is predominant in the *ffp* chords and the melodic phrases they initiate. The "celli" in the left hand are very significant against the renunciatory strain that ends this section of the movement. The descent must be into a region of great darkness.

The three low F's in bar 31 give only a hint of the warm glow that will now suffuse the whole picture. Sustain the tones to the utmost (of course with the pedal); and study carefully that relative intensity of the soprano and tenor voices which will give appropriate color to the new melody. You must make the most of this passage, for the sense of solace endures for only five bars. The violent protest that ensues is dramatic in the extreme.[5]

---

[5] Many good editions (Breitkopf & Härtel, von Bülow, Peters) repeat the harmony note, C-natural, against the melodic C-sharp at "three" and "six" of bar 35, and an analogous D-natural in bar 37. D'Albert, Steingräber, Schnabel, and Casella repudiate it. It does not appear in the original edition. The author, however, feels this interesting dissonance to be musically more "probable" than the D-flat in Op. 2, No. 1, upon which comment was offered in a footnote (p. 32) above. The mark *fp* for the bass G, in bar 36, must mean that the G is *f* throughout the bar, but that the left-hand chords (like the right-hand figurations) are *p*. Sustain the G (which must be struck with the thumb, after the arpeggio) by shifting silently to the little finger. The right-hand figurations require a very delicate stress on the middle note of each group, but no general *cresc.* Keep the rhythm unbroken when the accompaniment for these figures ceases (bar 41), but let an increasing sense of recitative appear. From the B-flat in bar 43 (as Schnabel suggests) a discreet rubato may be used.

Because there are more notes, the returning main theme (bar 44) is now much easier to play. Do not miss the bitter imitation in the bass at bar 46. With the soft pedal and a careful dynamic contrast, a wonderful color can be found for bar 50. From the beginning of the somber passage at bar 65, study out the most effective approach to the cataclysmic G-flat in the bass of bar 67; and try to get the utmost in finality out of the descent to the Coda beginning in bar 72. The Coda is difficult to shade. From the high F in bar 78, the author feels that a slight hastening is justified. It can be compensated for by a similar lengthening of the last three notes. Give full and firm value to the *rf's* in bars 82 and 83; but remember that this mark applies only to these notes. Keep as clear as their low register will permit the imitative voices in the following somber passage. Follow the general rule in giving a very slight accent to the C-sharp's in the final two-note phrases;[6] but make no departure from simplicity.

To imagine the right emotional note to strike after such a slow movement as this is as difficult as to write the movement itself. Beethoven calls his little piece *Menuetto;* but instead of the poised rhythm and the courtly elegance of that dance he finds a strain of such gracious gentility as will alleviate, without any shock of incongruity, the somber mood of the *Adagio.*

Observe that there is a continuous succession of strong and weak bars, as if the time were 6–4 instead of 3–4. Thus you must make no accent whatever on the first beat of bar 2, else you will break the melody into two disjunct phrases, and so fail to bring the melodic line to its stress-point (on D in bar 3) in an unbroken sweep. Be sure that the bass gives adequate support. In contrast to this legato, the phrases in bars 5 and 6 are detached, moving delicately to F-sharp. The rest of the section is analogous. The second section begins with an energetic figure by way of

[6] The first note of a two-note slurred group conventionally has the accent, no matter what may be its rhythmic position. The last note, through its staccato, can sufficiently suggest the ictus of the rhythm in most cases.

contrast. Without this, the Trio would seem uncouth. It serves here, however, only to enhance the charm of the main theme when it returns.[7]

The Trio is really but 16 bars long, with its altered repetition written out. Make the contrasts of *f* and *p* vivid, and observe the slurs which replace the staccato from bar 16. The triplets in the right hand are not easy to articulate, but if they are merely smeared in with the pedal the quaint theme will be ruined. The final high A of the Trio is often sustained with the pedal until the D. C. begins. The sudden silence implied in the notation is at first disconcerting, but is certainly in character with the whole Trio.

The *Rondo,* unfortunately, is out of character. For subject there is only an inquiring little figure of three notes (a kind of "motto"), with a soaring but inconclusive after-phrase, and a negative sort of cadence (bar 8). The subtheme (bar 9) hints at passion, which the B theme (bar 17), with its elastic sway, begins to round out; but its character is lost in the overlong chromatic scale, and is not recovered. The A theme, returning, thus gains no new meaning, even with its sudden plunge into B-flat, the key of the ensuing C subject. This theme begins with promising self-assertion, but the unison passage to which it leads, although vigorous, seems irrelevant. The returning motto seems suggestive, but accomplishes nothing in the slithering diminished sevenths with which it ends. A returns, somewhat elaborated, and proceeds, without recurrence of the B subject, to the Coda in which the motto is at last interestingly developed. Note that its rhythm is present in the syncopated chords, twelve bars from the end, and of course in the left hand thereafter.

The movement is hardly a brilliant success; yet we can hardly

[7] In this figure, Schnabel suggests *p* for the eighth notes after each *sf*, but introduces $<$ at bar 8. This is in accord with convention, since *sf* does not necessarily imply forte. To us, however, the intrinsic character of the phrase is vigorous, and it thus seems better to follow D'Albert's suggestion of *poco f* for the whole passage, with *dim.* at bar 8 for approach to the returning main theme.

think of it as a mere lapse into indifference. The notion is perhaps fanciful, but to us it seems like an adventure into the then unfamiliar realm of romanticism. This seems to us at any rate a clue to the proper tone quality for the opening. Certainly, the declarative tone of the first movement would be quite out of place.

In the *Sonate Pathétique* (completed, like the three sonatas in Op. 10, in 1798, but actually later than those works in conception), we find at once a clarifying of the stern purposiveness shown in Op. 10, No. 3. By comparison, indeed, it seems extraordinarily advanced. Even when it is badly played (as it mostly is) it commands our attention irresistibly. Its directness and force, attained within so short a time, offer an important revelation of the swiftness with which Beethoven's musical mind was maturing, and thus a significant addition to our "autobiography."

The word *Pathétique* connoted, for Beethoven, no sentimental notion of self-pity. The music is intently extraverted. Bold, Promethean defiance of apparently ineluctable circumstance—such is the "pathos" or feeling implied by both the word and the music. Such a work could not have been written before the French Revolution, or by a man indifferent to its implications. The modernity of it astounded his contemporaries (although he himself was doubtless unaware of its originality); but we can hardly see it in this light unless we put ourselves back into its time—a time when visions of a new order were as hopeful as in our own day.

The *Introduction* (the first to appear in Beethoven's piano sonatas) vastly exceeds in solemnity the opening of the Lullian or "French" overture which is its prototype. Drama at its highest tension is announced in the very first bar. Force and suspense seem the very substance of the rhythms, the dissonances, and the long, expectant pauses. To misplay any detail is to weaken and distort this impressive thought.

In any very slow tempo, our rhythmic attention, as it looks

forward to the next distant beat, is stretched to its utmost span. We measure these time spaces, as we listen, with high expectancy for that satisfaction which the next throb will give, if it comes at the precise instant that was forecast; and we are correspondingly frustrated if the beat is misplaced. Here the first chord, after its explosive attack, is unsupported by any subordinate rhythmic beating. It must therefore be recognized, when at last the music sounds again, as *having been* of that precise length which is now to be measured by the definitely marked rhythm. The time value of the sustained chord, that is, must have been counted, throughout, at the precise tempo of the following motion.[8] (Beethoven's indication, *fp,* which demands a forte attack for the tone, but an immediately following piano for the rest of its duration, is impossible to execute on the piano. The only solution is to play *p* at the first thirty-second note. Many editors alter Beethoven's mark accordingly.) Under no circumstances lengthen the thirty-seconds, but make them press forward to the next dotted sixteenths by playing them more softly than these longer notes. The E-flat (beat 3), with its sustained discord, is obviously the crisis of the piano part of the phrase. How to give this note its due prominence, and how to shape the dynamic curve of its release on the following softer D, is a problem that will not be solved at the first attempt.

Keep inexorably to your tempo in the following three bars. The *cresc.* in bar 4 is difficult to keep smooth. Pedal for each chord will help. Do not ignore the *sf* B-flat in the bass, at "three." The run must not be allowed too much freedom of tempo.

Allow no change whatever in speed at bar 5. Be sure to strike all the notes in the chords simultaneously, but make only a faint rhythmic accent on beat 2, and a little more on beat 3. Do not attempt to make the thirty-seconds in the *ff* as loud as the dotted

---

[8] The safest way is to count each sixteenth, throughout the *Grave,* thus: *one,* 2, 3, 4, *two,* 2, 3, 4, *three,* 2, 3, 4, *four,* 2, 3, 4. Only two slight deviations, noted in the text, will be allowable.

sixteenths. Hint at *cresc.* in bar 7, but soften the B-natural after the stress note, C. In bar 8, however, the eighth note, D, must continue the *cresc.*, and the F's must continue to increase so that the *sfp* in bar 9 is definitely the crisis of the whole Introduction. The real bass (B-natural, A-flat, G, A-flat | G), in bars 8–9, properly weighted, will contribute greatly to the intensification of this climax.[9] Keep the rhythm precise in bar 9, not only for the notes but for the silent fourth beat. The tied E-flat in bar 10 may be slightly lengthened, with some freedom for the descending run. The whole Introduction has the tension of tragedy, not that of personal suffering, and this large feeling-dimension must be maintained throughout.

The *Allegro di molto e con brio* snaps into instant action. The tempo should be such that one eighth note of the Introduction equals a whole bar of the Allegro. To play the Allegro at this speed is very difficult. A good deal of its character can be realized with a slower tempo; but the student should keep the faster in mind as a goal to be attained. At the outset, we are struck by a certain kinship between this principal subject and that of Op. 10, No. 3:

Op. 10, No. 3

Op. 13

In the D major sonata, there were really two motives: the descent of four notes (which was so largely developed) and the ascent to the culminant *sf*. In the *Pathétique*, after the propulsive

[9] In playing crescendo, remember that the lower register of the piano has much more volume than the upper. Unless high notes, forte, are well supported by low —and usually with the pedal—the high notes will sound harsh.

beginning, there is only ascent. Allowing for the minor key, however, the two ascents are almost identical (the dotted half, C, takes the place of the D–F-sharp–A), save that the *sf* in the C minor is made more shattering by the repetition of C and the rhythmic displacement of the *sf*. Here, also, the harmony intensifies the headlong drive. It almost runs out of its key into F minor at the first upward step, and is brought back (B-natural–C, bars 2–3) only to rush off again on its impetuous course. But note that (as in Op. 10) there is no *cresc.* in all this upward progression—only the *sf* at the crisis. Here, the *cresc.*, exceptionally (and with a high sense of character), comes on the ensuing *downward* progression, eventuating in the tense suspension of bars 7–8. (Do not miss the expansion of this dissonance in bar 16.) To control both speed and dynamics in this subject will require much study.

At bar 17, a transition seems to begin.[10] The excitement does not abate, however, and at bar 25 there is a return to the swift upward staccato of Subject I. Observe the rest in bar 27, in order to make the following *sf* seem as if the whole body of the music had plunged, during the silence, down the long chasm from the high B-natural to the low E-flat. Instead of being a mere transition, this passage intensifies the towering passion of the music. The descending two-note phrases that follow are the "diminution" (the rhythmic condensation into smaller space) of the preceding tremendous *sf* blows, and each must plunge downward with similar abandon. In reality, then, the two bars of wavering on B-flat–A are all that appear of actual transition, for in bar 41 the second subject appears.

Here, again, is high consistency of character. The key is E-flat minor (not the orthodox major). Also the motion in staccato quarters will not abate. But the essence of this subject lies in the

---

[10] The descending arpeggio in bar 19 will be much easier if the left hand takes the last three notes (fingering 1, 2, 3), with the right hand resuming (with the 2nd finger) on the first note of bar 20.

reiterated outcry, G-flat–E-flat, whose *sf* attack must be thickly pedaled and uttered with passionate intensity. The consequent phrases—two-note figures, with the ornaments (properly, "pralltriller," but often called "mordents")—will easily lapse into triviality if they are carelessly read.[11] If you play the passage at first without the ornaments, but with the proper, strong emphasis on the first of the two notes, you will see that the pralltriller is not a mere ornament, but an intensification of the note and so of the figure. This strain is a weaker continuation of the outcry, but it need not be made trivial. The closing subject appears at bar 79. The expectancy of the syncopated E-flats is an imaginative approach to the elemental energy depicted in the divergent scales, with their agitated figuration, which form the subject.[12] What a summation this is of the purport of the whole movement! The running passage (bar 103), although not forceful in dynamics, is still turbulent in spirit; and its lower intensity also allows a pointed reference to the principal subject, with a conclusion too emphatic to be gainsaid.

The poetic sense of the return to the *Grave* has often evoked comment. (It was not unprecedented. Haydn had introduced a

---

[11] The "mordents" are very difficult. The classic rule would place them on the beat: [musical notation] which at the terrific speed of this movement is almost impossible. But all good editors agree that to turn the mordent into a mere triplet of eighths— [musical notation] is abominable. Two grace notes *before* the beat, although contrary to classic rule, will more nearly embody the proper character of the figure. Even these, for most players, are very difficult.

To those who cannot manage the more desirable of the above alternatives, a fairly effective substitute may be offered: a single, quick grace note—in reality, the second of the two which properly constitute the ornament [musical notation] . This may be played almost simultaneously with the principal note. It is sanctioned by no rule, but gives a closer approximation to the desired effect than the faulty readings just mentioned.

[12] Von Bülow's suggestion of a relative weighting of —◡ for the two E-flats is admirable. Note that in the figurated rising scale which these poised notes initiate there is a similar character to that of the closing subject of the first movement of Op. 10, No. 3.

similar effect in the *Paukenwirbel* [*Drum-roll*] *Symphony*.) Only one point requires our notice: the enharmonic modulation in bar 3, where D-sharp takes the place of the former E-flat. Give the D-sharp slightly more emphasis than the E-flat received, and make the bass progression C–B-natural prominent enough so that the D-sharp now pulls upward, instead of downward, which was the tendency of the E-flat. In this way the shift to the remote key of E minor will be clearly felt. Do not too much obscure the melodic line (A–G–F-sharp–D-sharp) in the descent of the chords.

The development does not attempt to add force to what has already been forceful enough. Instead, it suggests an inner mystery in that force—an implication that we have had no time to grasp in the breathless haste of the exposition. The first phrase is not the principal subject, but is that altered form of it which was heard in bar 25. The melody in bars 5–6 of the development is from the first phrase of the Introduction, and, so far as is possible in the swift tempo, should hint at the somber character of that phrase. Beethoven wrote *cresc.* in bar 13, and gave no other dynamic sign until the *p* in bar 27. This at first seems an oversight. But if the natural contour of the detached four-bar phrases is respected, an effect of gradual crescendo can be produced, culminating with bars 24–27, whose increasingly heavy bass there changes dramatically to the sudden *p*. Casella counsels ⟩ in bar 16. If the rising figure of the bass has not grown too loud, however, the increase may well continue through the tremolando, with bar 17 then momentarily somewhat softer for the sake of further crescendo. (Similarly, of course, in bars 20–21.)

The harmony of the following passage (bars 31–34) is extraordinary. Make barely perceptible the threatening melody (C-sharp–D–C-natural–B-natural), which with its accompanying thirds is almost ultramodern in its dissonance with the bass G and the high A-flat. Do not detach the two phrases that the composer has purposely united with a single slur. (Casella's direction, *confuso,* if the playing suggests, but does not produce, confusion, is altogether appropriate.) The ensuing *cresc.* must be violent, with its culminant *sf* dominating both this and the similar, expanded passage at bar 45. The impetuous motion of the descending run (bar 51) must not be disturbed by rubato or by fussy dynamic shading. (Casella substitutes *sf* for Beethoven's *fp,* continues *con forza* for four bars, and diminishes thereafter—we think, with great loss of dramatic effect.)

The Recapitulation differs so little from the Exposition that no comment is needed. Hold the ⌒ before the last *Grave* exactly three bars; release the pedal precisely on the beat; and count the ensuing silences with great accuracy, so that the eloquent fragments of the somber Introduction may have their full effect. The pathos (in the sense we have suggested) of the last legato strain of the *Grave* has been carefully indicated by the composer. At the end of the brief *Allegro,* make the final chords sharp and decisive, without retardation.

Not only in itself, but as an imaginative antithesis to the character of the first movement, the *Adagio cantabile* is admirable. The mere sweep of the melody compels the most indifferent ear; but its exalted contemplation also commands the reverence of the most experienced hearer. The *Grave* kept the first movement from sounding overrebellious; but this imperishable melody opposes to the former turbulence a calm nobility which reveals, more clearly than any previous utterance, the dimension of its creator's mind. It is significant, as von Bülow remarked, that one of Beethoven's noblest confessions of idealism—the *Adagio* of the Ninth Symphony—is in a way a completion of this thought.

Beethoven's phrasing reveals the indifference current in his day to the use of the slur as a mark of punctuation in music. We venture (in the slurs printed below the notes) to suggest a phrasing which seems more in accord with the sense of the notes than that which the composer provided, and which appears above the notes. (The figures again suggest dynamic gradations.)

Here, for comparison, is the phrase from the Ninth Symphony:

No better illustration than this musical sentence can be found of the fact that pianistic legato depends on far more than mere physical continuity of tone. Only the most perfect gradations, whether of consecutive or simultaneous tones, will make us forget that felt hammers are striking wire strings. The next eight bars will have slightly fuller intensity, to permit of the richer figuration. The melodic value of the bass in bars 12 and 13 will be evident.

Many players obey a not unnatural first impulse to hasten the speed at bar 17. This is wrong. The melody emerges like a solo violin out of a thicker fabric of orchestral tone; but its lofty passion is the complement, not the antithesis, of what has gone before.[13] Beethoven's dynamic marks in the transition are: *cresc.* at bar 24; again (with no contradiction) *cresc.* at bar 26; *p* at bar 27, and *pp* at the second half of bar 28, with *p* for the returning theme. One must infer, with Schnabel, that *p* is intended at bar 25; but to us his suggestion of a slower tempo for this passage seems unnecessary.

The B theme (bar 37) is a kind of augmentation of the first

[13] Play the turns in bars 20–21 as four sixty-fourths: that in bar 20 in the time of the second sixteenth, and that in bar 21 in the time of the third sixteenth, of the beat. Since it is impossible to play the triple appoggiatura in bar 22 in the time of the following thirty-second, and still have any time left for the principal note, this ornament must have a little time for itself, with the succeeding figure slightly remodeled to keep its graceful contour unspoiled.

bar of the "violin" melody. The bass figure in bar 38 also faintly resembles the descending passage in bar 24. Whether these resemblances are intentional or accidental, they serve to knit the B theme to the principal subject. Do not ignore the implication of the dark key of A-flat minor in seeking for the appropriate tone color. Make no change in tempo. Brighten the tone at the enharmonic modulation in bar 42, but let nothing give flippancy to the dramatic staccato of the bass in bars 48–49.

The triplet figure that accompanies the return of A is violinistic, and very hard to play agreeably if the indicated staccato of the last two notes is literally obeyed. Casella counsels the use of the pedal, which seems to us admissible; but the phrasing of the accompanying figure will be utterly lost if different dynamic weights are not given to the two repeated notes (the second being faintly louder than the first). The staccato bass in bars 62–63 must be observed, but the pedal may again be taken for the second half of the bar. The *rinforzandi* in bars 70–72, followed by piano and the indicated phrasing, will give a suitable tone of regret to the conclusion.

Once more, the final *Rondo* will be found weaker than the rest of the sonata. Von Bülow makes a great point of the similarity of the opening figure of four notes to that of Subject II in the first movement. This point is sadly diminished in sharpness by the fact that this movement was written before the others, apparently as a part of a sonata for piano and violin. We might with equal force (and equal fatuity) point out a relation between bars 17–18 of the *Rondo* and bars 27–28 of the first movement. His emendations of the rather scanty dynamic directions are often debatable. The $\underset{}{\diagup}p$ for the three G's of the theme (bars 3–4) sounds fussy and consciously "artistic," even though this effect is a favorite of Beethoven's. Nor is it necessary to make the bass G in bar 170 the equivalent of the opening up-beat figure. But neither these nor other artifices will raise the expressive level of this movment to the height of the others.

A few hints as to technical detail may prove useful. Make the stac-
ato of the B-flat chord in bar 33 very short, thus giving more point to
the following *sf*. The A-flats in bars 37–38, and again in bars 51 and
following must be vigorously accented. In bar 38, begin the left-hand
figure with the 4th finger, and take the G of the upper voice with the
left thumb, to make easier the leap to the high register. (The same in
bar 148.) Play the descending run (bars 58–59 and later) with 4th
finger on E-flat and thumb on B-natural throughout. Do not forget
the character of the C subject (bar 99f.) against the crisp staccato of
the counterpoint. A slight retardation in bars 217–218 will enhance
the force of the final scale.

Even this brief analysis will point out how much more
definitely the character of the composer appears in this work than
in the earlier sonatas. Righteous indignation such as that of the
first movement, and the unassailable devotion of the second, are
not generated in shallow minds; and it is from the quality of
such utterances as these that we can infer the character of him
whose feeling they represent. You cannot conceive this music
save as the utterance of one who stands with his face to the future,
sensible that he may one day become its prophet.

# 4

# THE TRANSITION TO
# BEETHOVEN'S SECOND PERIOD

IF ONLY to correct a possible impression that an artist's progress is to be measured solely by his most strenuous efforts, we ought to study, at this point, the two lighter sonatas which make up Op. 14. But to do so would subtract too much from the space required for greater things. The first of the two you will find tinged here and there with romantic feeling—in the chromatic second subject of the first movement, and in the slow movement, which, as in Op. 10, No. 2, has the surface and the form of a Minuet to cover its kernel of bitterness. Op. 14, No. 2, on the other hand, has a kind of intimate humor, faintly sentimental (especially in the second subject of the first movement); prim and overcorrect in the *Andante* (though its self-conscious correctness is derided in the final fortissimo chord); and wholly mischievous in the *Scherzo,* which title Beethoven gave to the final movement, although its form is that of the Rondo.

These two works, however, are but relaxations from a far more serious task that was to be completed in the following year— the six String Quartets, Op. 18. Each of these, if we had space to study them, we should find to be a portrait of the composer in a characteristic pose. They would assure us that the *Pathétique* was no momentary, unaccountable flash of genius, but an achievement from whose height a whole new horizon could be scanned. The B-flat piano sonata, Op. 22, written in 1800, hardly consolidates the advance won with the quartets, even though Beethoven himself seems to have regarded it more highly than has the musical world since his day. This work, therefore, we also pass over.

With the *Sonata in A-flat, Op. 26,* however, the new maturity is in evidence. There is assurance so deep that it no longer asserts itself: so complete an identification of the composer with his idea that self-consciousness, which is still perceptible in the ungovernable passion of the *Pathétique,* is quite obliterated.

This is the first of three sonatas in which the first movement is not in sonata form. Instead, it opens with a set of variations on a fine original theme. Such a sonata was not, indeed, wholly an innovation. Mozart's charming little *Sonata in A*—perhaps the most lovable of all his piano pieces—had already set the example.

The Variation form, with the possible exception of the Fugue, is perhaps the most "musical" of all forms. It is almost incapable of imitation or parallel in other arts. Painting and architecture, it is true, often vary a motive; but they never vary their basic theme. Neither can a set of variations suggest, as the sonata form often does, the high contrasts and continuous tensions of drama, or the lesser undulations of narrative. Variation substitutes for the high possibilities of climax a kind of introverted concentration, often equally compelling, and sometimes even more vividly suggestive of character. But because it is the most musical of forms, it becomes, in the hands of an inferior composer, the most tedious of tortures.

Neither Beethoven nor Mozart was an inferior composer. Mozart's handling of his tiny, sunny theme is beyond criticism. The horizon that his work embraces, however, is far narrower than that which Beethoven scans. Indeed, it would be hard to find two works in which the antithesis of eighteenth- and nineteenth-century feeling is better epitomized. We shall therefore compare the two in some detail. This comparison is the more justifiable since there is some evidence that Beethoven (who was a jealous god) was in part moved to the making of this sonata by a spirit of rivalry. There is at any rate a remarkable similarity in the succession of character suggestions in the two sets.

To most of us, Mozart's theme will appear to "say" nothing. Yet it can hardly fail to reflect a condition of mind as untroubled as its own clear surface. But is the beginning of the second section:

as unimpassioned as our modernism complacently supposes? Or may these tensions have been more affecting than we can readily perceive? The variations should help to answer the question, for in them hints of character in the theme may be intensified.

The first variation is an incredible lightening of the gossamer of the theme; but against this very lightness the swerving thirds in bars 5 and 6, and the insistent reiterations of E in bars 3 and 4 of section II, take on a lyric vividness that is unmistakable. The second variation, less characteristic, accomplishes the necessary descent from the imaginative level of the first to that of the third variation, without, of course, hinting at what that is to be. The third is in the minor—a key-contrast whose interest for eighteenth-century ears was far higher than for ours. Its rounded phrases—the melodic interval of the diminished third, with the peak of the curve displaced to the fifth beat (bar 2); the intensification provided by the octaves (from bar 9); and especially the opening of the second section—are charged with a pathos utterly simple, but incisive enough to draw a furtive tear from many a courtly dame to whom the more ostentatious expression of grief would have seemed merely crude. The fourth variation, if only by its brightness, heightens in retrospect the pathos of the third; the fifth, very florid, is chiefly ornamental, but is in the same exquisite taste as the others; [1] and the sixth, almost chuckling, hints at many possibilities of further treatment with which, if he had not been a great artist, Mozart might have overweighted his dainty theme.

Beethoven's variations in Op. 26 follow so strikingly the same fluctuations of character that the resemblance can hardly have been accidental. Yet there is between the two sets a world of difference. Beethoven's theme, far more sober, is a kind of hymn— addressed, however, to humanity rather than to the Deity. We intend here no invidious distinction. It is merely a fact that Mozart's exquisite design is essentially aristocratic, whereas Beethoven's is, in the best sense of the word, plebeian—an echo of the fervent Protestant chorales which provided so sure a foundation for German musical culture. To play this theme musically is by no means easy, even though the technical demands are not great. But because the theme is a valuable study for those to whom this book is particularly addressed, we shall examine minutely the essential phrases.

At the outset we are confronted with the need for a more exact punctuation of the text than Beethoven provided. A perplexing variety of suggestions has been offered by the various editors. The emendations, to be sure, are only earnest attempts to indicate the real sense of the music, and Beethoven's own notation is for the most part clear. We offer, along with the original, but below the notes, what seems to us a rational phrasing.

The initial E-flat, obviously weaker than the following downbeat, must still be stronger than the A-flat which completes the three-note motive. These three gradations of piano are not easy to effect.[2]

---

[1] Reger's portentous variations on this same theme (for two pianos, and also for orchestra) are an amazement of ingenuity; but to our mind they go so far beyond the natural scope of the theme as to appear quite tasteless.

[2] To judge in advance the right dynamic intensity for the first note of a phrase (and especially for the first note of a piece, as here) is one of the most difficult of the pianist's problems. If the note is too loud, the rest of the phrase either must rise beyond its proper dynamic level, or must lose its proper inflection—unless,

The same problem arises in bars 1–2. The A-flat on "three" is up-beat to the next A-flat, analogously to the two initial E-flats; but this phrase is clearly of higher intensity than the first. As we read it, this phrase ends with the third G in bar 2; and this raises another problem of fine dynamic discrimination for these notes. (You have only to play the three G's with equal loudness to perceive the problem.)

The harmony for this phrase is so easy that it is often misplayed.

---

of course, the first note is the loudest in the phrase. The difficulty is far less if the phrase is begun too softly, for in that case there will remain "room to grow." Thus it is better to err in the direction of softness. But the artist will have in mind, before the first note is touched, a vivid image of the whole phrase.

Note that the alto and bass are dotted quarters,[3] and that they must
be sustained by the fingers; for although the pedal may be taken for
the slur, it must be released at the first phrase end, and this will cause
the up-beat, A-flat (if the fingers have left the harmony-notes), to
sound bare. Nothing is more indicative of the musicianly pianist than
his care for the true value of subordinate notes.

In bar 3, be careful to play the alto E-flat softly enough so that it
cannot be mistaken for a melody note. For the crisis, D-flat, von
Bülow and Casella arpeggiate (roll) the *sf* chord. This seems to us
quite out of character: justifiable only when the hand is too small to
reach the ninth. (Make the 5th finger bear most of the weight of the
attack, so that D-flat will emerge unobscured as the peak of the
melodic curve.) Be sure that the up-beat (four thirty-seconds) in bar 4
is preceded by silence, no matter how short. The two-bar crescendo
which most editions give in bars 5–6, will not appear unmusical if its
growth is placed chiefly in the second bar. (Casella, following the
original edition, omits this crescendo.)

By strict analogy, the phrase end in bar 9 would appear to be on
the third A-flat. The sixteenth-note slur, E-flat–A-flat, however, was
evidently chosen by the composer as the conclusion, with the following four A-flats as preparation for the down-beat in bar 10. We venture to substitute *portamento* for the composer's *staccato,* and bring the
phrase to an end on the third beat in bar 10, as in bar 2.

The *sf* F in bar 16 proclaims the importance of the tenor voice in
this section; but the higher phrase is also significant. Its shading
(obviously ⟨ ⟩) is difficult to manage against the natural
decrescendo of the tenor. At bar 20, help the legato of the octaves by
using a syncopated pedal with each beat; play the upper note of the
octave always louder than the lower, and study carefully the dynamic contour of the phrase. Subordinate the alto B-flats in bars 21
and 25, as you did the E-flat in bar 3. For the trills, a "turn" of five
notes (D–E-flat–D–C–D) will suffice; but that in bar 25 may well include seven—D–E-flat preceding the turn. Bar 26 is usually slightly
retarded, allowing space for the longer trill as an approach.[4] The

[3] In the original edition, the tenor E-flat is stemmed also with the bass, but
without the dot which the bass has. In bar 9, the tenor is only a sixteenth; but in
bar 27 it is also a dotted quarter. In many editions, the tenor in bar 1 is also
dotted—after all, a plausible emendation.

[4] To facilitate the playing of the trills, take the pedal for this third beat, and
release the first and second fingers (whose harmony the pedal thus holds) so

*cresc.* in bar 24 apparently ends with the *sf*. Do not arpeggiate this chord. In bars 31–32—the most intense in this section of the theme— a slight *rit.* seems to us allowable, with the two final bars played quietly *a tempo*. (A hint of this effect may be given in bars 13–14.) The staccato of the A-flats in the bass, in bars 16 and 34, must be elastic, not brittle.

The theme, throughout, must convey a sense of quiet fervency, with no apparent striving for effect. Every dynamic inflection will count either for or against the realization of this ideal; and you will find that to gain command of these inflections will greatly sharpen your discrimination in the playing of the en- suing variations, and of any other music.

The first variation, which should follow the theme without haste, but also without hesitation, should be in the tempo of the theme.

The characteristic figure of thirty-seconds (an ornament as appro- priate to this theme as were the delicate appoggiaturas in Mozart's first variation) is not a harmonic arpeggio, but a melodic grace. The pedal will ruin its delicacy. The bass, however, must move legato from bar to bar, and this is almost impossible with the unassisted hand. Take the pedal, therefore, *on the third beat,* releasing here the left hand. which at once prepares its next chord. Release the pedal exactly on the following beat, so that the staccato of the phrase end in the melody may not be obscured. Rubato for this figure is intolerable. Bring out the melody (B-flat | D-flat-C-B-flat) in the middle voice in bars 3–4, 11–12, and 29–30. The thirty-second-note figure being absent here, pedal each beat. In bar 17, where the left hand introduces the figure into an ornate version of the original tenor, you will find it more difficult than ever to play acceptably the melody in the right hand. The slight retardation recommended for bars 13–14 and 31–32 of the theme may also be employed in this variation.

The second variation, like Mozart's, descends from the high imaginative level of the first. Do not be deceived by the startling

that the upper fingers may perform the trill without constraint. The resultant blur is far less disagreeable than a clumsy rendition of the trills.

look of the page into the notion that this notation implies a Lisztian uproar.

After an initial *p,* Beethoven wrote no dynamic direction until the *rf* in bar 18; but it may confidently be assumed that the initial *p* is the characteristic dynamic sign for the whole variation. The editors of the best editions agree, often suggesting *leggiero* as a precaution. Use what we may call a legato pedal only for the slurs in bars 1–2, and so on. But when the melody thereafter appears on the weak beat, a slight touch of pedal, exactly with the note (which we may call a staccato pedal) will give a rounder tone. The *cresc.* that appears in the theme (and in the first and last variations) at bar 26 does not appear in this variation. Some editors recommend it, by analogy; but to us it seems artificial and unnecessary. The slight retardation we suggested at bars 13–14 and 31–32 of the theme, however, is possible here.

Mozart's third variation was but faintly tinged with pathos; Beethoven's is obsessed with gloom. Even the slow movement of Op. 10, No. 3 is translucent beside it. One thinks of Milton's

"yet from those flames
No light, but rather darkness visible."

If the figuration of Variation II compelled a slightly faster tempo than that of the theme, the persistent, dragging suspensions and syncopations here demand a return to the original tempo. A suspension is a note, originating usually in a consonant harmony, which is prolonged so as to sound against a new harmony to which it does not belong. It pulls strongly toward the new harmony, and presently moves into accord with it. This moving is the "resolution" of the suspension. But there is more in the condition of suspension than the pull of dissonance. Equally important is the rhythmic dislocation (syncopation) which here also occurs within the bar, but is strongest when the suspension is over the bar line. The crucial instant in the suspension is that in which its pull is most apparent: that in which dissonance and fundamental rhythmic beat coincide.

In order to sound at this point, the suspended note must be struck not merely with its normal weight as a weak or fractional beat, but also with the force of that strong beat which it anticipates. But again, if there is no fundamental rhythmic accent to mark the strong beat, the accented suspension may appear to the hearer as if it were itself the rhythmic accent; and in this case all that rhythm supplies to the pull of a suspension will be lost.

In this variation, therefore, the last sixteenth in each bar (the suspended—or, occasionally, merely syncopated—note) must be strongly accented. The real "one" in the following measure (the first note in the left hand) must nevertheless be loud enough to make itself felt as "one." The next two beats in the left hand will be much softer. The proportion of tone between the syncopated melody and the accompaniment is a matter for careful study. Although there is seldom as much time for the preparation of the effect as in this piece, the tonal and rhythmic values in suspensions are invariably managed in this way. We therefore edit very minutely a few bars of this variation, to illustrate as clearly as possible the dynamic process.

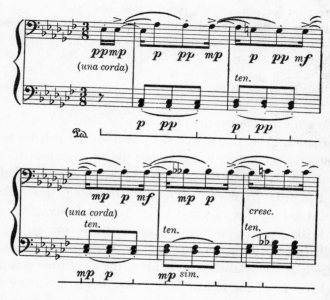

Even this tedious elaborateness does not indicate the finer gradations of *piano* that are essential; but it will outline the main details. To the author, the straining of the suspensions with their somber harmony is so great that he uses at each strong beat a suspicion of rubato —a very slight lengthening, not of the sixteenth-note approach, but of the crisis note itself. The left hand, that is, plays precisely in time, but the note of resolution is delayed, the delay being compensated for by a corresponding hastening of the following notes; but the last sixteenth must be inflexibly in tempo. (Nothing could be more repellent than the overdoing of this slight licence.)

The B-double flat in alto (bar 16) and the following G-flat in soprano are both marked *sf*. The G-flat, especially, cannot be too forceful. In contrast, play the A-flat–C-natural | D-flat in the alto, and the bass as well, markedly piano (the author plays *una corda*) so that the long soprano G-flat may audibly fall to F-flat. You will see that the composer's sforzandi in bar 21f. corroborate our slighter but similar accentuation of the music at the beginning. He leaves the bass unmarked, but it must of course give the strong-beat accent. He also detaches the two last sixteenths from the preceding notes which are beamed together. In music of this period, when the slur was not yet a very definite sign for phrasing or punctuation, the beam was often used as a ' phrase mark. It clearly represents Beethoven's intention here. Casella slurs from the last sixteenth in one bar to the sixteenth preceding the *sf* in the next. This reading is much easier to execute than the detached preparatory sixteenth which the original notation suggests, and seems to us allowable.

The sense of release that Mozart accomplished so beautifully in Variation IV is also achieved by Beethoven—not, however, by inventing a wholly new figure, but by an ingenious use of the very device by which the darkness we have just passed through was depicted: the device of syncopation. Many performers are tempted to turn this variation into a kind of Scherzo by taking a very brisk tempo. Yet the tempo of the theme (upon which Casella insists) seems impossibly slow. Perhaps the best advice is to play it as slowly as you can while at the same time you preserve the character of the music. Von Bülow suggests attempts at orchestral color which may stimulate your imagination, but are beyond the literal possibilities of the instrument. Schnabel's pointed avoidance of staccato for the delicate phrase ends is to us inexplicable. Delicacy is definitely indicated in the musical fabric; and to dull its sheen is to destroy the charm of this release from the preceding gloom. In his edition there is an unfortunate misprint in bar 27: the C on "two" in the right hand should be A-flat.

As in the preceding variation, the melodic accent is again on "three," the lesser accompanying accent is on the following "one," and the note of resolution is light. (Beethoven's caution, *sempre staccato,* for the left hand does not preclude this rhythmic accent.) The same values must be given in bar 5f., where the two sixteenths on "three," and later also on the following "one," are difficult to play with the proper discrimination. Observe that the last E-flat in bar 26 is the up-beat of the returning main theme, so that it must be clearly heard to progress to the A-flat on "two" after its tied continuation. In bar 26, Beethoven wrote *decresc.,* contradicting the dynamic indicated in the theme at this point. The bearing on bar 26 of Variation II is obvious. Also, the ⟨ ⟩ in bars 13-14 and 31-32 seems a kind of justification for our use of retardation at this point, both in the theme and the variations.

Variation V, once more like Mozart's in the profusion of its ornament, is the least imaginative of all. The melody is hardly altered. It appears, in the first eight bars, in the last note of each triplet; but these notes need not be especially marked, though you should be conscious of the melody's presence as you play. Thereafter, it is obviously in the alto.

Note that the left hand, at bar 17, has that melody in thirds which the right hand had in the theme. In bar 10, if the last eighth of the melody is too hard to reach with the right thumb, it may be taken by the left, thus:

(The right hand, from bar 9, having both melody and accompaniment to play, must function as if it were two hands: the thumb—which plays virtually all the melody—being the lower, and the fourth and fifth fingers the upper, hand. Practice the upper "hand" alone, sensing the weight as wholly reserved for the lower, until an even flow of tone is produced. Then add the thumb—which will need some assistance from the pedal to maintain the legato—making sure that the F in the upper line borrows none of the weight of the simultaneous thumb stroke. Add last the necessary, shading for the melody.)

The Coda is structurally unrelated to the theme; yet it forms a perfect epilogue to the whole set. The tempo must remain unchanged. The staccato of the bass simulates the pizzicato of 'celli and basses in the orchestra.

Since these instruments are not as quickly silenced as the damped strings of the piano, it is well to touch the pedal lightly with each note. Without more pedal than this, however, the portamento chords will require much care, and the legato of the melody even more. From bar 43, observe exactly the rests in the melody, shading with great care the antiphonal two-note phrases in bass and soprano. The *cresc.* in bar 49 will be enhanced if you adopt Schnabel's suggestion of a breath-pause before the final chord.

The humor in this Scherzo is more pointed than in any earlier example of this form. It is very difficult to play, but once mastered it is an inexhaustible delight.

Make the *sf* C (bar 1) very pointed. Reduce at once to *p* for the following notes, but be sure to maintain the legato of the melody, and still have enough tone for the sustained E-flat so that its progression to F may be clearly heard. Then, make the staccato F–D-natural–E-flat very sly, with no accent for the vanishing final E-flat. Bars 9–16 form the figurated repetition of the first section of the form, so that the conventional double bar does not appear. The staccato must be very light, the melodic E-flat and the unaccented final note having the same character as before. The second section presents no new subject. At bar 4 of this section, thump the bass A-natural vigorously to mark the rhythm against the suspended G-flat. In bars 11 and 12, following the original edition, modern editions set the sforzandi against the first beat of the bar. Many older editions (Liszt among them) put them on "two"—i.e., at the beginning of the ascending thirds. In spite of the heed which must be paid to the original edition, and to the experienced judgment of the editors, this older reading seems to us preferable. The sudden *f* at "three" in bar 10, after the preceding *p,* is equivalent to *sf.* Another *sf* on the next down-beat seems characterless. To shift the *sf* to "two," however, causes the first three notes to establish a cross rhythm which is consistently carried out in the two following phrases, and makes the sudden *p* at bar 13 more pointed. (Incidentally, the fingering $\frac{5}{3}$ for the weak down-beat is possible, but, with the *sf* on "one," another shift to $\frac{3}{1}$ is necessary.) Observe the notation exactly from bar 13.[5] Bars 25-28 may be slightly retarded. Preserve the melodic sense of the D-flat–C–C–C, with a breath-pause after the left-hand G in bar 28.

The humor of the theme is now more boisterous. The *sf* is delayed, falling on the melody-distorting E-natural, so that the delicacy of the phrase end disappears. The running counterpoint (taken over by the bass at bar 36) adds to the vigor, and the brief development of the final phrase of the theme forms an exciting conclusion. The left hand is very difficult. Avoid the 4th and 5th fingers as much as possible, even though the fingering seems at first awkward.

The quietude of the Trio seems subtly to relate the Scherzo to the soberer aspects of the whole sonata—a fact that will be more fully appreciated when the Funeral March is added to the picture. Only the textual reading requires comment. In the bass, at bar 10, the original edition gave F; von Bülow and others later gave A-flat; Casella and Schnabel return to the F, which is correct. In bar 13, also, the soprano F-flat is a dotted half note, not the half with detached quarter of the earlier editions.

The *Funeral March on the Death of a Hero* owes its inspiration to no known individual. The greater *March* which, four years later, formed the slow movement of the *Eroica* symphony, was the product of an idealization of Napoleon, whom Beethoven had supposed to be a man of high altruistic purpose. In either case, however, though he was doubtless quite unaware of the revela-

[5] Instead of staccato in the bass, bars 17–20, and two-note slurs, bars 21–24, von Bülow inexplicably gives portamento throughout. His editing of this whole sonata is so wilful as to be quite untrustworthy. His own expression marks, both in this sonata and the *Pathétique,* are also not distinguished from Beethoven's by smaller type, so that the student is inevitably misdirected.

tion, the man mirrored in the music is Beethoven's very self.

Beneath the obvious suggestion of a marching band, there is set forth an attitude of mind toward the experience of death. It is the interpreter's problem to make us share that attitude. Here is no self-centered grief, embraced in a rapture of agony. There is solemnity, appropriate to an event too big for lamentation; there is firmness equal to any endurance; there are moments of tenderness; but there is never the easy alleviation of tears. For the moment, heroism is begotten in us by the contemplation of the hero who is dead.

Solemnity and firmness must be depicted in the inexorable march of the rhythm: no mere leaden tramping, but rather a prideful step —a fitting gait for the somber ritual of death. Any suspicion of inexactness in time will detract from the essential dignity. Not only must the main beats appear precisely in their places; the sixteenth notes must always have identical time value, and the same feeling of approach to the following note.[6] The hand must be firm, so that all the notes of the chord (and of the accompanying bass) sound simultaneously; but, since the actual melody is more often beneath than in the highest voice, the melodic tone must be somewhat louder than its surrounding octave. The soft pedal is not necessary for the desirable degree of piano; but to use it, playing then somewhat more forcefully than in *tre corde,* will give a color to the tone that the author finds appropriate. The phase stresses are obvious. In bar 4, the three dominant chords should have the respective weights, ∪ ∪ —— . The pedal may be used, correspondingly, to mitigate an otherwise dry and inelastic staccato. The composer's dynamic directions are clear, and are identical in the repetition after the middle section.[7] To give force

[6] Count four to each beat, until the true position of the sixteenth note is ingrained in the musical consciousness. This will insure that the sixteenth will not be lengthened into something like the third eighth note of a triplet. Nothing is more nauseating than this March played as if it were written in 12/8 time. To give the sense of approach, play the sixteenth notes definitely softer than the following dotted eighths.

[7] Many good editions give a ◄══ at bar 13, representing what must have been a widely accepted tradition. It does not appear in the original edition, nor in Casella or Schnabel. In the doubtful case that it is authentic, the peak of this curve, at bar 14, would seem to be higher than the *sf* in bar 10, since the harmony is here more expansive in feeling. The same shading, however, within the range of piano, is equally affecting.

to the *f* and *sf* down-beats in bars 27–28, take a staccato pedal with each up-beat chord, leaving about an eighth rest of absolute silence before the heavy attack. (Sound that comes out of silence is more striking than sound, however loud, that is continuously approached.) Give all possible decisiveness to the cadence, bars 29–30. (Staccato pedal, however, is recommended.)

Casella is alone among the modern editors in recommending a greater number of notes than Beethoven wrote for the tremolando-like passages in the Trio. It is true that mere slavish timekeeping fails to suggest the drum roll that is obviously represented. But it is also true that Beethoven could have written, if he had desired it, the equivalent of the effect that Casella suggests. There is a cumulative-ness in the slightly conspicuous C's of the given notation which would be lost in the indeterminate rumble of the tremolando. The high staccato thirds, on beat 4, on the other hand, if cut very short, have such a thin, dry tone as to seem almost grotesque. We probably shall stand alone in recommending here a slight touch of the pedal, even though the composer indicated pedal for the rumble, and none for the chord.

The Coda, beginning eight bars from the end, has two divergent scale melodies, repeated in inversion. The greatest care must be given to their shading, and to their poignant harmony.[8] The *cresc.* with the ensuing *p* is difficult, but incomparably effective. *Una corda* with the ascending soprano phrase, and for the echo of the *sf* B-double flat, seems appropriate, with a slight retardation of the last three notes.

To Casella, the incomplete final bar of the March indicates that the Rondo is to follow without pause. Aside from the fact that the March began with an up-beat, whose value is conventionally subtracted from the final bar, it is doubtful whether the mood of the Rondo can be entered upon, whether by performer or hearer, without a moment's pause for the contemplation of what has passed.

The character of the Rondo, however, as the continuation or

---

[8] Do not misread the fifth bar from the end: B-double flat in the chord on "three"; F-flat in the chord on "four." (Experienced teachers, we hope, will condone this possibly superfluous advice.)

complement of the March, is not easy to grasp.[9] We have for principal subject rather a figure than a theme, and the character of that figure is not unmistakable. There are no high contrasts in the Rondo, and no pointed retrospects over the somberness of the March. Also, Beethoven gives as general directions for performance merely the tempo-mark, Allegro, and the dynamic sign, *p,* which governs for twenty-three bars. None of these things seems to mean much. But Allegro does not mean Presto (as Schnabel's alarming tempo-mark of $\downarrow = 160$ would suggest) nor does *p* imply a monotonous dynamic level. The piece is almost a "perpetual motion," all three of its main subjects being either made of or accompanied by a persistent figuration of sixteenth notes. The opening figure may be made brilliant by the fingers of a virtuoso, but its pattern, unforced, is no more than gently scintillant; and this quality is subdued rather than enhanced by the smooth lines of eighth notes that are presently added to it.

The motion begins on an elastic up-beat, with the rhythmic accents thus resting on the active chord of the dominant seventh, which colors the whole subject with its unstrained dissonance; and nothing more stressful appears in the mild modulations to related keys which form the transition to the second subject, beginning at bar 32. This is more an interlude than a subject, though it has a note of sprightliness not hitherto heard; and even the C subject, beginning in bar 80, offers no portentous intensification.

To us, the clue to this movement as a part of the whole sonata lies in its pointed extraversion. It represents the feeling of one who, after catastrophe, contemplates the course of normal life amid normal things. In that activity there is an implied invitation to join, impersonally; for it offers a hope, but no promise, of solace. The music, then, must be played undramatically, with neither urgent appeal nor aloof indifference.

The complex of suggestion offered by this sonata is far more intricate, and the total sense of the music is far more mature,

[9] Von Bülow even suggests that any desired rearrangement of the order of the movements in this sonata would be possible. This, at least, proves that he saw no continuity between the March and the Rondo. But it does not prove that Beethoven's vision was similarly defective.

than that which we found in the *Pathétique*. It is tinged with a humanistic feeling which Mozart hardly had the vocabulary to express. The currents of feeling awakened by the music, and their attendant association with circumstance and experience, are incapable of utterance in the literal medium of language. But our very awareness of maturity is evidence of the existence of these currents and our autobiography of the composer is thus the richer by a very significant chapter.

Yet, since we are concerned here with the transition to the second period of Beethoven's creative activity, the "maturity" of which we have spoken is only relative. Expansions are to occur of which the sonata we have just studied is only a hint; and, because so much more than we have anticipated is to appear in the second period, we cannot pass into that period without studying more examples of his growing insight. We have found that Op. 26, although it was not without precedent in containing no movement in sonata form, was nevertheless an adventure into an unexplored field of expression. The next-following sonatas tend in the same direction. Each of the two sonatas comprised in Op. 27 is entitled *Sonata quasi una Fantasia,* and the release of the imaginative fantasy is remarkably liberal.

No formal sonata had ever before begun with such phrases as we find at the beginning of Op. 27, No. 1. This is indeed the music of a dreamer; and the object of his dream is palpable. We do not, of course, know her name (it was certainly not the Princess Liechtenstein, to whom the sonata is dedicated), and we have no portrait of her in the music. The significant thing is that this music, in contrast to what we have so far studied, is introverted; and it finds extraordinary contentment in confessing its calm adoration. A few interpretative problems may be briefly considered.

The opening phrase is often read as if the bar line had been misplaced: as if the stress fell on the half note, G. This is a gratuitous misreading, and Schnabel has carefully guarded against it in his edition. Only when the proper rhythm for the beginning has been set forth can the later sforzandi on "three" become distinctive. The interpolated *Allegro* (6–8 time) is in pleasant contrast to, but hardly in character with, the *Andante*. The difficult leap from C to E in bar 7 can be obviated. Take the preceding E, F-sharp, G-sharp in the left hand with the 5, 4, and 3 fingers, so that the A and C can be taken with the 1 and 2. (Use the same expedient in bar 7 of the second section, taking the E in bar 6 with the thumb.)

The ensuing *Allegro molto e vivace,* if begun as fast as possible, will prove impossible at the end, where the syncopations enter with opposed legato and staccato. This passage is hard to keep clear; but it was certainly not written to be blurred. This movement substitutes for a Scherzo, and is essentially in that form; but its character—dark and spiritually tumultuous—is wholly appropriate to the preceding fantasy. The *Adagio* is in the same region of feeling as the *Andante,* but more declarative. Musical common sense will interpret it naturally. The trill on the upper A-flat of the octave in bar 6 can be facilitated by taking the lower A-flat with the left thumb. (The same in bars 22–23.) A slight retardation before the rapid run in bar 24 will permit unbroken motion in the eighth-note progression of the bass.

The very beginning of the *Allegro vivace* is awkward. Only energetic finger action will keep clear the low counterpoint in the left hand, and insure precise agreement of the two hands in bars 3–4. In the left hand, in bar 7, use the 4th for both G and D, with 1, 2, 3, 4 for the G, A-flat, F, D in bar 8. From bar 36 to 55, rock the hand from the wrist to keep the upper note of the broken sixths prominent. Use the same action in the left hand from bar 56, but especially from bar 66, to bring out the essential contribution of the tenor part. Although this is a Rondo, a kind of fugal treatment of the principal subject takes the place of the C subject, beginning at bar 106. Follow faithfully the composer's directions for dynamics. Make the *sf*'s on "one" in bars 132 and 134 heavily predominant over those on the preceding "two." The following episode (bar 140f.) is derived from that with the broken sixths. The brighter effect of the fragment of the *Adagio* in the key of E-flat is appropriate to the atmosphere of the Rondo. In setting the tempo for the final *Presto,* observe that you must finish with sixteenth notes, and that it will never do to begin too fast for the end.

The other sonata in this pair, Op. 27, No. 2, is the famous "Moonlight." This title was neither invented nor approved by

Beethoven. The sentimental yarns about its origin are all apocryphal. He was indeed smitten with the charms of the flirtatious Giulietta Guicciardi, but the dedication to her was an afterthought, the sonata having been originally intended for the Princess Liechtenstein. The popular title is really a nuisance. It not only reduces to insignificance our expectations of expressive meaning, but fails to accord, in any but the most superficial way, with the actual sense of the music.

It is true that the tone of the pedaled arpeggios in the *Adagio sostenuto* has a kind of luminousness, along with the gentle rocking of the triplet figure. Therefrom an idle mind might readily engender an image of moonlight on rippling water. But only if the somber melody is ignored. The harmonic curve of its long phrases is heavily weighted. The tense interval of the diminished third (bars 18 and 20), and the dark convergence of melody and bass on F-sharp in bar 23, shroud the whole vision in gloom which no moonlight could illumine.

The speed is so slow [10] that a lessening dynamic weight may shape each of the undulant triplets. Without this inflection, the whole piece will be perceptibly wooden. The melody must appear considerably above the dynamic level of the accompaniment— that is, the little finger, in the octaves, must play louder than the thumb; for the melody must not be heard in octaves. Also, its phrases must be led toward and away from their stress points with the utmost fluidity. The task is not easy.

In bar 8, the original edition has B-natural for the middle note of the second triplet. Many modern editions accept this without question. Older editions repeat the C-natural of the first triplet. The B-natural not only gives an uncomfortable parallel octave with the bass, but also a distorted progression to the C-sharp in the third triplet. We recommend C-natural. Intone the first G-natural of bar 10 so as to emphasize the shift to the darker minor harmony. Let the melody fall with tight-lipped aplomb to the B-natural in bar 15, and still more

[10] Liszt suggested $\quad \downarrow = 50 \quad$; von Bülow, 52. Casella's 60 seems to us somewhat hurried.

pointedly to the F-sharp in bar 23. The C-natural of the melody in bars 16 and 18 must be almost *sf* (in piano) if it is to remain audible against the indicated shading for the renunciatory figure in the bass. The melodic figures beginning in bar 28 have three notes only. The E on "one" in bar 30 should therefore not be so intoned as to be included in the preceding phrase. In bars 32–36, there is only figuration. It seems to us justifiable to intone the first note of each bar, keeping the rest *pp* until bar 35, where, after the weighted F-sharp, a slight *cresc.* (begun *pp*) will make possible an appropriate dynamic descent in bar 36. The D-natural in bar 39 is so meaningful as to justify a slight lengthening. The D-sharps in bar 41 must lead to the resumptive E in bar 42; but the cadential harmony in the two upper voices must also be felt. The end of the movement must be so approached as to suggest something like Hamlet's "The rest is silence."

The *Allegretto,* ensuing without pause, is as miraculous in its appropriateness as the *Menuetto* in Op. 10, No. 3. Liszt's metronome mark of ♩. = 76 seems to us more suitable than von Bülow's dragging 56, or Casella's oversprightly 84–88. Place the peak of the first phrase on E-flat in bar 2, with the continuation, staccato, diminishing gracefully to the end in bar 4. The following, wholly similar phrase really completes the first section of the form. The repetition is in the somewhat thicker, syncopated groups, which should have the same contour. In the *Trio,* the *fp* against the first bass note is your guide to the intensity of the sforzandi that follow.

The *Presto agitato* is very difficult to play, and few devices can be found to simplify it. To maintain the *p* until the sudden *sf* in bar 2 (for which alone the composer allowed the pedal) is no mean feat. The continuous *f* from bar 9 is very fatiguing, even with free wrist oscillation. The A in the tenor on "two" in bar 10 may be taken by the right thumb; but most students find this a doubtful aid. The sixteenths must not become inarticulate (though they are subordinate) when the second subject enters (bar 21). Do not attempt more than a "turn" (five notes, including the afterbeat) for the trills in bars 30 and 32. (Pedal this one beat, and so release the right thumb.) In bar 35, we favor rewriting the last half of the bar thus:

to correspond with the parallel passage at bar 66 of the second section. (Beethoven's piano still had but five octaves.) In bar 40, to retain force for the culminant octave E's, finger the rising scale with the thumb on A, E, and B. (Similarly in bar 70 of section II.) Von Bülow distorts the composer's sufficiently indicated phrasing in bar 43f. by dividing the beamed eighth-note chords into two groups of four. The seven chords after the detached "one" lead continuously to the next "one." (The same in bar 73f. of the second section.) Do not misread the sixteenths (section 2, bar 102) as thirty-seconds. (Von Bülow's accents are here quite appropriate.) Heavy accentuation on "one" and "three" in bar 113, and on "one" and "four" in 114 (and similarly in the following passages) will give life to what may otherwise degenerate into rather meaningless roaring. The trill in bar 123 may be somewhat prolonged, but the cadenza figure should begin impetuously, broadening only toward the three portamento quarter notes and the hushed *Adagio*. You will practice many hours before you can play clearly the final arpeggio figures. You will doubtless have noted that this is the only sonata-form movement in the three sonatas we have just studied.

Wonderful as the music is, the poetic theme of the "Moonlight" sonata is of course no novelty. In Op. 28, however, Beethoven spoke of a subject which hitherto had hardly engaged the mind of a creative musician—the subject of Nature. Beethoven's attitude is by no means that of Marie Antoinette and her silken-clad ladies-in-waiting, playing at dairy-maids; nor does it reflect the homocentric philosophy of the eighteenth century which permeates Haydn's "Seasons." It is probably akin to the deism of Rousseau; but of course Beethoven was not concerned with establishing or following any precise system of philosophy. It was enough for him to see, in the process of growth and multiplication, the fulfillment of a law to which he recognized his own subjection. Toward laws made by men he turned a critical and often a rebellious eye; but the commands that he deduced from nature as he saw it were inviolable. Thus none of his most famous contemporaries—not even Goethe, whose scientific investigations Beethoven would hardly have understood—found such deep intimate communion with growing things as did he

The title, "Pastoral," which is generally recognized as ap
propriate to this sonata, did not originate with Beethoven. No
has the music in any movement a direct reference (such as i
borne by the *Pastoral Symphony*) to particular aspects of nature
The sonata has no program. It merely utters the sense of well
being which, not only for Beethoven but for us, can come fror
that kind of experience whose quality is connoted by the wor
*pastoral*. If you try to associate it with any of the personal passion:
you will find your musical instinct frustrated at every turn. Bu
in the light of the pastoral assumption, every note is rich witl
meaning.

The quiet persistence of the pedal D, with its unruffled rhythm
the broad sweep of the ten-bar theme; the pervasive but incon
spicuous "activity." of the harmony, which almost translates th
melody into G; and the rich serenity of the tenor voice, added a
bar 11—all these are perfectly in character. The second strai
(bar 21), somewhat more exuberant, is still colored by th
pedal D. The transition (bar 40) begins at that level of interes
which the second strain just reached, and with its ensuing eage
figurations begins to throb with heightened interest. The gradua
approach to the second subject (bar 63) seems the very stuff o
anticipation; but the actual outline of the new thought is ob
scured for a time by the undulant, tentative phrases (bar 77
which at last form themselves into a second subject (at beat :
bar 90) that seems to have had no beginning, and has so ir
definite an end that, after the excited runs (104-108) it begin
anew and once more pursues its full course. Quite naturally, afte
all this, the closing subject is no more than a quiet epilogue.

The development is almost wholly taken up with the principa
subject. At bar 21 of this section a running counterpoint (appa
ently derived from bar 104 of the exposition) is added to the las
phrase of the main theme. After eight bars, the two element
change hands; after eight more, the thematic fragment is reduce

to two bars; at bar 57, the fragment is still further condensed, while the tenor has an inversion of the complete bar. This rhythmic condensation or "diminution" is a favorite device of Beethoven's. The high excitement wanes in a long descent on the F-sharp major chord. The closing subject is briefly alluded to, first in the major, then in the minor key of B; and at bar 107 the recapitulation begins. The brief Coda is a quiet reminiscence of the principal subject.

The technical difficulties are not great. The first bar is rhythmically "strong," even though the melody is silent. Since this begins on a weak bar, the phrase stress falls on the quarter note, A. Although the legato is unbroken, bars 5–6, with the up-beat, probably form a second phrase group, with a faint stress on D, bar 5. The stress in the final four-bar group is on E, bar 9. But the whole ten-bar period should be played in one sweeping curve. The pedal will be incessantly but discreetly used. There are no especial problems until bar 48, where the author and his pupils find this the easiest fingering:

The undulant eighth-note figures beginning at bar 77 are hard to equalize in the two hands, because the thumbs do not strike simultaneously, but each falls with the second finger of the other hand, and also because the melody is difficult to control in the extended position. (From bar 91, the inner figures, now fingered symmetrically, are easier.) A slight increase is essential in the four-bar groups beginning at bar 79, to make perceptible the phrase stress on the tied half notes; but do not allow these increases to obscure the definite *cresc.* in bar 87, which prepares strikingly for the entrance of the true second subject, piano, in bar 90. Keep exact time in the running passages, bar 104 and the like. Give an energetic accent to the third, E–C-sharp, in bar 131, diminishing the rising scale (but keeping it precisely in tempo) so that the right hand will still be audible at bar 133. Do not delay the entrance of the closing subject, and mark definitely the first of the two accompanying chords, so that the syncopated melody may appear in its true rhythm. If you fail to do this, you will have only a silly waltz tune. It is not easy to maintain the motion of the running passage in the development while preserving also the dynamic contour of the thematic fragments. The interchange of the parts must of course occur without pause or other interruption. Von Bülow and others dispute the authenticity of the sudden *p* at bar 65 of the development. The original edition, however, and all newer editions of consequence insert it.

To many students, the melody of the *Andante* at first seems without appeal. We are told, however, that this movement was a favorite of the composer's, and this fact alone should warn us against too much dependence on first impressions. Naturally, music in the character of the slow movements we have already examined would be out of place in this context. The pastoral quality, also, will be found only by implication; perhaps the most we can say is that there is no essential contradiction of that quality. The melody is neither tense with gloom nor buoyant with exaltation; yet it is by no means neutral. Its calm motion is impelled by a persistent staccato bass, which alleviates whatever of somberness belongs to the minor tonality. Even this is softly illuminated by the excursion into major at bar 5. The warmer second strain has a pedal A, which in some measure recalls the pedal D of the first movement. After the repetition of the main theme there is a lighter section, in the daintiest of tripping staccato; then the main theme again, with exquisite figuration of its repetitions, and a reminiscence of the second theme for a coda.

This simple music, however, is hard to play. The legato of the right hand is difficult to maintain against the staccato bass, which forbids any use of the pedal. The author has found the awkward-looking fingering

for the first two chords practicable, even for most small hands. In the following phrase, sustain each chord as long as possible, but with the slightest possible weight maintained after the attack. While sustaining each chord, lift the wrist so as to place the hand in striking position. In this way the interval of silence between the D's may be made almost imperceptible. In the bass, the first note of each beat will naturally bear more weight than the others. Having always to define the harmony, these bass notes must be carefully adjusted to the dynamics of the melody. In the second strain, with the repeated A's, the pedal is allowable.[11]

The delicacy of the B section is easily destroyed. The dynamic weight of the three chords must not be equal, for the rhythm will then have no ictus. Even if the first and third chords are made equal ($-\ \cup\ -$), the figure seems leaden, and disrelated to the following phrase. The author, therefore, plays $-\ \cup\ \cup$ , with pedal (even against the staccato mark) for the first chord. Play the thirty-second note before the ensuing arpeggio figure very short, with a decided accent on the first note of the triplets; but, above all, avoid any semblance of accent on the second of the two triplets. Make the most of the legato contrast in section II, where the pedal may of course be used; but observe that the staccato bass persists during four bars of the figurated repetition of the returning main theme. The pedal may not be touched until the bass is slurred. Hold the $\frown$ in bars 4 and 6 of the coda about five beats (eighths), being careful to observe the *cresc.* approach in a swelling portamento, with the ensuing *p* definitely contrasted. Take no liberties with the time as the triplets broaden into even sixteenths, or in the following bar. Play the turn in the last bar but one exactly in the time of the (slightly retarded) sixth sixteenth of the measure. (Schnabel, following the original edition, indicates B-sharp for the under ornamental note of the turn. Other editions consulted give B-natural, which we believe represents Beethoven's real intention.)

The humor of the *Scherzo* is certainly not urban, even though it suggests nothing that is conventionally recognized as rustic. Give no hint, in the first four bars, of the gay little figure to come. It is very hard to play these chattering little eighth notes clearly and in absolute tempo; but nothing must encroach on the

[11] Even considerably experienced students, of both sexes, have been known to miscount bars 7 and 8 of this section.

complete silence of the third beats. Similarly, give no warning
of the approach of the forte in bar 17. Since bars 3 and 4 of
section II have another pattern than the similar bars in section I,
the author plays bars 1–4 in a continuous legato, with the stress
point faintly marked at bar 3. Hold the ⌒ to make two additional bars.

The broken octaves in the *Trio* tax the left hand so cruelly
that the humor of the melody—the endless repetition of the one
ridiculous little phrase—is often quite lost. An increasing stress
on the F-sharps, although not prescribed except by implication
in the *cresc.,* eight bars from the end of section II, will enhance
the humor, and seems to us justifiable. Many editors recommend
a slower tempo for the *Trio* than for the *Scherzo,* and a faster
for the staccato section of the *Andante.* To our mind, these
changes involve a distinct loss of both continuity and character.
It is extremely difficult to articulate the eighth notes in the
*Scherzo* at a speed any greater than that at which the left hand
can execute the broken octaves of the *Trio.*

Something of the conventional pastoral character may be recognized in the *Rondo;* but there is nothing perfunctory in the suggestion. The well-being that has imbued all the sonata, so far
here rises to plenitude, far overriding any hint of rural scene or
action that may appear to be literally presented. The rocking
bass (which throughout the principal theme has again a persistent pedal note) is big with anticipation of the elastic melody
that emerges on the syncopated high A. The gracious curve of
this line, with its naïve staccato cadence, is a very ecstasy of contentment; and the continuation (from bar 9) only enriches the
mood. The transition (bar 17) is essentially a descending scale
disguised by shifts to higher and lower registers. Without "saying" anything, it still manages to maintain the impression of the
main theme, and it serves also to give spaciousness to the entrance of the B theme, in bar 28.

Here, indeed, the conventional pastoral contour is to be seen.
Figurated repetition of the characteristic figure brings a swif

rise to the exuberant shout (bar 43) with whose incomplete cadence return to the A subject is made. After the slightly figurated repetition of this theme, an elaboration of the original rocking bass forms a transition to the C subject. This is a fluid, four-bar strain, appearing first in the highest voice; then in the middle; then in the bass; then once more at the top (in octaves with added third); then, with full force, in the bass. Its culmination, in a variant of the figuration that closed the B subject, is of the highest exuberance. The normal repetitions of A and B lead to a brilliant coda which remains in character to its last note.

To give full value to the rising bass of the opening, allow the eighth notes to sustain, almost as if they were tied over to quarters— i.e., play legatissimo—and give a hint of crescendo up to the entrance of the theme. (Nothing, of course, must obscure the pedal D, nor the rhythmic rocking.) The phrase stress of the melody is on the high A; to keep the rest of its curve fluid, make no perceptible accent either on B or the final D of the phrase. Be careful to continue the legatissimo bass while playing the delicate staccato of C-sharp–D at the cadence. To us, the molto legato at bar 17 justifies the use of the pedal (except, of course, for the first half of bar 20). Casella, however, adds the caution, *e senza pedale*. Schnabel suggests a faster tempo for this passage. This seems to us purposeless.

Do not elongate the low E (*sf*) which introduces the second theme. The rhythm must continue unbroken. Put the phrase stress on the down-beat, A, and keep this stress in the ensuing imitations in the lower voices. Make thick sforzandi in bars 36, 38, and so on, increasing the volume so that the entrance of the passage in broken octaves may be very sonorous. Pedal the *sf* in bar 43 for half a bar; thereafter, keep the upper note of the broken octaves clear and bright; diminish the first half of bar 44 and increase the second, and you will hear the exuberant shout mentioned above. Articulate clearly, and in perfect time, the interpolations added to the returning main theme in bars 56–57, and especially in bars 118–119. Shape these phrases so as to give a delicate stress on the quarter note following the sixteenths.

Make no break in tempo at bar 67, where the transition to the third subject begins, but play the new phrase more softly than the previous one ended. Keep the right-hand figure legatissimo, with no pedal, while the left maintains staccato, with the second note of the figure lighter than the first. For the C subject (bar 79) take the pedal freely, building an apparently continuous crescendo (of course with minor dynamic shadings in each phrase) up to the *ff* passage in broken octaves. As in bar 43, the *sf* is especially applied to the sustained A; but the shouting is here even more exuberant. It is possible to make the descending scale sufficiently loud without the blurring pedal. Make no retardation as you approach the ⌒ in bar 113, and let the ascending octaves be as incisive as possible against the continuation of the scale in the left hand.

Do not elongate the rests in bars 167–168, as you approach the coda. Give the elasticity of portamento to the right hand in bars 169–176, with the left hand again legatissimo. Mark the two-note phrases in bars 183–186 by accentuation of the first of the two notes; but keep the normal 6-8 rhythm in the left hand. Beethoven did not indicate the pedal for the arpeggios which lead to the *Più allegro,* but to us the passage is unimaginable without it. The tempo in this final section will be chosen by the player according to his powers; but it should not be so fast that the figure in the right hand is blurred, or the characteristic rocking bass is made unrecognizable.[12]

[12] This difficult page requires long study. In the author's experience, both in playing and teaching, the following has proved the most successful approach:

Learn the right hand so thoroughly that there is no dependence whatever on the eye for the guidance of the fingers. Thus you may allow the eye to give undisturbed aid to the left hand in the measurement of the difficult leaps.

But more is needed than the help of the eye. The leap from the quarter note to the eighth is leisurely; that from the eighth to the quarter is dangerous. Therefore, the dangerous leap should be prepared for, as far as possible, during the moment of leisure. Taking the pedal with the quarter note (which is fortunately always the low D), release the hand at once, and move without delay to its striking position above the next eighth note. Considerably before the stroke, the hand should be poised for this note, with the finger and thumb almost in contact with the keys. When the instant for the stroke arrives, *pick up* (i.e., do not strike, with a downward motion) the octave eighth in that same motion which will both move the hand back to the low D and strike it. In this way, you move from an already established position to that distant note, and have but the distant note to prepare.

Now, if you look directly at a given note, you can usually strike it. The eye, therefore, before the hand moves to D, looks at D. But once the motion of the hand is inaugurated, the muscular measurement has been made, and the eye need not continue to stare at the note until it is struck. Thus, as soon as the location of D has been assured, the eye may look for the next eighth note.

The student will perceive that the process here described is applicable to a hundred other passages, different in detail but identical in technical principle.

# 5

# BEETHOVEN'S SECOND PERIOD

WHAT we have so far seen is proof that if Beethoven had died at thirty-one—five years younger than Mozart—he would still have left an indelible mark on the music of the world. What we shall see in this chapter will prove that those energies which already seem so great are really only coming to maturity. He was aware of this. "From today I will strike out on a new road," he said to a friend; and he demonstrated at once that this was no passing illusion of greatness.

The first efforts took the shape of three sonatas for piano and violin, Op. 30. The second of these, in C minor, exhibits the character we have already learned to expect when Beethoven chooses that key. It is an important document for his history as an artist, but of course lies outside our present field. The next work, almost contemporaneous, is Op. 31—three sonatas for piano solo, of which, however, No. 3 was written later (in 1802), and was at first published separately.

The first sonata in Op. 31 hardly lives up to Beethoven's promise of novelty. The others, however, are adventurous in the extreme: No. 2, for its blossoming romanticism; No. 3, for its intractable, often impudent, humor. Having space for detailed study of but one of these, we shall choose the easier and more popular—No. 2, in D minor.

After his excursions into fantasy, in Op. 27, we shall hardly expect the liberty enjoyed in that region to be forgotten. We encounter, in fact, a bold experiment in thematic invention and design.

The principal subject is not a pithy, epigrammatic phrase such as we have hitherto found. Instead, it contains, within itself, the high contrast which has formerly been exhibited in the two main subjects. The opening is merely a luminous, contemplative dwelling on the arpeggio of the dominant chord (*Largo*); but there follows at once an impetuous, almost irritable phrase (*Allegro*), which begins in D minor, but is too excited to stay in that key, and comes to a somewhat uncertain pause. The arpeggio then recurs, apparently in C; but the nervous continuation, now much expanded, at length discovers its true key, and, when it settles upon it (bar 21), presents the arpeggio figure in the bass, in rapid tempo, and answers it with a passionate phrase in the upper register. This gives the definitive form of the main subject.

The second subject appears, without episodic transition, in bar 41. This subject is also compound, but is not really new. Its first strain is derived from the *Allegro* phrase of the principal subject, and should have the same accentuation.

The recapitulation begins, as did the development, with the *Largo*. The two recitatives, added to the original thematic arpeggio, offer a high illumination of that contemplative phrase. The indication, *semplice,* cautions the player against a too dramatic rendition; but drama is present, nevertheless. Beethoven marked the pedal to be held without change throughout the recitatives. One may suppose that the lesser sonority of the piano in Beethoven's day made acceptable his rendition (which, Ries says, sounded as if it came from a great distance). The author has tried the doubtful compromise of holding the low chord with the left hand, throughout, and changing the pedal when the dissonance becomes too blurred. The development having dealt largely with the *Allegro* version of the arpeggio subject, Beethoven daringly (and wisely) omits its restatement, substituting new rhythms and figures (bars 1–12 of the final *Allegro*). At bar 31, the compass of his piano compelled an alteration of the passage originally appearing at bar 59 of the exposition. Here, he has indeed made a virtue of necessity, and the passage should be played as it stands. Even the soft pedal and very delicate fingers will barely suffice for a smooth reading of the final *pp* passage.

All the principal editions prescribe, for the first *Allegro,* an incessant changing of fingers on repeated notes. For the second *Allegro,* however, many editors recommend repetition by the *same* finger. In both passages, the first of the repeated notes is light, the second, heavier. It seems to us that in either case the first note can be taken with a lift, and the second with a release, of the weight of the hand, very little actual motion being necessary. In the first *Allegro,* that is, we recommend the following:

Note that the two G's are accented, but *not* the C on "one" in bar 5. In the second *Allegro,* we take the following, which is analogous:

In bar 22, Liszt has been followed by many editors in recommending that the higher phrase be taken by the left hand, with the sustained D held by the pedal. The resultant blur is unpleasant and needless. Take the sustained D in bar 22 with the 5th finger of the left hand, continuing the triplets with the right to the second A—i.e., to "two." The left hand can then take over the following notes (with 3–1) and continue to bar 24. The pedal then may be changed as desired for the melody. The same in bar 25; but from bar 30, the left hand may well cross, since the pedal will not blur.

Stress the F in the left hand, which so often appears in the pauses of the second theme. The second strain, bar 54, is possibly a kind of inversion of the phrase in bar 23. Detach the A (*staccato* means *detached*) very completely from the B-flat, so that the *sf* may have more point. (The same in bar 63 and similar bars.) Give the two-note phrases (bar 70f.) the normal stress on their first note. Do not be niggardly with the *cresc.* and *sf* at the close (bars 87–89).

Observe that there are quarter rests in bars 2 and 4 of the *Largo* with which the development begins, but that the A-sharp in bar 6 is a whole note. Take the low B-flat in bar 22 of the new *Allegro* with the left hand. Observe that the thirds in the two hands, from bar 32, are no longer in similar motion.

The *Adagio* offers us one of the frankest chapters in the history of the composer's heart. (The object of his affection is of no matter; it is the devotion that is revealed.) The opening is on a hesitant theme of detached phrases, in high register, cushioned on low, sonorous chords. Its passion is not so outspoken as that which we shall find in the later romanticists; but there is a clearer note of intimacy than had ever been sounded before. Tympani (bar 17) usher in the interlude which, with growing warmth, leads to the second theme. This is so worshipful in tone that it may be hard to understand in a day of overalls and bobby socks; but beneath its courteous restraint the glow is unmistakable. The form is A-B | A′-B′ Coda.

Liszt's tempo ( $\flat$ = 50 ) seems to us well chosen. Respect the rests in bars 2 and 4, else the high phrases will quite lose their purity, and the low chords will be overluscious. Respect also the sixteenth rests in bar 17f., although the tympani turn later into a figuration in high register which may be pedaled. Do not in the least abate the tempo in bar 30. All three voices are important here. The *cresc.* on the thirty-seconds, unless begun pianissimo, will not yield gracefully to the *p* in bar 31. Perfect measurement of the time is also essential for this flute melody—a wonderful blend of serenity and passion. Slightly oversustain the long tones so that the thirty-seconds may leap swiftly and eagerly to the following eighths. (Note that the alto, in bars 35–36, begins with a sixteenth, not a thirty-second.) The figurations in bar 51f. must again be delicately articulated in perfect time. If your arms are short, so that the left hand has difficulty in the high register, take over with the left hand at the thirty-second of the melody, and play the figurations with the right until the last two thirty-seconds in the bar. (The same in bar 53; but in bar 55, the left hand must resume two notes earlier.) Take the run in bar 94 all within the third beat of the bar. Sing appropriately, in bar 100, the imitation of the preceding octave melody; but give heed also to the meaning of the right hand.

The last movement is entirely in character with the rest, though both its form and its expressive tone are unexpected. This piece is almost a "perpetual motion" (more nearly so than the *Rondo* in Op. 26); yet it falls effortlessly into the sonata form. And its gentle gaiety is so tinged with warmth that we feel not the least surprise or regret on arousing ourselves from the mood of the *Adagio*.

The tempo is Allegretto, not Allegro. Liszt's ♩. = 80, although exceeded by some modern editors, to us seems perfectly suited to the music. The notation for the left hand is designed to permit the staccato of the melodic D to be felt. At bar 4, however, we stress and slightly sustain the E of the melody, which is the goal of the preceding three D's. Similarly with F in bar 8.

The fingering, 5,4,2,1, in bars 1-3, and 5,1,3,2, in bars 4-7, with the 5 released and the other notes sustained, seems to us a good substitute for the frequently used, but hardly allowable, pedal. Bars 15-16 may be pedaled throughout, and also the high A and D of bars 23 and 27. Keep the little finger bright in bars 35 and 37 (of course, without pedal). Accent the mordent in the two-note phrases, bar 43f. (this is the second subject), and increase slightly in bar 46 toward the *sf*. The similar two-note groups that follow, in broken octaves, may be slurred with the pedal. But against the staccato octaves (bar 57f.), keep the left hand as legato as possible, to substitute for the pedal.

The development will not be obscure to musical common sense, unless at bar 174f., where there begins a long succession of four-bar groups in which the *sf* occurs always in the second bar. (Do not mistake this for a first or third bar in the group.) The recapitulation begins with the last three notes of bar 214, which should be phrased accordingly, but with no preparatory retardation. In bar 381, the high F is difficult, if the notation is followed. Instead, take the thirty-second, D, with the left hand, and both the F's in one octave grip with the right. Then take over the lower F silently with the left thumb, for the scale.

The extraordinary capriciousness of Op. 31, No. 3, in E-flat, ought to be dealt with at length. Space forbids this, but we cannot forego a brief comment. Beethoven wrote *Allegro* at the beginning; *ritardando* over bars 3–5; a *fermata* over bar 6: and *a tempo* at bar 7. Many editors give a slowish tempo at the start (e.g., ♩ = 116) and a much faster tempo at bar 7 (Schnabel has 116 at bar 1, 126 at bar 7, and 138 at bar 8!). Liszt (126) and Casella (120–126), however, seem to feel that *a tempo* means what it says—that the original tempo should be resumed—and we heartily concur. The pianists are sometimes more extreme than the editors, making a kind of wailing Andante out of the first two bars,[1] and a ritardando thereafter that passes all bounds of musical decency. But if the first phrases are made urgent (as not only the word *Allegro,* but their intrinsic design may well imply) then the later excitement (e.g., bar 18f. and especially bar 9f. of the development section) will seem a natural outcome of the originally suggested character. The *cresc.* of the first *rit.* (bars 3–6) becomes portentous at the opening of the development, and again in the Coda. The outburst of forte F's in bars 44–45; the flightiness of the second subject (beginning at bar 46) and its explosion into the wild runs of bars 53–56; the quacking of the staccato bass (bars 78–81) and the immediate subsiding into gentleness—all these and many other details imply for the whole movement an ironic mood which is falsified by a sentimental beginning.

The *Scherzo* (which is in sonata form!) is in a wholly related

---

[1] Compare the similar dragged beginning of the *Fifth Symphony,* much in vogue at the end of the nineteenth century, which was at last effectually combatted by Weingartner.

vein. The only approximation to the gentleness that we ordinarily find in a slow movement is made in the simple *Menuetto,* which offers, in reverse, that surcease from a prevailing mood which, in Shakespearian tragedy is called "comic relief." For the last movement is impudence itself. In this sonata, surely, we have a kind of foretaste of the *Seventh Symphony.*

Liszt's edition of the sonatas presents them, not chronologically, but in the order (as he judges it) of their technical difficulty. This sonata, in his edition, is No. 18; but Op. 31, No. 2 is No. 24. We cannot understand why, for this one seems much more difficult, both to execute and to interpret.

Op. 49 contains two easy sonatas, quite out of their chronological place. No. 1 was written in 1799; No. 2, in 1796. Each has but two movements. The first of the two is more interesting. It has for opening a gently plaintive *Andante,* an admirable study in expressive playing for unskilled fingers; and it ends with a gay *Rondo,* quite extended in design. No. 2 has first a diminutive sonata form with a very brief development; then, a minuet which was worked over to fill a place in the popular *Septet,* Op. 20, for strings, clarinet, horn, and bassoon.

From this time on, however, the technical demands made by most of the sonatas are great. Beethoven no longer needs to restrain his imagination, for there is also great progress in the art of piano playing, and his high reputation allows him to command where formerly he had to consider. Yet, however great his demands upon the fingers, he still remains pre-eminently the music lover. And although the technical problems, from now on, are greater than can ordinarily be solved by many of those to whom this book is addressed, the music itself is not beyond their comprehension. We shall accordingly give more space to the character of these works, and proportionately less to technical details. This is done, indeed, to induce you to read and study his music, even though you may not be able to perform it. Often, as you will find, the main themes, and much of the structure generally, will prove quite easy to finger. And with little more than a clear sense of the themes (which contain the essence of the idea) you can gain a deeper insight into the composer's purpose than can be conveyed by listening, either to recordings or to actual performances. For these, although seldom technically faulty, are not always imaginatively brilliant. Beethoven wrote this music for you, as well as for the virtuosi; and you have the right (as you have with Shakespeare's plays) to interpret it for yourself. You will not be doing this if you let other people tell you what it says; and you will be gratified at the solidity of thought that comes from independent reading.

The little sonatas in Op. 49 contribute nothing to our biography. But the great *Waldstein* sonata (Op. 53) reveals a man even more mature than we should expect from the fact that more than twenty opus numbers intervene between the ironic E-flat sonata and this one. This work was written in 1804—the year in which the still more incredible *Eroica* symphony was finished. We often marvel at the dexterity of prodigies who accomplish at six what we shall hardly have attained at sixty; but measured by competent standards of mental growth, Beethoven's achievements in the years 1800–1804 are far greater. "What porridge had John Keats?" we ask; but we shall never know the answer.

Not only the *Waldstein,* but several other works written in this and the neighboring years—the *Violin Concerto,* the *Piano Concerto in G,* and the *Fourth Symphony* are the most striking—seem to stem from some extraordinary consciousness of well-being, rare in any human life. Because it is so rare, there are no good names for this condition—no words which we preserve from the degrading association with ordinary experience so that they may connote alone the quality of our great moments. The word *Euphoria* (literally, well-being) is too "learned" and unfamiliar. If you can hedge it about with barriers, and purge it of triviality, perhaps the word "serenity" will do—at least for a peg to hang our musical experience on.

The beginning looks, at first, like a mere rattling on two bars
of the C major chord. It is not that. The many E's are only
pulsations in what is really one long melodic E. It rises at last
to F-sharp and G, and quietly settles there.

There is a glint of something more vivid in the high response;
but this is only a flicker. The theme leaps the rails of ordinary
modulation and appears on the chord of B-flat, with new warmth
that vastly enhances the simple awareness of well-being we gained
from the theme at the beginning. We learn a little more, too, of
the quality of that high response, but its sense is not yet fully revealed. The music descends, soft-footed, to another beginning in
C; but this time the pulsations are swifter, the modulation is
upward, instead of downward; and the brightness begins to
gleam (but not to glare) with the B major chord (bar 23) upon
which the whole passage centers, though it is obviously the
dominant of E minor. This time, the descent is buoyant; but as
it rises, the music begins to step warily, for there is something
wonderful ahead.

This second subject (in the mediant major, E, instead of in
the dominant, G) gives us the needed context in which to interpret the quietude of the beginning. It is fulfillment itself—where
the thirst to be slaked is of the spirit. There is similar value in this
unexpected key to that which we felt with the first leap into B-flat.
Each is an illustration of the extraordinary significance of the
elemental musical facts. The repetition of the theme in the
middle voice is adorned by a delicate figuration of itself.
And now, once the sense of the theme has been fully revealed,
there is at last a kinetic impulse—not with a new theme, but
again with pulsations of harmony: to dull theory, mere triplet
figures on tonic and dominant, but to the more active imagina-

tion, a release of elemental force.[2] The closing subject, appropriately, is quite gentle, but insistence on the curious dynamic shading, *cresc.—p,* prevents any lapse in our expectation.

The development, again making use of the device of diminution, has several times to restrain the impulse to a forte outburst,
but at length (bar 27 of this section) the energy will no longer b
denied. Its vehicle, quite naturally, is not one of the principa
subjects, but is that same triplet figure in which it was at firs
suggested.[3] This long passage, although without a shred o
melody, is nevertheless a perfect culmination of the developmen
process. The essence of both of the main themes is quietude
(Not once is a recurrence of the opening two-bar phrase marke
otherwise than *pp,* though the third bar, developed alone, i
often forceful.) The frequent repetition of these themes woul
dull their precious significance; nor would their simplicity en
dure the harmonic distortions that development must entail. Thi
joyous outburst, then, is a spiritual welling-up—a kinetic re
sponse to the exalted quietude whose perfection could not b
otherwise acclaimed. (This is not an isolated instance. The heroi

[2] Note that in bar 56 a melodic phrase (E, B, A, D-sharp) grows out of th
first notes of the triplets; that this is hastened, in bar 58, by "diminution"; tha
it becomes only the two essential notes, E, D-sharp, in bar 59, and only on
note, insistently reiterated (the D-natural), in bar 60. The device has a learne
name, but it is simplicity itself, and fully efficacious where sophistication woul
have given a false lead to the musical intuition.

[3] From bar 27 to bar 51, Beethoven wrote no contradiction of the *f* wit
which this passage begins, nor any subordinate dynamic shading. Modern ed
tions, quite naturally, suggest this shading, which is quite clearly implied in th
notation itself: *cresc.* to the peak of the curve (e.g., the D-flat in bar 29), wit
some *dim.* thereafter. There are three similar four-bar groups, and six of tw
bars whose pattern is the last half of the four-bar group. In the original editior
the first bar of the four-bar groups is not slurred; the second is slurred by itself
and the third and fourth together. To our eye, this seems to imply a certain ir
cisiveness of attack on the first triplet figures which is obscured by the slur
that all modern editions insert, in this first bar. Schnabel indicates a kind o
marcato for the C, D, E, F, G on the strong beats in the bass, which is doubtles
the composer's principal point in the passage. (The upper voice, in the secon
bar of the group, has the high sixth against the bass, which may also b
emphasized.)

spirit is similarly maintained in a long passage in the development section of the *Third Symphony,* where there is no more than a titanic roaring on powerful, syncopated harmonies.) Nor is the long preparation for the return of the principal subject particularly concerned with thematic material. It is designed to make us aware of the sense of the main theme when it comes.[4]

There is nothing in the Coda which will perplex the student who has clearly conceived the sense of the movement thus far. It does, indeed, develop the principal theme [5]—but you have only to put this development of the thought back into the development section to see that it would be somehow all wrong in that place. For what it does here, after all, is to reveal the ineffable poesy of the second subject.

The slow movement is entitled *Introduzione,* quite properly, since this is not a self-contained slow movement. In consequence, this is the first (except the little pieces in Op. 49) of a considerable number of two-movement sonatas. Although this design was here an afterthought [6] it was an artistic "find" of no mean im-

[4] The Latin Europeans generally call this sonata *L'Aurore*—"The Dawn." Casella finds this passage of transition (which he insists should begin in almost complete confusion, and proceed to clarity) a probable source of the widely accepted title. It is quite possible to include any of the emotional characteristics which we have remarked in the themes within that poetic definition of the word "dawn" which alone would make it a tolerable title for the sonata. But we can hardly agree that this transition is the high point of poetic suggestion in the whole movement.

[5] The editors all remark (either by their words or their fingering) the difficulty of the left-hand part at bar 188f. of the development section. It seems to us that the following is a perfectly justifiable facilitation:

[6] Beethoven originally intended the rather sentimental *Andante favori,* in F, as the slow movement of this work. Ries tells of his characteristic outburst of temper when a friend dared to suggest that it made the sonata too long; but the unwelcome hint was taken, nevertheless.

portance. For the departure from the conventional three or four movements is no mere exercise of the economy of compression. Both this and the later examples strongly suggest that the origin of the two-movement form is in a different expressive purpose from that which generates the more inclusive form. In every case except Op. iii, the two-movement works present, instead of a wide variety, the same general feeling-character, only with a change of aspect. Drama, doubtless, is sacrificed; but something equally precious is gained. Spirituality does not necessarily demand dramatic utterance.

If you ask yourself what other "subject" Beethoven could have turned to after the extraordinary exposition of well-being which is set forth in the first movement, you will probably agree that there was no other; that he must either continue with this or stop. How anything more is to be imagined, and how such an image could ever be realized in tones, exceeds our dull comprehension—until it is accomplished. But Beethoven's solution of the problem is so effortless that we can hardly realize that there was a problem.

The *Introduzione*—fragmentary and indirect in design and statement, yet palpably profound in origin—is a parable rather than the orderly exposition of a thought. We must get its meaning by inference; but there are few who fail to grasp it. This music seems to explore the very source of well-being.

Consequently, when the *Allegretto moderato* (emphatically *not Allegro*) begins, we are already fully oriented. "Why, of course," we feel, "here we are!"—and so take for granted one of the subtlest inspirations in the literature of music. The theme, propelled by the low C, exhibits no trace of force, but its momentum is irresistible. The leisurely incessant sixteenths are the product, not the source, of that hidden vitality which is felt with the first low C and the two high G's, and pervades the whole movement. Not until bar 51 is there a crescendo whose goal is forte.

Almost immediately thereafter (bar 62), the B subject appears —a tumult of notes, at first, and kinetic, like the triplet figures in the first movement—but presently it becomes a vital, though somewhat fragmentary melodic line. At the end of this, the A subject, nude and towering, stands forth for a moment (bar 98f.); but there is swift subsidence to the initial, unforced utterance of the A subject.

The C subject (bar 175) has something of the same quality as the B, its energy being now colored by the characteristically darker hue of C minor. Once more the outline of the A theme is recalled, now harmonized (bar 271); but its subsidence is a long delight in the elemental rhythm of its first three notes, over which there are modulations newly figurated out of the familiar motion of sixteenths. The formal third entry of the A subject is shortened, and the B theme is made more sonorous than before; but the essential form is clearly evident. Irresistibly, the A rhythm emerges, in a long passage of dominant harmony (bar 378),[7] but the A theme, now initiating the Coda, assumes a much swifter pace.[8]

In spite of its speed, the Coda is no mere display of brilliancy. Two thirds of it is marked *p, pp,* or even *ppp* (which is very rare in Beethoven). The hoarse exultation of the *Finale* of the *C Minor Symphony* is in no way implied. The colorful modulation when the theme (as before) appears above the persistent

---

[7] Many editors (von Bülow among them) print the conventional whole rests in the silent bars just before the *Prestissimo.* But Beethoven, obsessed by the "one, two; one, two" of the rhythm, wrote "one, two" in these silent bars also— with two quarter rests!

[8] There is wide variation in the tempi suggested by the different editors for this *Prestissimo*— ♩ = 144 (Damm), to 𝅝 = 88 (Schnabel). The theme is of course "diminished" at its first appearance; but at bar 39 the basic rhythm, and at bar 83 the whole theme, will be found reaugmented, so that in this form it is essentially what it was in the *Allegro moderato.* Having in mind the character which seems to us indelibly stamped on the original theme, we cannot but feel that the *Prestissimo* ought not greatly to exceed the apparent sense of the change in time signature (2-4 to 2-2) implying *doppio movimento.*

trill is itself a denial of blatant excitement. Indeed, the whole
texture declares the rarity of the joyous experience out of which
this sonata must have arisen.

The next sonata, Op. 54, is also in two movements. For several
reasons, it is seldom played. It is both very difficult (Liszt put it
in his edition as No. 23) and rather enigmatic in character. It is
something of an experiment in the sonata form, the usual design
being hardly distinguishable. The first movement begins with
the suavity of the minuet, and then suddenly plunges into an
extreme contrast—a long octave passage, *sempre forte e staccato,*
with a few imitative phrases. The first part of this passage is
repeated, with the interpolation of two additional bars, and with
somewhat unexpected modulation. The minuet is then ornamented, rather than developed; the octave passages, abbreviated,
recur, and the end is a long development, largely by figuration, of
the minuet. The last movement (*Allegretto*) has but one theme,
a figure of rising, broken sixths, which is put through a great
variety of evolutions, and resembles, in the fertile novelty of its
treatment, the delightful spinning-out which Bach often con-
trives in the toccatas or the introductions to the Partitas and the
English Suites. But this is by no means backward-looking music.
In a day when far more startling devices have become commonplace, the modernity of this piece still stands out; and in this
respect the music already looks forward to the third period.

Whether the culmination of the second period appears in the
*Waldstein* or the *Appassionata* is a question that it would be
foolish to debate. Although it is technically more difficult to play
than the *Waldstein,* the *Appassionata* is easier to interpret; for
it speaks of emotion more frequent in our experience than serenity.
The title, although not bestowed by the composer, is as appropriate as any single word could be. The "passion," to be sure, is
not the tender one, but it is nearly as universal, and evokes from
almost any group of hearers immediate and unanimous assent.

Once more, at the very outset, we are amazed at the intuition that can find the commanding phrase. To mere critical analysis (and to some performers), the principal theme is hardly more than the arpeggio of the tonic chord of F minor. The simple device of placing the hands two octaves apart adds nothing to that critically observed fact; but it creates an impressive sonority and vastly increases the apparent range of the upward sweep of the theme. The purport of this sweep, however, would be lost without the aplomb of the preliminary drop.[9] The descent suggests some ineluctable finality, from which to rise is permitted, but from which escape is unthinkable. Note that for the repetition, Beethoven does just what he did in the *Waldstein:* leaps without transition into a foreign key. The G-flat major seems an alleviation; but the return to F Minor, in itself a yielding to inexorable force, is made ominous by the figure

in the bass.[10] The ensuing outburst (bar 14) is so difficult to play that it often fails to suggest a sudden release of the hitherto suppressed energy. Proof that this is the intention is shown in the violence that is done, in bar 17, to the principal theme—the time value of the low F being expanded in a great roar of syncopated chords, rising as if this were the actual thematic line, but followed, *p,* by the original upward sweep. (The ensuing as-

[9] Both to give the necessary shortness to the sixteenth note, which is characteristic of the whole rhythm, and to signify the tragic concentration of the thought, it seems to us desirable just perceptibly to elongate the C—the initial note. The upward sweep cannot then become indifferent, but will seem to have been generated by this opening figure. Only the faintest dynamic shading is permissible within the *pp* prescribed; but you will long since have discovered that a true legato—to the imaginative ear—is almost impossible at an absolute level of dynamics.

[10] The *C Minor Symphony* germinated in Beethoven's brain more or less at the same time as this sonata. How he was obsessed by this same rhythm, in that work, is well known. No wonder it spilled over into this piece whose character, although very different on the whole, is yet related to that of the desperately earnest symphony.

cending chords similarly expand the C's of the theme.) At bar 24 a transition begins, rhythmed in restless "triplets," [11] indeterminate in line but with several bitter discords, which soon makes obvious preparation for the entrance of the second subject (bar 35) in the orthodox relative major key (A-flat).

This, like the principal subject, is largely in arpeggio, and has the same rhythmic figure; but its import is far different. The warmth of it is as irresistible as the repression of the main theme; and we might be in doubt whether this warmth or that somber energy is to be the dominant force in the drama, if it were not that the two notes that form the feminine ending of this phrase (bar 41) are immediately reiterated, *f* and *sf,* and with strangely distorted harmony. The meaning of this distortion will be fully revealed at the proper time; but even now there is a portentous chill in the strangely colored scale that leads to the closing subject. Here, suddenly, is kinetic protest—both in the brief phrase four times ejaculated in bars 51–52, and in the insurgent bass, whose *sf* culmination re-echoes resentfully in the *piano* of the cadential figures which close the exposition.[12]

To enter upon the development without repeating the exposition was a novelty in Beethoven's structure, but it was dictated by musical common sense. One might as effectively repeat the first act of a play as the exposition of this sonata. The new atmosphere created by the preparation and announcement of the principal theme in E is like the raising of a curtain on a changed, yet familiar, stage setting. At the beginning, the theme is subdued, but by force, rather than by nature, as the unexpected sforzandi in bars 74 and 77 reveal; and its turbulence is suddenly and fully

[11] They are not true triplets, of course, since the time is 12–8; but in bar 13 of the Coda, Beethoven himself marks them so.

[12] Schnabel and D'Albert follow the MS. in placing the *sfp* (bar 61f.) only on the left-hand chord. Other editors (unjustifiably, we think) follow Liszt in placing it also on the first sixteenth thereafter in the right hand. A very slight *cresc.* on the A-flat sixteenths preceding the *sf* gives more body to the whole fourth beat, and accomplishes the purpose of the added *sfp*.

unleashed. Thereafter, the themes appear in the order in which they occurred in the exposition—each of them intensified. The second subject, whose generous warmth was at first disturbed only by that one throb of pain at the end, now turns out to have been far more tragic than it seemed; for its unrest is now spread over a larger area, and rises to a culmination that is little less than terrible. The passages that follow not only serve that purpose which we have already often noted—that of carrying on the feeling-*intensity* without further reference to the feeling-*character* —but make the four-note phrase (in the rhythm from the *Fifth Symphony*) stand out with threatening force.[13]

The recapitulation reveals no important differences from the exposition. The Coda, however, constitutes a second and even more intense development. This is really necessitated by the great dimensions of the whole movement; but necessity does not always mother such inventions as this. We are left with a kind of amazement that anything beyond the conclusion of this movement could even be projected. The rapid increase in intensity of the final phrase of the second subject in bars 213–217 is alarming, and generates another long passage of athematic eloquence;[14] but the tragic agony is even higher in the *Più allegro*. The incessant reiteration of the "symphony" motive (from bar 11) rocks the very earth.

Yet more *was* projected; and more was achieved. The theme of the *Andante con moto* is biblical in its simplicity. Its meaning is similarly elemental. There are almost no other harmonies than the primary triads (tonic, dominant, and subdominant); there is scarcely a melody; and there is no particularly novel fact of rhythm. But vital essences are not revealed through ornate sur-

[13] Casella follows von Bülow in counseling the doubling in octaves of this figure (bar 129f.). To us, the gain in sonority seems overbalanced by the inevitable loss of incisiveness.

[14] The composer prescribed the damper pedal from bar 233 to the sixth eighth note of bar 237, and all good editions not only preserve this mark but caution the player against ignoring it.

faces. Rather, they are thus made invisible; for a constant pre-occupation with surfaces provides us with few criteria for the elemental. Yet this theme, whether to the learned mind or the simple, comes home as if it were the very ore of truth—the source of passion and of pain alike.

Naturally, therefore, no contrasting theme would be thinkable. The structural device, accordingly, is that of variation. Here, also, the process of variation is without artifice. The first variation moves essentially in eighth notes, the second is in sixteenths, and the third in thirty-seconds; and for epilogue there is a return to the theme, with the brief phrases now shifting in register from low to high, while two passages of sober recitation emerge beneath the higher strains. There is an indeterminate ending, on a long, pianissimo chord of the diminished seventh, and a sudden jolt as the same chord, in the higher register, is struck fortissimo. Without pause, we are thus projected into the *Allegro ma non troppo.*

What we shall find is an unrestrained release of that often inhibited passion which was portrayed in the first movement. In this similarity of character, the sonata thus resembles the *Waldstein,* where the last movement was also the complement and fulfillment of the first. And since the brief slow movement likewise runs into the last without pause, it is not wholly unreasonable to think of the *Appassionata* as still another two-movement sonata. Nor is this the last we shall encounter.

This *Finale,* however, is not a Rondo, but another huge sonata form. The impetuous rhythm of the opening fanfare, and the excited running figures that follow, make possible a pianissimo statement of the tempestuous principal theme (bar 20). There is at first only the restless figure of sixteenths, but their repetition is intensified in the incisive ejaculations added in bar 28; and in bar 36, these ejaculations become the leading thought, attaining an almost desperate energy as they return to the original figure at bar 64.

There could be neither time nor place for a contrasted subject in such a turmoil as this. Instead, at bar 76, there is a brief legato strain which soon attains a larger sweep, but which abates not at all the high tension already so long maintained. The swift figure of the principal subject—somewhat reshaped, and with declarative chords above it (bars 98–99) that recall the "symphony" rhythm—then brings the exposition to a close.

The development begins in ominous quiet, the chord of the diminished seventh once more assuming the elemental mystery that Bach felt it to possess. At bar 142, there is added a new phrase of melody—if that can be called melody which has (save for its cadential figure) only two adjacent notes; but of its significance in contributing to the discourse there can be no doubt. As in the first movement, the development ends in athematic figures and arpeggios which, at the end, allow the first moment of pause since the opening fanfare. The recapitulation is without any novel additions; but the whole of the development and recapitulation—instead of the exposition—is marked for repetition.[15] The catastrophic Coda is indescribable.

We append here a few observations on technical problems, although most of these are beyond facilitation.

In bar 14, division of the difficult passage between the two hands is often suggested; but since the parallel passage (bar 149) has to be taken with the right hand alone, we see little value in the evasion. In bar 17 and like passages, do not mark sharply the 12-8 time—but also, do not distort it! In bars 28–29, take with the right hand the repetition of the third, B-flat–D-flat, written for the left hand at the fourth main beat of the bar (the tenth eighth-note of the twelve). In the second subject (bar 36), it seems to us that the rhetorical stress lies primarily on the weak beat, C, and secondarily on the "four," B-flat; but in bar 38, the stress lies on the strong beats, with the B-flat slightly the more intense. In bar 60, take the first C-flat of the right

[15] Von Bülow protests this repetition as imposing too great a tax on both performer and listener. In our experience, Gieseking is the only notable pianist to obey the direction. But few indeed are they who can make this an addition to the sense of the music.

hand with the left thumb, the right thumb taking the following D-natural.

The calm, from bar 65 on, must not be indifferent, yet the *pp* can endure no perceptible variation. The hint of rubato which we suggested for the up-beat to bar 1, if not overdone, is useful in bars 65 and 66, but not in bar 78! Observe that the 3rd, 6th, 9th and 12th counts in bar 126f. are eighth notes. Bar 203, parallel to bar 64, may in our opinion have the slight retardation that implies the end of a great division of the form. Make the eighth notes at the end of bar 219f. very incisive. In bar 11 of the *Più allegro,* it seems to us that the second *sf* is the more emphatic. The quarter notes in the left hand, also, cannot be without ictus, else the relation of this to the "symphony" rhythm will be lost.

Bearable words, not only for the character but even for the execution of technical detail in the *Andante con moto,* can hardly be found. In the first variation, observe the eighth rests against the legato of the left hand. In the second, the melody—easily discoverable in the sixteenth-note figures—is of course to be made clear, but not overemphasized. In the third, at bar 5 (counting from the last "second ending"), take the two thirty-seconds, C and D-flat, with the idle right hand. Note particularly that the first sforzandi, in bars 2 and 3, occur in piano, whereas forte rules in bars 4 and 5. The editors are unanimous in their opinion that this same contrast should continue throughout the variation, even though Beethoven wrote no *p*'s, but only the *f*'s (in addition to the *sf*'s) to indicate his meaning. In bars 18 and 20, the high G-flat of the left-hand figure can conveniently be taken with the right thumb.

In the *Finale,* at bar 37 and similar passages, be sure to observe the rest. The following *sf* will gain immensely by appearing out of (melodic) silence. In bar 64, and in similar passages, omit the second sixteenth in the left hand rather than delay the entrance of the figure in the right. Note that the melody, in bars 76f., is not in the left hand, but is in the D-flat, C, B-natural, C, and so on, of the high figuration. This is proved at bar 86, where the left hand has the melody, and the right a new figure of accompaniment.

Let us pause for a moment to add a few notes to our autobiography. What manner of man is this, who has just spoken? Although only thirty-six, he is hardly the same person as he who, two or three years ago, lost himself in the fantasies of Op. 27. The ready sensibility to egoistic pain which evoked the "Moonlight" sonata is perhaps not lost, but it is merged in a larger sensibility. The passion of the *Finale* of that sonata seemed as intense as human nerves could endure; but how much more comprehensive (and comprehending) is that region of the mind which is disturbed in the *Appassionata!* There is a novel sense of excellence in nature throughout the *Pastoral* sonata; but the serenity of the *Waldstein* stems from a sense of rightness in the universal scheme of things. Nor do these concepts appear as mere personal opinions, or momentary excitements. They are convictions, rooted deep in the experience of a man who feels that his experience has proved them sound; and having no longer any doubt of the efficacy of his judgment, and having at the same time an abounding affection for humanity, he speaks as a prophet—as a very Elijah—impatient with a humanity which needs to be shown how to decide between the glories and the trivialities of life. No cloud of uncertainty obscures his vision, and he declares his visions as if they must be for all men the axioms which they are for himself.

Many men, perhaps, see as clearly, and draw their convictions as justly, as he. But they are not artists who can embody their thought in language that people like ourselves can understand; so that their wisdom cannot be communicated otherwise than by personal contact. Nor do we always look to the artists for wisdom. We mostly suppose them to be absorbed in the quest of the breathless perfection of beauty, which they treat as a thing wholly disassociated from the humble things that make up our lives. This man, however, lives in no ivory tower. He speaks to us believing himself to be on our own level; so that although he exhorts, we are never offended.

# 6

# BEETHOVEN'S THIRD PERIOD

CERTAINLY, with the great works we have just studied, Beethoven's position among the great musicians was assured. How his mind could have grown so fast is beyond explanation. But—still more amazingly—this extravert, this man who now thinks with godlike assurance, is about to discover a still vaster spiritual world, and to grope, within himself, for the interpretation of mysteries which had escaped his extraverted vision. To us, these mysteries are so obscure that his language about them often seems enigmatic. Perhaps that is because he no longer speaks in his former tone of absolute assurance; for we, being ourselves but gropers, put our faith only in those whose conviction seems unassailable, and do not willingly follow a groper.

This change from extraversion to introversion considerably retarded Beethoven's production. Thus, after Op. 57 (the *Appassionata*), there are no more piano sonatas until Op. 78. And what we find in that work is a tiny sonata whose two movements together are shorter than the first movement alone of either the *Waldstein* or the *Appassionata,* and whose theme seems even more diminutive. Study well, however, the tone of the four-bar introduction. For here (and in all that follows, though it is not there quite so evident) is a new feeling-quality: a kind of gentleness that we have not encountered before. It feels like a benignant hand, laid for a moment on a cherished head; but although that which follows is hardly more than amiable banter, the amiability (colored by the introduction) is so pervasive that the banter takes on the significance of a parable.

We have not hitherto found Beethoven a sparkling composer; but the second movement—again the perfect complement of the first—sparkles throughout, and is yet without a trace of garishness or glitter. Beethoven was fond of this sonata, recommending it to those who were infatuated with the *Moonlight*. It is much harder to play, however, than it seems at first sight, for the gentleness we have spoken of is hard to impart, and without it the music may easily appear meaningless.

Op. 79 is much easier to play, but seems to us less interesting. Its first movement expands the *Ländler* (the predecessor of the Waltz), somewhat as Op. 54 expanded the Minuet, into the dimension of the sonata form—but more consistently, for there is no violent contrast. The *Andante* is a tiny Barcarolle, and the *Vivace* a gay little dance, behind which lurks a sly but kindly humor.

Op. 81a is the only one of the thirty-two to have a confessed "program." The three words, "Farewell," "Absence," and "Return," suffice to indicate the general character of the three movements; and the word, *Lebewohl* (Farewell) is set over the first three descending notes (G, F, E-flat) of the introductory *Adagio,* to give to those notes (which will recur in varied contexts) the significance of a primary motive in the piece. Both in their descent, and still more in their harmonization (compare bars 1–2 of the introduction with bars 7–8), they imply an appropriate but by no means frantic regret. The principal subject of the *Allegro* is less characteristic of the immediate business of leave-taking (though the notes G, F, E-flat are conspicuous in bars 2 and 3); but the descent from the *sfp* B-flat in bars 7–8 is not without the hint of a sinking heart. The second subject is prepared for by a syncopated version of the *Lebewohl* phrase, and the theme itself begins pointedly with those notes. The development is very short, but the Coda, largely concerned with this phrase, gives adequate compensation. The collision of tonic and dominant harmonies (bars 163–167) doubtless gave, in 1809, a considerably modernistic touch.[1]

In the slow movement, Beethoven for the first time translates the direction *Andante espressivo* into German that means, very literally, "In going motion, yet with much expression." The music is here highly characteristic, not only in expression but in formal design. There is of course no agonizing; but the persistent dissonance and uncertainty of key reflect wonderfully the sense that pervades a household where there is an empty chair. The form is not developed into the rounded unity of a completed discourse. The second subject (bar 15) is only half drawn, and though both strains are repeated, with intensification, the whole design is tentative. The last six bars make admirable preparation for the "Return."

Here, for a moment, there is indeed the high excitement of greeting;[2] but Beethoven wisely does not try to maintain this level of excitement throughout. Instead, there is a phrase of simple contentment, growing steadily in richness and sonority, until it eventuates (bar 27) in a high ejaculation—the very affirmation of a renewed and purposeful existence.[3] The ensuing lighter counterpart is delightful, and introduces the second subject,

---

[1] The hunting horns in *Tristan and Isolde* (Act II, Scene 1) indulge, somewhat more daringly, in the same opposition of two harmonies.

[2] Von Bülow sees in the ejaculations of the left hand in bars 5–8 an analogy with the musical phrase of greeting (also in *Tristan,* Act II, Scene 1) which Isolde emphasizes by waving her scarf in time to the music. That stage business, to most Anglo-Saxon eyes, seems sufficiently childish; and we find von Bülow's implication unwelcome.

[3] This passage sounds noisy and meaningless if it is hurried (as it often is), and if the sforzandi are kept at full intensity throughout the eight bars. The original edition has, for the four notes in bars 27–28, *ff, sf, sf, sf;* but bars 29–30 have no dynamic marks. How this can mean anything but a lightening of the force during the descent, we cannot see; but even Schnabel suggests *sf* for each note in bars 29–30. Bar 31 has *ff* for the A-natural, and no further marks, but the same style is too obviously implied to require indication.

whose two combined melodic phrases will be used in "doub
counterpoint" (that is, with the upper phrase becoming th
lower, and the lower, the upper) in the development section. Th
recapitulation is considerably abbreviated by compacting th
principal subject, and for Coda there is a brief and beautiful id
(*Poco Andante*) which establishes on a high plane the hint
contentment that we found in the theme at the beginning.

More than five years elapsed before Beethoven added anoth
to his collection of piano sonatas. That is a greater interval tha
we have yet encountered, and we should naturally expect a simil
difference in style. But if it is there, this difference is not on th
surface—unless simplicity is to be the principal characteristic
the new manner. Simplicity, however, may be deceptive; and w
shall find with careful reading, a more metaphoric illuminatio
of emotional character than we have hitherto encountered. Ar
since this sonata, although by no means easy to interpret, is most
of moderate technical difficulty, we shall study it somewhat mo
closely. We shall find in it another important chapter in ou
"autobiography."

There is little learning—which Beethoven seldom cares
parade—but much wisdom: the kind of wisdom implied in Pa
cal's saying, "the heart has its reasons, of which reason know
nothing." The quality of such wisdom, being perceptible by i
ference rather than by factual observation, is hardly amenable
language. But close scrutiny may reveal in the substance of th
music the basis of inferences not wholly untranslatable into word
We must at least make an attempt to discover them.

There is first of all a striking contrast (in spite of their simila
ity in design) between the first two phrases. Not only the *f* an
the *p,* but the melodic design, suggest an opposition of vehemen
and gentleness. The forte phrase has detached eighth notes f
the up-beat, the "three" of the first bar, and the last note; but i
the piano phrase, these notes are all quarter notes (the last tw
portamento). The forte phrase ends with an upward leap; th

piano phrase moves stepwise throughout. But in these simple-looking five-note groups, the stress points are not easy to determine. The final A of the first phrase is the highest note, and the apparent goal of the motion; but if the staccato is observed, the loud note sounds uncomfortably harsh. Thus the major emphasis seems to fall on the first down-beat, G. The parallel note to the A, in the piano phrase (i.e., the B), is a quarter note, and easily bears the greater stress. If this is so, the whole eight-bar period sets forth a subtle antithesis of feeling in which the vehement somewhat yields to the gentle. But we may hope for more light in what follows.

· The curve of the ensuing strain is wholly gracious, though its intrinsic warmth is made almost urgent by the many syncopations.[4] The final sweep down to the low E on the submediant chord is extraordinarily rich (as the ritard and the fermata imply), and the whole descent from the point of dynamic stress—surely, the syncopated C, rising to A (bars 10–11)—requires the most careful shading. But this strain, like the first, has an indeterminate ending, so that we are compelled to include the following phrases also in the whole pattern of the principal subject. Here the feature is the enormous leap from the high E to the low F-sharp. For, although the stress point is expressly deferred by the composer to the later F-sharp (bar 20), the repetition of the leap gives a quicker *cresc.* and a *fp* to the F-sharp in bar 22 as the culminant point in the whole strain. Together with the ritardando to the long-delayed establishment of E minor as the tonality, these markings offer a problem in shading which is not easily solved. These are perhaps the essential features to be observed in interpreting the whole composite theme. What, then, is that inference of feeling which we obligated ourselves to draw?

It is not easy to form. No event, no act, no circumstance is here depicted, but only a state of mind—a state so complex that three

---

[4] Do not forget the dynamics essential to the playing of syncopations. (See the comment on Variations III and IV in Op. 26.)

quite different musical strains are required to delineate it. We cannot say, with confidence, what that state *is;* but we can say what it is *not,* and to that extent, at least, we know what it is. One does not, to such strains, strive for military glory, nor seek profound philosophic truth, nor memorialize the eyebrow of one's mistress. Neither is there thought of death, nor the wistfulness of melancholy retrospect—though this last suggestion will probably seem less untrue than the others, for we have seen vehemence overcome by gentleness; and that will hardly happen without a deep background of experience which contributes to the final state of mind.

This is a noteworthy change from the Beethoven we have so far found in his music. In the earlier works, whatever their theme, he was forthright and often indignant in utterance. Here, he has become tentative, but through understanding, not through timidity. In Op. 31, No. 2, or in the *Moonlight* sonata, his self-steeped passion accrues to adoration or despair. Here, it is sublimated into almost selfless tenderness.

What follows is largely to the same purpose, and we shall attempt no more verbal elucidations of its quality. Beethoven wrote no other direction than *pp* for the rising octaves from bar 24. They are obviously in the rhythmic pattern of the two first notes of the sonata, and you may either let that fact appear of itself, or may aid your hearer's comprehension by hinting at that emphasis which you gave those notes. But you need no more than a hint, for the fact appears at the peak with the *f* and *sf*. Beethoven marked no dynamic change for the two chords following the downward scales. Many editors suggest *mf,* which we think justified. The *cresc.* in bar 43 is impossible on the tied notes. We therefore begin the *cresc.* on the up-beat. Note that the two-chord figure (bars 47–50), although rhythmically shifted, is related to that with which the sonata began.

The second subject (bar 55) at first appears as a mere descent of fifths and fourths, with a fragment of melody at the end; but these bare intervals are at once turned into graceful figures, perfectly complementing the implications we have found in the principal subject. Nothing can alleviate the difficulty of the accompanying sixteenth notes;[5] but once they are past, no more than a bar (67) of announcement is required for the entrance of the closing subject. (Note that the suspended G–F-sharp in bars 69–70 is an echo of the same notes in bar 55.)

The immediate topic in the development is the principal subject. Measure precisely and articulate definitely the reiterated eighth notes, throughout. In the original edition, only the first up-beat (bar 84) is marked staccato, but the same effect is doubtless implied for the whole passage. In bars 85, 87, and so on, the final eighth note should be slightly heavier than the preceding; and this difference will become more marked as the energy increases (from bar 89). In bar 113, be sure that the C (the first note of the subject, in the left hand) sounds out clearly above the B-flat, and learn to manage the pedal throughout this beautiful tenor solo so that there may be richness without blurring. A slight increase in speed is counseled by most editors as the climax of this passage is reached (bar 132); but the quaint imitations which from this point prepare for the recapitulation (bar 144) are best taken in the main tempo.

The brief Coda emerges almost insensibly from the closing subject. The ritard. (bar 233) must not begin before it is marked; but the fermata in bar 235 implies that it should amount to a considerable broadening. And do not spoil the exquisite simplicity of the end by retarding the final phrase.[6] A slight enlarge-

[5] Von Bülow tolerates

and the like as a substitute; but the subtle vivacity of the figure seems spoiled when the tenth above the bass is thus brought into prominence.

[6] In his sketch book, Beethoven noted the ending of the movement with several marks of expression—among them, poco ritard. for the final phrase. Since this does not appear in the original edition, however, we must conclude that he changed his mind during the composition of the piece.

ment of the preceding long drop is natural, however, and seems almost essential for the proper emphasis of the F-sharp.

As we might expect, since this is a two-movement sonata, the last movement is a clarification of the general sense of the first. "Not too fast, and very songfully" is the composer's direction; but the precise tonal meaning of this will be discovered only after many trials. The lightness of the motion must be preserved, but without any tinge of triviality; and that is by no means easy to do.[7] In the repetition in octaves of both this and the following strain, be sure to make the upper note brighter than the lower. It is not easy to "draw" acceptably the delicate *cresc.–p* of the cadence (bars 7–8).

Beethoven indicated no shading for the second strain of the theme (bars 8–10f.). Von Bülow, for the repetition in octaves both here and later, marks a phrase stress on the E and the D-natural bars 17–19. To us, this sounds sentimental and overdone. Whether it be in single notes or octaves, the phrase seems to us to culminate in its final note. Make the grace notes in bars 29–30 very short, and play them before the beat so as not to distort the delicate motion of the sixteenth-note figures. In bar 34f., the rhythmic figure of the last two notes of the cadence reappears, but shifted to "one" and "two." But we should also note that this is another version of the rhythm of the two opening notes of the first movement. Articulate very clearly the accompanying sixteenth-note figures, and mark generously the contrast between *f* and *p*. Thus the liquidness of the ensuing strain will be more conspicuous. The $<$ $>$ in bars 41–42, and 43–44, is Beethoven's own mark. Since it is difficult, however, to get a smooth *cresc.* for the long C-sharps (bars 42 and 44), the author begins the

---

[7] In the author's experience, it is not the melody, but the sixteenth-note accompaniment, which is hard to manage. If it becomes thick and smeary (with too much pedal), the melody will refuse to flow; if it is brittle, the melody will not sound legato. Be sure to silence the eighth notes of the bass elastically (with a bare touch of the pedal) as if they were plucked by the 'celli and contrabassi of the orchestra.

murmuring sixteenths with the pedal in bar 41, holding it to the B in bar 42. The murmur emerges into clarity in bar 46 [8] but returns, much enriched, in bar 49. This is the B subject. Be sure to allow no discrepancy in the tempo at bar 61f., where for a moment there is the equivalent of 6–8 time. There is no new C subject—only a brief development of the strain first heard as if in 6–8 time.[9] In bar 283, we feel that the *f* belongs less to the right hand than to the figure in the left, which, for clarity in the ensuing imitations, must be definitely started here. The last *three* sixteenths in the left hand in bar 231 obviously replace the *two* which have hitherto formed the up-beat to the principal subject. This unexpectedly warm version of the theme (even more than the phrase in bar 50) demands the most careful study. The contrast in register for the succeeding phrase is easily emphasized by giving melodic value to the chromatic ascent in bar 235; but to make the tone glow as it should, whether in the higher or the lower region, is a problem in dynamics and pedaling too subtle for exact description.

The Coda is entered upon by deferring the final chord in the cadence of the second strain of the theme—by deferring it, indeed, almost to infinity; for though the E often appears, it is never a final note, but instead the initial note of a new version of the cadential figure. Only after the brief reference to the main theme in bars 277f. does the original cadence appear. The accelerando beginning in bar 288 after the long ritardando is most

[8] The last two sixteenths of the left-hand passage (C-sharp, D-sharp, in bar 46) can be more conveniently taken with the right hand, along with its E and F-sharp. The same in the parallel passage (bar 188).

[9] Von Bülow suggests a grotesque remedy for what he feels to be the grotesqueness of the sforzandi in the transition back to the principal subject in bars 137–139. To our ear, these accents are the culmination of the swerving figures preceding, and—far from being detached, as he suggests—should be included in the phrase and approached in unbroken legato. (Some French and Belgian editions "correct" the sixteenth G-sharp, before the *sf* F-sharp, to an F-sharp an octave below the *sf* note. This was apparently for conformity with the dominant seventh harmony of the bass; but it represents a harmonic squeamishness hard to understand in these days.)

difficult to shape effectively. Schnabel sufficiently refutes von
Bülow's opinion that the hastening is only a gradual return from
the retarded to the original tempo. (The labored impression
given by a literal observance of von Bülow's words is so intolerable
that one cannot but wonder whether the words were as carefully
chosen as they seem to be.) But we cannot, either, manage the
tiny naïveté of the *a tempo* without a brief breath-pause, which
Schnabel forbids.

The next sonata, Op. 101, is the last of these works with which
this book will deal. It is technically beyond the power of the majority of those to whom our effort is addressed; musically, it is
also probably beyond the imagination either of the author or most
of the virtuosi; yet it offers so deep an insight into the quality of
Beethoven's third period that our "autobiography" will be incomplete without it.

The sonata was published in 1817, with a dedication to the
Freiin (Baroness) Dorothea Ertmann, who, in 1803, had been
a pupil of Beethoven. There is much testimony as to the perfection
and the interpretative interest of her playing, as well as to the
beauty and the quiet charm of her person. Beethoven called her
his "Dorothea-Cecilia," and to her, more than to any other pupil,
he seems to have imparted the secret of that moving style which
—especially in improvisations—was his own.

Before coming to Vienna from her home in Frankfort am
Main, Dorothea had married an officer in the Austrian army.
Some time before this sonata was written, her only surviving
child—a little boy—died. She was so distraught with grief that
her health was gravely endangered. For some time (as she told
Mendelssohn, many years after), Beethoven could not bear to
come to her house. At last, however, he asked her to come to him;
and when she came, he went at once to the piano, saying, "We
shall speak to each other in tones," and played, without a word,
for an hour. Dorothea wept, and was comforted.

There is no evidence whatever that any strain of this sonata was conceived on that day. It is true that the dedication was not given to the publisher until the sonata was already in the press, because, as Beethoven wrote, "I wanted it to be a surprise." But whatever the connection with the episode, the music has certain qualities that make it appropriate, not to the death of the child—for the man who was himself too gentle to touch a wound with ill-chosen words would hardly have offered a dirge—but to the quality of understanding that could make Dorothea forget.

We have found something of the depth of his new gentleness in our immediately preceding studies. But we have seen nothing like this, which you may without too much difficulty find for yourself in the first movement. It is the very anticipation of ro-manticism at its highest intuitive pitch. The form is more free (in the first movement) than any which Beethoven had so far created—unless in the string quartet in F minor, Op. 95—but the impression upon the hearer is lucidity itself.

With melody so fluid that it seems to have been already in mo-tion before it comes into sight, there is a beginning on the domi-nant harmony, made still more fluid by chromatic progression and by cadences that avoid any strong emphasis on the tonic. Such harmonic evasion was not new. It had been much exploited by Bach (see, for example, the *Prelude in C-sharp minor,* Book I of the *Well-tempered Clavichord*), but for no such expressive pur-pose as this. For we have here a more immediately personal com-munication—a more "subjective" attitude—than had ever before been uttered in music.

At bar 25, a cadence is at last completed in the dominant. What follows, however, is no "second subject," but only a quiet inter-lude whose main line is at first in the bass, and then migrates to the high register, only to waver for a time on syncopated chords, and subside again to the harmony of E from which it started. Then, at first tentatively but soon with extraordinary fervency, the first fluid theme is swelled to an irresistible appeal, never declarative but always persuading, through the utter frankness of its inherent sympathy. Insensibly the music arrives at a kind of recapitulation (bar 60), and there is a brief epilogue (bar 88), with just enough of added strangeness in the harmony (93–94) to make real the already incredible communication.

There follows another extraordinary image. The direction is *Vivace alla Marcia;* but human feet never marched so lightly as this. One would think it a kind of "Midsummer Night's Dream" music, save that there is an undercurrent of human warmth that prevents it from escaping into the colder region of mere fancy. Conventionally, the *March* has a *Trio* whose curious melody turns into a canon in which, by a momentary interruption of the imitation, the lead is taken from the upper voice and given to the lower. Conventionally, also, the *March* returns after the *Trio,* with a scintillant close in F major.

But now comes a moment of spiritual exaltation which has few rivals in any literature. After the F major close of the *March,* the first chord (the dominant of A minor) gives a strange remoteness to the long initial E of the melody. With a gentle swerve, the harmony comes to rest at the third beat; but the melody, subtly animated, floats up to C and droops again to the active leading tone before it completes its first long phrase on the tonic. The next phrase (they are all of two bars) strains for a moment toward a higher region, but falls, without protest, though with a kind of regret that is deepened by the sinking of the G-sharp to G-natural against the last note of the melodic phrase. But the momentary hint of pain is alleviated at once. With motion so quiet that the long upward intervals seem effortless, and with a bass that by its descent exalts even more the height to which the melody rises, the next seven notes seem almost to illumine eternity. And as if in humility before the vision, the final phrase of the sentence begins, far below, and comes to rest in the quiet tonality of the major.

What follows is an aftermath of ecstatic contemplation of the vision just revealed. Although it becomes almost passionate, it is still governed (as Schnabel pertinently remarks) by the *una corda* which Beethoven prescribed at the beginning and released only toward the end of the contemplative little cadenza that leads so pointedly to a little reminiscence of the first movement. Whether or not Beethoven "found" this music during his improvisations for Dorothea, it is music for the alleviation of even greater woes than hers.

The final *Allegro* (which word Beethoven qualified by a German phrase meaning "fast, but not too much so, and with resolution") is a full-fledged sonata form [10] in which the long development section is a fugue on a somewhat altered and expanded version of the principal subject. The fugue, of course, is a form quite capable of standing by itself, and of being developed to far larger dimensions than this. Beethoven was sufficiently skilled, even in his earlier years, to write conspicuous examples, such as that which concludes the Variations for piano on the theme from the Ballet, *Prometheus* (Op. 35), or the last movement of the great string quartet in C, Op. 59, No. 3. But while the fugue is indeed a particular form, it is also a manner of developing a theme, and is thus available, when the subject is suited to that manner, for use in the sonata or other forms. The dainty subject of the slow movement of the *First Symphony* is set forth in the fugal manner; so is a considerable section of the *Rondo* in Op. 27, No. 1; and in both the first and the last movements of the *Eroica* symphony there are extended fugal passages.

In Beethoven's last period, both the general manner and the conventional form of the fugue appear much more often than formerly. Polyphonic texture (the use of melody, rather than of mere chords or their arpeggios, as the accompaniment for a main theme or melodic line) is still more frequent, as the first move-

---

[10] Casella, remarking in the *Appassionata* the innovation of the unrepeated exposition, speaks also of Op. 90, 101, 109, and 110 as following the same plan. He must be speaking of the first movement, since the exposition in the last one is repeated; but, to judge from his comment on the fugal character of the last, he seems unaware that this is a true sonata form.

ments of this sonata will show. To those who look only within
the substance of music for an explanation of its quality, this later
manner of Beethoven's thus seems a somewhat recondite mystery—
the evolution of a "purely" musical mind, solving purely musical
problems for the edification of the few who are capable of understanding the art in its pure essence.

He whose autobiography we have been extracting from his music
hardly appears to have been that sort of man. Nor is any such notion suggested by his daily life or his letters. He was, indeed, a
recluse. He was so deaf that he had to converse with friends and
strangers through the humiliating medium of a paper and pencil;
he was perplexed by the confusions of a world emerging from war,
and by the behavior of his nephew and ward who caused him
endless distraction; but he was most absorbed in the endeavor to
set forth what seemed to him ideas that were the proper spiritual
concern of all humanity. What is the *Ninth Symphony*—with
which he was not yet actually occupied, but which it had long
been his purpose to make, on Schiller's *Ode*—but the exposition
of four ways of life, of which the last, the way of human brother-
hood, is set forth as the true way?

These later visions are naturally less simple than the demonic
rages which, as we have seen, seized him in the earlier years. His
whole manner of utterance, therefore, ceases to become declarative,
and becomes conditional. And for that kind of utterance, the
polyphonic musical substance is most suitable, not merely because it
is more complex, but because the harmonies that arise out of polyphony are no longer the bare and often hard facts of tonic, dominant, and so on, but are incidents in the progress of a musical
fabric that is conceived as the equivalent or the symbol of a subtle
and evanescent state of mind and feeling. Beethoven, in his last
days, became a polyphonist because he had to—because no other
manner could fulfill his expressive purpose.

We need go no further with the analysis of the last movement
of Op. 101. Its intricacies are such that a whole chapter of dull

words might be written to describe what, after all, is far more than the mere structure which alone such words would reveal. Instead, we shall leave the reader to his own ingenuities in exploring this and the still later works, hoping that what we have already set forth will yield some clue to their understanding.

# 7
# ROMANTICISM —
# FRANZ PETER SCHUBERT

~~~~~~~~~~~~~~~~~~~~~~~~~~~~~~~~~~~~~~~~~~~~~~~~~~~~~~~~~~~~~

FOR the true amateur—the true music lover—there is a special corner of the mind in which, like keepsakes and other mementoes of precious moments, he stores some of the piano pieces of Franz Schubert. There is seldom occasion to make display of these things. They commemorate no great historic occasions, nor do they represent the travail of great spiritual discoveries, such as we sometimes found in the sonatas of Beethoven. Schubert's is the most intimate music ever written; for he wrote out of almost incessant inspiration, and thus revealed, with almost every note, that world of the imagination which he seldom left.

Through his effort to interpret the new world which the Revolution inaugurated, Beethoven was made a romanticist. Schubert was born one; and so, since he was twenty-seven years younger than Beethoven—and yet lived but a year beyond the death of the great master—no adjustment was needed to enable him to live in the romantic world as his natural habitat. We shall soon encounter other romanticists; and since that word is very differently understood by different people, we must at least try to define the meaning we intend it to convey.

To many, especially today, the word "romanticism" implies an unruled activity of the fancy and a corresponding indulgence in wishful thinking. It is taken as a synonym for sentimentality. But that is by no means the sense in which the romanticists understood themselves and their purposes. They were, indeed, dreamers—or at least, idealists—men whose search for a better world began in the imagination, rather than in a "realistic" cognizance of literal facts. But the images upon which they built were drawn—as truly as those of the realists—from life. The Revolution, even for the common man, represented more than the escape from subjection to tyranny. Not the King, but he himself, collectively, was now the State; and his collective imagination was the source from which the pattern of the State must henceforth be derived.

In this new world, in consequence, the artist became a new figure. He was no longer the mere purveyor of pleasure to a privileged aristocracy. He was the instigator of that in the imagination which was to be enacted into reality: "the unacknowledged legislator of the world," as Shelley called him. Like other legislators, past and present, he sometimes proposed silly laws; but we have just fought a second world war to preserve precisely that which the romantic artist, more consciously than his predecessors, proposed as the basis of the common good—the unfettered conscience of the common man.

That conscience is not a mere formulated rule of behavior. It is a compound of experience and aspiration—the two often in conflict—working toward a goal too uncertain to be defined. But since it is thus uncertain, the only guide toward it is the imagination. He who imagines is thus the real leader toward it. Even he, however, can judge of the rightness of his direction only by the fact that his image evokes assent from other minds—or rather, from other hearts; for there are involved here, and very deeply, Pascal's "reasons of the heart" to which we have already referred. Artists have always based their work on those reasons. But the work of those who were liberated by the Revolution is stamped with a special character; and it is this character which

—as we understand the word—ought to be implied by the term "romanticism."

By nature, then, the work of any romanticist, being individual, is autobiographical. Out of Schubert's works, however, we can trace no such narrative of growth as we discovered in the sonatas of Beethoven. That growth perceptibly reflected the humanism and the philosophy of the Revolution. But Schubert was incapable of conscious philosophizing. His impulses were as liberal as Beethoven's; but he knew them only as the emotional attitudes of the immediate moment. Such a work as Beethoven's *Ninth Symphony* is therefore unthinkable from Schubert, even if he had been allowed the twenty-five years of life that were needed for the gestation of that really philosophic music.

Schubert was, and remained all his life, a singer. But by sheer genius (doubtless aided by a most fortunate absence of pedantic training) he had discovered a far different solution for the problem of combining words and music from that which had been the rule of the musicians before him. He had devised a kind of song form in which new phrases of melody were provided whenever the words brought new currents of feeling into his poem; and he had done this in a way that had been thought impossible, for he had managed it without destroying the continuity of the musical idea. You will find a wonderful example of this kind of writing in *Der Wanderer,* a song which he wrote in 1816, and in which, without any sense of incongruity, eight different melodic strains are used to depict the gloom and the nostalgic memory of the "hero," who, like the composer, was everywhere a stranger in the ordinary world.

This gift of melody (the richest, surely, ever possessed by a human being) made him impatient of the laborious devices by which the learned musical forms are developed. The sonata, indeed, was for him a somewhat infrequently chosen form, and it was only in his later years that he turned with any strong determination to instrumental music. To 1815 belong at least 195 compositions, almost all for voices (among them, two Masses, a *Stabat Mater,* four *Singspiele*—a kind of opera with spoken dialogue—and another Operetta); but there are only four piano sonatas of minor interest, an immature string quartet, and a few smaller instrumental pieces. Two years later, he took a sudden interest in the piano, and wrote the three sonatas, Op. 122, in E-flat, Op. 147, in B major, and Op. 164, in A minor; but it was only in 1823 that he added another (Op. 143, in A minor). In 1825, there are three more: Op. 42, in A minor, Op. 53, in D, and Op. 120, in A. In 1826 came a very important work—really a sonata, but for some reason called by the publisher a *Fantaisie, Andante, Menuetto et Allegro,* in G; and in 1828, three great works, published posthumously, in C minor, A major, and B-flat major.[1] In these later years there is a considerable mass of smaller pieces, among them many dances, many of which cannot be dated accurately.

Let us begin our study with one of these simpler pieces—the *Impromptu in A-flat,* Op. 142. Technically, it is not at all difficult, but if carefully played it offers an illuminating approach to the character of much of Schubert's music.

In the quiet rhythm, there is but one debatable problem: the relative weight of the first and second beats in bars 1 and 2, and in similar passages. A clue is given in the notation—the half-notes on "two"; but musical common sense will also tell us that there would be little point in the repetition of A-flat in bar 1 unless the second note was to be louder than the first. If we scrupulously obey the *pp* and the *sempre legato,* there will be little danger of overdoing the emphasis. (The pedal, though not indicated, is available.) In bar 3, the forward glide is a dynamic approach to the C in bar 4. But if you make a continuous increase from the first B-flat in bar 3, you will either get too high an in-

---

[1] The opus numbers represent the order of publication, but since Schubert's first published work, the *Erlkönig,* appeared only in 1821, there was already an immense list of works ready. Those were chosen which seemed most likely to sell, and the order in which they had been composed was not considered.

tensity for the C, or fail to make the increase perceptible. Beginning, then, with a B-flat on "one" appropriate to its eighth-note up-beat, take the A-flat a little softer, and then grow through the next B-flat to the C which is your goal. You will not be aware of the diminution, but will feel the sense of continuous legato. And you will again perceive that legato cannot be produced by mere continuity of tone from one note to the next, but depends also on a continuous, though very slight, dynamic fluctuation.

The repetition of bars 1–8 is made in the higher octave, but only in the right hand. The change of color, however, is almost vivid, and requires no new dynamic level for the second period. The indicated repetition for the whole section (and for the second) is so out of accord with twentieth-century nerves that it is probably best to ignore it.

The sudden *f* suggests an unsuspected intensity in the quieter thought. The up-beat is now an eighth note, and the stress is expressly marked on the first beat. But there is no contradiction of our phrase design in the first section, for the second E-flat is here the end of the motive, whereas the second A-flat (bar 1) continues on, legato, to the B-flat. The heavy staccato chords in bar 3 may be pedaled at the attack, but must be released so as to give the detachment that staccato implies. (Because of this staccato, you may prefer to give a continuous crescendo throughout the bar; but a similar treatment to that which we suggested for bar 3, section 1, is also possible.) The *fz* in bar 9 is in the governing *ff,* and this is obviously the loudest note in the whole passage. Be sure that B-double flat in the bass is clearly audible when, in bar 10, the bitter chord of the augmented sixth (Schubert's favorite harmony) sounds against it. The ensuing *fz* is in piano, and both this and the next augmented sixth chord in bar 12 must be given the color appropriate to their yielding echo of the former high intensity. (*Una corda* is surely justified.) The turn in bar 11 may be slightly delayed, initiating a *rit.* that continues to the · fermata in bar 14.

The *Trio,* with its easy triplets, usually tempts the temperamental to a tempo quite out of accord with Schubert's apparent meaning. He wrote no sign for greater speed. An ill-judged *molto più mosso* yields only an aimless scurrying in which all relation is lost with the character of the preceding portion. Observe that the accents on "two" in the first two bars correspond to those which we read into the opening strain. Bring out the last note of each triplet in bars 3–4, and in like passages, which continue the melody. Likewise, in the second division, keep the little finger bright throughout the approach to the *ff* in bar 11. Observe exactly the rests in the left hand, which greatly intensify the forzandi. These marks do not appear in bar 15; but Schubert wrote no diminution to the ensuing piano, and the omission is not likely an oversight. The transition back to the first part may fade somewhat in time as well as in dynamics.

The subtle melancholy of this piece—the utter unconsciousness of pain, and the absence of all rebellion or even of protest—reminds us of what Matthew Arnold somewhere calls "the almost intolerable pathos of Burns's verse." Quite certainly, if it were conscious, it would be neither pathetic nor intolerable. Your fingers will not be too busy to allow you to think of these qualities as you play, and you will find, in this and many other Schubert pieces, studies in fine gradations of feeling such as are seldom to be met with in any other composer.

The *Impromptu in G-flat,* Op. 90, No. 3, a little more difficult, but yet very congenial to the hand, has something of the same quality but is intrinsically more animated. The indication, *Andante,* and the many whole and half notes, which to the eye suggest slow motion, are belied by the 2–2 time signature. (The piece was originally written in 4–2 time (₵ ₵), but modern editions divide the 4–2 bars into two.) With only two beats in a measure, the triplet figures [2] are swift with subdued excitement

---

[2] The notes are not marked either as triplets or sextolets. (A sextolet consists, properly, of three groups of two notes each, played in the time of four

from the beginning. (Although the pedal will be used almost constantly, these figures need not be blurred.) Here, even more than in the *A-flat Impromptu,* the singer is manifest. There are but few phrase patterns in his song, and the repetitions are many; but just as a good singer or speaker knows how to change the color of a repetition so that it has a new meaning, the pianist may vary these strains so that they never lose for a moment their poetic interest.

The tempo is about $\downarrow = 72$. Mark, but within the prescribed *pp,* the stress point on B-flat in bar 3 so that the ensuing *cresc.* may subside to the *p* in bar 8; and color the cadence (bars 11–12) so that its simplicity (by contrast with the half-close in bar 8) will be without affectation. The urgency of the next strain will then be suggestible without too much force, and the *pp* of bar 25, maintained to bar 32, will allow the *cresc.* at that point to color vividly what is essentially the repetition of bars 17–24. The *pp* at bar 41 (for what is essentially a repetition of bars 25–32) will then, by contrast, give the necessary color, and make possible a portentous *cresc.* in bars 48–49. Observe that the longer melodic notes absorb from the dynamic gradation of the triplet figures a shading which, in reality, is impossible on a single note. Such illusions as this are frequent in sensitive piano playing.

This piece is really in the simple A-B-A form of the operatic aria and the song. Bar 49, then, is the beginning of the B section. Its whole substance is more agitated in character than the A, but its speed needs no hastening to give that effect. Rather, you must gain it by allowing the bass and tenor to assert themselves. Even so, the assertion must not be too violent, else you will quite ruin the climax of the whole section, which, prepared for by the ominous *fz* in bars 72 and 76, appears with the precipitate melodic

---

normal notes of the same time value. Two triplets are also six notes in the time of four, but the accentuation, usually very slight, marks the rhythmic difference.) Here, the pattern sufficiently indicates the triplets. If the accentuation were intended as that of sextolets, the time signature would have been 6-4.

figures (79) and reaches its peak in bars 87f., where the heavier
bass-notes are in octaves. There is also ample possibility of color
in the transition back to the A section, beginning at bar 101. Liszt
(who transposed the piece into G major) made a new version
of this section as far as bar 133, with the melody an octave higher,
with full chords in the right hand, and with long up-and-down
arpeggios in the left hand instead of the original figures. This,
of itself, makes a new color for the repetition, and apparently
lightens the problem of interpretation. But there was nothing in
the character of the A melody which demanded any such change
in register, and the whole piece becomes, through it, both sentimental and tawdry. The Coda, if the rest is well done, will give an
interesting but not difficult problem of interpretation.

Somewhat more troublesome for the fingers, but much easier
to interpret, is the *Impromptu in A-flat,* Op. 90, No. 4. The
arpeggio figures are not as difficult as they look. Learn to grasp
each chord in the whole succession with the same fingering as
that which you will use in arpeggiating it, thus:

and when you can find these without hesitation you will have
little difficulty with the sixteenths, for the thumb will always show
your second finger where to go. The C-sharp minor section is
extraordinarily dark and passionate. Mark the bass well, in bars
11–13, so that the straining of the diminished third in the melody
(C✕–E-natural) will be fully realized. In the second section,
climb impetuously through bars 3 and 4 to the augmented sixth in
bar 5, and be sure that your *decresc.* reaches *p* in bar 7, else the
whole line will become "obvious." The C-sharp major key at
bar 17, section 2, seems calm; but there is brewing a most extraordinary harmonic moment—bar 29—where the chord of the
augmented sixth, instead of resolving as before, leaps bodily to

what is really the D major triad, and goes on to achieve almost unendurable tension with another diminished third in the melody at bars 31–32. Wagner might have learned something from this passage.

Considerably more difficult is the *E-flat Impromptu,* Op. 90, No. 2 though for the most part the scale passages lie comfortably for the hand. ♩.= 69 is a sufficient speed, for the middle section as well as for the first. The form is obviously A-B-A. The striking color of the key of B minor in contrast to the original E-flat is a heavy contribution to the fiery energy of the dance tune. The sudden *p*'s must be realized to the full, and also the reference to the triplet figures of the A section in bars 23, 27, and the like. (The single triplets on "two," at the beginning, are from the same source, but that fact is not likely to be realized by the hearer until it is revealed in bar 23.)

The lovable theme and its engaging variations which form the *B-flat Impromptu,* Op. 142, No. 3, will hardly need comment, if you can manage those which have already been discussed. For the "two-against-three" of Variation 3, see the footnote, p. 34, above. The rest, we believe, will interpret itself.

Beethoven gave a somewhat depreciatory title to his smaller piano pieces. He called them *Bagatelles*—but although they are by no means trivial, they represent what must have been a minor field of his musical interest. Schubert's small pieces are more characteristic of himself, and his interest was evidently more discriminating, for he gives them two different generic titles. Besides the *Impromptus* there are also *Momens Musicals.*[3] There is no very clear distinction, either of form or character between the two, but the "Moments" are on the whole shorter, and are more in the nature of little, fugitive flashes of feeling, captured on the wing, and—in one case, at least—allowed to escape again.

[3] This is probably Schubertian French. Properly, it should be *Moments musicaux;* but to English ears (and perhaps to German) the proper phrase sounds unmusical, and it looks even worse to the eye.

There are six of these pieces, every one a gem. We shall begin
with the fourth, in C-sharp minor.

Its Moderato tempo was intended to govern the whole piece;
but Liszt (unwisely, as we think) seems to have played the first
and last parts Vivacissimo agitato. The bass must be very light and
staccato against the persistent legato of the right hand. (Some
·students still need to be told that you cannot get the effect of
staccato with the pedal held down.) Since most of the figures are
arpeggiations, it is allowable to play legatissimo (that is, holding
a note partly or wholly for the duration of the following note—
or even notes). You will find that there is a melody latent in
these sixteenths—not hard to see, but requiring a fine discrimination to shape against the softer sixteenths, which must never lose
their articulateness. Having avoided the pedal from the beginning,
you will see how grateful its effect is when at last it is prescribed
(bar 22). But do not spoil a third available color value (that of
legato in both parts) by using the pedal. The middle part seems
at first quite cosy and restful; but there is a sensitive spot (at
bar 11) which winces and hesitates, and can find relief only in
the alarming-looking key of F-flat major. (Do not be unduly
alarmed. However many the accidentals on the page, there are
only black and white keys on the keyboard; and this will soon
turn, for your fingers, into the equivalent of E major.)

The tiny "Moment" in F minor, No. 3, is the most popular of
Schubert's piano pieces. Berlioz might have said of it, as he did
of the *Allegretto* in Beethoven's *Eighth Symphony,* that it fell
straight from heaven. The piece looks easy to play, but it is not
so. To get the two grace notes to run perkily enough to the C's
without at the same time thumping the A-flat takes more practice than you would suspect; and there are several similar problems. Do not make an elaborate effort to alter the color every time
a short section is repeated. There are indications for such color
in the longer final section, and to anticipate these will dull their

sheen when they do come. You will spend many minutes (or perhaps hours) in trying to make an effective "vanishing point" at the end.

No. 2, in A-flat, has in full measure that unconscious but intolerable pathos to which we have already referred. Be careful, as you begin, to shape the up-beat so that it really moves forward to the real "one"—not only by appropriate dynamic gradation, but by sensing the flexible rhythm. The first four-bar period is made to seem almost irregular in design through the unexpected reiteration of the up-beat figure on "one" of bar 3, and the immediate quelling of this activity. The second four-bar group is still more disturbing, with its *fz* on the long chord. After this stroke, the rhythm loses all momentum until the next phrase begins,[4] and the next phrase, depressed into E-flat minor, can achieve only a doubtful smile as it ends in major. The greater asymmetry of the second period (nine bars long, where the first was eight) makes its quiet conclusion even more intolerable.

The muffled thudding of the bass in the F-sharp minor section emphasizes the immobile repression of the melody. The pedal may be used for this figure, where the thud represents the staccato, and the slur over the two eighth notes will be suggested by softening them perceptibly after the first note. But the thud must not become a crack! There is somewhat greater fluidity as the first six-bar period is expanded to eight bars, but the repression again becomes almost complete as the transition is made back to the first strain. The forte repetition of this second section, later, will give no interpretative difficulty if the sense of its first appearance has been grasped. Keep the E-flats in the Coda (nine bars from the end) somewhat prominent, both in the tenor and later in the soprano, and let the figure of the main theme dwindle and fade to the weary cadence.

This must conclude our study of the smaller pieces. Nor have

[4] This does not mean that it should be played out of time!

we space for detailed examination of the great *Wanderer Fantaisie,* Op. 15, written probably in 1820, upon themes from the extraordinary song we have already mentioned. It is extremely difficult.[5] Schubert could never get through the last movement. There are four great divisions which together resemble the large outline of the sonata: *Allegro con fuoco, ma non troppo* (only the torso of a sonata form); *Adagio* (on that part of the song which has the words, "And what they say is empty sound. I am a stranger, everywhere"); *Presto* (a *Scherzo*); and *Allegro.* The rhythm of the opening is derived by a species of diminution from that phrase of the song which forms the theme of the *Adagio,* and both the *Scherzo* and the *Finale* will be seen to be based on various transformations of that same theme. They who hold Schubert incapable of development should first study the ingenuity of this piece.

In the familiar editions of the piano sonatas, only ten works appear. There are at least eleven others (some of them quite early, and one incomplete) among which there is one of the finest of all: the so-called *Fantaisie* in G. (The original publisher seems to have been alone responsible for the title: *Fantaisie, Andante, Menuetto et Allegretto,* under which it appeared. Unlike the first movement of the *Wanderer Fantaisie,* this is a full-fledged sonata form.) The first movement is largely in a similar vein of melancholy contemplation to that of the A-flat *Moment Musical.* The *Menuetto,* a curious mingling of Haydnesque stateliness and more modern freedom, is often played separately. It is not very difficult, and you will find it inexhaustibly appealing.

Among the ten sonatas in the available collections there is not a dull moment—at any rate for those who have discovered the

---

[5] Liszt substituted, for many of Schubert's more unmanageable passages, new figures which are more pianistic or more sonorous, but which also take from the music a certain character that it cannot afford to lose. He was so enamored of this work that he also arranged it into a piece for piano and orchestra. Effective as this is, it of course loses even more of the original sense than the revamping just mentioned.

subtle poetic sense which imbues the work of this unique genius.
None of them is easy, in spite of their intimacy and unpretentious-
ness. Schubert was too little the virtuoso to explore, for its own
sake, the peculiarity of his instrument. He contents himself, when
intensifications are needed, with figurations mostly familiar in the
technique of the day. What he means is obvious enough to the
eye; but to the ear alone these passages are sometimes very hard
to make effective. Many of the sonatas also appear, at a first
reading, unduly long (a frequent reproach with other works
also); but this judgment seems, to the initiated, to be based on
almost complete misunderstanding of the unworldly imaginative
mind of the composer.

We have space for extended consideration of but one sonata
—the last, in B-flat. The opening theme of this incredibly beautiful work is Schubert's very self—gentle, unobtrusive to the
point of shyness, stunned by worldly noise. You would hardly suspect the melancholy of this theme if it were not for the quiet but
ominous rumble (bar 8) which seems like the voice of the ghost
in *Hamlet*. A release of warmth in the extension of the theme
(bar 20f.) is exquisitely accomplished by a new texture for the
accompaniment, and the emergence of the original line, forte
(bar 36), seems to suggest almost untrammeled happiness. But
the sudden chill in bar 45 belies this implication. The transition
to the second theme (beginning in F-sharp minor) is itself a composite theme (like the second subject of Beethoven's "Return" in
Op. 81a), and indeed it fulfils a good deal of the purpose of a second subject. Of the two combined phrases, the tenor is soon proved
the more important by emerging as a solo line. Note how the
sudden gasp of uncertainty recurs (bar 72) even though the
lilting phrases that follow seem to ignore it. The true second
subject is probably that hidden in the rhythm of the chords from
bar 81. The melodic line will become more visible in the development, but it must be foreshadowed here. Keep the arpeggios
very staccato, using pedal only for the two slurred notes of the

first triplet in the bar. It is important not to fumble the rhythm in the pauses from bar 95 to 99.[6]

The almost shockingly dramatic fortissimo trill at the end of the "first ending" is hard to forego; but it can hardly be denied that a repetition of the whole exposition is fatiguing. The second ending, with its sudden overturning of the B-flat key into C-sharp minor, is sufficiently startling.

For the first 55 bars of this section (counting from the C-sharp minor signature) there is perhaps no very subtle point made, though you will observe the emergence (bar 14) of the melodic line out of what was before a rhythmic succession of chords. And that which follows *looks* obvious enough—too obvious to some [7] —but the subtle pathos of it is incomparable. First, the second subject sets forth timidly on what seems an intended excursion from the now established key of D minor into F major; but at the very doorway the new key is forbidden, and D minor, with no show of force but with an ominous suggestion of submission to a hidden power, is reasserted. The same effort by the bass has the same result, and a rumble from the underworld hints at the strange moments of chilled hesitation which we found in the exposition. Now the main theme tries for a similar escape, and is as inexorably turned back. Even though, at the second trial, the B-flat key seems to have been reached (bar 76f.), the ineluctable

[6] If you think of the melodic progression, from bar 91, as being essentially this

it will perhaps help you to see the quite rational continuity of the passage.

[7] Harold Bauer, in an edition of this sonata which is announced as an attempt to make the beauties of Schubert more accessible, has deleted the whole passage about to be discussed, and has even more violently maltreated the final movement.

gravitation of D minor draws everything, even the rumbling quasi-tonic, B-flat (bar 81), into its orbit. Release does come— as soon it had to, else there would have been catastrophe—at the next attempt, but the darkness of D minor has left an indelible mark. For in the recapitulation the higher register in which much of the former matter appears has no corresponding brilliancy; and the Coda, although we cannot but be conscious of its recession from desire, seems to speak of the tiny area of its remaining pleasure as if it were enough.

The region of the *Andante sostenuto* is that to which our vision was reduced at the end of the last piece. But the darkness of C-sharp minor has fallen upon it (as it did for a time in the *Allegro*); the place is strange and hushed, and everything moves on tiptoe. In the melody there is neither fear nor active sorrow, nor any appeal for sympathy; but here, nevertheless, is music to break our hearts. Whether it be orthodox or not, the author plays *una corda* throughout the whole first section, finding that even the *f* in bar 12 cannot otherwise be appropriately colored. The *ppp* of the last few bars can still be perceptibly managed. You must deviate not one hair's breadth from the measured tempo in the thirty-second and the two following eighth notes throughout the accompaniment, else the hush will be broken, and the pointed omission of the thirty-second, as the first section nears its end, will be pointless.

The middle section is frankly elegiac; yet the sense of the past is somehow so strong that we can contemplate, rather than participate in, its regret. The triplet sixteenths lighten remarkably the color of the repetition; but at the end of the section they can also be made to fade and dwindle apprehensively, so that the bar of silence before the return of the theme is pregnant with the sense of the immediate scene.

The *delicatezza* with which we are cautioned to play the *Scherzo* is not very difficult to obtain—in the melody—if the prescribed *p* is allowed to rule; but the tripping articulation essential to the accompanying figures is not easy. Observe that only two notes in the whole *Scherzo* are marked *f*—and those are *fp* (section 2, bars 22 and 34). The hiatus, so frequently used in the middle of this section, produces a rhythmic complication. Bars 41 and 46 extend the periods to five bars, and as a consequence, bars 51–52, the echo of bars 49–50, stand by themselves. We feel that a slight *rit.* for these two measures keeps the irregularity from being deceptive, and also shapes more engagingly the return to the main theme.

In the *Trio*—as appropriate to the *Scherzo* as the *Scherzo* is to the rest of the sonata—the *sfp* on the strong beat in the bass must of course be preceded by an accent on the syncopated chord, and that chord may well be pedaled, the release being with the note following the *sfp*.

To be able to invent music as demurely saucy as this *Finale*—music which is infectiously gay, and yet without a trace of boisterousness—is to possess a musical imagination of the highest order. The main theme is only a whimsical chuckle, but what an infinity of amiability inspires it! And how it is set off by the first loud G, and the later, always startling but never alarming explosions of that same note! And how insouciant is the pendant phrase (bars 19–22) with its perky, staccato bass, and the impish echo in sixteenths (bar 22) of its first three notes!

The second subject (bar 86) is very hard to play. The right hand can get no help from the left, and must therefore manage the legato and the delicate shading of the melody along with the supporting sixteenths of the accompaniment. The syncopated bass of course forbids the pedal, though for a time, when the bass is legato (bar 112) the pedal is implied.

Two bars (precisely!) of silence launch the third subject (bar 156) without the return of the first theme. This is not the usual pattern of the Rondo, and indeed this movement rather approximates the sonata form than that of the Rondo. By contrast with everything that has preceded, this new subject seems tempestuous; but its energy soon turns to geniality (bar 186). In all that follows, be sure to keep the sixteenth notes very short, so that they never coincide with the last note of the triplet accompaniment. Do not miss the piquant turn given the main theme (from bar 225) by the sixteenth-note up-beat which replaces the original eighth note. There is vigorous development of this subject (not easy to play), so that the character of the sonata form is still further preserved. The Coda (from bar 490) with its gay *Presto* is indeed a little boisterous—but who would not be, with all this provocation?

Partly because Schubert was not a virtuoso pianist, but more because he instinctively sought that community of mind which is engendered when people make music together, he wrote a large number of pieces for piano duet (for two players on one instrument, not for two pianos). Since this book is intended for those who have a similar love of music, we must look at a few of these pieces before we turn to the work of other composers.

The notion of playing duets has gone sadly out of fashion since the radio and the phonograph have presented us with ready-made music that we can so easily turn on—or off. The great symphonies have all been arranged as piano duets (Schubert's, of course, among them); and there are few who have learned to know the symphonic literature in this form who will not agree that to play a symphony in such an arrangement is to hear its essential substance more clearly than is possible from the orchestra itself. For although the piano has no such possibilities of color as the orchestral ensemble, it is incomparably the clearest of all instruments, and, possessing enormous dynamic range, is capable of representing almost any rhythmic vitality.

The unready reader, also, will find in duet playing a most valuable remedy for his trouble. Especially if he finds a companion who reads more readily than he, the drive of continuous motion will spur him forward and accustom his eye to the discrimination of that which is most essential in the musical idea—

the rhythm, if he plays the lower part, and the melody, if he plays the upper. The delight of ensemble playing—perhaps the highest enjoyment of the true amateur—is a pleasure to which the playing of duets is a valuable introduction. The pedal may sometimes provoke debate, since it can be managed by only one of the two players; but the one who is charged with its management will soon learn to listen acutely enough to other than his own music so as to avoid damaging the ensemble by too exuberant an enrichment of his own part.

Schubert left twenty-one opus numbers of piano duets, ranging from simple Ländler, Marches, Polonaises, and Variations, to extended Rondos and two complete sonatas—one in three movements (Op. 30, in B-flat), and one in four (the "Grand Duo" in C, Op. 140). The familiar *Marche Militaire,* from which Tausig made his brilliant concert piece, is one of three Marches in Op. 51.

In the *Grand Rondeau* (Op. 107, written in June, 1828) you will find re-created one of those moments of intimate musical communion which were the breath of life to Schubert. If you are a very sophisticated person, you may find the unhurried grace of the opening theme too naïve for your taste. But if you go on, a forgotten corner of your sensibility will almost certainly come to life under the persuasion of its euphony. The melody is amiability itself. Between its leisurely notes the sixteenths of the *secondo* part twinkle graciously. The second strain (bar 8) is no more urgent than the first, and repeats its eight bars, as the first strain repeated its four, without any heed to the passing of time. No one can restrain a smile when the first strain comes back with an unexpected sparkle in the descending scale that accompanies it. Five C-sharps, in bar 33, answered by four E-sharps in the thirty-second-note figuration, initiate the smooth transition. The B subject (bar 69) is in the expected dominant, but is faintly tinged with a desire to move into the minor mode. Even this faint shadow of unrest vanishes, however, in the fluid passage of colored harmonies (92f.) of which Mozart had probably invented the prototype, and which leads back to the A subject (103).

The C subject (138), after a few measures of energetic motion, turns out to be no more than a variant of the B theme, only with more modulatory harmony, and with its accompaniment enlivened. (By this use of what is essentially development of earlier matter, the *Rondo* is thus made to resemble the sonata form. We found the same process in the last movement of the B-flat solo sonata.) Both the A and the B subjects, whose return is not long delayed, are considerably adorned; the Mozartian passage is made more luminous; and the last appearance of the A subject, sung in the warm tenor register, has a similarly luminous accompaniment, made out of the original figurations.

The *Grand Duo,* Op. 140, is more than a piano sonata. It is of symphonic proportions; and in the opinion of a scholar no less learned in the lore of Schubert than Professor Otto Erich Deutsch, it may well have been a sketch for the lost "Gastein" symphony.[8] It was written at Zelész, in Hungary, in the summer of 1824. Schubert was then on a second sojourn at the residence of the Esterhazy family, with whom Haydn, long before, had found employment for thirty years. (This was not, however, the "little Versailles," built by Prince Nicolaus Esterhazy, at which Haydn worked for so long.) As before, in 1818, Schubert was music master to the Countess Esterhazy and her three children, of whom the eldest (Carolina) apparently now awakened a vivid but ephemeral disturbance in his heart. The *Duo* was not published until 1838, when Diabelli issued it with a dedication (*par les Éditeurs*) to Clara Wieck, the famous pianist who was soon to become the wife of Robert Schumann.

[8] Sir George Grove, instigator and original editor of *Grove's Dictionary of Music and Musicians* (the most valuable dictionary of music in any language), wrote the original article on Schubert which has been retained, with minor additions and corrections, in all the later editions. He was firmly convinced that this "Gastein" symphony really existed, although no trace of the actual work has ever been found. You will find the story of it, as he understood it, in that article, which remains the best brief account of Schubert's life and work.

The *Grand Duo* is in C, but its main theme, like that of the introduction to the wonderful last *Symphony in C*, hovers on the border of A minor. The whole texture is orchestral, rather than pianistic, but the qualities of certain of the orchestral instruments are so clearly implied in the substance of the music that the players' imagination is almost deceived into the supposition that they are indeed an orchestra. Nothing could be more certain than the image of the 'cello tone given at the first entrance of the second subject (on an up-beat, bar 49) or that of the violins in answer (bar 57). Not only is this theme identical in rhythmic pattern with the first phrase of the principal subject; its developed continuation, from bar 66, forms both the transition to the closing subject and that subject itself. This shows how far Schubert was advancing in the use of that kind of structure which had by now been fully established in Beethoven's practice. Moreover, the development section itself is almost wholly concerned with this rhythm, and thus shows all the coherence which could be expected of any symphonic composition, and gains much in expressive allusiveness. The recapitulation, too, begins with no perfunctory restatement of the exposition, but with the principal subject heavily reinforced; and the whole movement is summed up in a Coda which is not only appropriate but illuminating.

The slow movement is equally mature in texture, while at the same time the grace and gentility of Schubert's personality are not in the least obscured. That Beethoven was his model, however, is evident from the second theme (beginning at the return of the four-flat signature), which cannot help but remind us of an episode in the *Larghetto* of Beethoven's *Second Symphony*. The *Scherzo,* although vigorous and energetic, does not attain to the unimaginable excitement of that in the great *C Major Symphony,* but it is an illuminating preliminary. The *Finale* emphasizes that ambiguity of key which was notable at the beginning of the *Duo;* for after the long initial E, the subject really begins in A minor, even though at the eighth bar it is safely in C. The persistent, scurrying sixteenths of the counterpoint also faintly remind us of the last movement of Beethoven's *Fourth Symphony,* where, however, there is a less exuberant gayety than that which this piece, quite appropriately, sets forth.

Was ever a truer portrait painted of a human face than is drawn, in the few pieces we have studied, of the mind and heart of this extraordinary genius? When he speaks in music, he has. no reserves. He never strikes an attitude, or feigns, for the sake of impressiveness, a gravity which may make us conscious of the artist. He often seems, to contemporary vision, naïve. But is our sophistication (which is the background and the source of this judgment) really a superior wisdom? Or is it merely a safeguard against the revelations of spiritual emptiness which such insight as his must inevitably expose? The still, small voice is particularly inaudible to those who reap the whirlwind.

The artist's real business is with human impulses themselves. They are at once the most familiar and the least understood of earthly facts. For as facts—as things once accomplished—they appear only in the guise in which they can be represented or symbolized; and we are ourselves mostly so naïve that we suppose the surface of these symbols which we have ourselves chosen to adopt (out of that personal or conventional preference which we call "taste") to be the true index of their content.

It was because he sensed the extraordinary penetration of Schubert's insight into these ultimate realities of human impulse that Liszt spoke of him as "the most poetic musician who ever lived."

# 8

# ROBERT ALEXANDER SCHUMANN

~~~~~~~~~~~~~~~~~~~~~~~~~~~~~~~~~~~~~~~~~~~~~~~~~~~~~~~~~~~~~~~~~~

THE tide of romanticism flowed high in all artistic fields during the early years of the nineteenth century. Byron, Keats, and Shelley, the great exemplars of that manner in England, all died in the early twenties; but the impress of their vision was felt long after. Goethe, the foremost figure in German literature until his death in 1832, had begun as a romanticist, but later, because of his dislike of the excesses of the weaker literary brethren of that school, became a kind of eclectic classicist. Heine, however, born in the same year as Schubert (1797) was during his youth a close counterpart of the great composer. (Unfortunately, his *Buch der Lieder* appeared only in 1827, so that Schubert had time to set only six of his poems. Among them is that gripping embodiment of the nameless terror which haunts the spiritual night of all humanity, the *Doppelgänger*.) But there were many other romanticists in Germany, whether poets like the brothers Schlegel, Tieck, Uhland, Chamisso, and Wilhelm Müller, or novelists like Jean Paul Richter and E. T. A. Hoffmann.

Of all these the full influence impinged upon the youthful mind of Robert Schumann. He was one of six great composers who were all born within the span of five years: Mendelssohn and Chopin in 1809, Schumann in 1810, Liszt in 1811, and Wagner and Verdi in 1813. All of these, except Chopin, had deep literary interest and some facility in writing; none was more susceptible to the inner sense of poetry than Schumann. His ancestry was not at all musical, but his father was a publisher and in some measure an author, and had sympathy with Robert's tastes, even if he had no understanding of his greatest talent. His mother, however, the daughter of a physician, had a kind of horror of the social career of an artist, and stoutly opposed Robert's ambitions until it became apparent that the law, for which she had destined him, was in nowise suited to his mind. This was the more unfortunate since his father died when Robert was sixteen. But already his mind was forming, under the stimulus especially of the novelist Jean Paul, whose fantastic tales he read and reread, and whose imaginative habits he considerably acquired. His musical talent, however, had been manifest from the first. He tells us that he had begun to compose at seven, and there are many tales of the facility of his improvisation. At the children's parties, for example, he would improvise little musical portraits of his playmates—portraits so vivid that they were recognized at once.

This disposition to see personalities and characters in music, together with the fact that he had no teacher of consequence during his whole youth, determines much of the form and the quality of his piano music. There is also the influence of Johann Sebastian Bach, whom he understood more imaginatively than any of his contemporaries, and from whom he learned the secret of a kind of polyphonic harmony which we shall soon encounter. Living thus largely to himself, he peopled his world with fictions —all, however, drawing their breath of life from himself; and in this way he began to find in himself a kind of dual personality which in some degree resembled two characters, Vult and Walt, in Jean Paul's *Flegeljahre* (Years of Adolescence). His more fiery self he called Florestan; his more melancholy and poetically contemplative, Eusebius. Many of his earlier compositions were signed, according to their character, F. or E.

The first published works are all piano pieces:[1] twenty-three successive opus numbers, all written during the years 1829–39. We shall begin our study with a piece that is well within average technical powers—the ever-popular *Papillons* (Butterflies), Op. 2 —and shall observe it rather minutely, as being especially suited to those for whom this book is mainly intended.

If there is any real meaning to be attached to the title, these are social butterflies: gay participants in a Carnival rout which ends with the striking of the hour of six, and the dispersal of the revelers to their beds—or breakfasts—we are not told which. To the whole piece—which is a sequence of twelve numbers, mostly very short and, except for the *Finale,* showing almost no thematic relation to one another—there is a six-bar *Introduction:* a suave line of unharmonized melody, faintly reminiscent of Weber's *Invitation to the Dance.*

Do not try to make this the prologue to a tragedy. Schumann has marked the stress point on the G-sharp in bar 3, and the echo is obvious in bars 5–6. In the first four-bar phrase of No. 1, stress the high G, but do not make another accent on the D in bar 3, else you will split the one phrase into two. In the second four-bar phrase, however, the high G is secondary to the final D. Section 2 derives, for four bars, from the cadence in bar 8. Make the eighth notes very staccato, with the accent on "two" very firm; then make vivid the suave contrast of dynamics and phrasing indicated in the notation.

In some editions, the first note of No. 2 is wrongly given as a sixteenth. (It should be an eighth.) In the interlocking octaves, after the swift arpeggio ascent, play the two thumbs louder than the two little fingers. Only so can you get any real continuity in the melodic line. In the last section, observe the rests in the melody; fit the intervening sixteenths very precisely in their place, keeping them appropriately

[1] Songs began to pour forth in 1840 (the year of his marriage to Clara Wieck); the next year came three symphonic works, and the next, chamber music; and in 1843 he won a great success with a choral piece, *Paradise and the Peri,* after Moore's *Lalla Rookh.* Thus he completed in four years his introduction to all the significant forms of composition except the opera and the Mass, in which fields he later also ventured, but less successfully.

soft; and then make as suave as possible the legato of the melody (from the tenuto F) against the continued detachment of the bass. The alternative version (in small notes, in most editions) for bars 5–6 is universally preferred.

The heavy accents at the beginning of No. 3 evidently apply throughout section 1; but strong and weak beats must be differentiated, and you must make dynamic room for the *sf* E (bar 4) and F-sharp (bar 8). This high energy may well be lessened in section 2, though the general character is the same. The little canon in section 3 will be spoiled if the left hand makes an unguarded thump when the right hand plays its strong accents (and vice versa). To avoid this is not as easy as it looks.

In No. 4, stress the first eighth in bars 5 and 7, rather than the dotted quarters in bars 6 and 8, and observe the rests in the left hand (bars 5–6) to make richer the more sustained chords in bars 7–8. The second section, up to the *rit.,* is so gay and dainty that it may well be taken faster. The general rule that the first note of a two-note phrase has the accent is also to be followed here, with the left hand's "two," in consequence, extremely light and exactly in time.

Out of the milling crowd one might now think that two especially attractive young people emerge (No. 5), their faces glowing with something a little more personal than the excitement of the Carnival. (Note the direction, *basso cantando;* and note also the eighth rests in this part.) The ⟨ in bar 1 is original; the ⟩ in bar 2 is editorial, but natural; for although the stress point is thus the B-flat in bar 2, the following accents cannot without clumsiness be all of even weight. The F-sharp in the bass (bar 5) leads forward (as that in bar 1 did not) and therefore must not be minimized. Its goal (G) is doubled an octave higher in the tenor, which now melodically supplants the bass. In bars 9 and 10, mark clearly the contrasts G-natural–G-flat and F-natural–F-flat in the successive chords, as well as the melody and the ensuing bass. Schumann wrote no *p* at bar 13, but it seems to be implied, both by the nature of the new phrase and by the swells in bars 13–14. Do not ignore the recurrence of the original bass rhythm at bar 15. The ⟩ at bar 18 seems to imply a *p* for the beginning of the melody in octaves. We feel that the real end of the piece is on the F at bar 25, which we approach with a slight *rit.,* and as graceful a curve as possible. The rest is only a charming effect of sound, and has no syntactical relation to the piece. It easily bears a slight *accel.-rit.* along with the marked swells.

More boisterous revelers take the foreground in No. 6. In addition to the marked sforzandi (Schumann wrote them only in bars 1–2, but they are implied—and often printed—in bars 3–4), thump vigorously the A's in the bass, and after the climactic A (bar 5) observe the proper accentuation for the two-note group, G–F. In section 2, many editions mark pedal for bars 1–2. This is impossible, of course, for the rhythmically similar bars 3–4. It seems to us better to avoid the pedal in bars 1 and 3, and to slur the first two notes only of bars 2 and 4, and so on (of course with the pedal). The tempo for this section must surely be definitely (but not distressingly) slower. In section 4, the notes marked *sf* have no staccato dot. In bars 1, 3, 5, and 7, then, pedal from "one" to "two" only; but in bars 2, 4, 6, and 8, which are legato, pedal more generously.

The superscription, *Semplice,* and the caution, *pp.* in No. 7, are warnings against sentimentality—but not against all beauty of tone and design. Observe religiously the rests in the left hand, and where they occur, take all possible pains with the shading of the melody. In the swaying little waltz that has now been introduced, do not let the *mf* give the effect of *f*. We advise pedal at beats 1 and 3 (rather than throughout the bar), as giving greater clarity, as well as sufficient aid to the right hand, which has a difficult accompaniment to play along with its melody. Schumann's prodigality with accents (at "one" in every bar) should not be interpreted as an excuse for incessant thumping. The implied motion is like that of skating, with every "one" the propulsion of a new, gliding stroke.

Drum hard for the first three notes of No. 8, but release the pedal on "two" so that the ensuing legato phrase may begin clearly. Observe the two-note phrases from bar 5. In section 3, the "roll" of the chords is doubtless the reason for the *poco rit*. Even with this concession, no very satisfying execution can be found. The accent in bar 3 anticipates unobtrusively the general accentuation in the last eight bars. Note the effect of this in comparison to section 2, where the same notes are differently shaded.

The eight-bar introduction in No. 9, although marked *Prestissimo,* can hardly be played as fast as what follows. Let it jangle bravely, with a vigorous forte in bar 2, and not much diminuendo. Thus the unexpected character of the main part will be more striking. This main part poses the hardest technical problem in the *Papillons*. Whatever fingering you choose, make the habit of it invariable by slow practice with each hand alone *until you feel no hesitation in any*

*progression.* (Be sure that both wrist and elbow are free from tension.)
You will still have some difficulty when the two hands play together,
but once more you will find that the removal of even the least uncertainty is attainable with patience.[2] Deviate but little from the governing *pp* throughout, and make no *rit.* whatever at the end. The swift
dancers must just vanish.

From bar 3 to bar 8 in No. 10, use the third finger for E in all chords
where that note occurs. The *Vivo* tempo, thus far, can hardly be fast
enough for the next eight bars, which refer to No. 9. The *Più lento,*
in spite of its great force, will be in the tempo of the same phrase in
No. 6, and will be similarly phrased. In the following little waltz,
the real difficulty is to measure the force of the accented third beat in
the somewhat awkward left-hand figures so as not to destroy the continuity of the two-bar phrases. At bars 9–12 of the second section, the
exquisite harmonic inflection of the preceding four bars seems to us
to demand a slightly slower tempo, as well as the tonal contrast of *pp*.

No. 11, a kind of *Polonaise,* looks more difficult than it is. In the
opening chords, and elsewhere, play the anticipatory sixteenths more
lightly than the eighths. The *accel.* at bar 2 seems to us musically impossible unless bar 1 is taken somewhat slower than the main tempo
of the piece. For the fingering of bar 3, section 2, see our comment on
Beethoven's Op. 31, No. 2 (p. 89). In the *Più lento,* the right hand
has only broken octaves to play, a fact often unobserved, which makes
the left hand's task easy. The two accents inside each beat are not
vigorous, but imply a kind of fattening of the tone which enriches our
sense of the melody itself. Attempt no rhythmic novelty in bars 11–12,
and keep the grace notes short and very smoothly legato.

The *Finale* begins with a thumping old peasant waltz, known as
the "Grandfather-dance." (Its words begin, "And when the Grand-

---

[2] The following seems to us the best fingering for the first eight bars:

The apparently awkward shift at bar 5 is justified by the beginning of a new
phrase at that point.

father the Grandmother grabbed.") The single accent, marked on the up-beat, is a hint, perhaps, of that purposeful seizure. Anything more impish than the four bars of 2–4 time would be hard to imagine. (Bars 2 and 4 are heavier than 1 and 3.) Make the grace note very short, and articulate every sixteenth in bar 2, with the left hand staccato and very light beneath them. The second ending, however, may be retarded and pedaled. The combinations of the Grandfather-dance with the theme of No. 1 are at first easy (though you will not find at once the way to keep alive the character of each tune), but there are presently some rhythmic complications that nothing but careful counting will solve. The low D cannot possibly be sustained as long as the notation demands. Schumann marked the pedal to be held during the whole passage; but one imagines that the piano of his day had less duration of tone than ours, else he would have found the blur intolerable. You may well substitute the sostenuto pedal, using the damper pedal normally *after* the low D has been thus "caught." The final long dominant chord cannot be effective if begun *ppp* as the composer marks. Take the sixteenths *mf* and even *poco cresc.* to an accent on the high A, holding down every note. (You may pedal only until the releasing of the low A.) Now release one finger at a time, slowly enough so that after each release the remaining lowest note will sound out like a solo voice. (But there will not be much left of the last A, whatever you do to sustain it.) [3]

The *Papillons* was written in 1829–1831. There is little to be seen of the intellectuality which is so much prized by the rhetoricians. Indeed, to the eye of a purist, the form is chaotic. But this confusion is more evident to the eye than to the ear; more disturbing to the intellect than to the musical sensibility. No. 1 follows well enough the general Introduction, and within its diminutive dimension is an orthodox two-part form. No. 2, however, has another Introduction, thematically quite irrelevant to what has gone before, and also to what it introduces. What it introduces is indeed no more than a gleam in the eye; but even a purist would hardly forbid such things, nor insist that a gleam must be developed until it has become an empty stare. It

---

[3] Vogrich, inexplicably, has marked pedal for the whole duration of this passage. That merely makes Schumann's notation meaningless.

is the same with all the little pieces that follow. There is no formal reason why they should appear. Some of them (e.g., No. 6) have three ideas in a space hardly large enough for two, and the character of the next piece is never predictable from the present one.

Yet they do hang together, and there is something vital in their continuity, for there is not one of the twelve numbers that could stand alone. Together, however, they have what Schubert gave to the "song composed throughout"—a unity of mood which is self-evident, and is capable of making a concrete whole out of apparently discrete parts.

In our further study, we can hardly expect to find any logical sequence, such as we found in Beethoven's works. Therefore we shall take up the easier pieces first, and the harder ones later, leaving the ultimate portrait of the composer to form itself like a composite photograph.

Quite easy for the fingers, though somewhat alarming to the eye, is the *Romanze in F-sharp,* Op. 26, No. 2. It is really a sort of duet, in which two rich voices sing against a cushion of undulant harmony. The parallel thirds of the singing voices might be thought tiresome if their sentiment were less true; but this happens to be the perfect representation of a kind of emotional reality, which, when it is intimately our own, never seems sentimental. And Schumann makes it very intimate.

Sing sonorously (but piano) with the thumbs, but give just a touch of brightness to the little-finger notes in the right hand, which occasionally double the melody. Pull tensely on the syncopations in bars 5, 6, and 7, making the bass at "four" heavy enough to give the necessary rhythmic lump. Schumann did not himself indicate that the repetition should be *pp,* but to make it so is surely justifiable. In bar 9, the soprano must emerge unmistakably as solo. Phrase the B and A-sharp as a single group, with the C-double sharp on "four" gently marking the rhythm in the suspension. The rest, to D-sharp, is a single group, with the stress on F-sharp, in bar 10. The nostalgic harmony at bar 11 is created by the D-sharp in the bass, which departs from the therwise sequential repetition of bars 9–10. A slight crescendo on the pproaching F-sharp–E-sharp will make possible the darkened color ssential to this rich seventh-chord.

Observe that at "four" in bar 13 the bass takes up an exact imita-on, at the fifth below, of the tortuous soprano melody. This passage s one of the fruits of Schumann's study of Bach, who knew very well ɔ what intensity such chromatic harmonies as these could rise, when ɪey are produced by purposively moving melodies in combination.[4] "he low D-natural in bar 16 must be very sonorous, with the suspen-ɪons in both voices clearly audible above it. Take the ensuing repeti-on of the duet very quietly, but get the full sense of the C-sharp in ɪe bass, which produces the second inversion of the tonic harmony. "his unstable chord gives the duet a certain forward motion toward ɪe most intense moment in the piece. At this climax, take over the ʌ-natural of the right hand with the left thumb, leaving the right hand ɪee to play impressively its insistent recitation. Be sure that you do not bscure any of the imitations of this phrase in the ensuing develop-ɪent. In the Coda, do not let the upper note in the octaves of the ɪeme predominate, for the notation expressly extends the two sing-ɪg voices after the accompaniment is silenced, and the lower A-sharp ɪust therefore not be obscured. (Some editions—even Steingräber—ɪark the pedal to the very end, which of course makes the careful otation meaningless.)

Now let us look at a happier piece—much easier to play than ɪe *Romanze,* though it moves faster—the carefree *Arabeske,* )p. 18. The infectious melody almost plays itself; nevertheless ou will spoil it if you do not articulate clearly the figure of ac-ompaniment, which is divided between the two hands. But do ot thump the eighth notes. Nothing forbids the judicious use f the pedal. The ensuing *Minore I* sounds quite new, but you ɪill see that its melody is derived from that of the beginning. "he phrases again shape themselves, and you have only to observe ɪnsitively the dynamic markings to grasp the whole character. "he brief interlude before the return of the first part is very char-cteristic of Schumann's "Eusebius" mood. The sign, *ritard.,* so

---

[4] Compare the three-part invention in F minor, which is a wonderful ex-mple of triple counterpoint.

frequently used, has (as very often in Schumann) essentially th
meaning of *rubato,* and applies only in the bar over which i
stands. Do not ignore the reference to the beginning in the rhyth
mic figure in bars 11 and 15, and give room at the end for thi
figure to begin engagingly the returning first section.

The *Minore II* is more fiery, in spite of the composer's temp
indication, "a little slower." The jerk of the up-beat is sharpene
by the sixteenth rest (instead of the original dot), and the figur
of the accompaniment adds this same rhythmic propulsion t
the exuberant upward sweep of the melody. Keep the sixteenth
consistently short (compare our comment on the *Funeral Marc*
in Beethoven's Op. 26). Vogrich added a staccato dot to the [
of the melody in bar 3 and like passages. The effect is not un
characteristic, but he might have used it less frequently wit
advantage. The poetic epilogue requires imaginative shading o
its appealing melody, but gives no trouble if the many ties ar
carefully observed. You must pedal generously. The triplet in ba
6 occupies exactly half a bar, and should give no trouble if i
is so spaced. Make broad and eloquent the figure of the up-bea
which forms the final phrase.

If Eusebius seems to be the animating spirit of the *Arabesk*
Florestan is unmistakable in the second of the *Fantasie-Piece*
Op. 12—*Aufschwung,* which is "Soaring." The beginning veril
shouts with the sheer joy of living. The two swells and the *s*
in bar 2 locate with certainty the peak of the opening phrase; bu
it is often spoiled by two equally loud bangs on the first beat
(The *sf* in bar 3 applies to the bass rather than to the melody.
Make the succession of leaping C's (bar 4) give full affirmation t
the consequent phrase. Release the pedal with the G and the (
(bars 5–6) and soften these notes somewhat, so that the melod
may leap over the sixteenth rest in a *grand jeté,* as the dancers cal
it. (At the return of the first phrase, the left hand—which ma
well play all the melody in bar 1—may still take all but the D-fla
Unless you have a very big hand, this is much the best way.)

With the second strain, in D-flat, we really leave the ground. Do not spoil the illusion by making bumpy accents all the way up to the B-flat, which is the indicated peak of the phrase. (The eighth notes are weaker than the quarters, but the sixteenths must also be audible.) In the descent, note that only three eighth notes are separately stemmed (and are thus melodic); the second phrase is all in dotted quarters. From the double bar in bar 8 of this section, the staccato marks are to be interpreted as accents. These melodic notes, however, must not be shifted from their off-beat position, any more than the stemmed eighth notes beginning in bar 10. (The different notation for the melodic phrases seems to us to imply a smoother legato for the high than for the low phrase.) The *ritard.* in bar 15 has its normal meaning. In bar 17f., give warm sonority to the A-flat, A-natural, and so on, of the tenor, and observe that the last four notes of the melody are again dotted quarters.

The middle section, peculiarly, begins a bar after the change of signature to two flats. It takes a good deal of practice to find the right dynamic proportions between the melody and the rising scale passages (bar 10 after the change of signature). Unless you begin *p,* you will never succeed. In bar 16, swell the final F of the phrase to *sf,* but take the ensuing arpeggio immediately *p,* holding the pedal throughout. Thus you may get full value out of the contrast between the C-flat (16) and the C-natural (18) of the harmony. Pedal the *sf* G in bar 20, but only to the beginning of the staccato climb, and be sure that the sustained C is audible. At bar 22, after the culminant note of the staccato approach (the "one"), we find it best to play the arpeggio *pp* against the pedaled chord on "one." Vogrich suggests *misterioso* for the quiet chord sequences at bar 41f.—appropriately, we think. A slight rubato will also be needed in bar 51, to make the significant B-natural of the harmony count. Budget your energy during the growing fragments of the returning main theme, so that when the full utterance of it appears you will not long since have reached your highest level. (Here, of course, the left hand cannot help out the right. Leave out the high D-flats where they cannot be reached, but do not double the C's of the melody.) Schumann marked no *rit.* at the end, but you can hardly make the final cadence affirmative enough without it.

One more small piece must be studied in some detail before we go on to the more rapid consideration of other works. The first of the *Fantasie-Pieces* (*Des Abends*—"At Evening") exhibits the rhythmic ingenuity that is very characteristic of Schumann's musical thought. The melody looks as if it were in 3–8 time; but you will see that the time signature is 2–8, and that the accompaniment has two quite normal triplets of sixteenths to make up this measure. The F and the E-flat of the melody are thus both syncopated against the true measure accent;[5] and to realize it you must obviously give to the left-hand eighth note, A-flat, that gentle weight which will make it a definite "two" in the measure. But against this, which persists throughout, the curve of the melodic phrases must be made to appear almost endless. To achieve this effect, make no dynamic accent whatever in the melody on "one" of bars 2, 4, and the like, and stress only those melodic notes which have rhetorical emphasis in the phrase— for example, the B-flat in bar 12. Do not allow the shifted position of the melodic notes in bars 5–7 of the E major section to disturb the rhythmic continuity. The shift is only an ingenious kind of rubato, written into the fabric.

We shall turn now to larger pieces, and first of all to the *Davidsbündlertänze* ("Dances of the David's-leaguers"), Op. 6, which in our concert experience, at any rate, seem to be inexplicably neglected. The "League of David" was only a figment of Schumann's imagination, but it was a great progressive force,

[5] Many of the older commentators, Christiani among them, used to insist that Schumann's notation was a mere intellectual complexity, and that the piece should be played as if it were in 3–8 time. Having once felt the true sense of the notation, you will probably think disrespectfully of these respectable gentlemen.

nevertheless. He thought of it as a spiritual union of forward-looking musicians, going out with sling and stone to do battle against the musical Philistines, who were as numerous in Schumann's day as in our own. Eighteen pieces are brought together in this work, and united by that same invisible thread of common feeling which makes a single piece out of the *Papillons*. There is at the beginning a rhythmic "Motto," by Clara Wieck; but there is no trace of it thereafter unless there be a hint of it in the first two bars of No. 3. Indeed, there is but one actual recall of an earlier theme in the whole work—that of No. 2 in No. 17—yet the spiritual unity seems unbroken. The character of the dance is often present, but there are mostly idealizations of rather than provocations to, actual dance steps.

No. 1 is a sort of waltz, but its flavor is much richer than is required for that dance. The fluid, unforced propulsion given by the initial figure of six eighth notes, the subtle variety of the melodic outcome of these figures, and the infectious passion to which the whole piece rises—these are things which seem, even today, wholly original. In the first edition, almost all the pieces were signed, by their initials, as having been conceived by Florestan or Eusebius, or both. This first one is by F. and E. The second, quite obviously, is by E. alone. Its melody, which is in the dotted quarters of bars 1 and 2, and is sufficiently indicated by the notation throughout, must be colored, but not obscured by the surrounding notes. (You may be sorely tempted to squeeze too much out of the lovely high G's in bars 1 and 2.) The harmony at the repetition of section 2 seems abrupt. To minimize this, bring out the F-sharp and E of the accompanying figure, which lead back to the D-sharp, and be sure that the A-natural in the bass (bar 1, section 2) counteracts the A-sharp of the preceding melody.

No. 3 had in German the direction, *Etwas hahnbüchen*—"somewhat clumsily"—in the first edition, and in the second, *Mit Humor*. Both are mostly kept in later editions, and both are appropriate. No very elegant steps are suggested at the beginning, but there is good, earthy vitality. (The first section was not repeated in the first edition.) In the following section (*Schneller*—"Faster"), the imitation between bass and treble is not carried very far, but is the more amusing for its abandonment (bar 5). The difficult tenths in the left hand (22f.)

have been ingeniously facilitated by von Sauer (Peters Ed.).[6] Bars 39–41 are almost literally quoted in the *Promenade* of the *Carnaval,* Op. 9, at the opening of section 2. Schumann calls our attention (in *Florestan,* ibid.) to a quotation from *Papillons;* but does not acknowledge this one. Carefully avoid the pedal, ten bars before the end, to point the momentary recall of section 2, and to give full value to the sonority when it is indicated four bars later.

No. 4 gives us our first contact with a novel treatment of the suspension. In the excited tempo of the piece, the "pull" of the dissonances turns into a fascinating jangle that seems like the mere staggering of accompaniment and melody. (The same device is vividly used in the *Finale* of the *Piano Quintet,* Op. 44.) In the brief second section, bar 1, observe the eighth rest before attacking the dotted half note, G. (The notation for G is mathematically incorrect, but is musically sensible and obvious.) Take no pedal for the last three eighth notes before the final chord, and accentuate the middle note to give a forceful approach.

If No. 4 was obviously by Florestan, the next piece is as certainly by Eusebius. Even though many of the pieces in the *Davidsbündler* may be beyond your technical powers, do not deny yourself the satisfaction of an attempt at the naïve No. 5. The like of it is not to be found in musical—or verbal—literature. (Ignore, however, Vogrich's ostentatious fingering. You can find a simpler and better one without effort.)

No. 6 is hard. The dissonant bass figure is awkward, both technically and musically; but if the first note in each group—usually the real bass of the harmony—is made pretty solid, the ensuing dissonance on the first of a two-note slur need not, by its necessary slight accentuation, obscure the sense. The melody, also, has two-note phraselets which, especially when the notes are tied, must have a perceptible accent on the first note. The larger phrase groups, however, need not be distorted, and have an unmistakable stress point. In bars 9 and 11 of section 2, the *sf* can of course be played only on the one note (G or D) which is not tied—but this is not a melodic tone. The *sf* must therefore occur on "three," instead of on "four," as marked. To enforce the sense of the phrase crisis, we lengthen the "four" (with pedal), thus making it really legato with the following C-sharp and F-sharp.

---

[6] Take the bass in octaves merely—G, F-sharp, and so on—and insert the tenths—B, A, and so on—an octave higher between the octaves of the right hand. The harmonic effect is clear, and the rhythm is no longer blurred by the inevitable rolling of the tenths.

(Although the melodic sense is similar at bar 2 of section 1, this extreme need not be resorted to.) Vogrich's *molto più mosso* for the Coda seems to us quite out of character, even for Florestan, the obvious author.

Eusebius's melancholy No. 7 is another piece which may safely be attempted by the less skilful. Note that the right hand does not play until bar 4. In section 2, bars 2 and 6, take the last note of the arpeggiated grace with the right second finger while the left hand leaps to the low bass note. In this way, the bass may coincide with the *sf* treble, and you may get enough tone so that you will not be tempted to miscount the following long notes. Two bars before the final return of section 1, emphasize particularly the B-double flat in the high tenor, which coils so tightly around the G–A-flat of the melody.

No. 8 is Florestan in a saucy mood. The "vamping" in bar 1 becomes difficult for the left hand in bar 2, but you can lighten its burden considerably by taking the three C's and the B with the right thumb. No. 9, in the original edition, had the superscription, "Hereupon, Florestan stopped (*schloss*—presumably the banter of No. 8) and there was a painful twitch about his lips." We find little suggestion of pain in the enormously forceful, irresistibly propelled melody. Rather, it seems a towering passion of a more heartfelt kind which causes the twitching lip. For although the dissonance at the first note may have seemed more bitter in 1837 than now, the twenty-four consecutive sforzandi are hardly the natural expression of the tearfulness that Schumann's words imply. Do full justice to the charming smile with which the piece ends.

No. 10 presents what is in a sense the opposite of the rhythmic problem we found in *Des Abends*. The notation looks like 6–8 time, but the music must sound, from the beginning, in the indicated 3–4. To give this value, play the third eighth note, A, slightly staccato, and with more weight than it would have if it were the weak "three" of 6–8 time; then follow the *sf* F with a D also louder than it would be in 6–8 time. If you learn to think the rhythm properly in this way, you will convey its proper sense to your hearer. (This piece is also by F.)

No. 11, evidently by Eusebius in a regretful mood, is another easy piece, but one whose value will grow upon you as you return to it. In No. 12, Florestan appears as a relative (perhaps rather distant) of Till Eulenspiegel; and in No. 13 his wild humor rules until, as he pauses for breath, Eusebius seizes the opportunity to sing, in contrast, what is almost a hymn. The long repetition indicated by the *Da Capo* is usually (and, we think, wisely) omitted. Whether the Coda is by F. or E. is hard to say; but if it is F., he is much subdued. (It is not easy to keep the repeated eighth-note chords light enough—especially in the right hand—and at the same time play a well-shaded melody.)

Eusebius obviously brings forward the fluid waltz (No. 14) from whose graceful background figure one suspects that Arensky found inspiration. This little piece, also, is for any amateur. F. and E. are joint authors of No. 15, a reply to the bouncing mood of the beginning being found in a very broad and passionate melody which will need to be played almost forte if the swells in the arpeggiated accompaniment are to be vividly surmounted.

No. 16 is unsigned, since it runs into No. 17 without a break; but it is doubtless by Florestan. The brief staccato phrases have their melodic stress on the last notes (D and B), for which Clara Schumann, in her edition of her husband's works, indicates the pedal—but only to the next eighth note. We think it justifiable to play the three forte chords in bar 4 slightly ritenuto. The interlocking octaves in the ensuing canon are awkward, but the characteristic sforzandi make them obligatory until the last two bars, where the voices can be more conveniently redistributed without harm to the thought. The version of the first theme in delayed afterbeats, with the curious lump of accentuation on the dotted eighth (section 2, bar 8f.) seems like an extraordinary anticipation of modern jazz. A more delectable region than that which is represented in No. 17 would be hard to find; but it is difficult to maintain the sense of distance which the superscription, *Wie aus der Ferne* ("As if from afar"), imposes. The recall of No. 2, at the end, is as exquisite as the emergence of No. 17 out of the boisterousness that preceded.

"Quite superfluously," runs the superscription of No. 18, "Eusebius thought of the following; but with it, great happiness shone in his eyes." It was indeed a poet, not a virtuoso, who composed this piece. Only gradually, perhaps, will you come to see how perfectly it brings the whole work to an end.

No work more characteristic of Schumann's imaginative mind ever came from his pen; but several others—which we must try to discuss in much fewer words—show its gradual maturing.

The *Carnaval,* Op. 9, is a fulfillment of the promise of the *Papillons,* which it followed after three or four years. The *Pré-*

*ambule* seems to exhaust the possibilities of increasing excitement, but it is as nothing compared to the final *March of the Davidsbündler against the Philistines,* where the *Grossvatertanz* is again an almost predominant note in the unconfined joy. A more infectious gaiety was never embodied in the stuff of art. The intervening pieces all have titles, some of which, like *Chiarina* ("little Clara"), *Chopin, Paganini,* are almost needless in explanation of the portrayal of familiar figures in the musical world. Others, like *Pierrot* and *Arlequin, Pantalon* and *Colombine,* limn the stock characters in the *commedia dell' arte,* and still others, persons whom we only slightly know; but all are in carnival costume and in carnival mood. Throughout, certain notes whose letter-names are found in Schumann's own name, or in that of a little Bohemian village called Asch,[7] are to be found in the varied themes. The three germs of melody appear, in "breves" (notes of twice the value of a whole note or "semibreve") in the score. Clara Schumann's edition notes that these "Sphinxes," as they are called, are not to be played; but modern opinion (rightly, we think) does not agree.

Still another Carnival piece, the *Faschingsschwank aus Wien* ("Carnival jest from Vienna"), was written in 1839, reflecting the composer's brief residence in that city. This piece is much easier to play than the *Carnaval,* though it is by no means a musical advance beyond that wonderful work (how could it be?); but since it is within the technical grasp of many an amateur, we may note a few of the more troublesome or otherwise interesting passages.

The E-flat section of the first movement presents a succession of suspensions or syncopations in which, until the sixteenth bar, not one down-beat is struck. How, then, is the hearer to know that these are syncopations? Two things can be done to help him.

[7] The German term for A-flat is As; that for E-flat is Es, and that for B-natural is H. Thus, Asch can be musically "spelled" in two ways: either A, Es, C, H, or As, C, H. The four musical letters in Schumann's name are obviously Es, C, H, and A.

First of all, make no retardation whatever at the end of the preceding section, so that the established rhythmic expectation will not be disturbed. Secondly, give to each "three" the rather incisive attack (even in piano) which any syncopation must have; feel the unplayed down-beat yourself; and release the following "two" very lightly and staccato, so that a similar attack will be possible on the next "three." When at last (bar 8 of this section, and later) an actual down-beat is played, it should merely confirm a rhythmic intimation already clearly given. Note that the rhythm of the opening bars which prevailed before the syncopated section governs also what follows.[8] The irruption of the *Marseillaise* toward the end of the section beginning in F-sharp was a piece of impudence, the tune being then forbidden to be heard in Vienna.

The phrase marks in the E-flat portion of the section beginning *Höchst lebhaft* are a precise indication of the sense of the music; but curiously enough, they may easily misdirect the player. Make the eighth rest, of course, after the eighth note, by releasing the pedal (the chord will sound more elastic if you use your foot); but do not shorten the half note (which you will also pedal), which must sound as the poised goal of the upward or downward leap. Observe that in the brief interlude in this section the slurs are from the half note to the eighth. The different sense

---

[8] In bars 57 and 59 after the return of the first theme in B-flat, some modern editions give

where the original had D-sharp (instead of C-sharp) and A-sharp (instead of G-sharp) in the eighth-note figures. The D-sharp and C-sharp are doubtless irrational, according to the harmonic conventions of Schumann's day. Yet they are not only far more logical, since they preserve the line of the original figure, but—once the mind perceives that logic—are more well-sounding. It seems a pity to suppress this little adventure into modernism, which has many prototypes in Bach. (Vogrich, in his edition of the *Carnaval*, likewise condemned an augmented triad in the *Eusebius* as a "musical impossibility" because its B-natural occurred against a B-flat of the melody!)

will be conveyed by making these eighth notes lighter than the former ones, and by releasing the pedal as they are struck, so that their staccato is "dry."

Any amateur can finger the disconsolate little *Romanze,* which seems like a wide-eyed little wallflower, too timid to join in the wilder gaiety. But those who have sensitive ears will find much exercise for the imagination, both in discriminating the insistently repeated phrases and in coloring the gentle alleviation of the brief middle part.

The perky *Scherzino,* too, is not very difficult, except for the imitations (bar 17f.) where the half-note octaves can hardly be bound legato to the succeeding eighth notes without the use of the pedal. The following, we think, makes that use inconspicuous:

(Schumann certainly intended pedal for the rumbles in bar 33f.; yet he writes the same staccato eighth note above them.)

The *Intermezzo,* if Schumann had not by now given up the habit of signing his pieces, would certainly have been said to come from F. A more exuberant passion could hardly be expressed. Yet this piece is less difficult than it looks. Your chief difficulty will come with the imitations, very low in register and subsiding in intensity, at the end. Only experiment—beyond our powers of verbal description—will reveal the necessary management of dynamics and pedal.

We shall doubtless be charged with a blind spot in our musical vision, but we cannot see that the last movement lives up to the rest of the work. It is gay enough, but it seems like the tag end of a party, when everybody wants to go home, but nobody knows how to break off the festivity.

The culmination of the improvisatory style which we have found in the *Fantasie-Pieces,* the *Davidsbündler,* and the *Kreisleriana,* is reached in the great *C Major Fantasie*—to our mind, Schumann's most significant composition for the piano. Schumann himself said that he had never written anything more impassioned. To call it improvisatory is scarcely just, for there is quite enough coherence to hold together the longest single piece we have yet examined (the first movement). Indeed, there is so clear a recapitulation, at the end, of what may be called the exposition at the beginning, that there is definite resemblance to the sonata form. Yet both the subject matter itself and the middle part of the movement are by no means in that convention, and the two following movements are so little like what is to be found in the orthodox sequence that no other title than that which Schumann chose could be acceptable. It is a usual experience for even mature students to be somewhat confused, on first contact with this piece. But though the episodes may at first seem to outweigh the principal subject matter, the intended balance is soon perceived; and when the whole piece can be seen in perspective, it takes a place in the musician's affections among the richest imaginative creations in his literature.

The main theme, which begins by adding the ninth to the already established dominant harmony, is an early recognition of the passionate intensity of that interval (a value that was soon perceived—and overemphasized—by Richard Wagner). The tonality is nowhere ambiguous, yet there is in the whole statement of the initial theme not one C major (tonic) chord. A modulation to E-flat major (bar 28) and a vigorous episode in C minor (bar 33) ensue, together with a more gentle and luminous version of the principal theme, without the tonic's ever being conventionally established. (This is not, of course, out of any desire to be shocking. It is only evidence of Schumann's belief that any musical idea must somehow evolve its own form.) After a color-ful episode, quite obviously transitional (bars 53–62), we look for a second subject; but what appears is a still more quiet utter-ance of that derivative of the first theme which appeared after the C minor episode.

There follows an excited passage in forceful syncopations—palpably the equivalent of a beginning of development, though this figure has not before appeared. The first theme is quietly referred to; then (bar 105) an excitement more expectant, which builds up to a most intense insistence on the main motive; but this dwindles and disappears in a long, vague, descending scale. It introduces a quite new theme, marked "In the Tone of a Legend" (though exactly what that implies is not wholly clear). The tempo is really *Andante con moto;* the fable—if there was one—must have involved rather sorrowful happenings, for there is a hint of despair in the insistently repeated notes and in the cadence of the phrase, and something of a sense of protest in the rapid crescendo (bar 26, this section) and the ensuing strain of melody. Another excited, but underived, passage brings a force-ful reference to the legendary theme; and then, with the rhythmic figure that had underlain this still persisting, a marvelous version of the main theme of the *Fantasie,* floating first above, then in the midst of the figure. A happier episode leads to the legend again, this time very forcefully, and so to what we have called the re-capitulation.

One who seeks a cure for spiritual paralysis should subject himself to the middle movement of this *Fantasie.* It is a March—quite literal and unashamed—but driven by an exaltation im-possible to be enacted by mortal feet. Even the fluid motion of the quiet subtheme (bar 22) is activated by anticipatory sixteenths, whose eagerness will not be subdued, but emerges, in its own right, to such effect that when the quiet line returns (bar 40) it has gained a more purposeful quality and covers a much larger area. (Observe the augmentation in the bass from bar 76.) The new theme marked *Etwas langsamer* ("somewhat slower") is another example of Schumann's imaginative use of syncopation. Every note of it, for three bars, anticipates by one eighth note the beat of the measure to which that note really belongs. (For the manner of performance, see our comment on the E-flat section of the first movement of the *Faschingsschwank*.) The character is no longer frankly march-like; but the rhythm at the fourth bar still shows the anticipatory eagerness of the sixteenth-note motion, and perhaps it is because of that that we find this theme wholly appropriate to what has gone before. The continuation (bar 18 of this section) gains much warmth from the still novel use of syncopation, and emerges (bar 28) into a delightful capering, more dainty than can be adequately suggested by the composer's mark, *scherzando*. (Pedal, with stress on the first note, the slurred two-note group; make the next six notes delicately staccato.) This merges imperceptibly into the subtheme, and so to the final return of the sweeping march tune. The Coda, electric in its excitement, yet appropriate (since it derives remotely from the subtheme), poses also a terrific technical problem which would perhaps have been restrained if the *Fantasie* had not been dedicated to Liszt.

The last movement is perhaps Schumann's most poetic utterance. To attempt to describe its spiritual nourishment would be like an evaluation of nectar and ambrosia in terms of their vitamin content. More than musical common sense is required for its understanding; but the technical difficulties are not great, and you can at least taste the unique flavor of this music. Schumann's indications are not altogether logical. *Langsam getragen* means, essentially, slow and sustained; *durchweg leise zu halten,* keep it soft throughout. But the section marked *Etwas bewegter* (a little faster) rises to a fortissimo affirmation, and not only is there no mark for the return of the original tempo (which would be hardly needed, since the musical meaning is obvious), but the *Etwas bewegter* itself, unless so slight as to be virtually imperceptible, will allow no proper space for the vitally important dissonances (the progressions of B-natural to C, A-natural to B-flat, G to A-flat, and so on, in the bass) which provide half of the meaning of the melody itself. Even so, you can get much spiritual sustenance from this imperishable page.

It is evident here that Schumann, although not himself a virtuoso, contributed a great deal to the technique of piano playing. We ought, then, to take some account of these efforts. The earliest, written before the wilful injury to his hand which—fortunately for us—compelled him to devote himself wholly to composition, are six *Caprices,* after some of the twenty-four extraordinary compositions of the same name which Paganini published as Op. 1. Until Paganini appeared in Vienna, in 1828, no one had dreamed that the violin could speak in this amazing way. The whole world was agog with excitement. Thousands were drawn for the first time into the concert hall—and many found good reason, in less vivid music, for going again. But Liszt, with the piano, and Berlioz, with the orchestra, found inspiration for countless technical discoveries—valuable for music of a depth beyond Paganini's own reach—which never would have been made if it had not been for his example.

Schumann was as amazed as the rest of the world, and being at the threshold of an intended pianistic career, was prompted to experiment, for which the Caprices were not only the model but the substance. Op. 3 deals with six of the originals; Op. 10 (written in 1833, a year after Op. 3) also contains six. By comparison with the brilliancies of Liszt's transcriptions (such as the *Campanella,* from a violin concerto) or original inventions (the *Transcendental Études,* and others), Schumann's efforts seem a little colorless. Yet the second Caprice of Op. 3, on a kind of Hunting Song, is still often heard.

A more original study is the brilliant *Toccata,* Op. 7. Difficult as it is, this piece is very much more than a technical exercise. Two vigorous bars of a syncopated figure usher in what proves to be a very soundly constructed piece in the form of the first move-ment of the sonata. The principal subject has incessant motion in double notes (in sixteenths), and that motion is maintained throughout with negligible interruptions. (Bach conceived the Toccata as a sequence of varied rhythms; the use of one persistent rhythm is a nineteenth-century idea.) There is a fascinating transi-tion, on figures that have the healthy vitality of Bach, which leads to a sonorous phrase for the tenor (the second subject). The sixteenths maintain the essence of the principal subject as a figure of accompaniment. The development makes great use of the two opening bars, and introduces also a new passage in oc-taves which presently becomes the countersubject of a fugato on the opening figure. There is a brilliant display of unexpected rhythms in the Coda.

By far the most important of his technical explorations are the *Symphonic Études,* Op. 13. They were written in 1834, were first published in 1837, and were issued in a revised edition in 1852. The work is in the form of a series of variations on a theme announced as "by an amateur." The amateur was a certain Baron von Fricken, the father of Ernestine von Fricken with whom Schumann fell violently (but temporarily) in love while she was a fellow pupil, with the composer, of Friedrich Wieck. As varia-tions, the *Études* are intellectually hardly remarkable. Indeed, the third and the ninth *Études* are not variations of the theme at all, but quite independent pieces. But the fact that they fit satisfac-torily into the scheme of the whole work is proof that something besides the intellectual problem of variation—something more interesting to the composer than any solution of that problem—was the creative spur for the whole work.

Before the extended epilogue, there are eleven studies (nine variations). A mere glance at the successive numbers will show what a variety of rhythms and figurations must have crowded the composer's imagination. (At least five more, not included in the final versions, were written. They are published in several modern editions as "Supplemental Variations." They are all of considerable musical interest, but it is impossible to find a place for them in the existing sequence, and it is hardly satisfying to hear them after the rousing *Finale.*) In this epilogue, the Baron's theme appears only incidentally, and in a fragment. There is instead a "main" theme from an opera by Heinrich Marschner, *Templar and Jewess.* In the opera, this phrase has the words, "Who is the highly-honored knight?" It is beyond the intended scope of this book to study the variations in detail, but we must at least mention the last one before the Finale. It has an incessant, murmuring figure of accompaniment against which melodic voices (true variants of the theme) pile up like the instruments of the orchestra into one of the most colorful fabrics of tone ever evoked from the piano. But the discrimination of tonal judgment and the rapid shifts of attention required for a perfect performance can be attained only by a finished artist.

It seems a little strange that after so skilful an example of the sonata form as that which we found in the *Toccata,* Schumann should have found the composition of a full-fledged sonata something of an incumbrance. Yet the *F-sharp Minor Sonata,* Op. 11, seems to suggest that condition. The *Introduction* is, indeed, the man himself—absorbed into such oblivion of all but the immediate subject that he quite forgets the average hearer's expectations, and extends his *Introduction* to almost sixty bars. As an exordium, this is portentous; but the main subject of the *Allegro vivace* sounds indecisive and in a way preparatory. (It has two phrases: one, unharmonized, on the dominant and its fifth; the other, a brief, scampering figure that escapes at once toward C-sharp minor and is too restless to establish itself either there or elsewhere.) The transition, beginning in E-flat minor, has a new color and the more passionate character which is indicated by the composer; but its goal remains tentative, and a long recall of the main theme is required before the relative major key is reached. The second subject, which thus at last appears, is a veritable balcony scene in brief; but it has been so long delayed that it stands in the position of the closing subject, and a brief reference to the main theme brings the exposition to a somewhat disconcerting end. The development is so vivid and ingenious as to make us forget the unstable exposition, but it deals (of necessity) so largely with the impetuous sixteenths derived from the main theme that the recapitulation seems superfluous. Yet a corrective Coda is unimaginable.

The slow movement, though we are expressly directed not to play it passionately, seems a kind of outcome of the lyrical second subject. Here and there, also, the open-fifth figure of the first movement is hinted at. The piece is very short, and exquisitely proportioned. Liszt, in a published critical article on three of Schumann's compositions, denied the rightness of the direction, *senza passione,* finding in the music "the most passionate abandon."

The sturdy humor of the *Scherzo,* on the other hand, is delightfully mitigated in a swifter, more delicate, alternative strain, and there is, for Trio, an *Intermezzo (alla burla, ma pomposo—* "jokingly, but pompously") eventuating in a laughably over-emphatic passage of pianistic recitative.

Liszt's opinion of the *Finale* seems to us just and discerning: "The *Finale* is extremely original. Nevertheless, however logical the course of the main ideas, and in spite of the rapture of the peroration, the general effect of this piece is often broken up, interrupted. Perhaps the length of the developments contributes to the uncertainty of the whole. Perhaps, too, there is need for an indication of the poetic import." [9]

It is a little perplexing to find the next sonata, Op. 14, announced as the "Third," whereas Op. 22 is announced as the "Second." It is true that the G minor, Op. 22, was begun in 1833, and the F minor, Op. 14, was written in 1835 and published in

[9] As quoted by Frederick Niecks, *Robert Schumann* (Dutton, New York).

1836. (A revision was published in 1853.) But the number was apparently not given in the first edition. Instead, at the request of the publisher, the description, "Concerto without Orchestra," was added—a not wholly inappropriate phrase, yet one that caused much comment. (To make the resemblance to the concerto form more complete, the *Scherzo* was deleted from the first edition.)

This piece has never won great favor with either the pianists or the public. Yet, to our taste, it seems the most interesting of the three. It is not only more brilliant, but also seems to offer a more subtle revelation of the composer's personality. The form, unless in the last movement where the nature of the material makes development all but impossible, is far more shapely than in the *First Sonata,* though it cannot be denied that the G minor is still better. But there is in the F minor something of that rare tang which we noted in the *Davidsbündler,* and which seems to us more precious than the perfection of form.

The brief *Introduction* is highly expectant. Its initial octave phrase hints at (though it does not rhythmically present) the main theme, whose brave flourish on a staccato down-beat begins a descending line that needs no more than four bars to arrive at a sense of full conviction. An alternative phrase of three notes, interestingly imitated, makes welcome the reassertion of the main thought, and with similar brevity transition is made to the second subject. This makes tentative entrance, as befits its gentle character, so that it is hard to define its precise limits, though its identity is unmistakable. Hop-skipping chords ensue, whose rhythm soon provides the pattern of an exquisitely harmonized chromatic descent, sufficient—since the exposition is not to be repeated—to serve as a closing subject.

An "intellectual" development of such materials as these, if it were possible, would be repellent. The purpose of development, however, is rather exaltation of the sense of the subject matter than an exhibition of constructive cleverness; and Schumann here rightly chooses to be the artist rather than the craftsman.[10] The recapitulation begins with the restatement of the *Introduction*, and the main theme is slightly but interestingly expanded. The Coda, to our notion beginning eight bars before the *Animato*, restates most of the development. This may be taken, however, as a return to the old practice of repeating the second section of the sonata form. The actual epilogue is brief and sufficiently affirmative.

The *Scherzo* is almost of symphonic proportions and substance. It is forceful and hardly humorous; but its energy, even though cushioned, is abundant and infectious. The *Trio*, into which several references to the main subject are interjected, is largely lyrical. Because of the interpolations of the main theme, it was possible interestingly to disguise the actual return of the first section.

The slow movement is a set of variations on a melancholy little theme by Clara Wieck, curiously (perhaps femininely) formed of three different four-bar phrases, each of which is literally repeated before the next occurs, and none of which returns to exemplify the sacrosanct A–B–A form. There are but four variations, none of them pretentious, but each of them vividly characteristic—especially the last, in which the hitherto somewhat repressed feeling becomes intense and eloquent. An ineluctable finality is conveyed by the last six bars, all on the one chord of F minor, dying away in the one unchanging rhythm of the first two bars of the theme.

The *Finale* is marked *Prestissimo possibile,* but both this and the metronome mark  $\quad \downarrow = 96 \quad$  suggest a speed too fast to allow any clear grasp of the ingenious detail. In the main theme, the last two sixteenths of each triplet are obviously to be taken as thematic, although they are not separately stemmed. (The

---

[10] An arpeggiation of the hop-skipping chords was devised, in both the development and the Coda, in the first edition; but in the second, the original rhythm was substituted—wisely, as most editors seem to agree.

scale-wise progression, upward in one strain, downward in two, is obvious.) A derivative from the main theme, at bar 9, has a figuration of its harmony that often confuses student readers. The last two notes of each triplet harmonize, not the first note of that group, but the first note of the *next* triplet. If it were loosely played, this would give the effect of a mere rolled chord; but of course the actual triplet spacing must be carefully exhibited, and it is for this reason that we deprecate a too fast tempo. The effect is rather like that of a photograph made with the camera somewhat out of focus. This device is very largely employed throughout the movement.

There is then a subtheme, warm and quiet, whose brief phrases are made into a dialogue between the soprano and the low bass. The triplet figurations accompanying this theme are in the conventional harmonic arrangement (i.e., all three notes belong to the harmony of the beat on which they appear), but at bar 37 the distortion noted at bar 9 returns, and there is a long approach to the second subject. The dialogue between the two hands, on this figure (bar 48f.), has a clinging suspension at the end of each melodic phrase, which, in its cumulative excitement, prepares wonderfully for the lilting subject itself (bar 60, *con anima*). One can hardly blame Schumann for repeating this whole theme, with its approach; but it does get him into grave difficulties. For the development of the main theme (bars 102–119) cannot much intensify the already high excitement, and it is necessary to subside into the subtheme to gain relief from the long-persistent "distorted" triplet figure. Even so, the culmination (*Molto a capriccio e sempre stringendo—Vivacissimo—Più presto,* from bars 146 to 166) is beyond practicality, whether of performance or understanding. What follows, also, until the Coda (bar 333, again *Più presto*), is only a repetition of what has gone before. Vogrich and other editors suggest cuts which relieve the listener's fatigue, but at the expense of a considerable sense of truncation in the whole form. It may be that this sonata can be enjoyed only by rather extensive concessions to the composer in the matter of form; but it still remains an imaginative effort of a very high order.

The *Second Sonata,* Op. 22, is without these defects. The same insistence on impossible speeds appears in the superscriptions of the first movement: *So schnell wie möglich* ("as fast as possible"); *Schneller* ("faster"); *Noch schneller* ("still faster"). But if the word *possible* be interpreted in relation to the idea, instead of to the fingers, Schumann's intention can be realized. Indeed, the sense of the music is so clearly set forth in the notation, and is so readily apprehensible to almost any hearer, that we shall forego detailed comment on it.

Having looked at a good many of the larger compositions, which do indeed prove that the genius of Schumann lay in his unique imagination rather than in his command of the logic of extended discourse, let us return to one more example of the swift and suggestive sketches, compressed often into the tiniest of forms, in which his vision was most clairvoyant. The *Scenes from Childhood* are doubtless the most satisfying collection of such pieces. They were written in 1838, before he had any children of his own; but they are a kind of prophecy of that intimacy which he was soon to enjoy so fully that there is no similar tale to be told of any other musician. He told Clara that the music had been prompted by an incidental remark of hers that he seemed to her like a child. (The point of this remark lies in the fact that it was addressed by a girl of eighteen or nineteen to a man some nine years her senior.) "I felt as if I had wings, and wrote about thirty neat little things from which I have chosen twelve and called them *Kinderscenen.* You will like them, but you must forget your virtuosic self. . . . I am very proud of them, and make a great impression—especially on myself—when I perform them."

He was irritated by the literal sense in which the critics (and probably the public) took the titles. One of them, he writes, "seems to think that I place a crying child before me and then seek for tones to imitate it. It is the other way round . . . the superscriptions came into existence afterwards, and are, indeed, nothing more than delicate directions for the rendering and understanding of the music." Nevertheless, the titles are often so in accord with the sense of the music that the question of priority is of little account.

The pieces are mostly quite easy to finger, but they are not so to interpret. Fine discrimination is needed if a performer is to convey all the allusion which careful study will reveal in the music. Neither, for the present writer, do the titles always illuminate the musical meaning. That given to the first piece, *About Strange Lands and People,* is for us made into an enigma by the notes. (But there is no enigma in the notes themselves.) Nor have we the wit to imagine a *Curious Story,* such as is supposedly told in the second. Both pieces, and most of the others, are no more than expressions of the moods into which we might be thrown if some detail in the painting of a quiet foreign village, or the narrated antics of some bouncing but amiable person, had left their mark on our subconscious. From the description of the game of tag in *Haschemann,* we cannot tell who is "it," but the scampering and the gaiety are there. On the other hand, few could fail to sense, and even to see, in the music of the *Pleading Child,* the upward gaze of reproachful eyes. *Glückes genug* is essentially contentment; but this is a state of mind which needs no image of a state of body to complete it; and in the *Wichtige Begebenheit* ("Important Event"), the importance of the event, rather than the occurrence itself, is what is set forth in the music.

Not without reason is *Träumerei* known to all the world. Neither painter nor poet could better limn the wide, arrested gaze of eyes fixed on a world that grownups can no longer see. *Am Camin* is a picture, not of the glowing coals in the fireplace, but of the quiet security in the background of the children's minds as they sit before the hearth. We can, indeed, see the tipsy, unsteady gait of the *Knight of the Hobby-horse,* and there is no harm in our completing our picture with a tossing flaxen poll, and a face constrained to the task of managing the unruly broomstick; and we may, if we choose, embody in a mental image the face *Almost Too Serious;* but we may also understand the mood itself, unembodied. We can hardly play, however, in spirit only, a game of "Boogey-man."

Almost more wonderful than *Träumerei* is the pictured end of the children's hour. Low and quiet, the melody moves with the cradle from side to side; and up above, there is the shadow of its sway, or the echo of its rocking (it is no matter which), always later, and always vague like the drowsy eyes within. The comfort of sleep comes nearer, and in a little while, there is a sigh. The Poet himself comes in, and Schumann says he speaks; but the sober and affectionate tones seem rather like the unspoken thought of one who comes to see that all is well.

After 1839, Schumann composed far less frequently for the piano, and, for the most part, less characteristically. Until that year, as we have said, the piano was his only medium of utterance, and it may be that experience with the more colorful voices and strings and orchestra dulled for him the interest of his first favorite. To be sure, when he combined the piano with the strings, as in the *Quintet,* Op. 44, the *Quartet,* Op. 47, the three *Trios,* Op. 63 in D minor (to our mind, the finest), Op. 80, and Op. 110, and the two *Violin Sonatas,* Op. 105 and 121, the old delight returns—as it did also in the one full-fledged *Concerto,* Op. 54. But it is seldom indeed, in the later piano solo music, that he strikes the wonderful note of spontaneity that sounds, almost unfailingly, in the earlier pieces.

The most important works after Op. 28 (*Three Romances,* of which we studied the second) are: Op. 32, *Four Piano Pieces, Scherzo, Gigue, Romanze,* and *Fughetta;* Op. 68, the *Album for the Young,* also called the *Christmas Album*—forty-three pieces, of which Nos. 1–18 are for actual beginners and the rest for more skilled hands; Op. 82, the *Waldszenen* ("Forest Scenes"), which includes a miracle of pianistic delicacy, "The Prophet Bird"; Op. 99, *Bunte Blätter* ("Pages of Many Colors," or, as usually translated, "Variegated Leaves"), from which Brahms chose a theme for a most remarkable set of variations, which we shall study in detail, in its place; and Op. 124, a collection of small pieces, written at various times between 1832 and 1845, and published in 1854.

There are also four groups of pieces for piano duet which, like those of Schubert, are invaluable for practice in sight-reading, and are at the same time poetic utterances of no mean import. The first of these is called *Bilder aus Osten* ("Oriental Pictures"). There is a little preface which relates the pieces to the composer's reading of some stories from the Arabic, as told by the poet Rückert, who was master of some thirty languages, and who translated voluminously from Oriental authors. (These were stories from the Arabic of Hariri.) The composer warns us that some of the pieces will prove to be of a strange and singular character; but they remain, for the author, quite simply German, and thoroughly enjoyable as such. The next set is "Twelve Pieces for Piano, Four Hands, for Little Children and Big." Among these, two seem to us of especial interest—the ninth, *Am Springbrunnen* ("At the Fountain"), and the last, called *Abendlied* ("Evening Song"). This latter is one of the finest melodies that ever sang in Schumann's brain. It is likewise an admirable study in the playing of melody, for the primo player has nothing whatever to do with his left hand, and can give his entire mind to the shading of the single line. The secondo part is not difficult, either; but as an accompaniment to such a melody, it will give the player an ample problem in appropriate tone color. The nine "Ball Scenes," Op. 109, include dances of many nationalities, and the "Children's Ball," Op. 130, is a set of six easy dances.

Schumann's piano music by no means reveals his full artistic stature, but it is perhaps the frankest revelation of a personality to be found in literature.

The artistic kinship of Schumann and Schubert is evident. Although each belonged to the great family of the Romanticists, it is not in this particular that their similarity is most striking. Each grew to maturity without that formal induction into the learned mysteries of composition which had been *de rigeur* in the age of classicism. It was indeed essential for the Romanticist to evade or to defy this formality; but Schumann's evasion or defiance was more conscious than Schubert's. The musical atmosphere of Vienna, in Schubert's day, was still largely tainted with the odor of decadent classicism, as may be seen, not only in the public indifference to his work, but in the opposition to Beethoven and even to Mozart, who, in his Vienna period, was rapidly assuming the romantic attitude. It is because he breathed this atmosphere that the undertone of pathos, of which we found so much in Schubert, is not a note of rebelliousness or of protest, but of involuntary isolation. It is merely that of an artist absorbed in a world of endless beauty and interest, which he sees with clairvoyance but is somehow unable to interpret to his fellows. Of the tragedy of his own artistic frustration he seems hardly aware. Although he reveals himself in every phrase, toward the task of tonal portrayal he is essentially an extravert.

Schumann, during those years when instruction is an effective molding force, was even less instructed than Schubert. His imagination, if less profuse, was equally spontaneous; but the natural outlet of it was dammed, not only by parental opposition, but by his own lack of pugnacity in forcing a channel. What did come forth, until he was liberated, was improvisatory and quickly dissipated; what remained within was nurtured in introversion.

The *Davidsbund* was what might nowadays be called a defense mechanism. The members of that league were those who thought as Schumann did. He did not join the league, he made it. He did not let others join, he made them join—and made them over so that they might be eligible to join. (Everybody, in his way, tries to do that, but most of us fail altogether, or, if we persist, become curmudgeons.) Schumann's introversion, being the product of force, was gradually dissipated as the pressure was removed. His piano music is the record of that dissipation; and when it was complete, he turned to other vehicles of utterance. Of his effort within this larger field, his piano music gives little evidence; but of the earlier work there is enough to show the liberation of a mind almost unique.

## 9

# FRANÇOIS FRÉDÉRIC CHOPIN
## Rondos Mazurkas
## Nocturnes Études Waltzes

F OR Schumann, the piano remained a sufficient vehicle of expression for some ten years only. For Chopin, it remained sufficient all his life. The implication of these facts is fairly obvious. We shall find it realized in our study of Chopin's music.

Into the stream of romantic music in Western Europe, Chopin came as something of an alien. He had had, from his teachers (Zywny for piano, and Elsner for composition), some introduction to the methods of that historied art. The Warsaw Conservatory was to the Poland of his day rather like what the New England Conservatory was to the America of the "gay 'nineties"— a most valuable medium of contact with the musical ideas of the great (German) world, but in itself incapable of being the well-spring of an indigenous musical art. Out of its offerings, Chopin absorbed rapidly what was of value for his own imagination. He enjoyed also the advantage of life in an enlightened—rather than a ponderously cultured—family. To his parents, his imagination was neither an amazement to be exploited, nor a faculty to be confined within the walls of orthodox convention. Taste and gentility ruled in the doings of every day, and had neither to be acquired by envious effort nor fortified by invidious critical disparagement of that which was not accepted in high places.

The boy's strength, whether spiritual or physical, was not superabundant, but he was no mere weakling. He was doubtless a little squeamish—as those are likely to be who have little contact with the rough edges of the world. From the beginning, his creative images were virtual rather than real; but virtual images emanate also from real objects. And he had, also from the beginning, a power of lending credibility to his images which is the possession of but few.

Without this credibility, his work would have been welcomed far less widely. We do not question the "veracity" of Schubert or Schumann, for what they speak of is mostly within the boundaries of our own experience or intuition. Chopin presents to us the image of feelings that originate we know not where; yet he makes them seem as natural as those originating within our ordinary circle of experience. And his utterance is thus the more appealing, not for its strangeness merely (since strangeness is often repellent), but because it seems immediately true; and finding ourselves capable of these unfamiliar visions, we cannot doubt that we have been spiritually enlarged. If his imaginative excursions led us into some frankly unreal world (as those of Berlioz often do), we should hardly follow. But what he shows us has verisimilitude such as can neither have emanated from unbelief in himself nor can evoke skepticism in us.

He often deals, of course, with things (or rather, with the emotional products of things) that we all recognize as real. It is also true that in these utterances he strikes a less profound note than do those artists whose actual notion of the world seems more like our own. But there are times when reality palls upon us—when we feel that we are indeed "bounded by a nutshell," and when the pleasure of seeming to rule infinite space seems wholly desirable. This, of course, is mostly a youthful dream, and it is thus natural for Chopin to be the favorite of those who are beginners in their exploration of the imaginative regions revealed by music. But the world of the Romantics was also a youthful world.

The piano had already become, in the period that our study has covered, a pre-eminent instrument for the satisfaction of the musical instinct of thousands. Chopin, who knew how to make the piano sound as no one had ever made it sound before, soon came to exert the strongest attraction upon those youthful minds of which we have been speaking. And the proof that what he saw and felt was, after all, rooted in some sort of reality is to be found in the fact that even yet, when a supposedly disillusioned world has heaped scorn upon dreams not previously guaranteed to be disillusioned, Chopin can still bemuse and fascinate a multitude.

It is noteworthy, but not unnatural, that his interest in other music than his own seems to have been slight.[1] His sensitivity to colorful pianistic tone was so keen that one can well imagine music which lacked that quality to have been, for him, all very well, but just not quite the real thing. Certainly, there was no other music to which he could apply that unique gift of touch out of which his own compositions were in large measure generated. This aloofness meant, of course, a slow isolation from the rest of the musical world—an isolation that it may be foolish to regret. For more intimate contact, if it had not resulted in sheer perplexity, would have brought about only an attempt to absorb influences and ideas alien to the very essence of his genius; and it is not easy to imagine any very happy results from the disruption of such creative sensibilities as his. He was quite aware of his

---

[1] We shall presently see something of the *Ballade in F,* which he dedicated to Schumann—partly, no doubt, out of recognition of the favorable criticism of his Variations on *La ci darem la mano* which Schumann had published in the *Allgemeine Musikalische Zeitung* in 1831 ("Hats off, gentlemen, a genius!"), but more probably to return the immediate compliment paid him in the dedication of the *Kreisleriana.* The copy of that piece which Schumann had sent him was found on Chopin's shelves after his death—with the leaves uncut.

apparent disadvantage. He once spoke of himself as "like the E-string of a violin on a contrabass"—a remark that indicates both a keen critical judgment of himself, and a significant lack of artistic vanity.

The opus numbers of his works indicate fairly accurately the order of their composition. We might, then, by following their chronological order, expect to find a logical exposition of his artistic growth. But that growth, although it was certainly an advance in technical mastery, was also (as we have just seen) a kind of recession from the great world of music. And since his music is mostly cast in small forms, it will be as well to take it up according to the various types into which these small forms may be classified. The advance and the recession will both be amply illustrated in the successive examples of almost any form.

## The Rondos

His Op. 1 is a *Rondeau.* There are three others (Op. 5, 14, and 16), of which Op. 14 is with orchestra, and so outside the scope of our study. These are altogether the least important of his pieces, and he has no late examples. Yet we shall find it interesting to look for a moment at the equipment of the young composer who at sixteen published his Op. 1 in Vienna. Although the full flavor of his later style is lacking, the skittish main theme shows such skill in the varying of its sprightly rhythm as betrays both a musical sensitivity and a consciousness of values belonging only to the accomplished artist. The transition to the second theme is confidently, if not daringly, modulatory, and the figurations, if not yet wholly individual, imply something of that uncanny sense for pianistic effect which is invariably exhibited in the maturer works. The second subject is in E major—a vivid contrast to the original C minor. Its melody is more Bellinian than suits our present taste, and the delight in figuration soon absorbs his mind so wholly that there is no time for a restatement of the main theme before the C subject appears. This is in A-flat, and is a fragment of rhythm rather than a theme, but it is both brief and appropriate. The rest is recapitulation, with the C subject thrown in, and a brief Coda. The other *Rondeaux* are more elaborate and somewhat more brilliant, but not much more significant. Op. 3 is an *Introduction and Polonaise* for piano and 'cello. Chopin was very fond of the 'cello, and later wrote one fine sonata (Op. 65) —almost his only successful venture outside the field of music for piano solo. Op. 4 is a solo sonata, published posthumously, which we shall look at when we reach the stage where such compositions were more within his grasp.

### The Mazurkas

But already with Op. 6 and 7—two books of Mazurkas—we encounter music more individual in flavor. The Mazurka is distinctively a Polish dance, usually somewhat slower than the Waltz, but in the same 3–4 time, and it has great variety of rhythm. Daring and impulsive steps are suggested, implying moods and excitements far outside the range of the more conventional German dance. Nowhere is Chopin more original or more engaging than in these dances. In the very first (Op. 6, No. 1, in F-sharp minor) an emotional note is struck which no German composer would ever have imagined—not even Schubert, though his Waltzes and *Ländler* and *Deutsche Tänze* are equally true to their race. We find at once the frequently characteristic strong accent on "three," and the intermingling of triplets and dotted rhythms with more suave and willowy movement.[2] Even more vivid is the subtle harmony. The F-naturals (at ritenuto, end of section 1), when they move to F-sharp, seem to clinch the cadence in the A major key; yet in an instant we are in F-sharp minor again. What an adventure into keylessness is the contradiction of

[2] See, for instance, how rhythmic details from bars 1 and 2 are combined in bar 5; how the rubato return of the original strain is quite adequately prepared for merely by writing two eighth notes on "two" in bar 8, to replace the preceding ♪♪ and how fresh and endearing is the flowing figure of the cadence.

B-sharp and B-natural at the beginning of section 2! And the jangle of the grace notes in the third section (which, of course, is a tiny Trio, with a *da capo* of the first part following) is as stimulating as the triangle in the orchestra.

In No. 2, after eight bars of tentative muttering over a "pedal" fifth,[3] nothing could be more unexpected or more charming than the lilt of the following strain; but no Anglo-Saxon would ever anticipate the sudden energy of the cadence. No. 3 begins with the pedal fifth, and shows a similar degree of contrast, but a quite different total character. Do not miss the delicate blush of color in the figurations following the brief repeated section. No. 4 is of course too diminutive to admit any vital contrast; but within its slight dimension it is as original as any of the others.

It is of course beyond our available space to speak in detail of each of the fifty-one Mazurkas. Nor are general directions for their performance likely to be helpful when in each individual piece features will appear which could not be covered by such comment. Metronome marks were provided by the composer for the earlier opus numbers, and appear in the posthumously published Op. 67 and 68 (which are also early works). For the later ones, only the usual Italian directions are given. The tempo is a vital question in such an unpredictable dance as the Mazurka; but Chopin evidently decided that instinct, rather than verbal direction, had to give the ultimate answer to that question. He was laborious and almost finicky in his attention to detail, and was especially careful in the Mazurkas to give meticulous indications of his meaning. If we study minutely a single striking example, we shall find that musical common sense, conscientiously exerted, will prove equal to the interpretation of his notation. We may take the next in order—the Fifth, Op. 7, No. 1.

What *Vivace* means is partly indicated by the metronome mark, $\downarrow \cdot = 50$. An excited tone for the whole piece is indicated in the *f, cresc.,*

---

[3] The drone bass, like that of bagpipe music, was invariably used in the earliest popular Mazurkas.

*ff*, and *fz* ➤ all appearing in the first three bars. The rhythm is immediately impelled by the figure

which appears on the first beat of every measure in section 1. But the supposedly characteristic accent on "three" is not indicated, and if we arbitrarily insert it we shall only impede the upward spurt of the melody. This propulsion, evident in the long upsweep of the melody, is, however, somewhat confusingly notated. The staccato of the first note (in both bass and melody) and the following sixteenth rest, are both apparently negated by the pedal mark. Similar instances will be numerous, and we must resolve the difficulty. We may safely infer that the staccato dot on the bass note is really a sort of accent, and does not imply extreme shortness for the tone. But

cannot be similarly understood. The eighth note, F, *must* sound detached. We *can* make it so by sustaining the bass note for an instant—until the treble F has been released—and catching the bass with the pedal barely before the hand has to move to strike the following chord. But also, if the attack on the treble F is sharp, while the following sixteenth and quarter notes are less loud, the detachment we seek will *appear* to be real, even if the pedal is taken on the beat. From Chopin's notation we must infer that this was his intention.

The dynamic problem of the whole upward sweep, however, still remains. The *cresc.* will actually be aided by the dynamic difference between the sixteenth and the preceding eighth which we recommended above; but the stress points in the three similar phrase groups are not yet determined, except in bar 3, where the *sf* stands on "two." But to give the same shape to the two preceding phrases will make the whole line pedestrian. It seems to us that the solution is indicated by the bass note, B-flat, on "three" of bar 2, where by analogy with bar we might expect a chord. This B-flat, in the rhythm of the bass, is obviously an up-beat to bar 3. The D of the melody on "two" thus appears as a kind of "halfway point" in the whole ascent; but it may have only that elastic and "continuing" sort of stress which will keep

it moving, and the following E-flat will be but little softer than this
D. The up-beat bass, B-flat, can help to initiate the rapid *cresc.* up to
the final *sf*. (This may seem to the reader absurdly minute; but it
represents the kind of problem which either a musician or an actor
has often to solve, at much greater pains than we have had to take
here.)

At bar 4, with the sudden *p*, the initial figure

becomes coquettish and a little hesitant. Structurally, it forms a two-
bar addition to the apparently normal four-bar period just completed;
and the coquettish figure is now interpolated between repetitions of
the graceful antic of bars 7 and 8, so that another six-bar group is
formed—this time 2 + 2 + 2 instead of 4 + 2. Both the *p* (which is
sudden, even with the ➤ for preparation) and the accent on the sixteenth note present difficulties. The direction, *scherzando*, seems to us
to justify a rubato lengthening of the sixteenth rest, and so a slight
delay in the entrance of the accented sixteenth note. This, of course,
may appear only in this one bar; but a hint of the same effect may be
given in bars 9–10, rather by shortening the sixteenth to a thirty-second
note than by actual rubato. The downward leaps of the ninth can
hardly be intelligible if the pace is hurried.

The demureness of the second section is actually more coquettish
(because it is so very simple) than the frank allurement of the first.
Observe that in bars 5–7 there are even, instead of dotted, eighth notes,
whose primness must not be lessened, even in the prescribed *stretto*.
Here the legato must be accomplished with the smallest dynamic
gradations that will keep the phrase alive. (The direction, *senza
Pedale*, must of course be respected.) The *poco rall.* in bar 7 makes
possible the graceful shaping of the two-note groups which break the
final triplet. (We think a slight *cresc.* on these four notes is justified,
since it enhances the impetuosity of the returning first idea.)

The direction, *sotto voce*, in section 3 certainly implies the soft pedal.
The real harmony for the whole duration of the drone bass is a kind
of mixture of the two augmented sixth chords called the "German"
and the "French" sixths:

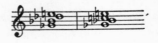

The initial F may either be understood as implying a major seventh chord on the VI of B-flat minor, or as a kind of "leaning-note" before the augmented sixth chord. To inexperienced ears, the passage is weirdly dissonant, but musical common sense will soon recognize it as legitimate. Chopin marked the damper pedal to be depressed throughout the first seven bars. Only thus will the drone bass have its proper effect; and only in a whisper can the melody be subtly enough uttered. He who can resist the enticement of this sloe-eyed phrase is a puritan indeed.

Before we turn to a larger piece, it may be well to list a few of the easier Mazurkas, with a few comments on their character. No. 6 (Op. 7, No. 2) is much easier to interpret than No. 5. Keep the opening strain very restrained (but not indifferent!) so that the sudden energy of bars 7 and 8 may have full effect. In section 2, be sure to sense the different harmonizations of the same phrase (bars 2 and 4), making the last one a suitable preparation for the swaying curves of bars 5–7. In the first part of the A major section also, give no hint of the energy that will be released, with the same thought, in the second part.

No. 16 (Op. 24, No. 3) is a tiny piece, and so has relatively slight contrasts. Take the triplet after the fermata in bar 10 *a tempo* and with a kind of twinkle before the very suave legato needed in bar 11. Study carefully the two-note phrase groups in the left hand, in section 2. This phrasing must not affect the shape of the melody above. (Observe that in the third beat of bars 2, 4, and 6 the chords are not eighth notes, but quarters.) You will enjoy devising a way to make the Coda vanish imaginatively.

No. 24 (Op. 33, No. 3) has tireless charm, but has hardly an obscure passage. Feel the G on "three" in bar 8, in the bass, as up-beat to the returning melody. The forte prescribed for section 2 cannot, surely, imply harshness. A very warm sonority with care-ful dynamic shading of the melody, and a somewhat softened beginning of the new strain at bar 9 seem to us essential.

No. 40 (Op. 63, No. 2) is full of harmonic and melodic subtleties. The suspensions in bars 2, 6, and so forth, can be made to "pull" only if the first bar is felt as introductory, and the drive of the motion begins with the bass (C, in bar 2, A-flat, in bar 6, and so on). To reveal all the harmony implicit in the chromatic melody from bar 13 will tax all your skill in dynamic shading. The little figure of four eighth notes at the cadences in bars 24 and 32 becomes a counterpoint at bar 33. It is not easy to make this line clear, and still subordinate it to the real melody, above.

No. 44 (Op. 67, No. 3) and No. 47 (Op. 68, No. 2) are of moderate difficulty, and easy to interpret. Of the larger or more subtle examples, our space will permit the consideration of but one. With some hesitation, we select No. 17 (Op. 24, No. 4), in B-flat minor.

The introduction is notated as two convergent syncopated lines. These two voices do produce harmony; yet the intended effect is that of a single melodic line, incomparably fluid, and attaining its true melodic beginning (bar 5) with an evocative dissonance. The melody is still notated in two voices (though it should sound as if in one), but at bar 13 its true sense is set forth. The characteristic accents on "three" appear in alternate bars, but are so reinforced by the changing harmony that they need no other emphasis than that which will make this harmony count. At the end of the first section, do not too much soften the B-flat, which must be audible against the bass in the first bar of the new section. In this new figure, we find that same contradiction of pedal and staccato which we noted in No. 5, above. Here, actual silence for the rests seems to us imperative, with the harmony nevertheless sounding, underneath; for without it the fluidity and grace of the rocking figure will inevitably suffer. But we have here an advantage not enjoyed in the forte phrases of No. 5. The staccato is now piano and the tone can be silenced with the briefest touch of the damper against the string. Thus, if the foot is lifted with this note, it may easily depress the pedal again so soon that the bass note will still be "caught" by the pedal before it is released by the finger.[4] It is

---

[4] To silence the low strings, which are long and relatively very heavy, complete contact of the damper for an appreciable time is required. If you strike a low note forte with the pedal depressed, you will find that you may make three or four instantaneous releases and depressions of the pedal before the tone

possible that the effect Chopin intended was that which we have described in the footnote below, and which is at least approximately indicated in this notation. This "trick" of the foot—often used—is usually called a "half-pedal." Observe that at the mark, *scherzando,* in bar 4, the first two A-flats are sixteenth notes, whereas in bar 5f., the similar notes are thirty-seconds. This, together with the accent on C-flat (bar 4), surely implies a graceful rubato for the beginning of this delicate passage. (Play the thirty-seconds essentially as grace-notes.)

In the unharmonized passage following the return of the first thought, there is harmonic suggestion comparable in strangeness to that which we found in the third section of No. 5, but far different in character. Sotto voce and almost without dynamic shading, it gives an extraordinary hint of elemental pain. The ensuing section, however, brings quick release. It is marked *con anima,* which means "with soul," and is not to be confused with *animato* (animated), which directs an increase of speed. The many contrasts of *f* and *p,* all with four-bar phrases, make this section difficult to play interestingly; but the composer's directions, if sensitively followed, are quite sufficient.

The epilogue is a poetic pearl of great price. Its slight thematic relation to the rest of the piece is heard in its vague recall of the momentary somberness of the unison passage. Indeed, it seems somehow to be the final and sufficient explication of that unexpected thought.

### The Nocturnes

The form which next appears in the serial list of the solo pieces (Op. 8 is a Trio for piano and strings) is the Nocturne.

is wholly silenced. A single release of the pedal, however, will silence the higher strings. The following will provide an experiment:

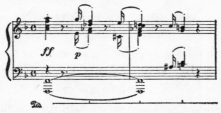

Not much, to be sure, will be left of the low F after three contacts between the damper and the string; but if the foot acts very quickly, the tone will be clearly audible after the first release.

Mozart had used the Italian form of this word, *Notturno,* as the title of a chamber work for strings and two horns. The more familiar French spelling, as well as the conventional poetic character implied by the word, seems to have come from John Field, an Irish composer and pianist whom Chopin met in Paris in the winter of 1832–33. The two men were not very sympathetic. Field's reputation, however, was high, and Chopin once wrote rather proudly of some commentators among the pupils of Kalkbrenner and Herz who regarded him as the equal of Field. The older man, from his altitude, looked somewhat contemptuously at Chopin, whom he described as a "sick-room talent." But Field's Nocturnes are today of little interest save as a minor source of Chopin's finer examples.

The reference to the sick-room is more appropriate to Chopin's Nocturnes than to any others of his works. But even that opprobrium belongs mostly to the mawkish pianists who, for many years, used these pieces for the purveyance of overgenerous portions of the food of love. A sounder critical objection would perhaps be that there is in them the play of fancy, rather than of imagination; but even this is not always true.

Op. 9 comprises three Nocturnes. The first, unquestionably, is boudoir music, adorned with ornaments and cosmetics that cannot disguise the doll-like face to which they are applied. The second has been played to exhaustion; but that very fact should warn us—who are really the exhausted ones—that such popularity as it has for fresher minds than ours is not won by sentimentality alone. The third, being more lively, is less patently nocturnal, but is for most ears more interesting than the first. The melody is hardly more distinguished, but the ornaments, at least, are more subtle. The variant of the opening strain at bar 9 employs the diminished third to a degree then unprecedented, and the other figurations are often similarly recherché. None of these pieces, however, wholly refutes Field's criticism.

Op. 15, however, is a different matter. No. 1, in its quiet portions, if not wholly free of the odors that taint Op. 9, No. 1, strikes a truer note of feeling. The sound of the middle section is more portentous than its meaning, and the whole character seems not clearly related to the rest. The other two pieces in this group, however, are outstanding. The *Nocturne in F-sharp,* No. 2, seems to us the first full revelation of the imaginative stature of the composer. We shall therefore examine it closely.

The melody, throughout, absorbs into itself the ornamentation which, in the earlier pieces, was palpably plastered on to the surface of a somewhat banal line. The emotional point is revealed at once. Its first phrase, cushioned on the elastic seventh chord, gains through the "leaning note" A-sharp a singularly heightened warmth. Nor is this lost as the phrase rebounds, effortlessly and with exquisite grace, from the low C-sharps. (We feel that in spite of the portamento mark, the first phrase ends with the first eighth note, C-sharp. The second, then, is up-beat to the next phrase.) Repetitions—the first, slightly ornamented, the second, sequentially raised—absorb our attention always more fully; and the long upward leap in bar 6, with the wide arc of the ensuing curve, firmly establishes the implication of passion that was inherent in the beginning. Neither has the gradually developed cadence (bars 7–8) the usual perfunctory character: it remains fully relevant to the mood. Even the floridity of the restatement (bars 9–16) is wholly appropriate, and the transition to the middle section unexpectedly heightens the already grateful tension. (Note that the bottom of the melodic curve in the opening strain was made of three reiterated notes, and that the peak of the curve in this transition is made in the same way.)

The *Doppio movimento* ("doubled speed") is not derived from the earlier matter, but is unmistakably related in character; obviousness in the succession of four-bar phrases is disguised by the continuity of motion (for example, in bar 8) to the sequential continuation. The climax of the whole curve (bar 17) is not on the down-beat but on the ensuing C-sharp with its resounding, unexpected harmony; and the recession fades into extinction on the one dotted rhythm that has obsessed the whole section. The epilogue—of course, a return to the beginning—although more ornamented than ever, is still without a trace of superfluity. The cadence (bars 8–9 of Tempo I) is suddenly and vitally intensified, and the concluding passage is not the mere tinkle of sound which it at first appears, but is an echo, both in its smaller detail and in its larger curve, of the original opening phrase.

Here, certainly, is a poet. He voices, to be sure, the aspirations of the 1830's, with which those of the 1930's professed to have little in common. But the later 1940's are not so sure of themselves, and are finding, in their perplexity, something not wholly foreign to the nostalgic passion of the earlier day. Chopin is a little aloof, for he knows that his are uncommon visions, and that they must be kept uncontaminated; but there is here none of that vanity of romanticism which supervened upon its too unquestioned acceptance. Both for its comparative playableness and for its essential poetry, this Nocturne is deservedly a favorite, and a valuable preparation for greater works.

Some technical problems may be profitably considered. The accent on the first note is undoubtedly authentic; yet if it is allowed to override the natural stress on the down-beat it will ruin the main phrase. (We suspect that the mark is a survival of an old convention in piano playing that every phrase should have an accent on its first note. Chopin was criticized, in Vienna, for not observing this rule.) Taking advantage of the fact that it is hard to tell whether a note is louder or longer than normal, we interpret this mark as an agogic, not a dynamic, accent. The two C-sharps, which Chopin groups together, portamento, cannot form a separate phrase. We take the first of these, therefore, as ending the initial phrase, and the second as up-beat to the C-sharp on "one" of bar 2. The appropriate dynamics for all these C-sharps will be found only with study. The thirty-second notes in bar 2, if played strictly in tempo, lose elasticity and grace. We therefore elongate slightly the tied thirty-second, C-sharp, and hasten proportionately the following thirty-seconds—arriving, however, at the high C-sharp precisely on the beat. The quintolet in bar 3 must not be turned into two notes plus a triplet. (The C-sharp of the bass must fall halfway between E-sharp and D-natural.) In bar 6, we take the pedal with the staccato B of the bass, against which the tied F-sharp of the melody seems to be harmonized by the subdominant triad before the more dissonant chord that follows. (In bar 6 of the final section, Chopin prescribed the pedal.) Practice the left hand, in bar 7, alone. The three voices must be audible if the harmony is to be understood. The low A-sharp, when the repetition begins in bar 9, seems from the arpeggiated notation to take precedence not only in time but in loudness over the higher, and the ensuing B-natural may be similarly weighted, though of course the true register of the melody is now the higher. The notation is here a graphic picture of rubato. (The Peters edition has arbitrarily contracted these two arpeggiations into mere rolled chords.) Intone the left-hand D-natural in bar 11 (which must not coincide with the first note of any triplet in the ornamental variant of bar 1) so that its progression to C-sharp will be clearly heard. In bar 15 observe the same caution as in bar 7.

The *fz* C-sharp in bar 17 is in piano, and should give no more than quietly sonorous support to the melody. Begin the chromatic slides in bars 18 and 20 at the last instant compatible with smooth execution. Be sure that the interesting chords in bars 22–23 give all possible addition to the meaning of the melody. In bar 24, the sixteenth notes form two sextolets, not four triplets (as are erroneously marked in Peters), and must be appropriately rhythmed. The quintolets in the *Doppio movimento* can be heard as such if that direction for speed is not exceeded. (The left hand will be fitted against them as in bar 3.) The elaborate notation making a separate voice out of the second and third sixteenths in the quintolets and later seems to us superfluous and incapable of any clear utterance. Observe exactly the changed rhythm-pattern at bar 9, where the left hand now coincides with the beginning of the triplet in the right. Save up for the striking value, already remarked, of the C-sharp in bar 17. The final low octave C-sharp may be held until the right-hand phrase has faded. (We even take the liberty of sustaining it through the pause, and thus coloring the up-beat of the returning A section.)

In bar 6 of Tempo I, make the high A-sharp even more intense than the preceding F-sharp (*fz*). Play bar 7 so as to make the unexpected leap to D-sharp in bar 8 as pointed as possible. In bar 9, take the triplet and the following G-sharp in one group, as marked, with both dynamic and agogic emphasis on the G-sharp, so that the ensuing chromatic descent may be spacious and delicately colored. The *fz* in bar 10 is in *pp*. The entrance of the first triplet of thirty-seconds may be slightly delayed. The sextolets from bar 12 must be properly rhythmed. Retard only the last sextolet, and that but slightly. We take the liberty of sustaining the thirty-second, C-sharp, against the final widely dispersed tenth.

Even more remarkable, though less immediate in its appeal, is the third number in Op. 15. The MS. is said to have borne the words (run through with a pen), "After a reading of *Hamlet*." Although it would be hard to establish any direct association between the music and any episode in that play, the texture of this piece is so unusual for Chopin that it seems certain to have originated in a source that he did not ordinarily tap.

More than any other of Chopin's works, this is a song of solitude. Such spiritual bleakness as this was seldom productive of musical inspiration until the later years of Brahms; and it seems to us a significant indication of breadth in Chopin's musical mind —of breadth which remained, for the most part, unexplored. It is a frequent enough mood in the experience of a nervously overexcitable person such as Chopin was; but it is seldom expressed by such a person until it has turned into more violent feeling. There is here, of course, far more than "spiritual dryness." There is a sense of awe—not so vast or so profound as that which a more philosophic mind would conceive, but to meet with it at all in Chopin is something of a surprise.

Technically this is one of Chopin's easiest pieces; interpretatively it is not so. The superscription, *Lento,* is accompanied by Chopin's metronome mark, $\text{♩.} = 60$. This is simply impossible; yet no commentator seems to take any direct exception. The additional direction, *languido e rubato,* and credible reports (by Huneker) of Anton Rubinstein's "very slow" tempo, seem to us to indicate that the mark should be nearer $\text{♩} = 60$. The accent on the up-beat is here a different matter from that in No. 2. This D is not only the first note of a two-note phrase, but is also a kind of reciting tone, recurring often (bars 7–12, and so on) in the melody, and appearing in the bass when the parallel phrase is centered on F (bars 19-22). This first D may of course be slightly lengthened (as may the A-sharp in Op. 15, No. 2), but not the later ones. Against the forte F (bar 4) the bass figure must have a kind of hollow aplomb—a sense of the inexorable—not easy to render unless the prescribed languor is kept within narrow bounds.

The sudden chill that comes with the *sotto voce* phrase (bar 51) implies *una corda,* and the *fz* D-sharp of the bass, here and elsewhere, should convey a veiled, rather than a literal threat. The modulations throughout this and the ensuing climactic passage are altogether extraordinary, and prove Chopin to have been, from the beginning, one of the great harmonic liberators of the nineteenth century. The augmented fifth chord (56-57) is but the beginning of an excursion into harmonic regions hardly dreamed of before this piece was written, and the culmination (77f.) seems to us the most genuinely tragic moment in all Chopin. How amazingly right—and how wholly unexpected—is the alleviation that comes with the vanishing of the deep bell, and the entrance of the religious strain that is neither hymn nor chant, but is the epitome of both! [5] At bar 120ff., the many *fz* signs imply that more of crescendo has been needed in the approach than has been indicated. Give these sustained *fz* notes full intensity; pedal only with the slurs ("three" to "one," bars 120-121) and prolong the sustained note so that it is audible for an instant *after* the staccato chord on "two" has been silenced. These notes are the counterparts of trumpets and trombones cutting through the strings and winds of the orchestra. Where the trumpet notes make continuous melody (e.g., 126f.), be sure that they are clearly sustained. The singular impressiveness of the major ending can be enhanced by prolonging the preceding dominant chord very slightly beyond its normal proportion in the prescribed ritenuto. This major ending is the more striking in that the *fz* D, four bars from the end, had all the appearance of a tonic, so that to reach the tonic G is itself something of a surprise.

Op. 27, No. 1, in C-sharp minor, begins with great promise. Over the rocking accompaniment, indeterminate in tonality, the melody creeps chromatically upward as if to glimpse some region beyond its normal vision. This sense that revelation is im-

---

[5] Chopin's slur beginning at bar 85 was surely intended to cover only three bars—as is proved by the release of the pedal at the C-sharp, and the direction, *a tempo.*

minent is not only maintained but heightened—first by the silent
bar (10), big with the sense of the augmented sixth, and then
(bar 17) by the diminished third, more tense than the augmented
sixth of which it is the inversion. But the middle section is dis-
appointing. Its two-bar figure seems a still further induction,
rather than the assertion that we expect; and when after still another approach the long-sought objective is reached (*con anima*)
we seem but meagerly rewarded for our long suspense. No ora-
torical flourishes—not even the magnificent attitude that is struck
with the return to C-sharp minor, or the resounding recitative
in which the attitude is dissolved—can make alluring the return
to the condition of mystery; and the sweetness of the *calando* is
almost an affront—the apparition of a needless *deus ex machina*.

The next Nocturne, however, which at the outset promises such
sweetness as will endure but little light, accomplishes so much
more than is in the apparent bond that we are compelled to admiration. The wide curve of this melody arises out of something
more than aesthetic exaltation. It sounds the authentic note of
that romanticism of which the French were now (in 1836) the
leading purveyors. But this exquisitely finished manner was not
devised solely for the exhibition of external charm. Even within
the drawing room, where the gentle "action" of this piece takes
place, its aspiration, as well as its pianism, is recognized; and its
passion, although attenuated for modern ears by a manner that
seems hardly capable of honest utterance, is nevertheless real.

The flexibility of the piano has never been better exhibited.
The spacious figure of accompaniment provides both a rich
sonority and a continuity of motion that can be minutely hastened
and retarded without disturbing its essential forwardness; and the
melody, therefore, can be nourished at any desired moment with
contributions that seem to be entirely absorbed into itself. There
is hardly a phrase which the awakened imagination will not thus
enrich. Study of the detail will be found fascinating, but we can
take space to describe only the most salient points.

Be sure that the B-flat (bar 6) fades appropriately for the feminine ending after the A-natural. Support the ensuing strain firmly with the descending bass up to its end in bar 9. If the final F proves inaudible when tied (as is probable), it seems to us better to restrike it. Ornamental as they are, bars 10–16 have a core of true expressiveness which is more fully revealed in bar 18f., and in the subtle enharmonics of bars 22–24, where you will find much exercise for your finest judgment of tone gradation. This transition seems to us to imply a somewhat fuller emphasis for the returning theme. (Chopin wrote no dynamic mark after the ⟨ in bar 25.) Strive to make audible, without restriking, the C-sharp in bar 34. The culmination of this episode (bars 40–45) is again highly meaningful, and the sense of the abbreviated bass figures (44–45) should be fully realized. The ensuing repetition of the theme should doubtless be the most forceful; but you will find it no mean problem to execute the cadenza in bar 52 con forza, as marked. In bar 60, after a forte ascent, De Pachmann played the descent *pp*, with exquisite effect. The retreating phrases of the diminished fifth in the epilogue (bar 62f.) must not be obscured by the added graces (bar 66), which must be very soft and very close to their ensuing principal notes. In the *calando*, use no rubato, but only dynamic shading, so graduated that the two voices may remain distinct. The "seven against six" at the end can be accomplished only by feeling the whole span of the half-bar as the unit of time, with the seven sixteenths unretarded.

The next piece, in B major, in which a quietly elegiac tone is maintained without affectation or sentimentality, is quite within the range of modest technique. The sudden intensity of bars 5–6, with the stretto and the ⌢, greatly illuminates the sense of the whole strain. Do not allow the tone to become harsh, or the legato broken, through inadvertent thumping of inessential notes. The tenor, from bar 8, is valuable. Read accurately the voice-leading in bar 12. In bars 40 and 61, the G-sharp which anticipates the trill on A-sharp is melodic, and moves to the F-sharp–E, which are to be taken with the left hand. The closing recitative is as right, and as unexpected, as the religious strain in Op. 15, No. 3. Measure exactly the even eighth notes and the triplets to make them ominous. (The soft pedal will give the needful dulness of tone.) Make the thirty-second-note figures forceful and abrupt. In spite of the *a piacere,* keep religiously to the proportions, though not to the absolute values, of time indicated in the notes. Cling a little to the high E in the eighth-note recitation, whose every note must be articulate. The A-sharp in the last bar but one was written as an appoggiatura, but many editions print it as a quarter note, which is indeed its proper value. The weight of authority seems to incline to the major chord at the end, though many editions give it as minor.

The tone of the *A-flat Nocturne,* No. 2 in Op. 32, is so repellent to twentieth-century ears that we may well dismiss it without study. The main portion of the next, in G minor (Op. 37, No. 1) is probably not more "true," though one is reluctant to doubt its patent grief. The middle portion, however, is remarkable. For twenty-four bars the chords, with but one exception, have their roots in the bass. The solemnity of its rhythm, combined with this biblically simple harmony, makes this a notable musical utterance, however its significance may be obscured by the self-induced melancholy that surrounds it.

The *Barcarolle* (by which name the Nocturne, Op. 37, No. 2, might have been called) seems to have gone out of favor; but if the thorny passages of double notes are lightly and elastically played (which is not easy), the piece can regain its original charm. It was once averred that the quiet middle section contained Chopin's most beautiful melody; but that, today, is hardly a tenable opinion. Only the greatest care in the choice of the phrase stress in the middle portion can prevent an intolerable monotony of thumping.

The *C minor Nocturne,* Op. 48, No. 1, seems to us to display the same uncertainty of purpose as that which we noted in the C-sharp minor, Op. 27, No. 1. There is drama in the detached, recitational beginning, and in the soaring phrases that are soon generated out of it; there is dignity and even nobility in the sotto voce strain in C major; but the attempt to intensify this quality through the mere force of theatrical octave passages is only bewildering. And the thickening of the accompaniment for the returning main theme (in the *doppio movimento*) makes for heaviness and confusion, rather than for decisive affirmation.

It seems to us indisputable that the later works of Chopin reveal (along with that increase in skill and delicacy which so conscientious an artist must acquire) a notable deterioration in imaginative quality. Stagnant air and artificial light (sometimes expensively shaded) form the environment of most of the remaining Nocturnes. There is a momentary pulse of life in the *Molto più lento* section of Op. 48, No. 2; but repetition soon dulls its energy. Op. 55 contains nothing but salon music. Op. 62, No. 1, often called the "Tuberose" Nocturne, has indeed the heavy fragrance which that title suggests, and as with many odors, there is a momentary evocation of poetic imagery; but there is still more of the skilful device which, after long nurture within the narrow confines of "Art," is often mistaken for poetry. The melody of Op. 62, No. 2, had been drained of feeling by sentimental opera writers, long before this piece was written, and the middle section is only artificially animated. The posthumous Nocturne published as Op. 72, No. 1, was written in 1827. It is alive, but adolescent.

### The Études

We may turn next to the *Études,* the first of which are labelled Op. 10. There are twelve pieces in this group, written between 1829 and 1831—that is to say, by a mere boy; but although this boy had already discovered secrets in the piano as remarkable as those which Paganini had revealed in the violin, there is no trace here of Paganini. The secrets are Chopin's own, and even Liszt, the greatest virtuoso of his time (and perhaps of any), displays by comparison a far more derivative invention.

This book having been designed for music lovers rather than for virtuosi, it is beyond our scope to enter in detail into the many

questions of technique presented by these *Études*. We shall choose
for discussion only a few—those which may with some pleasure
be attempted by pianists of moderate skill. And this necessity
leads us first to the discussion of the three smaller *Études,* without
opus number, which were published in 1840 in a *Méthode des
méthodes du piano* by Moscheles and Fétis. They present elemental problems in a comparatively simple form, and are at the
same time of high musical interest.

Indeed, the first, in F minor, which deals with the rhythmic
problem of four notes against three, is irresistible in its appeal.
The piece has already begun when its first notes become audible
—a wavering figure that comes out of silence and disappears, leaving behind it an undulation of the harmony of F minor. When the
melody comes again within hearing, it has another contour, but
the same fluidity, and we find at last that it was the end of this
strain which we glimpsed when the piece began. Although it
floats like a cobweb in the air, it bears a burden of feeling which
no cobweb could support, and this nameless but familiar mood
grows and wanes and sinks at last to earth, with three soft chords
of F minor for requiem. There is hardly a more poetic page in
all Chopin.[6]

The second, a problem in the maintenance of staccato and
legato in one hand, is as valuable technically as the first, but is
both easier and less interesting. The problem is obscured, however, by the frequent pedal signs (for you cannot play staccato
with the damper pedal down), and these, at least for practice,
should be ignored. The third is a study in playing two notes
against three, for which a mechanical process is available. Count

[6] There is no mechanical process by which the four notes against three can
be mastered; but if you can play two bars of this mixed rhythm correctly, you
will be able to do the rest. The 25th and 26th bars give a convenient sample.
Play each hand separately, counting only two to the bar, in what you are sure
is an unchanging speed. Then, having learned the easy figure of the left hand,
set it going and *forget all but the notes G and B, which fall on the beats.*
While you continue this figure, begin to think the right hand; then begin to play
it. If you persist, you will succeed.

as if the time were 6–8, and put the second and fourth eighths of the left hand between the last two notes of each group of three: i.e., count one, two-*and*-three, four, five-*and*-six, and put the left-hand notes on each *and*. There is here also a problem in the rapid adjustment of the right hand to shifting chord positions; but that problem, if a reasonable fingering is adhered to, is merely one of effort. The music, brought up to the Allegretto tempo, will be found charming, with unexpected harmonic interest at bar 25.

The first of the *Grandes Études* (Op. 10, No. 1) is extremely difficult to play at its proper tempo. Yet it is a valuable study in extended position for students who are far below the technical power to play it at its proper speed. The wide oscillation of the wrist which the figures demand is a commonplace in modern playing, and can hardly be better acquired than through this piece. Bar 31, in the established fingering-pattern, is painful, and may be facilitated by the use of

$$\mathcal{7} \quad 2 \quad 3 \quad 1, \quad 3 \quad 2 \quad 3 \quad 1, \text{ etc.}$$

The second, a streak of wildfire, has to be fingered with the 3rd, 4th, and 5th fingers for the chromatic scales, throughout. (These fingers have the same task in double thirds, so that this is in a way a preparatory study for Op. 25, No. 6. It is hardly less difficult.)

The third begins with the loveliest melody that Chopin ever wrote. (This is his own considered statement.) In the first part, there are no real difficulties; yet the dynamic shadings and the rubato which alone make a tolerable performance require almost as much study as the ensuing tangles of double notes. The fourth, vigorous and healthy, also makes severe demands upon the left hand. Few facilitations can be found.[7]

[7] The quarter notes in the right hand, bar 27 and part of 28, can be taken with the left, as far as the hand can reach them. The right hand, in this way, gets a valuable rest. Note that the slur from the up-beat to the C-sharps in bar is a motive hightly characteristic of this piece, recurring in bars 4–5, 7, 11,

The fifth is the famous "Black Key" Étude—a piece whose technical ingenuity is so consummately brought off that a hearer would hardly suspect it to be the solution of a difficult problem in composition. Although a brilliant performance of it is beyond any but an accomplished technique, the student of more moderate equipment can gain from the practice of it a valuable sense of confidence in the use of the hand in that forward position which is essential when the thumb is constantly ready to strike a black key.

The sixth, in E-flat minor, is technically not very difficult to play. It requires, of course, a very accurate dynamic discrimination to keep the melody sounding above the figure of eighth notes, and at the same time to keep that figure alive. The third sixteenth of the figure is almost invariably the note which has to be gently "squeezed" to get the full harmonic flavor of the figure. But so little relief is offered from the tone of melancholy which is sounded at the outset that practice of this Étude soon becomes emotionally fatiguing.

The next four studies are so difficult that the analysis of them hardly falls within the province of this book. The twelfth, however, the famous "Revolutionary" Étude, again offers valuable practice to those who cannot perform it adequately.[8] Its fiery

---

16, and so on. The final flourish, bar 4 from the end, can be made much stronger by dividing it thus:

[8] To make the leap from bar 2 to the chord in bar 3, take the pedal with the 4th beat; release the hand at once, and poise it above the octave G; "pick up" —that is, do not strike with a downward motion—this octave, and throw the hand, thus lifted, to the chord at the 3rd bar. (Similarly, of course, in the many similar passages.) In bar 7, accentuate G and B-flat (against the established rhyhtm) but resume the normal stress at "two" in bar 8. (From the middle of bar 6 to bar 9, give the left hand less energy than the right: you will conserve strength and gain clearness.) In bar 27, descending, finger 1235, 1235, with the 3rd finger on the low B-flat of bar 28. Bars 29-32 are the hardest in the piece. The stress falls persistently on the 2nd finger, and must be audible.

energy is communicated to the player (if not to the hearer) even with relatively slow speed, and the piece is thus a strong incentive toward an ultimate goal of mastery.

The second book of the Études begins with what in America is usually called the "Aeolian Harp," but in England (on the authority of an improbable-looking story recorded by Kleczynski) is called "The Shepherd Boy" (who "takes refuge in a peaceful grotto from approaching storm. In the distance rushes the wind and the rain, while the shepherd gently plays a melody on his flute.") This piece is much harder to play than it looks, and offers little benefit to the fingers of the amateur. The next, however, is very valuable even to the unskilled. The rhythmic problem is curious. Such accentuation as will *compel* the hearer to recognize the triplets in the right hand would doubtless ruin the fluidity; but if you do not *think* the triplets, your fault will be at once apparent in a dull and shapeless line. If your left hand can span a tenth, you can sustain its harmonies, almost throughout, without the pedal. (The initial bass note has the harmonic value of a sustained whole note almost throughout.) At bar 13 from the end, extend the slur from the E-natural to the high D-flat, and play a slight *rit.* on these notes, with a very slight breath-pause after the D-flat. Then accelerate the remaining notes to the *a tempo* in the next bar. Eight bars from the end, detach the initial C, beginning anew with the high A-flat, and play *cresc.* to the high F, the real crisis note, in the next bar. Three bars from the end, make the appoggiaturas long, giving to these notes and the intervening D-flat the value of a retarded triplet of sixteenths.

The third Étude, in F, is musically one of the most fascinating,

---

The *ff* at bar 37 must be tremendous. To prepare for it, take the pedal for two sixteenths on the first three beats, and for *all* of the fourth beat, in bar 36. Diminish the melody in bar 38, but crescendo with continuous pedal from "three" to yield another crisis at bar 39. Take the A-flats in bar 40 with the 5th finger. The last beat of bar 56 may be broadened somewhat. Some performers confess their exhaustion at bar 65 by taking a sentimental *pp* instead of the *ff* there marked. Broadening of the tempo is preferable to this feeble device.

but is too difficult to yield much benefit to the average student. The fourth and fifth are less interesting musically, though the middle of No. 5 may tempt the ear for a time. The sixth, in double thirds, is of extreme difficulty, so that we omit analytical comment. The seventh, however, although of extreme musical subtlety, presents few physical problems, and—if the reader has not wholly outgrown the romantic period—is likely to prove of the highest poetic interest.

It is obviously a duet, probably between a 'cello and a violin, with piano accompaniment. Ignore any dotted bar lines in the opening recitative, if they appear in your edition. (Mikuli gives the 4th and 5th notes, C-sharp, B-sharp, as quarters; others give them as eighths, which is doubtless right.) The dotted quarter, A, is the goal of the preceding notes, and may be somewhat prolonged; the B-natural and the homologous A are the (more subdued) stress points in the ensuing sixteenths. Start the 'cello melody firmly, and float in its accompaniment, rubato. The violin begins with an imitation which must be clear and sustained above the much softened accompaniment; but do not lose the contour of the 'cello in bar 3 (of the 3–4 time), nor the continuity of the violin. Indeed, from bar 5 to bar 9, the violin almost predominates; but do not miss the somber droop of the 'cello in bar 8, and allow it to resume leadership in bar 9. Although the warm ninth chord at bar 12 deserves careful preparation, do not miss the darker harmonies (with D-natural and F-natural) that follow, and be sure that the long notes of the violin do not fade from sight. In bar 15, the C-naturals are increasingly bitter, and that value is realized in the violin (bar 17) against which the 'cello gives to the A's the echo of its former emphasis of C. The color of the major key, from bar 18, is vivid in proportion to the preparation made for it in the preceding passage.

We make sustained melody of the upper voice in bar 21, thus introducing the more insistent violin phrases which follow, and which are of equal value with the 'cello all the way to the E-flat major cadence in bar 29. Here, with the beautiful enharmonic modulation the violin now definitely takes the lead, the 'cello having only a persistent figure to play. Whatever may seem the best pedaling during the sixteenths, take a new pedal with the last (the low B), sustaining until the "one" of the next bar. In the violin melody itself, note that

the last note of the bar is only once (bar 30) of the same length
as the last note in the 'cello. This, of course, is for differentiation of
the voices, and must be carefully executed. After the ⌢ in bar 37,
resume decisively the dark color of the main thought. (The F-natural
in the 'cello, bar 40, should be phrased with the following C-natural,
not—as Mikuli has it—with the preceding E.) Do not ignore the tragic
tension of the harmony in bar 56, and step carefully with the sixteenths
in bars 58–59. Note that the cadential figure in bar 63 is often sequentially repeated for epilogue, thereafter. The slurs, which seem to
be Chopin's, since they are repeated in all the editions consulted, are
misleading. The meaning of the passage must surely be this:

No. 8, the study in sixths, is as difficult as that in thirds. No. 9
(the "Butterfly") has no brilliancy at all unless the 5th finger is
able to predominate over the thumb, throughout; and that feat is
so fatiguing as to make the study impossible for any but the most
accomplished technicians. The study in octaves (No. 10), being
mostly in conjunct motion, is easier than if there were more
frequent skips; but its musical interest seems to us relatively low.
The last two are again of extreme difficulty, though No. 12 is
more manageable than No. 11.

### The Waltzes

The *Waltzes,* long among the most favored of Chopin's pieces,
have now mostly lost their savor. They are of course idealizations
of the somewhat plebeian dance (by comparison with the Minuet)
which delighted the Viennese for a century after the more stately
measure went the way of monarchy after the Revolution. But it is
no longer easy to recapture the sense of grace and elegance that
they once conveyed. The first, Op. 18, is the nearest to the true
dance of them all—and on that account, perhaps, is among the
most permanently pleasing. It is frank and healthy, restrainedly

passionate in the D-flat section, and altogether bewitching in the B-flat minor portion, with the grace notes. The *Waltz in A-flat,* Op. 34, No. 1, is somewhat more pretentious as a composition, and by that much less compelling as a waltz. The next, however (Op. 34, No. 2), is a kind of *Valse triste,* and the very incongruity implied in those two words is inherent also in the music. It is not very difficult to play, and will last long in the affection of any music lover. The next is decidedly, in contrast, a *Valse gaie;* but its gaiety is ephemeral. The passage with the grace notes is rumored to have been suggested by Chopin's cat, jumping onto the keyboard while he was composing—a story no more likely to be true than that of George Sand's tail-chasing puppy, which is supposed to have suggested the D-flat Valse.

Op. 42 in A-flat is probably the most "distinguished" of the Waltzes. If it were to be danced, Schumann thought that "half the ladies should be countesses at least." The mingling of duple and triple rhythm gives at first a curious suavity to the surface of what soon proves itself to be a true, though highly stylized, dance. This is salon music of a very high order: colorful, easy to understand, and so difficult to play that a competent performance will evoke high approval from those who play the rôle of Schumann's countesses.

The *Valse in D-flat,* Op. 64, No. 1, mentioned above in relation to George Sand's little dog, is also called the "Minute-Waltz," from some senseless tradition that it ought to be played in that brief time. Being fairly easy, it has been "played to death"; yet it is intrinsically charming, and as an evocation of a time when delicate trifling had its price, it will hardly be wholly forgotten. The next, in C-sharp minor, is much more substantial, though not less poetic.

Observe the ➤ in bar 1 by obtaining just that lesser volume for the D-sharp (bar 2) which will perfect the actual legato. Rhythmic interest in these two bars may be heightened by playing the "two" an instant too soon, and the "three" apparently (but not really) too late, with slightly heavier emphasis than the "two." Begin bar 3 precisely on time, but very lightly, and observe rigorously the time values in the graceful figure. In bar 10, and bar 12f., always take the first of two repeated notes as approaching the second—that is, the first much lighter than the second; but without that detachment of the two-note groups which would be indicated if the notes were slurred in pairs. The legato implied by the long slurs must still be felt, and this is not easy to insure. The second section (*Più mosso*) might be taken a little deliberately the first time, with increased speed for each of the repetitions. The last eighth note in each figure in bars 1–4 is often emphasized and sustained into the next bar. This is an interesting effect; but we think it wiser to produce it only occasionally—perhaps at both opportunities in the repetition following the D-flat section, and once during the final repetition. The *Più lento* confesses an adoration too intimate to be whispered in the glare of the ballroom. Only a hint of the rhythm of the waltz is audible. Note how, against the descending arc of the melodic curve, the harmony continually strives upward —with the A-natural in bar 2, the D-natural in bar 4, the E-natural in bar 6, and so on; and how the almost incessant syncopation keeps the melody rhythmically afloat. You will find few passages in Chopin that better repay minute study.

The third, even by comparison with the first of the three pieces in Op. 64, seems to us negligible. This is the last of Chopin's Waltzes to be published during his lifetime. Among the posthumous publications, however, we find several highly interesting pieces.

That in A-flat (Op. 69, No. 1) is as gracious, superficially, as the one last dismissed; but it seems to us to emerge from a richer vein of feeling. It is not difficult; but it must be read with care. (Compare bars 1–2 and bars 8–9 of section 2, marked *con anima*.) The *Valse in G-flat,* Op. 70, No. 1, is far less difficult than it looks (or sounds), and will give many a timid student a certain measure of needful self-assurance. The very long skips are quite safely "anchored" on black keys, and soon become congenial to the hands. In the *Meno mosso,* bar 2, and elsewhere, observe that the phrase begun in the preceding bar ends with the eighth note after the dotted quarter, and that the two following notes are an up-beat. (Careless players read the eighth note as if it were a sixteenth, and join it thus to the up-beat.)

The most sparkling of all the Waltzes is that in E minor, published posthumously without opus number. It is difficult, and has been made more so by the senseless speed at which the virtuosi love to take it. (The tempo mark, *Vivace,* given in most editions, is not in the original, which has no mark. It is certainly a justifiable suggestion; but *Vivace* does not mean *Prestissimo,* nor is such haste suggested by the composer's indications of *grazioso,* or *dolce e legato.*) The passage in bars 9–14 of the second section is a valuable study in extended motion for both hands, and the Coda demands great firmness in the fingers if its vividness is to be at all adequately realized.

# 10
# CHOPIN'S LARGER WORKS
## Scherzi Ballades Polonaises
## Préludes Impromptus Sonatas Fantaisie

~~~~~~~~~~~~~~~~~~~~~~~~~~~~~~~~~~~~~~~~~~~~~~~~~~~~~~~~~~

### The Scherzi

AFTER the Waltz, the Scherzo is the next large form to evolve in Chopin's hands out of what was originally a minor type of composition. The *First Scherzo,* in B minor, Op. 20, is a bolder adventure than Chopin had yet undertaken, whether in form or expression. Its form is still recognizable as the vastly expanded design of the Minuet with Trio, out of which the sonata-scherzo had grown. But no one had ever contrived to give it such dimensions,[1] nor had even Beethoven unleashed so bitter and sardonic a humor. The first section even has the conventionally marked repeat, and the second—beginning with the usual modulations, and ending with a return to the first section—is also repeated; but this repetition is written out. The *Trio* presents a far greater contrast of mood and tempo than is usually to be found,[2] but it has likewise precisely the conventional form.

This piece is very difficult technically, and is all but impossible

---

[1] The last movement of Beethoven's Op. 14, No. 2, is called *Scherzo* but its form is really that of the Rondo, and its dimension far smaller than that of the *First Scherzo* of Chopin.

[2] Compare, however, the Trio of the *Scherzo* in Schubert's great quintet for strings, in C.

to interpret effectively. It begins at such a high level of excitement
that at the peak of the second section a limit is reached which
can hardly be transcended. The performer—since Chopin provides nothing but repetitions, except for the Coda—has thus to
bear the whole burden of increasing the tension; and only super-
human skill and strength can accomplish that task. It is unfortunate that this is so, for the musical idea is of extraordinary
vividness—the very epitome of Chopin's unique musical personality—and nowhere, in spite of its turbulence, does the excitement
ever seem artificial.

Even today, the two forceful, dissonant chords that introduce
this piece sound a compelling threat. The rhythm of the main
subject—there is, indeed, but one real subject—is shattering; its
elementally simple harmonies (tonic for eight bars; subdominant
for eight more) are so disguised by the accented appoggiaturas
that we can hardly believe them to be so simple; and its melody
is as intractable as wildfire. The broadened conclusion of the
first section (it is hardly another subject) is the perfect representation of passionate resentment—unyielding, except to the physical
necessity for breath. The second section, still with no other than
the original thought in mind, climbs to an intensity all but unendurable, and descends with flailing arms to the reassertion of
the original thought. Never before had a piano uttered such
sounds as these.

The *Trio* is the very antithesis of the *Scherzo*—languid and
bemused where the *Scherzo* was frantically overwrought; but it
is nevertheless the only logical contrast. Its luscious weakness does
indeed betray the overexcitement of the *Scherzo* as self-induced;
but such subjective passion was, for its moment, as "true" as the
more objective emotions that nowadays are supposed to be the
concern of artists. The forceful interpolation into the *Trio* of
the two bitter chords of the opening looks, from the objective
point of view, melodramatic. But in its highly subjective setting
it is amazingly right.

The *Second Scherzo,* Op. 31 (1837), is the most popular of the four separate Scherzi. It begins in B-flat minor, and is always spoken of as in this key; but the main theme, and also the end of the whole piece, are in D-flat major. The primary dance form is more disguised than in the *First Scherzo.* The introductory phrases, together with the sweeping melody that ensues, are indeed identifiable as the first section of the original form, and this section is conventionally repeated. The next section, however, beginning in A major, and also repeated, is so wholly different in substance and character that it cannot be taken as the completion of the first. Neither is it a Trio. It comes too early for that, and is followed, after its repetition, by an imposing development of both its own substance and that of the first section. The first section then returns (but not the second), and there is an extraordinary Coda. Altogether, the form approximates more closely to the Sonata than to the Scherzo. But there is a logical continuity that makes the form perfectly coherent, whatever may be its theoretical name. There is more variety of matter than in the *First Scherzo,* and though the nervous tension is thus more relieved, the whole impression is one of higher significance.

Chopin has seldom set down more clearly his musical intentions. Yet the opening of this piece is so often distorted that a few warnings seem necessary. Do not be misled by the ejaculatory character of the first phrases into any departure from strict time. *Sotto voce* does not imply a blur. The two hands must play the triplets perfectly together, with no accent on the A-natural, and with the culmination on the F. Only so will the veiled threat (which will be duly realized in the Coda) be impressively conveyed. Do not hasten, either, the forceful descent of the chords in bars 18–19, or carelessly displace the *fz* on "two" of bar 22. Every note in the descent of the main theme from the high F (49) must be audible, with proper propulsion from the left hand (on "three-*one,* three-*one*"). In the continuation, observe meticulously the many ➤ signs, and make the left hand in bars 62 and 64 softer than the right in 61 and 63. The ensuing broad song needs only a careful study of its phrase contours to be effectively played. (Too sharp an articulation of the accompanying figures will defeat this end.) The climax will best be attained if the *più cresc.* (109) is begun almost in piano. We find the precipitous descent (127) easier to play with the requisite force if it is divided between the two hands.

At the beginning of the A major section, the C-sharp is the melodic tone, but the E–F-sharp above it must be audibly led. At bar 13 of this section, observe precisely the rests in the left hand. Pause slightly on the C-sharp before the ornament (17), and allow a sense of ritardando to prolong the delicate ringing of the instrument. The similar ornament at bar 43 would doubtless have been introduced at bar 42 if the compass of Chopin's piano had permitted its extension to the high G-sharp which corresponds to the final C-sharp of the other passage. Surely this emendation is to be recommended; and if you adopt it, begin the ornament a bar earlier than is indicated by the notation, to correspond with the design of the earlier passage. In the following theme (45), whose entrance may be made somewhat rubato, heed carefully the design of the melody as indicated by the rests—at bars 48, 52, and 56, but *not* at 60, where the rhythmic contour is changed; keep the figure in the alto clear and rhythmic, and observe the caution, *legato,* in the bass. The running passage at bar 70 is usually taken at a faster tempo than the preceding. This is desirable, for even with its melodic bass the passage has relatively little interest. The culmination (94) must be powerful. To this end, the descent may again be divided between the two hands.

The development begins with the startling roar initiated by the low D following the bar of rest after the E corresponding to bar 100 of the first A major section. (We shall number this beginning as bar 1.) The ensuing passages lie badly for the hand, and the octaves in the left hand are very important. No alleviation of the difficulty can be found. At bar 25 (*agitato*) where the figure of bar 45 of the A major section is developed, take the pedal for the whole bar only where the dotted half notes appear in the thematic figure (i.e., bars 26, 28, and so on), leaving staccato the "one" of bars 25, 27, and so on. (Chopin indicated the pedal for every bar alike; but he appears to contradict his indications by his somewhat erratic notation of the bass, which is occasionally phrased as we suggest—e.g., in bars 28–9, and 36f.) The reappearance of the main theme, now in E (50), is followed by an exciting development of what were originally subordinate phrases. We feel that not only *cresc.,* as marked, but also *accel.* is desirable, up to the *ffz* in bar 73. The following descent, in that case, will have to be broadened. Indeed, we are inclined to take this descent as a kind of flourish, without any marked rhythm. The low F, in any case, comes as up-beat to the forceful sequential passage that concludes the development; but this, because of its titanic energy, has to be broadened in tempo.

The effect of the sustained (instead of the staccato) F at the end of the opening figure in the recapitulation is extraordinarily alarming. (We shall number the first bar of this return again as 1.) How wise Chopin was not to enlarge here upon the somewhat florid phrases which he inserted at bars 16 and 40 in the repetition of the first section! The broad melody returns, in its place, with no important alterations save at the close, where it is remarkably uplifted. To initiate this effect, bar 107 may swerve slightly from the strict measure, and still in the *piano* marked at 106. Study the left hand carefully here so as to realize all the needful values in the increasingly dissonant harmonies. A slight *allargando* along with the *molto cresc.* of bar 122 will give added force to the D-flat chord, 124. With this chord, the tempo must again be strict, and must remain so, no matter what the difficulty of the rising figures in the right hand. Make the culminant notes of these figures staccato and very forceful; pause for no flourish at bar 148, but go right on, always imperceptibly accelerating. Squeeze every ounce of dissonance out of the extraordinary harmonic sequence from bar 164. (Chopin's phrasing here seems to us ineffective.) Beginning with 164, we group A-flat–A-natural, A-natural–B-flat, and so on, together. Likewise, we play the final detached chords (189f.) with considerable breadth. Note that the grace-note chord in the final bar is also, like the F, an octave higher than it is written.

The *Third Scherzo,* in C-sharp minor, Op. 39, was written in 1838–39. Its beginning approaches more nearly than the others to the vigorous and incisive rhythm which so often appears in the Scherzi of Beethoven. In form, it resembles the *Second Scherzo,* but is somewhat less developed. The introductory figure, in the Second, is a vital part of the whole structure. Here, it remains merely introductory. The main theme—sometimes unharmonized, sometimes forming an accompaniment to a somewhat subordinate melodic line—maintains its incessant, biting staccato throughout the whole first section. The second section (*Meno mosso,* D-flat major), like the second section of the B-flat minor Scherzo, is broader and more lyrical, but it has far less variety. Its theme is almost a hymn tune, and there is a faint resemblance, in the handling of it, to Bach's fashion of improvising interludes between the phrases of the hymn in his *Choral-Vorspiele*. But this is a resemblance with a difference, for Chopin's interludes are prismatic clouds, departing from, rather than enhancing, whatever of religious solemnity is to be found in the theme. One can hardly deny a somewhat annoying regularity in the persistent recurrence of these colorful passages; but neither can one deny that the fact of color is itself remarkably intensified in the middle of this section. When the first section returns, it is merely abbreviated, instead of being developed. The *Meno mosso* is now in E major. It lacks the passage of heightened color, but is effectively broadened and dimmed by reduction to the minor key of E. The Coda, swift and excited, is without thematic relation to the main themes save for a hint of the principal strain at the close.

This piece is by no means easy, but having few thematic materials, it presents correspondingly few technical problems. There is fortunately no temptation to a distorted rhythm in the *Introduction*. The four quarter notes in the 3–4 measure are merely four notes making up one bar of the main tempo. If the tenth chords in bars 6 and 14 are too large for the hand, the F-sharp may be added to the down-beat by a swift passing of the second finger over the thumb; but it is better to omit this higher F-sharp altogether than to weaken the chord by rolling it. Observe that the octave passage from bar 27 is marked staccato only in the two bars preceding the sustained G-sharps, but that from bar 57 the staccato is incessant. The earlier passages are thus to be understood as merely non legato; and to make them distinct in quality from the more brittle staccato figures will give another valuable contrast in addition to the marked distinction between *f* and *p*.

In the *Meno mosso*, the final chord of each choral phrase is of course to be held with the pedal throughout the ensuing ornament. This compels a very careful study of the dynamics of the ornament. The hint of melody in the highest notes (the resemblance to the descent from E to G-sharp in bars 31–33 is probably not accidental) will come out of itself; but to control the delicate and fluctuant *piano* of the whole fabric requires long practice. Most of the difficulty will be found in the left hand, which, for some time, will probably insist on playing too loudly. Even more difficult (and more important) is the perfect synchronization of the two parts. It is hopeless to try to give any pattern of variety in the many repetitions of this figure. Make the chorale phrases as varied as is consistent with their character, playing the ornaments almost undeviatingly *piano*. In the *più lento* of the E major section the chorale is itself marked *sotto voce*. The "clouds" must therefore be more ethereal than ever—an effect which is automatically somewhat aided by the softening of the hymn, but is made more difficult by the slower tempo. To image this whole episode as receding into a remoter distance will perhaps help to achieve its difficult perspective. The chorale vanishes, at last, in vague ascending figures.

The Coda begins at bar 48 of the *più lento,* but its theme begins on the following (weak) bar. The rhythm is here somewhat confusing, for the reminiscence of the chorale occupies but five measures, and the interpolation of three more (54–56) is so phrased as to appear to be a part of the ensuing phrase of the hymn. Since the rising sixth, G-sharp–E-sharp, is the essential interval in these three bars, and since that same interval begins the actual chorale-phrase ensuing, it seems to us that the three interpolated bars should be made the conclusion of the preceding five, with a fresh beginning at bar 57. Play the left hand in the Tempo I with great clarity against the stimulating figures in the right hand, drawing every ounce of value from such details as the chromatic descent in bars 3, 7, and so on. Only fingers of steel can realize the vivid excitement of this conclusion.

The first three Scherzi are irritable and often ironic, possessing these "humors" rather than the more boisterous humor implied in their title. The Fourth, in E, Op. 54, in contrast, is amiable almost throughout, and has no humor at all. It is the longest of the Scherzi, but is so only because its many cantilenas are unwilling to end until they have been spun out to perilous thinness. It seems to us strange that so nearly insipid a piece could have been written in the same year as the *A-flat Polonaise.* The student will find in it but few difficulties which will not have been prepared for by a study of the Waltzes and Nocturnes.

## The Ballades

Properly speaking, the Ballade is a folk song, commemorating some stirring or sentimental event, such as we find in "Chevy Chase," or "Edward," or "Barbara Allen." The vocal Ballad, raised to the status of art as in Schubert's *Erlkönig* or Loewe's *Die Uhr,* is still a composition based on a story, and would have far less interest if the image of the story were wholly deleted from our image of the musical meaning. Nevertheless, the music does not itself tell the story, but only illustrates it; and illustrates it by setting forth the tension of tragedy, the lilt of joyous excitement, the bitterness of frustrated desire which it is also the purpose of story-telling to awaken in us.

Chopin wrote four Ballades. It is possible that he had, in each, some story with which the music was associated. But he did not tell these stories, and we shall help ourselves not at all by beginning our study of the music with a program. Turned into actual episodes, the succession of moods in any one of the Ballades would yield a most irrational yarn. The music, however, is wholly consistent.

The *First Ballade* (in G minor, Op. 23) is in our opinion the finest of the four. Schumann expressed the same thought to Chopin. Indeed, he said that he liked it the best of all Chopin's works; and the composer answered, "I am glad of that, it is the one I, too, like best." It is not the most finished—that praise certainly belongs to the Fourth. It is not the most excited—that quality we should find in the Second. It is not the most romantic —that, doubtless, we should have to say of the Third. The First, however, after long acquaintance, seems the most elemental of all, and thus the truest. We shall study it, therefore, more minutely than the others.

Play the arresting passages of recitative at the opening with a solid attack on the low C; hold this a shade longer than its proper value in the Largo tempo, and begin the eighth-note ascent *p,* making the successive C's the stress points in the ascending line, with a slight hastening in the middle and a broadening at the end of the passage. Be sure to release the final F-sharp gently. The crisis of the next phrase is on the A, and its end is on the dotted eighth, E-flat. The next five notes must then meaningfully reiterate the preceding five—of course, more softly. Give full time to the ensuing silence, and make the final notes decisive and firm.

Release the pedal with the beginning of the 6–4 time, but sustain the B-flat as marked. The rhythmic motion begins with the bass D, so that the B-flat need not be measured exactly. Make the curve of the melody continuous to the C in bar 3 of the *Moderato,* with the stress on the preceding D. In the accompaniment, stress slightly and pedal the second of the two chords, releasing it only as the following melodic note is struck; and in bar 3, be careful to release the pedal exactly with the eighth rest on "four." This sudden silence marks, as effectively as would a note, the rhythmic beginning of the ensuing phrase, and it emphasizes also the hesitancy of the melody itself, which always pauses, indecisively, on an active note. With the high G, bar 15, there comes a hint of purpose, reiterated in bars 17–18, which pervades the melody thereafter. Do not make the florid figure in bar 26 into a mere ornament, but let it be imbued with this new vitality, as the gathering energy of bars 27–28 seems to suggest. In bar 29f., be sure to sustain the tied E-flat, D, and so on, so that they are clearly audible against the bass. The *f* and *agitato* at bar 33 are always taken to imply a much faster speed (observe that there are now rests where there were tied notes, before); but the *sempre più mosso* (37) warns us against a too great spurt. In bar 41f., be careful not to allow the double notes in the figure to suggest a triplet grouping of the eighths. Observe the rests in bar 45f., and note that the two "horns," as we may call them, which introduce the second theme, first appear in bar 49. Do not ignore the compelling line of the bass, from this point on. In bar 57 we find the fingering: 253512, 312312|5 conducive to the vanishing effect which is obviously intended.

The second theme is surely one of Chopin's most moving melodies. But the stress in the first phrase on the clinging G, against which (and similarly in bars 63, 69, and 71) the left hand makes a compelling curve with its last three notes. Also, against the insistence of the high B-flat (64), the sequential harmony—especially with its highest notes, B-flat, A-flat, G, F, E-flat—makes a contrapuntal enrichment that must not be wasted. From bar 75 to 85 there is no melody, but instead, a kind of atmosphere in which the passion of the second theme still lingers. The descent (bar 86) to the ominous, low E and the return of the first theme must be carefully delineated, else that theme, with its sudden, frantic crescendi, will be pointless. (Take the octaves of the melody with the right hand.) The purport of the second theme, which emerges suddenly out of the first at bar 99, is much enhanced by the fine dissonances, A, G-sharp, F-sharp, E-sharp in 103f. Note that these notes appear also in the third and sixth beats in the left hand, which must not fail to realize their value. Make no accent in the rising octaves in bar 112f., but only a gradual *cresc.* from *mf,* giving your all only at the *ffz,* bar 117.

Some editions give a *cresc.* in bar 119, rising to *f* at bar 123. We think it better to begin the long rise from that point piano, with continuous *cresc.* to bar 129. Emphasize the high G, bar 131f., rather than the down-beat, F-sharp. The left hand is here much harder than the right, but it will spoil the charming passage if it is faulty. From 139 to 141, emphasize the high note in each half bar. From 143, although the composer has stemmed E-flat, E-natural, and the like, as quarter notes, we feel that the C-flat–B-flat, D-flat–C, and so on, in the upper voice of this harmony are of greater importance. The culmination on the F-sharp minor chord, bar 147, will thus be much more convincing. The point in all the ensuing turmoil is revealed in the sonorous version of the second theme, bar 159. Make this very full throated, with much sonority from the left hand. Toss the quintolets in bars 163–65 ecstatically, and bring out the melody under the B-flats in 167. After the decisive conclusion (173) we have again a continuation which maintains the current of feeling without actual repetition of the thought. Make no *dim.* until it is indicated, thus giving full value to the sudden subsidence into tragedy that is so wonderfully achieved in bar 186. (The sixth eighth note in this bar is surely E-flat.) Make the pedal D's very somber beneath the first theme by the accentuation recommended at the beginning. Do not hasten, but rather expand, the two final bars before the *Presto con fuoco.*

This whole Coda is very difficult. We find it to be Chopin's nearest approach to that mighty disturbance of the soul which Beethoven portrayed in the *Appassionata.* Indeed, the phrase A-flat, G, F-sharp, G (bars 9–10) is identical in pattern with one of the most pregnant moments in the *Finale* of that sonata. The wild excitement from bar 35 is still another incoherent but powerful maintenance of a mood already established. In bars 44 and 48, finger the left-hand scales with the 4th on B-flat and the 3rd on F-sharp throughout. Make the ensuing G minor chords (*ritenuto*) very solemn. Begin the *accel.* broadly enough so that you have a real accelerando, not a sudden presto. Observe the staccato of the final note of the figure, so that the whole musical body seems to fall onto the low *fz* in bar 47. We find it better to broaden the last three octaves in bar 54.

We must speak at far less length of the other three Ballades. The Second, dedicated to Schumann, opposes tenderness and violence in the starkest fashion—as elementally as in many old English ballads. (Huneker asserts that it was inspired by Mickiewicz's poem, *Le Lac de Willis.*) Chopin's melody is often called effeminate; but the quiet song that forms the chief thought of this piece is essentially feminine. It is as shy as an anemone—aloof from passion and incapable of conflict; yet, in its own way, it is warm, gracious, and even devoted. It is abruptly confronted by "the very torrent, tempest, and whirlwind of passion"—incoherent and self-willed; it is stirred to unexpected depth by that contact, and is at last broken by it; but its nature remains untouched and unchanged.

Schumann asserts that, as he heard Chopin play the piece, it ended in F major, and supposes the impassioned episodes to have been afterwards inserted. It must have been a very different piece from that which was published, for the end is now in A minor. This ending seems to have been taken as an affront by some of the more doctrinal-minded critics. Hadow thinks it a deliberate straying away from a logical conclusion; but does the "logic" of such conflict as this consist in the mere obedience to a rule that musical compositions should end in the key in which they begin? The end is indeed unexpected; but in the light of the antithesis involved it is inevitable. Chopin is seldom as brilliantly logical as he is here.

Chopin's long slurs somewhat obscure the natural punctuation of the theme. We take six of the initial C's as introductory, with the seventh, after a hint of hesitation, as the real up-beat. The high F (bar 4) is surely the crisis and the end of the antecedent phrase, with the consequent strain weighted on the G in bar 6. Slight gradations of dynamics will be discoverable throughout that will remove all trace of stiffness from the exquisite melody. (We feel that the E in bar 22 should form the end of the preceding period, not the beginning of a new one, even though the composer has so slurred it. Compare the "feminine" ending of the first period, bar 6.)

No lightening of the difficulty of the *Presto con fuoco* can be found. Even though the figures in each hand are conventional, the two parts will not go together without error until they have been assimilated to each other by long practice. In the rallentando before Tempo I, keep the stress in the middle of the bar, not on the downbeat. In bar 6 of Tempo I, count out the rests in the retarded time indicated by the *slentando*. The broken melody will then resume its motion without a jerk. From bar 14, the phrasing in the bass should be throughout:

In the *Agitato,* take the first of the two repeated chords lightly, with a lift of the wrist, and the second heavily, with a downward impulse of the hand, the fingers themselves leaving the keys only far enough to permit the forceful downward stroke. Only one note in each group of six can be really forte, and where there is a note on the fourth eighth, this will be the predominant accent. The tremendous chord of the augmented sixth which precedes the simple strain of the first theme really has the ⌢ which Chopin placed over the following rest; for this chord is prolonged by the pedal until the last eighth of the following bar. (Here, of course, is the justification for our reading of the six C's at the opening of the Ballade.) The Schirmer edition, in Joseffy's editing, has an unfortunate misprint of F-sharp for the bass note. It is of course F-natural.

The *Third Ballade* quite loses touch with that rudiment of life out of which folk ballads are made. In its thematic substance there is nothing stern, nothing which of itself is the breeder of drama. Yet the C-sharp minor section presents a development of the two main themes which is more logical in a purely musical way than in almost any other work of Chopin's. The piece is so familiar that we need not offer comment on its many technical problems.

The Fourth, which is still harder to play than the very difficult Third, implies a background of experience still farther removed from ordinary life. Both these pieces are more like romantic novels than ballads. The Fourth is probably Chopin's
most aristocratic composition. It represents the very summit of
his artistry, but it reveals also that loss of contact with life which
we have already noted in the later Waltzes and Nocturnes.

The music comes into being on ten elastic G's, so harmonized
as to leave us, at the end of the preamble, expectant and uncertain.
The theme that now appears exhibits a sensitive fatigue that at
once arouses our sympathy. Although there are but two brief
motives in the whole theme, they are so delicately handled that
after twenty-nine bars of it, with only slight additions of ornament, it still has not seemed redundant. Indeed, after a brief
interlude (bars 37–46) its second motive can return, preparing for
a much more richly harmonized version of the whole theme (bar
58f.). The very considerable agitation which is its product (bar
72) is not, however, allowed to expand.

The second theme (80) has something of the character of the
opening of *Ballade II*. For once, Chopin's notation pretty clearly
indicates the real syntax of the theme; but the stress points must
be very subtly brought out, else the wonderful line will become
pedestrian. With bar 100, passion begins again to assert itself;
but as in bar 72 it eventuates in floridity. There is a hint of the
principal theme (121), and all at once we hear again the essence
of the romantic introduction, now so interwoven with fragments
of the main theme as to appear quite fresh. There follows a passage of close imitation, unusually "learned" for Chopin, which
yields some very interesting harmonies. The main theme then
emerges in its original shape; but from bar 152 it is newly
figurated with a grace beyond attainment by any other composer.
Impassioned passages arise out of these figures, and make an approach to the return of the second theme, which now acquires
a wholly unsuspected intensity. The sweep of it is irresistible, but

it seems to us a less convincing outcome of the theme in its original form than is revealed in the middle section of *Ballade II,* where its second theme is developed. The *stretto* marked for the sequence of strangely progressing chords (198–200) is in some editions prolonged to include the three *fff* chords that leave us expectant on the dominant of F minor (202). Other editions (which we think more rational) mark this conclusion *ritard.*

The quiet harmonies that follow complete the preparation for the Coda, which, however, is not thereby restrained. There is in the whole conclusion no reference to the main themes of the piece; but it seems, nevertheless, quite related. It is very difficult to play—unless, as some do, you take it so fast that the detail cannot be heard. The whole composition, indeed, is beyond the technical powers of those to whom this book is chiefly addressed. Only a few hints, therefore, will be offered.

At bar 58f., only the figure of sixteenths can be clearly audible against the theme and its main bass. All other notes must be put in the background—no simple task! Against the reminiscence of the introductory figure (125–6), allow the left-hand figure (beginning with the B-flats) to emerge, and let the three notes E-flat, E-double flat, D-flat in the right hand lead pointedly to the harmony of bar 127. Similarly, let the three B's in the end of bar 128 grow so that the suspension of the final one will lead, through the ensuing A, up to the E's which recall the introduction. In the little cadenza which closes this passage, we find it much easier to take the two notes, D–F (which are preceded by a grace note, G), with the right hand. Observe delicately the rests in 153—do not pedal over them. In the Coda, the thirty-seconds after the dotted sixteenths are to be played as if they were the third sixteenth of the triplet, simultaneously with the corresponding note in the triplet figures. The fingering in bar 223 is in most editions so clumsy that we offer the following:

Or the left hand can take the single note in each triplet; but we find this less comfortable.

## The Polonaises

Chopin's Polonaises are often described as expressions of his passionate attachment to his native land. It is probably true that, being thus instructed, we manufacture an image of Poland out of this music, just as we make Tchaikovsky's music into a portrayal of Russia; but the fact remains that in 1939 the *A major Polonaise* sounded hourly over the Warsaw radio as a sign that Poland still breathed, and was indeed, for the Poles of the twentieth century, just what Chopin had felt it to be for those of the nineteenth.

The earliest of his published works in this form was the *Andante spianato and Polonaise,* Op. 22, which is with orchestral accompaniment, and is thus outside the scope of this book. The earliest of the solo works was Op. 26—the *Polonaise in C-sharp minor,* and that in E-flat minor. The first is played by every schoolgirl, the second, far less often; yet it is to our mind far more interesting. The first (like Op. 22) is in a lyrical vein, far removed from the more militant examples of later years. It presents no problems of importance, either technical or interpretative. The second, however, is highly characteristic, certainly, of the composer in his more turbulent moods, and possibly of his nation. It will bear a few detailed comments.

*Poco riten.* and *accel.* mean exactly what they say. But to appreciate a ritenuto, you must first have an established tempo to be "retained" (in the old sense of "held back"). You must therefore be fatally precise in the rhythm of the first five notes, beginning the following chords, in their slower tempo, at the precise point indicated by the rests. Keep their tone sullen and veiled. The *accel.* begins in the same tempo, with a somewhat clinging B-flat, and a gathering rush on the following notes with the E-flat sharply cut off. The *riten.* in bar 6 may well be more pronounced than in bars 2 or 4; thereafter, the incisive *a tempo* must be precisely as it was in bar 1. Chopin's pedal for the ensuing chords is pretty "thick"; to use it continuously throughout the *cresc.* in bar 8 seems to us enough. Be careful that the eighth-note chords are always more heavily weighted than the sixteenths. The scale in bar 10 may be begun with the last B-flat in the left hand, without serious detriment to the thought; but be careful to bring out the left-hand eighths, B-flat, A-flat, A-natural. In bar 13f., we advocate the repeated finger for the repeated note as in Beethoven's Op. 31, No. 2. Note that the ⌢ over the bar line implies a pause, but no retardation of bar 20, which, although *p,* must be as nervous as the preceding music. Observe exactly the rests, the staccato, and the *pp* in the ensuing section: the *cresc.* will thus be much more alarming. In bar 11 of this section, hold the E-flat and G-flat with the pedal to allow an incisive stroke on the sixteenths and eighths of the bass. The indicated rhythmic division of the thirty-seconds should be maintained, but with no accent in the progress of the downward swoop until the low A. (Bar 13 will bear a shade of delay before the attack on the high G-flat.) Play the hollow diminished sevenths of the transition *una corda,* but not melodramatically.

The *Meno mosso* has a strain of melancholy in spite of its major key; but this tone is only hinted at, even in the legato phrases. They must be scrupulously contrasted with the staccatos. Observe the high value of the slurs in bar 22.

The Coda, only four bars long, is of the extremest tension. Again, Chopin's directions, *accel. e stretto,* the two ⌢ , and the rest, mean exactly what they say. Release the pedal with the eighth rests, and pause about one beat. Play the second of the *ff* G-flats, both high and low, with terrible force, waiting (with pedal) on the quarter note, G-flat, until the *pp* recitation can be delivered with appropriate pathos.

Op. 40, No. 1, the "Military" Polonaise, is too familiar to require much comment. It has a few difficult spots (for instance, the last four sixteenths in bars 1 and 3), but it is more tiring than difficult. Make "two" in bar 1 lighter than "one" (and similarly throughout similar phrases), else you will have nothing but noise. In the D major section, Chopin wrote a most significant slur from the high D down to the low one (bars 1–2)—and then contradicted it with a pedal mark. We think it best to observe the staccato phrase end, with a strong accent on the following half note. In the ensuing section, do not misread the thirty-seconds in bars 1 and 3 as appearing also in bars 5 and 7.

The *C minor Polonaise,* Op. 40, No. 2, is much easier to play, and is in many ways a noble and affecting piece. It seems to us, however, that the opening strain of the A-flat section is so lush as to be out of character with the rest.

The next, the great *Polonaise in F-sharp minor,* Op. 44, would have stood as the most imposing contribution to this form if it had not been overshadowed by Op. 53. Its difficulties are not so much in the way of unusual technical demands as in its requirement of a degree of strength which only the most robust possess. Its mood (save for the high contrast of the middle section) is the gloom characteristic of the F-sharp minor key, and is otherwise unrelieved (D-flat major is only the enharmonic of the dominant of F-sharp minor). The Mazurka's quarter notes are equal in time to the eighths of the Polonaise proper (*doppio movimento*), and there is a curiously piquant quality in this fragile melody in contrast to the stern stuff that surrounds it.

It is probably needless—in view of the vogue with which the jazz bands have endowed it—to speak of the great *Polonaise in A-flat* at any length. Brilliant and stimulating, where the F-sharp minor is morose and almost depressing, this piece has not only every quality requisite for popularity but also most of the virtues of permanently appealing work. Taken at the intended tempo (Chopin was distressed, even in his day, by the "speed-bugs") the piece is less difficult than it sounds. Though it is possible (and profitable) to play it in a forbiddingly difficult way, it is legitimately within the right of every student of reasonable advancement to try his hand at it. We shall offer but few comments.

Release the pedal precisely at "two" in bar 1, and similar passages, to mark the rhythmic beat, and continue in the indicated tempo. Beware the whole-step progression in bar 9, from F to G—it is in the highest voice only. Observe the ⏤ marked in phrase after phrase of the main theme (to pound the "two" will destroy its characteristic exuberance), and reduce the octaves, E-flat–A-flat, staccato, to *mf* so that the two sixteenths may increase to a vivid "one" in the next bar. Play the grace note, bar 18, virtually simultaneously with the following F (not as a thirty-second preceding it). But the  〰

in bar 27 will almost inevitably become a triplet of thirty-seconds, in the time of the sixteenths. Begin the scale (30) on "two" and piano, and sharpen the articulation as you reach the top. (Begin that in bar 46 a half beat earlier.) In bars 39–40, be careful to fit the left-hand sixteenths and the right-hand thirty-seconds exactly into the rhythm—it is easier said than done.

Some students have to be cautioned not to turn the eighths, D-flat–D-natural, in bar 52 into sixteenths. Do not hasten the speed at bar 57. Rather, intensify the proud rhythm of the underlying chords. Take the high B-flat on "two" in bar 80 with the left hand, for adequate force.

Properly, the tempo does not change with the E major section; but many pianists increase the speed here—greatly to the detriment of the melody, to which the stunning octaves are, after all, only an accompaniment. The left wrist, for these octaves, cannot possibly be the fulcrum. Instead, it will become stiffer as the tone increases, and the motion of the hand, once the passage has become shaped in the muscles, will be found to come almost wholly from the elbow and the shoulder. (Busoni used to rewrite the left hand against the chords in bars 20–22, continuing the octave figure in one tremendous crescendo throughout the whole passage. The effect was of course overwhelming; but it has not been much emulated.) The ensuing fluid episode (bar 11 after the change of signature) will seem irrelevant only to those who do not recognize the need for a period of relaxation after such tensions as are here exhibited—or to those who try to exaggerate the contrast by sentimentalizing this episode. Note that in the last beat of the fourth bar from the end there is the rhythmic equivalent of four sixteenths—not of a dotted sixteenth followed by a thirty-second.

The *Polonaise-Fantaisie,* Op. 61, although made by the exercise of mature artistry, seems at the present time artificial and essentially cold. The three Polonaises in Op. 71 are posthumous works, written in 1827–28–29. They have the *da capo* form of the *C-sharp minor Polonaise,* and are of interest rather to one who is searching for minute details of style than to the music lover who seeks more immediate stimulation. We may therefore turn from this form, which, although of high interest, is not the most adequate vehicle for Chopin's individual genius, to:

### · The Préludes

In no other collection of pieces—not even in the *Études,* where he could ignore the question of difficulty—did Chopin reveal his artistic self as fully as in the twenty-four *Préludes,* Op. 28. The title, *Préludes,* has of course quite another implication than in Bach's *Well-tempered Clavichord,* where it signifies an actual introduction. Yet many of the pieces, by their very brevity in proportion to the weight of their thought, leave the hearer with a sense of expectancy, and are in that sense preludes to reflection; and it may thus be said that Chopin has given a new meaning to the word—a meaning that other composers, often at a loss for titles, have been glad to adopt. Several of these Préludes are quite within the technical skill of the amateur. Others are of extreme difficulty. Their imaginative interest, however, is quite independent of their technical demand; and we shall find a good many of them of high importance for the purpose of this book.

No. 1, in C, reveals a momentary spurt of passion, caught at its very summit, and brought to an end almost before we have had time to realize its character. Hence it is often played twice through; but to us this seems a more than doubtful experiment. The sense that a feeling has been caught on the wing is quite lost.

Note that the rhythm is two triplets of sixteenths in 2–8 time. The bass, therefore, must give an unmistakable "one," and the crisis, in each figure, comes not on the first note of the right hand, but on the third—i.e., on "two"—with a slight diminution to the final sixteenth. This puts no slight burden on the little finger, for each bar must have the contour ⟍ ⟋ , yet so discreetly marked that the larger contour of each long phrase, up to the climax in bar 20, is fully perceived. Observe that the melodic phrase in bars 24–25 begins on the beat—a most ingenious device for subduing the excitement; for the syncopation, resumed in bar 26, can now be made gentle and evanescent.

The harmony of No. 2 was in its day (and even now almost remains) ultramodern. That the essential figure in the accompaniment is B–A-sharp–B–G, and so on, is shown by the notation only in the first two bars; but this strangely tortured curve is of course implied throughout. Its gloom, however, will be dissipated if this line is made too clear against the harmony. The successive dissonances yield a subtle flux of intensity—alleviated in bars 6–7 after the accumulation of bar 5, but increasing to a sharper bitterness in bar 11, and even gaining, in spite of the *dim.*, an added measure of awe as the inevitable end approaches. The actual melody, whose brief phrases eventuate in the inexorable repeated notes, must be in sharper focus than the writhing phrase of the accompaniment. Nowhere in music, unless in Schubert's *Doppelgänger,* can one find so concise an epitome of nameless fear.

No. 3 has a left-hand figure more difficult to master—but of course less fatiguing—than the "Revolutionary" Étude. The melody is all too likely to be ignored in the player's absorption with this figure. The rests, in the rising line, imply a lilt in the melodic motion which will bear a good deal of separate study. The sustained legato of the descent (bars 5–6) is pointless without this approach. This is even more true of bar 16f.

No. 4 is easier to interpret than No. 2, but it is by no means an elementary piece. The immobility of the melody requires both subtle shading and a more definite punctuation than is indicated by the composer's ten-bar slur. Give the hint of a new phrase with the B-flat in bar 4, and the G-sharp in bar 8. Even so, the melody will have little meaning without equally subtle management of the harmony. Pedal, throughout, all repetitions of the same chord, and allow the repetitions, after the first, merely to throb with the same harmonic sound. But whenever a chord changes (e.g., E-flat, bar 2; F, D, and G-sharp, bar 3), be sure that the new tone colors the throbbing sequence. Observe the ⌒ over the rest, and do not in the least "roll" the three final chords.

No. 5, very characteristic of Chopin, is also very difficult, especially for the left hand, which may easily lose dynamic control of the extended figures. The syncopation in bar 1 must not be allowed to suggest duple rhythm (6–16). Stress the first G in the left hand, and the E in the right, enough to mark these notes as not the weak notes of triplets; for unless the accented B is heard against the true measure accent there will be no syncopation. The twinkling of the figures from bar 5, likewise, will not "come off" until you can trip over the notes quite nonchalantly.

No. 6 is almost certainly the Prélude with which the title "Raindrop" ought to be associated—if, indeed, there is any historic justification for that association. Its grief is more sonorous than that of No. 4; but in neither piece do we find that conscious parade of sentiment which sometimes makes the Nocturnes repellent. The melody must of course suggest the 'cello. Its dynamic curve is so wide that it seems to us impossible to continue very long the *sotto voce* of the opening. Do not minimize the melodic phrase in the right hand in bars 6–8. The rhythmic insistence of bar 13 certainly demands a full tone, with the E–F-sharp of bar 15 *una corda* and slightly extended in rubato. The three accents on the B's in the right hand are doubtless intended to apply throughout the piece. The dynamic difference here indicated is difficult to produce, but of high import for the whole thought.

No. 7 is a Mazurka in miniature. The gentle grace of its motion is (to our ears) often spoiled by a too slow tempo. *Andantino* does not mean *Adagio*. Do not make of the third repeated chord a dull reiteration of two already burdened steps. Take those steps rather on tiptoe, and put your heel down softly on the third one. The sprawled chord in bar 12 is impossible for most players with Chopin's fingering (thumb on both A-sharp and C-sharp). Rather omit the low A-sharp than weaken the rhythm by rolling the chord. Make the retardation at the end all but imperceptible.

No. 8, in F-sharp minor, is the least suggestive of the title, *Prélude,* of all the pieces so far encountered. It is described by Niecks as depicting anxiety and agitation; but these words, in our opinion, imply more of pain than is actually set forth. There is passion, in abundance; but its sweep—maintained through 32 bars by four times that number of identical rhythmic figures—seems to us akin to what Schumann called *Aufschwung*. The direction, *molto agitato e stretto,* in bar 20 is rather an effect gained by contrast with the preceding ritenuto than the great increase in speed which the words imply.

No. 9, for most students, is not immediately attractive—probably because, by comparison with most of Chopin's pieces, its melody lacks all suavity of curve. But if the accompanying triplets, without overbearing the stately march of the melody, are kept firm and inexorable, this piece can be profoundly impressive. The least departure from the solid rhythm (unless at the return to E major, bar 8) will be ruinous.

No. 10 is a kind of will-o'-the-wisp, not very hard to play or remember, nor—when the piquancy of its one little figure has become a little worn—very interesting.

No. 11, on the other hand, has a peculiar daintiness which will probably retain its charm long after the considerable technical difficulties have been mastered. The problem is to maintain the fluidity of the motion (which must not be too swift) while the articulation remains clear and scintillant. The reader will long since have discovered that the secret of fluidity lies in smooth dynamic gradation. The very subtle gradations here required are by no means easy to attain. Do not be misled by the recitative-like appearance of the close. The composer marked no *rit.* and none is desirable.

No. 12 seems to us to be agitated in exactly the sense of Niecks's comment on No. 8. It is so difficult that it is usually abandoned by all but the most skilful; but even though it be only partially mastered, it is an excellent study. Attack the first eighth in each beat with a slight drop of the wrist. If the finger which is to take the next eighth note is at the same time shaped for its attack, the stroke can be made—almost completely, and with little effort— by the lifting of the wrist, which of itself drives the shaped finger downward.

No. 13 tempers its warmth and quietude with a certain melancholy. The piece is by no means hard to play, but one should not make it easier than it is by delegating to the right foot that whole problem of legato which belongs to the left hand. Note that although the fifth eighth note of each figure is usually the weightiest, there are other notes, not always in similar places in the figure, which have considerable harmonic value. Only when these values are realized will the long notes of the melody assume their full interest; but these, of course, must also be appropriately graduated.

No. 14 seems like a preliminary study for the last movement of the *B-flat minor Sonata,* Op. 35. At a first reading, you may discover neither melody nor harmony; but both will emerge, with practice, and yield an extraordinarily suggestive thought. To make the two parts coincide in every detail is also a valuable discipline for the fingers.

We have already studied the first eight bars of No. 15 very minutely. The rest of the first section will follow by analogy. Some intemperate performers make the C-sharp minor section absurd by taking, suddenly, a much faster tempo. The composer gave no sign for this, nor is there any justification for it. An imperceptible hastening of the repetition (from bar 17) may be tolerated, but to make the excitement hysterical will ruin the whole psychology of the piece.

Contrary to the usual fashion with repeated notes, the G-sharps, even more than the preceding A-flats, need to be even, monotonous, and increasingly threatening; but they must not override the melody, which is in the upper voice of the left hand. It should not be—but it often is—necessary to point out that the bass of the first beat in bar 2 of the C-sharp minor section is D-sharp, not C-sharp. The melody at bar 35 (D-sharp, C-sharp, C-sharp, B-sharp) and at bar 37 (D-sharp, E, C-sharp, and so on) must override the other right-hand notes— not an easy task. Difficult to produce at the right value is also the dissonance of G-sharp–A in bar 44, and the "dying fall" of the three-note phrases with which the section ends. Do not sob over the return to the opening melody. It offers, indeed, but a meager measure of relief; but after the terror of the middle section, it is enough. Do not, either, make elaborate drama out of the recitative, even though to contrive a convincing dynamic shading without tempo rubato will cost you much study. We think it well to keep the A-flat in the final chord still perceptible as the significant monotone it has been, throughout.

No. 16, in B-flat minor, is so difficult that we shall offer no comment beyond a high appreciation of its brilliant vitality. None of the Études, probably, is more difficult.

With No. 17, on the other hand, the moderately skilful may cope. The uncomfortable entangling of the hands will seem, at first, like a needless burden; but when you find the colors growing richer, at bar 19, you will see that Chopin's demand is justified. The variety of harmonic suspense in this and the corresponding episode (43f.) is undiscoverable in any earlier music.

The counter-melody at bar 20f. should be brought out more by the thumb than by the little finger of the left hand. Be sure to realize fully the C-natural against the A-sharp in bar 22, and the B–A-sharp in the left hand in 24; and in the similar passages following, study the similar values. In the *ff,* bar 35, use only such intensity as will allow the melody to keep its curve. Soften perceptibly the second note of the melody in the beautiful sequential passage, bars 51–53, and contrive to keep the G-natural audible against its fascinating harmony as it moves to A-flat in bar 55. The *fz* A-flats from bar 65 should be kept at a single, unchanging loudness, while the melody pursues its way as if unconscious of their ringing. How loud they are to be you can determine only by experiment. They are so weighty that a little space of time beyond their strict value may be allowed them.

No. 18, which at the very outset is cast in a vein of high excitement, reveals before the end the superficiality of its mood. The ejaculatory style is easy enough to catch, though the notes themselves are not easy to play. But the piece contains little nourishment for the spirit.

No. 19 is probably the most difficult of all—quite beyond the powers of any but the most gifted student. Nothing in all Chopin illustrates so well the unheard-of flexibility of wrist which was the most novel feature, in his time, of his manner of playing. Older pianists, like Moscheles, and many younger ones, such as even Mendelssohn, found his demands beyond their powers. It is a pity that this piece is not more accessible, for it is one of the most sanely joyous utterances in the literature of the instrument.

The melody obviously lies in the first notes of the triplets in the right hand, and the phrasing, although not indicated, is unmistakable. The right hand will group the notes as they are printed—that is, the second and third eighths of each triplet "go with" the first. But this is not so in the left hand, where the second note of each triplet begins the group and the first note of the next completes it—the longest leaps thus lying, not within the groups but between them, so that each group thus consists of three notes all in downward motion. To group the right-hand figures thus would be to increase their range, which is mostly within the octave, and so to make a needless difficulty. But at best this piece poses a tremendous technical problem.

No. 20 is surely one of the most trenchant epigrams in musical literature. Like any verbal epigram, it can become stale if it is too often repeated; but the fault is with the hearer, not with the idea. Although the stress in each one-bar phrase is on the third beat, the *ff* at the beginning suffices to prevent our understanding the "three" as if it were "one." No more than *p* and *pp* for the second and third four-bar groups seems to have been indicated by the composer, and these seem to us the best guide to the composer's intention, though a slight crescendo toward the end is in keeping with the dignity of the music. It helps also toward solving the problem of the final chord, which is offensive if too loud, and flabby if too soft. (Do not misread the final E in bar 3 as E-flat.)

No. 21 is amiable and colorful, but familiarity usually makes it appear somewhat overwarm. It is quite easy to play, once the wedge-shaped figures of accompaniment are mastered. In bar 13 from the end the last note is G-flat, not G-natural.

No. 22, although very difficult, offers irresistible temptation to energetic temperaments. To shape the bass effectively, make its phrases two bars long, with the second a little weaker than the first, up to bar 15. Begin the high D-flats (17) about *mf*, with the crisis on the ensuing C, and diminish as you descend. (The persistent *ff* is impossible for any but pianistic giants, and is also nearly meaningless.) Do not ignore the right hand, whose upper notes, carefully shaped according to the prescribed ➤, are indispensable to the sense of the lower line. The little finger must far override the thumb if their full value is to be squeezed out of these notes.

No. 23 is a perfect embodiment of the ineffable charm which the poets are always praising in music. But you will make of it little save a superficial glitter if you ignore (as Cortot and many other virtuosi do) the tempo mark, *Moderato*. Every note in the chain of incessant sixteenths must not only be audible but must exhibit a delicate ecstasy of motion, always perfectly sure where it is going, but having no earthly reason for going there save that there is an infinite delight in it. There must be no haste, nor any sentimental rubato; but unless you contrive, within the limit of piano (which is never exceeded), the most subtle dynamic contour for your line, you will turn a miracle into a mere manipulation. The trills in the left hand must only murmur as they give rise to the ensuing curve. In bar 3, the left hand must articulate precisely with the right. "Squeeze" slightly the dominant sevenths on the last half of beats 2 and 4, and also, in bar 4, the diminished thirds (B-flat–G-sharp) with their attendant notes. At bar 18, in spite of the eighth note, A, and the rest thereafter, we make the following G of the right hand into a continuation of the melodic phrase. The E-flat in the last bar but one continues exquisitely the motility of the whole piece into the silence of its unfinished close.

No. 24 offers a compelling portrayal of a mind in a legitimate frenzy. There is not a superfluous note, nor a phrase out of drawing, nor an instant of aberration from the point at issue. Not even Beethoven, who always finds the simplest terms for the most cogent thoughts, can speak more directly to his purpose. Even his eyes seldom blaze more resentfully.

It is of course very hard to play. Again we feel that there is danger of too swift a pace. The figure of accompaniment culminates on the eighth note, but unless the preceding sixteenths are articulate the whole incisive figure becomes a confused noise. Also, the swoops of scale and arpeggio, in a reasonable tempo, can be played without distorting the inexorable rhythm; but if the motion has to be retarded, these passages become rhetorical and empty. How threatening, after the continued forte is the sudden piano on the strained interval of the augmented fifth; and how alarmingly the drive of the theme is intensified by the ensuing octaves! The descending run in thirds seems as if it must be the ultimate climax; but it is only the beginning of the end. Give especial emphasis to the G-sharps against the high F's with which the descending arpeggios at the end begin. (Their meaning is really that of an augmented sixth against a B-flat which is only implied. The G-natural in the passage is an interesting defiance of contemporary harmonic convention.) The D's at the end are cataclysmic—all the more so because they re-echo those upon which the preceding passages have ended so defiantly. They have their full effect only on a concert grand piano.

The twenty-four *Préludes* were published in 1839. Two years later, Chopin published, as Op. 45, a single piece with the same title. It is exquisitely dressed in harmonies which, at that date, no other composer in the world could have invented. The tone is somewhat nocturnal, the melodic phrases being all of a questioning, indecisive design. But one must put oneself back into the days when romanticism was unchallenged if one is to enjoy its delicate flavor. The cadenza is nevertheless an extraordinary patch of harmonic color. (Obviously, only well-trained fingers can strike all these notes with the requisite delicacy, and precisely together; but without this delicacy and precision there is only the effect of spilled water colors.)

## The Impromptus

Chopin left four Impromptus, one of which, the *Fantaisie-Impromptu*—written in 1834, but thought by the composer to be unworthy of publication—has attained a posthumous popularity greater than any of the others. That which is called the First— the *Impromptu in A-flat*— was "propagandized" by George du Maurier in his famous novel, *Trilby,* in which the heroine, under the hypnotic spell of an evil genius, who bore a considerable physical resemblance to Paganini, was enabled to sing this purely pianistic piece. This all happened before the day of the jazz hound, however, and even Svengali would have scorned to devote the music of an artist to the pedestrian pursuit of an erotic rainbow.

The Impromptus are by no means Chopin's finest efforts. The "Trilby" piece (Op. 29), for those who can manage its rather formidable difficulties, is an agreeable adventure in pianism. It is much more coherent in structure, but intrinsically less imaginative, than the Second, in F-sharp, which was once by far the most popular of the lot. Its pensive opening figure, in the left hand, generates after a few bars a more lyrical strain, the very epitome of the romanticism of the 1830's. There is high contrast in the insistent rhythm of the D major section, and a remarkably "modern" modulation into F major, where a triplet figure (an elaboration of the opening) accompanies the return of the main theme. This melody, however, after modulating colorfully back into its original key, is dissipated in a passage of swifter figurations, with a sustained line (hardly a melody) in the left hand. The first six bars of this are forte; the repetition is piano. The contrast is very difficult to manage, since the leggierissimo thirty-seconds are easily smeared by the pedal, but the sustained line in the left hand (not conspicuous in the forte passage) is hard to design, along with a sufficient harmonic substance, without the pedal.

The *Third Impromptu* (in G-flat, Op. 51) begins with an apparent allusion to the opening of Op. 29—for what reason, we cannot discover. It is more difficult than the earlier piece, but—as with many of the later works of Chopin—its more sophisticated structure cannot disguise its rather commonplace substance. The *Fantaisie-Impromptu* is much the easiest of all, except that the Coda does considerably tax the little finger of the right hand. The problem of four against three which is so largely exemplified is exceptionally easy to handle here, so that those who are bothered by that problem may well take this as an exercise. (Two against three may be similarly easily mastered in the middle part.)

## *The Sonatas*

The form of the sonata was naturally uncongenial to the fanciful mind of Chopin. He wrote one early example (Op. 4, published posthumously) which is a fairly remarkable work for a boy of eighteen, but by no means represents the best of which he was capable, at that age. Only in the *Minuet* (where the device of imitation plays a rather uncertain rôle) and in the *Larghetto,* which is a not unsuccessful venture into the then unusual rhythm of five beats to the measure, does he seem at all free of the burden of form.

Op. 35, in B-flat minor, however, whose slow movement (the famous *Funeral March*) is familiar to the whole world, is a very different matter. It has been vehemently praised by many, and as vehemently condemned by others; but it cannot be ignored. It is extremely difficult, so that minute discussion of its problems is hardly within the scope of this book; but some comment is demanded.

After four obscure and somber bars, a nervous rhythm is generated, and in due course a still more nervous principal theme— the very counterpart of almost uncontrollable agitation. Seldom indeed can such high excitement as this be embodied successfully in the principal theme of a sonata form. For a sonata theme must

undergo the test of development; and if it cannot be made to grow
in meaning and intensity, the failure of the movement is assured.
Chopin's theme, in this prospect, is unpromising; but it seems to
us that he solves his problem successfully, and even brilliantly.

The composer's pedal marks are irreconcilable with the notation of
the musical thought. Even the four preparatory measures seem to
us to require clear articulation, rather than the incoherent murmur
which the continuous pedal produces; and the theme itself, blurred
and mumbled by the pedal for three bars, becomes a sample of mere
impressionism—quite the opposite of what the notation of the music
suggests. Nor is it of any advantage to murmur the beginning of the
theme in order that its higher reaches may be made vivid. You have
every right to dislike the musical idea as something overwrought and
almost hysterical; but you cannot remedy the fault—if you take it as
that—by minimizing its vividness.

It is perfectly in character to have the second subject appear after
no more than four bars of transition (33–36). Nor is that subject irrelevant to the picture. Its pathos is indeed self-conscious, but its
decency—considering the provocation to pathos—is remarkable, and the
continuation (the succession of chords in triplets of quarters) offers
sufficient variety and a sufficient increase of harmonic intensity to
bring the exposition to a convincing close. The development is so
wholly related to the principal theme (although a counter-strain, related both to the introduction and to the second subject is provided)
that it would have been the height of absurdity to begin the recapitulation with the original version of the main theme. Hence the recapitulation begins with the second subject—a structural error, if it be one,
which Beethoven also committed, for a similar reason, in Op. 31, No. 2.
The brief Coda is wholly appropriate.

The *Scherzo* had to follow the first movement, if the *Funeral March*
was to be followed by the ghastly *Finale*. This sequence puts a considerable burden on both performer and listener—and was doubtless a
burden to the composer. Chopin's solution of the problem would have
been brilliant if he had not been misled into composing the sentimental
*Trio,* which has a feeble amiability, almost as inappropriate to the
nervous excitement of the *Scherzo* itself as is the *Trio* to the *Funeral
March.* The pedal marks, in the opening of the *Scherzo,* are again
contrary to the notes. The accent on the quarter note, E-flat, in bar 1,

is practically the equivalent of a slur from that note to the ensuing F, which is marked staccato. The pedal on that F, however, destroys the incisiveness of the whole phrase. Otherwise, the sense of the music is unmistakably indicated. But it requires no mean technical power to produce it.

One has only to compare the *Funeral March* in this sonata to that in Beethoven's Op. 26 to see that there is here a personality of far less weight. Not the dignity of death is celebrated, nor the fortitude with which the brave confront it. There is instead a frail abandonment to the luxury of tears. Yet Chopin's management of the hypnotic power of monotony (in the incessant alternation of the two chords in the bass) is dreadfully effective. The *Trio* has been recognized from the first, by all who are not the slaves of sentimentality, as pitifully inappropriate. We only wish it were merely that; for to us the *Trio* seems to bring to the surface the spiritual weakness which is implicit in the March itself.

The *Finale* is a tour de force. Pianistically, it reveals a possibility of color never before imagined, unless in the *Prélude, No. 14*. Harmonically, there is weirdness which sometimes (bars 21–23), as an evocation of the spirit of evil, seems to us more vivid than anything which Berlioz (who dearly loved to conjure up devils) could imagine. Our readers are not likely to play this piece too fast; but there is a recording which quite obscures the fact that there are twelve eighth notes in every bar.

The *Sonata in B minor,* Op. 58, was written in 1844, six years after the B-flat minor. Its first movement is more diffuse than one would expect, after the conciseness of Op. 35; but this piece is driven by no such compulsion as the former one. The technical demands are at least as great, but the impression it leaves is hardly one of spiritual satisfaction. Beethoven might have been able to strike developmental fire out of the principal subject. Chopin can only manipulate it. The second subject is no more poetic than the weakest of the Nocturnes, so that the chief interest lies in the connecting passages, which are often exciting in themselves, but contribute little to the whole thought. The *Scherzo* has neither humor nor any stern irony, but is merely graceful; neither can the *Largo* be saved from banality by the few genuinely human impulses in the E major section. The *Finale,* however, a sort of Tarantelle, comes to life—too late, unfortunately, to resuscitate the other movements. This is a sonata for the virtuosi—not for the lover of music.

## The Berceuse, the Barcarolle, the F-Minor Fantaisie

Three large pieces, not in those genres in which we have found most of Chopin's compositions to be cast, remain to be considered. All three are of consummate technical artistry, but only one of them appears to survive in the affection of the general music lover.

The *Berceuse,* Op. 57, is an amazing harmonic feat. The figure of accompaniment, sounded as prelude for two bars, persists throughout the piece with not only its initial note, D-flat, but— until sixteen bars from the end—the simple foundation of tonic and dominant harmonies, essentially unaltered. Over this quietly rocking figure a fluid strain of melody begins:.a phrase without an end, which at first repeats itself with ever-softening cushions of harmony about it, and then dissolves into a variety of arabesques, so exquisite in their sonority and so varied in their color as to make us quite forget that melody has disappeared. Only at the very end does the real melody recur; but we are not disappointed, for it was long since evident that in this regal cradle there was never a baby at all. (If you are unconvinced, compare this piece with Schumann's *Kind im Einschlummern* from the *Scenes from Childhood.*)

Similarly unreal, but of even greater brilliancy in its accomplishment of a difficult feat, is the *Barcarolle,* Op. 60. The difficulties to be surmounted by the performer are here very great, but the reward is hardly proportionate, even though, in the Coda, there is a patch of sequential harmony whose like no one had invented, up to that day. The whole impression is too sumptuous for association with the lazy undulations of a pleasure boat and the unconventional garb of its occupants.

These two pieces illustrate a tendency that we have already often remarked in Chopin's work—one that is the product, as we see it, of his increasing isolation from the active world of music, and his preoccupation, not primarily with problems of technique, but with the cultivating of those refinements in tonal sensation to which, by his very nature, he was abnormally sensitive. His withdrawal was in part compelled by his frail health; but it was also an inevitable product of his temperament. Yet, although we cannot give unqualified praise to those overrefined works which came forth from his ivory tower, we must remember that it was that same unique sensibility which was the source of the more virile pieces that contributed so much to the true literature of the piano.

One later work, indeed—the *Fantaisie in F minor*—demonstrates a considerable survival of his powers. We may close our study of Chopin with a fairly minute examination of it.

Although its form, after the first third of the design has been completed, is mostly filled out by repetitions, the matter is all of Chopin's best, and the repetitions, appropriately colored by transposition, are consequently not tedious. The music has much of the character of the Ballades, a sense of narrative being almost constantly present; but there is no more need to invent a story of our own than to accept, as a program for the piece, the preposterous notion (apparently fathered by Liszt) that the music originated in a quarrel and a reconciliation between the composer and George Sand. The music is on the level of the most sensitive poetry of the romantic period; it arouses in us the same tensions and excitements which it is the purpose of that poetry to evoke; but the music is a sufficient vehicle for the conveyance of this feeling-character, and any concrete narrative, instead of being a help, would be only a hindrance to our understanding.

The *Fantaisie* begins with a quiet march rhythm. The first low phrase, unharmonized and somber, comes to a halt and is answered by another tranquil strain in the high register; but from this strain all trace of somberness has disappeared. The intriguing antiphony, which betrays no sense of conflict, in spite of the opposite character of the phrases, is continuously removed from the initial darkness by remote modulations into warmer and warmer harmonies, which, nevertheless, are always adroitly brought back to the original tone center of F minor. At length the march disintegrates into an arpeggiated figure whose curve presents no more than a hint of melody, but which, gradually hastened, prepares for the passionate utterances that form the main matter of the discourse. The first of these (bar 73) seems, even as it appears, to have been long since begun, so that its turbulent syncopation needs but five bars in which to reveal the character of its excitement. Four more measures suffice to introduce a contrast as great as that which we noted in the march—a theme with wings, if ever there was one, that glides and spirals in an ecstasy as joyous as the former strain was urgent. The swirling arpeggiations that follow (bar 85f.) maintain this new elation without insistence on the theme itself. (We have met with the same device in the *Ballade in G minor*.) The excitement, however, instead of relaxing, builds up still higher, so that the actual climax is not a single moment of crisis, but a passage of considerable breadth (bars 109–126). This leads, without transition, to another march tune—appropriate, perhaps by association with the opening strain of the *Fantaisie*, but quite unrelated to it in substance.

What follows is repetition of matter already familiar, with the swirling figures now leading to a dwindling reminiscence of the passages that woke the original *Tempo di Marcia* to life. Three descending octaves (already heard in a more intense context) introduce a singularly appealing *Lento sostenuto*—a melody in Chopin's highest vein of seriousness, quite underived from any of the earlier matter, but perfectly in the imaginative character already set forth. The spell is rudely interrupted by a recall of the swirling figures, and what follows is again a repetition, with some rearrangement, and an excited hastening of the gayer march tune.

There is then a brief reference to the *Lento,* and, for Coda, a sound-effect made of the swirling figures. Appropriately to the general character of the piece, the close is not in F minor, but in A-flat major.

To realize the quiet solemnity of the opening march, be sure that the staccato eighth notes, C, B-flat, A-flat, are softer than the preceding quarters. The high register of bars 3-4 must be emphasized by clear tone in the melody and a considerably softened accompaniment. Lead the C's at "one" in bar 5 legato to the low C's on "two" to re-establish the march rhythm. (This, of course, by means of the pedal.) Bring out the bass in bars 8-10, but do not ignore the upper voice as you do so. The C-flat in bar 12 is so significant, harmonically, that it may be a little elongated. The repetitions of the new melodic strain that appears in bar 21 should reach their greatest warmth of tone in bar 25. (One way to achieve this effect is to give these last phrases a somewhat thicker bass.) Study carefully the charming brightening of the color in bar 27. The *fzp* (or its equivalent) appearing in many editions in bars 37 and 39 is apparently not autographic, though it is appropriate, if not overdone.

The 2-2 time, indicated in most editions at bar 43, is attained, according to most editors, only gradually (*poco a poco doppio movimento*). Joseffy omits the indication, but the passage is obviously constructed on this implication. Elongate slightly the last triplet before the chord bearing the ⌒, counting out the full time of that chord in this retarded tempo. The true accelerando will therefore really begin at bar 47, with bars 54 and 56 taken somewhat faster than bar 43.

The syncopations from bar 68 are sometimes hard to manage against the triplet accompaniment. If so, omit for a time the two last notes of each triplet, playing only the notes that fall on the beat. You will soon gain an unshakable certainty of the basic rhythm, and will be able to add the omitted notes without difficulty. Curve the figures in thirds (bar 73f.) by shading dynamically up to the "one." The new melody at bar 77 is marked *p* in most editions, but there is little doubt that this is an editorial addition. Even so, it is a fair question whether Chopin meant this new strain to be taken forte, or neglected to insert the mark for piano. Since this melody appears three times in the *Fantaisie,* we compromise by taking it twice in piano, but the third time make a crescendo in the approaching bar, and play with the fullest sonority compatible with appropriate dynamic shading. The swirling figures (bar 85f.) will in any event be taken forte, for the following passionate phrase (bar 93), unless so approached, will lose half its vitality. The two-note groups, beginning in bar 95, should be so phrased as to fall into groups of two beats—two-*three,* four-*one,* and so on, and this same phrasing should be continued throughout the whole ensuing passage (101–109).

The passage of divergent octaves (109) is less difficult than it looks. The right hand is relatively easy, since it moves only in one direction —continually upwards. The left hand, which goes upward as well as downward, is harder. To master it, delay a little the speed of the upward F-sharp–G, measuring the downward arpeggio thereafter as if it contained no D-natural. When once you can continue this essentially downward progression to its end, you will find that you can insert the D without feeling that you have had to change the downward motion; for the distance is only a half step. The black keys, in either hand, give you secure location, and you will soon find that, with a slightly cautious beginning, the whole passage will come off triumphantly.

The *fz* chord in bar 119 falls on the half note in the middle of the bar. In the parallel passage (bar 64 after the *Lento*), older editions give the same notation except that the first note is an eighth. Joseffy and the more modern editors, however, put the chord after an eighth rest only—i.e., a quarter note earlier, with the half notes of the chord dotted. This is doubtless the correct reading and is palpably more intense. In bars 124–5, the inner voice of the right hand (D-flat, C, B-flat) should be clearly audible against the rising notes of the bass to give full meaning to the reiterated A-flat's of the highest part.

The new march melody (bar 127f.) must be kept legato, and its accompaniment rigorously staccato, throughout. (In the parallel passage, later, the hastened tempo ultimately makes the effect impossible, and the composer has consequently modified his notation.) The pedal must not be touched. Black keys, in the melody, can be taken with the 4th or the 3rd finger, alternating with the 5th on the white keys; but where two white keys occur in succession, the weighted 5th finger, with a little practice, can learn to attack the second key with what is so nearly a glide that the legato will not be perceptibly broken.

In the *Lento sostenuto,* study the dynamic contour of the melody with extreme care, modeling your design after the image of the singing voice. The danger of wooden thumping is greatest from bar 9, where there is for a long time no division of the beat. We feel that a slight hastening of the tempo from bar 12 to bar 15, with a compensating retard in bar 16, is a justifiable aid toward the solution of the problem. Most editions, at bar 22, divide the first beat into two eighth notes, G-sharp and F-sharp. Joseffy indicates as preferable the G-sharp as a quarter note; and to us this avoidance of sentimentality is commendable.

In that reminiscence of the *Lento,* near the end, which is marked *Adagio sostenuto,* the three eighth notes in the figures of the short recitative are often marked (and more often played) as triplets—i.e., with a slight accent on the first of the three notes. The eighth rests preceding (in all editions) belie this reading. To us, the triplets, by comparison with the even eighths (of which, then, the second will receive the slight stress) seem weak and undignified.

The *assai allegro* which indicates the speed of the brief Coda is probably intended as the equivalent of the *doppio movimento* finally attained at the *agitato* marked at bar 68 from the beginning. It is doubtless not intended that the figures should be clearly articulated, but that there should be a kind of orchestral swelling and diminution of the final A-flat chord.

# 11

# JOHANNES BRAHMS —
# THE EARLIER WORKS

WE turn now to music which is generally regarded as far more "intellectual" than that of Chopin. That word need not be—though it often is—alarming to the average music lover. For it implies, not that the music of Brahms is obscure, or repellently lofty in tone, but that it deals with emotions that are not trivial, and does not attempt to make an appeal to the senses sound like an appeal to the heart. It is true that Brahms had a great mastery of the learned processes of composition—of counterpoint and all its intricate devices; but no one (unless a sophomore pursuing his first course in musical form and analysis) would contend that music is profound merely in proportion to its intricacy. Indeed, Brahms's profoundest music is by no means his most intricate. The true measure of profundity is in terms of meaning—of reference to significant human experience—not in terms of structure.

Brahms had a deep respect for competent structure, since he found out very early that adequate expression is impossible without it; but no more than did Bach does he make snobbish display of contrapuntal tricks. He had also a healthy contempt for the display of strong emotion for which no sufficient provocation appears—for the kind of thing that sensible people call sentimentality. We are all of us, probably, sentimental about some

things, and Brahms was no exception; but he was no public purveyor of emotional intoxicants.

His was not the kind of boyhood in which such bar tending is
learned. It was, indeed, once proposed that he should be exploited
as a pianistic prodigy; but that scheme was fortunately abandoned
before it was entered upon. Although a mere tacit acceptance of
membership in the Wagner-Liszt party would have assured him
of what would now be thought quite honorable professional support, he could not conceal his aversion to the principles of that
party—and did himself serious damage by publishing his senti-
ments. Yet he had no ambition to become the accepted leader
of the opposition. Hence, when at the age of twenty he was announced to the world by Schumann as a very Messiah, come to
free the world of the sins of the "futurists," he was far more
alarmed than elated, and slackened very considerably his work
on actual composition, in order to give his time to perfecting his
technique of composition and his already remarkably mature
understanding of his art.

This step made of him, for a time, something more of a con-
servative than he already was by nature, but it did not make of
him a pedant. It only deepened his conviction—already implanted
by his teacher, Marxsen—that the essential method of classical
music was not exhausted, and that the appeal of the colorful art
of the futurists was itself in danger of that fate. His fear of
sensuous allurement was probably exaggerated, but in our
day, when Wagner and his disciple, Strauss, have largely lost
caste, Brahms still slowly climbs the heights of general popularity.

He wrote a great deal of music before composing the *Sonata
in C* which he finally published as Op. 1, and most of that music
he destroyed. Almost all that survives is the *Sonata in F-sharp
minor,* Op. 2, and the *Scherzo in E-flat minor,* Op. 4—written
when he was eighteen, and the earliest of his existing compositions. Although our interest in the *Sonata in C* is rather for what

it reveals of the mind of its youthful author than for what it excites in our own, we shall look at it somewhat closely.

We are astonished, at the beginning, by the identity in rhythm and the considerable likeness in design between the principal theme of this sonata and that of Beethoven's Op. 106. An exalted model, surely! What can he be going to say that has not already been better said on this theme? But our discomfort at the resemblance soon ceases, for even with an identical rhythm, the energy displayed by the two themes is of a different character. Two harmonies, tonic and subdominant, are hammered on in the Brahms theme, whereas in the Beethoven the tonic alone is the anvil.[1] Brahms's fondness for counterpoint is at once evident in the imitations appearing at bar 17f. After this device is abandoned, little more is needed for transition to the second subject. This theme is in the relative minor instead of the more orthodox dominant key, and consists of two different strains. The first appears with the up-beat F-sharp in bar 38; the second, in bar 51; and the first, disguised, recurs in bar 59. A swifter figure (63) seems to announce a new theme for closing subject, but instead the second strain of the second theme is used for that purpose.

That same strain, in canonic imitation, begins the development, and in one form or another the two strains of the second subject are present in most of this extended section. The principal subject, however, is combined with the second at bar 17 of the development (we count from the change of signature), and is hinted at in several other places; but it plays a minor rôle in the whole design. The recapitulation is quite orthodox, with the second subject group now in C minor, as is logical. The principal subject comes decidedly to the fore in the emphatic Coda.

The love of the straightforward melody of folk song was strong in Brahms. Although he became one of the most aristocratic of composers, he remembered without shame his plebeian youth; and

---

[1] The progression from the initial tonic to the subdominant harmony is so frequent in Brahms as to constitute a conspicuous feature of his style.

in the melody of the people he found, all his life, a sturdy virtue which—as against the pretentious trickeries often evident in the "new" music of his day—he sought to retain in his elaborated works of art. The slow movement of this sonata has, as theme, the precise transcription to the keyboard of an old German love-song, intended for a solo tenor and a male quartet. Translated, the text of the song which Brahms prints below the music runs thus:

> (Solo) With stealthy step the moon doth rise,
> (Quartet) Blue, blue little flower;
> (Solo) Through silver clouds it climbs the skies,
> (Quartet) Blue, blue little flower.
> Rose in the vale,
> Maid in the hall,
> O, loveliest Rosa!

The not very coherent sense of the words is made by the music to seem rather despondent. On this theme, Brahms writes three variations and a Coda, and the same emotional strain is pursued in the first two of the variations. The third, in C major, is brighter, but the Coda, with steps as stealthy as those ascribed in the poem to the moon, recedes into melancholy. The lowly sentiment is remarkably exalted by the variations.

The *Scherzo,* in E minor, 6–8 time, is vigorous and incisive, frankly acknowledging Beethoven as its model; but there is little if any of actual humor. The *Trio,* in 3–4 time, but faster, so that its quarters are about equal in speed to the eighths of the *Scherzo,* offers a less striking contrast than this unusual rhythmic shift would lead us to expect. The scheme of modulation is here quite adventurous, but the music is in the vein of passion rather than of humor.

The *Finale* begins with a transformation of the opening theme of the first movement into 9–8 time. What follows, after the first four bars, could be interpreted by the ear as in 6–8 time, but is really in the established 9–8. This illustrates a love for cross-rhythms which we shall find frequently exemplified in later pieces. The general form of the movement is that of the Rondo. The B subject, in G, floats its melody on an undulant left-hand figure, and pursues its quiet way for a considerable time before any intimation of excitement appears. The A subject then recurs, on the dominant of C (instead of in its original tonic tonality) and with frequent changes in its tonal base as well as alteration of its original design. The C subject, in A minor, begins in 6–8 time but includes also an episode in the former 9–8 measure. As transition to the A theme, the principal (6–8) strain of the C subject is alternated, in a kind of mild development, with the A theme. When the first subject returns complete, it is momentarily on the dominant of F. This departure from rule (the A subject, in the Rondo, conventionally always reappears in the tonic) is too mild to be called inconoclastic, but is a positive indication of an independent mind in these matters. There is a swifter Coda, whose energy is whipped up by frequent insistence on the augmented triad.

This music portrays a mind extraordinarily occupied, considering its youth, with "grown-up" ideas. It lacks neither passion nor the disposition to idealistic dreaming; but it is never loosed from its moorings by excess of intensity in either mood. It is definitely romantic, but it does not reveal the sudden flashes of improvisatory inspiration which we often found in Chopin and Schumann. It is evident that the composer, who was soon to be announced as the awaited Messiah, came not to destroy; but we are not yet certain that he will be able to fulfil.

We may forego detailed mention of Op. 2—another piano sonata, in F-sharp minor—written a year or so before Op. 1, but published with this number because the composer recognized it as of lesser value. It displays more of the brilliance of virtuosity, and less of the emotional stability that is so marked a feature of Op. 1. If we take the works in the order of their opus numbers, the next piece for piano is the *Scherzo in E-flat minor,* Op. 4, a piece that has historic as well as intrinsic interest. For it was through this Scherzo that Liszt first made acquaintance with Brahms's music. At the urgent suggestion of Joseph Joachim, but largely against his own instinct, Brahms paid a visit to Liszt at Weimar, in 1853. Too nervous to play his pieces before the great pianist, Brahms was amazed at the facility with which Liszt, at sight, read both the *Scherzo* and a part of the *C major Sonata*. But he was constantly uncomfortable in the great presence, sensing the faith of the "futurists" as incompatible with his own, and found his self-confidence as a composer not at all bolstered.[2] Thereafter came his visit to Schumann, and the famous article which Schumann published in the *Neue Zeitschrift für Musik*, praising Brahms as "the one who must come" to reveal the true path of the music of the future.

The *Scherzo*, which is less difficult than either of the sonatas, and probably retains, for the twentieth century, higher interest, was composed in 1851, and is the earliest to be completed of all Brahms's published compositions. It has two Trios, but no other unusual feature of form. Like the Scherzi in the two sonatas, this has energy and a compelling rhythmic élan. Unlike them, it has a spark—however faint—of actual humor, at the outset, where the character borders on the grotesque; but when this disappears, as it does in the Trios, the tone becomes amiable (in the first) and even passionate (in the second). There is little, however, of frank gaiety, or of the irony that is often Chopin's species of humor. Was it perhaps because he had little sense of humor

[2] William Mason, in his *Memories of a Musical Life,* describes the occasion, at which he was present. He tells of Raff's comment on a resemblance between Brahms's Scherzo and that of Chopin in B-flat minor, which somewhat offended Brahms, who had as yet never heard any of Chopin's music. Mason also relates how Brahms, during Liszt's playing of the *Sonata in B minor,* which he had recently finished (and in which the technique of the transformation of themes is carried much further than in Brahms's C major Sonata), fell sound asleep in his chair. Liszt, he says, seeing the sleeping boy, rose from the piano and left the room without a word. This story is doubted by Kalbeck, who insists that Brahms, who had been invited by Liszt as his house guest, stayed two or three weeks at Weimar.

(in music) that in the later works in sonata form, Brahms often replaced the Scherzo with an Intermezzo?

This piece is not very difficult to play. Be sure, as you begin, to give that stress to the second of the three notes in the up-beat which will keep this figure from sounding like a triplet. Count the rests between the phrases meticulously. Be sure to sustain the long B-flat (bar 10) so that its ascent in bar 12 will be that of a continuous line. You may pedal bars 17 and 18, but keep the staccato very sharp thereafter, using no pedal even in bars 21 and 22. The repeated three-note figure (23f.) is the most definitely humorous feature of the piece. Keep it clearly staccato, both here and from bar 45, where it accompanies the new legato melody. Against this same melody, which appears, staccato, against the three-note figure of bar 45 at bar 61f., the figure must be clearly distinguishable. Adequate fulness of tone at the climax (69), however, can hardly be realized without the pedal, which we depress for two beats, leaving only the "three" really staccato. This pedal is all the more needful in view of the *poco a poco più sosten.*

The C-flat in the left hand (86) may more easily be taken by the right thumb. Note, from bar 110 to 114, the augmentation of the phrase in bars 106–109. Bars 112–113 must sound like one very broad bar of three beats (with the main accent on "one") preparatory to the *sff* in 114. The *strepitoso* at 122, to our mind, must be expressed without hastening the time—by incisive clarity in the notes, and no accents during the descent, which will quite spoil its precipitousness.

*Trio I* tempts most students to a much more frequent use of the pedal than is justified. The staccato octaves in the theme need have little force, and cannot hop gayly if the pedal weights their steps. In the *scherzando* figure (9f.) note that the G-flats (bars 9 and 12) are accented, but do not apply this accent to the other up-beat quarters. Against the tied F of the *piacevole* figure (37) give weight to the F in the left hand to mark the down-beat, and then soften the rest of the phrase. (Similarly at 46f., 60, and so on.) The need for an accented B-flat to mark the beginning of the left hand in bars 63 and 69 seems to us to preclude observance of the composer's ⟨ in bars 64 and 70. From bar 122, preserve carefully the character of each of the two combined melodies. The one-bar rest after the final B-flat of the Trio completes a four-measure period; the three-bar rest following begins another rhythmic period whose fourth bar contains the up-

beat of the Scherzo proper, to which you now return, playing it without repetitions. You need not fear monotony if you have caught the
vital rhythm. The ⊕ marks the point at which *Trio II* enters.

In this Trio, the ascending bass has a counterpoint in the descending
inner notes, A-sharp, G-sharp, G-natural, F-sharp, of the chords in the
right hand, which notes must therefore be audibly marked. We play
the turns in bars 8, 14, and the like, as triplets of sixteenths (e.g., in
bar 9, C-sharp, B, A-sharp), filling the time of an eighth note only,
and leaving the following notes precisely in their indicated time. In
accompanying the ensuing melody, do not ignore the change of harmony at "three" in bars 72–73. The word *sostenuto* does not properly
mean either *ritardando* ("retarding") or *ritenuto* ("held back"—i.e.,
in a somewhat slowed-up tempo), but Brahms, in this Trio and often
elsewhere, uses it indiscriminately in either sense. At bar 56, extended
by the dashes, it obviously means "retard"; at bar 136, qualified by
*poco,* it seems to mean *ritenuto,* but the needful *a tempo* thereafter, is
missing. (We put it at bar 150.) At the end, *Più sostenuto* can mean
nothing but *meno mosso.* This is almost Brahms's only sin against
clearness.

Brahms's next work, the *Sonata in F minor,* Op. 5, is the last
of his piano sonatas. He abandoned neither the instrument as a
vehicle of expression, nor the form itself, which he used in many
chamber works; but the sonata as a solo piece no longer attracted him. He did, indeed, plan another, but it grew too big for
one performer, and, after many experiments, turned into the
great *Concerto in D minor,* Op. 15.

The F minor Sonata is definitely of higher interest than its
two predecessors. Its difficulty is great, so that we shall make no
comment on the technical problems; but we should fail in our
attempt to give, along with our study of the individual pieces,
some notion of the composer's character, if we did not call attention to its most striking features.

That character is strongly outlined in the principal theme. This
is hardly a melody, but is rather a rhythmic-harmonic outburst
of towering energy, embracing almost the whole of the keyboard
in its sweep. To this is added, in striking antithesis, a somber

strain, restricted in range to the minor sixth, and inhibited in action by the insistent rhythm of the pedal point figure in the bass. Transition begins, after recurrence of the main thought, with a combination of the two ideas—the upper part, derived from the somber phrase, being accompanied by a rhythmic figure from the opening theme. The second subject, highly introverted, is lyrical but almost static in motion. Constant modulation enhances its mounting tension.[3] The closing subject is no more than a wisp of chromatic cadence, repeated.

The development, exploiting the figure that initiated the return of the main theme after its contrast, soon abandons the vigor with which it begins. The somber strain of contrast is the topic, and this is enriched by a second melody, really a variant of the original strain, which gives an impression of high complexity if the two are kept clear against the pedal figure, now in the right hand. At bar 88 an extraordinary revery begins, sprouting from this same phrase—a long baritone melody in the purest romantic vein. The highest note in the harmony, from bar 109 on, draws a tense line of ascent which greatly heightens the harmonic color. A momentary return of the main theme is thus provided for; but it subsides into mere suggestion of this thought. The recapitulation is abbreviated by omitting the second (contrasting) strain of the principal subject, but is otherwise complete. The Coda (190) does not attempt to expand the main theme, but reaches appropriate intensity by a few incisive rhythmic strokes.[4]

[3] The *a tempo,* bar 39, implies the tempo of the piece thus far. The texture tempts the player to greater speed, but the climax (52f.), with its broad approach, makes a faster tempo at the outset of the theme sound trivial. The *accelerandi* (56 and 61) give additional evidence of, and compensation for, the slower motion of the second subject.

[4] The two thirty-second notes in the principal subject *can* be played in proper time when they appear as single notes. In octaves, the long leap to the following note often makes strict observance of the rhythm impossible. No one can leap from the high B-flat in bar 19 to the low D in bar 20, or take those in bars 200–202, in time. In these passages it is absolutely necessary to lengthen the last thirty-

The *Andante espressivo,* and also the *Rückblick,* were written before the other movements of the sonata. The *Andante* has as motto three lines from a poem by Sternau, called *Junge Liebe* (Young Love). The sense of the three lines is about as follows:

> The evening darkens, the moonlight shines;
> There are two fond hearts united in love
> And clinging in blissful embrace.

The rest of the poem is in the same vein, and is little better than our version of it. Brahms, however—remember that he was twenty—seizes upon the poetic image and sets it forth in a "translation" far superior to the original. You can see that the meter of the first line of the verse is reproduced almost exactly (without a repeated sixteenth for "the") in Brahms's melody. (We shall soon meet with another instance of this kind of correspondence.) Both the curve of this melodic line and the enriched harmonic color of its continuation are in the romantic vein, but the utterance is so unforced that the word sentimental cannot be used to describe it. The contrasting strain, in high register, is similarly appropriate to the poetic impulse, but not to the sentimentality, of the following verses, which speak of the scent of roses so far permeating the air as to hint at the presence of angels.

The next division, in D-flat, seems at first sight to have no melody; but if you play the upper notes in the left hand as a continuation of those in the right, you will find one, and will be gripped by it when the delicacy of the beginning grows into passion. The whole episode is repeated (unfortunately?), with a slight but significant change in harmony. The opening strain

---

second; and we are of the opinion that this expedient should be adopted throughout. The notation would be

which is a comparatively slight distortion.

recurs, more richly accompanied, and at last subsides in a murmur suggesting evanescence. But all this, long as it is, is but the prologue to a new strain, exalted enough to be taken as a kind of benediction.[5]

The *Scherzo* is more consistent and economical in structure and design than any of the earlier examples. It lacks, again, almost all trace of real humor, and the almost ecclesiastical *Trio* is a strange contrast to the exuberant energy of the main substance. The return, after the *Trio*, is upon a long bridge studded with fragments of the main theme.

The fourth movement is an interpolated Intermezzo entitled *Rückblick* ("Retrospect") which gazes with sorrow and frustration upon the long love scene of the *Andante*. Kalbeck finds some scraps of information about a girl whom Brahms met on a walking tour in the Rhine valley after his visit to Weimar, and can thus readily interpret the music as representing the ashes of those roses whose scent overpowered the poet Sternau, and, of course, Brahms as well. We are less sentimental nowadays, and probably more just in our estimate of the real poetry of the music.

The first two bars of the *Finale*, a Rondo, set forth a somewhat plebeian dance measure; but this initial heaviness is at once relieved by a high, syncopated phrase, graceful and elastic, and it is this character, rather than the sturdiness of the opening, which dominates the theme. The climax is a brilliant cascade of broken sixths, and this also accomplishes the transition to the B theme. This is a conventional kind of tune (which perhaps did not too much delight the composer, since it does not recur), in the slightly unconventional key of the tonic major (F) instead of the relative major (A-flat). The most important matter in the piece is, however, the C theme (138)—a broad phrase in D-flat which soon develops a curious resemblance to Haydn's "Emperor's

---

[5] There is a resemblance both of substance and character in this closing episode to Hans Sachs's monologue, in Act II of *Die Meistersinger*. Kalbeck, perhaps overconfidently, ascribes it to the fact that Wagner heard Brahms play this sonata at Vienna in 1863.

Hymn." (This was probably quite unobserved by the composer.) At bar 164 a canonic imitation begins, which is but a hint of the many contrapuntal ingenuities that will later be worked on this theme. The four initial notes, F, E-flat, D-flat, A-flat, descending, are also in the pattern of the "Cambridge Bells," of which much use is made in the *Finale* of Brahms's *First Symphony;* and their ringing in the swing of the march rhythm gives the whole passage a high and sane exhilaration. At the Coda (249) this theme (*Più mosso*) is transformed into even eighth notes, and becomes (although not pedantically exact in its design) the accompaniment of the original form of that theme. Minglings of this with the main theme, and a further hastening of speed, produce an impression of abandon which we have hardly found, thus far, in Brahms's music.

The form and substance of this sonata often give a hint of unwieldiness. There is, indeed, no waste; the substance, except for the Trio of the *Scherzo* and the B subject of the *Finale,* is distinctive; the handling is imaginative and ingenious; yet the whole impression is of an idea not quite in focus. But the mind that conceived it is evidently growing by leaps and bounds.

The next piece in the order of its opus number (but not in order of composition) is a set of *Variations on a Theme of Schumann.* It is his interest in this form of composition, rather than any dissatisfaction with the sonata form, which really explains Brahms's abandonment of the piano sonata. Remembering that Brahms is now gravely concerned to prove himself that champion of true musicality whom Schumann had announced, and remembering that the Variation form is perhaps the severest test of the whole capacity of a composer, we can understand why the next compositions we shall have to study will be, with one exception, sets of variations.

Op. 9 is not his first effort in this form. The two sets, one on an original theme, and one on a Hungarian song, which were published as Op. 21, were written almost a year before that on

Schumann's theme—and are not only less skilled but less musical. The theme of Op. 9 is from Schumann's Op. 99, and is the first of five "Album Leaves" comprised with various other compositions in a collection called *Bunte Blätter* ("Variegated Leaves"). The variations were composed as a kind of tribute to the stricken composer of the theme, who was now confined in an asylum at Endenich. Clara, Schumann's anxious mate, also wrote some variations on the same theme, and both sets were published by Breitkopf in 1854.

Some of the variations are very difficult, but most of them are manageable, and the work is of such extraordinary interest (although it is for some reason seldom played) that we must examine it closely. The burden of the theme is a quiet melancholy, expressed with a reticence that gives it the immediate stamp of truth. The three C-sharps whose gentle insistence forms the core of the thought descend in almost identical curves that remain within the compass of a fourth, except for incidental up-beats. The middle section strives upward, with singular intensity, from the same C-sharp. The harmonies for the four phrases that form the beginning and the end are slightly but meaningfully differentiated, and the performer has a most interesting problem in discovering the subtle shades of emphasis that will realize their value.

Variation I presents the theme in the bass, unaltered until bar 15. Thereafter, the three C-sharps rise to three D's and then to three D-sharps, with two strangely potent notes (A-sharp, bar 18, and E-sharp, bar 22) distorting the harmonic progression, yet directing it to its proper close. Do not spoil bars 15–16 by haste or rhythmic indecision.

Variation II shows a curious abbreviation of the theme. One bar of 9–8 time equals three bars of the theme, and the fourth bar is omitted. Thus, at the end of bar 2 we have already reached the equivalent of the double bar which marks the end of section I of the theme. Each of the next four bars corresponds to two bars of the theme; but, since the close of the variation would have been rhythmically shapeless after only two more measures, the variant of the middle section forms the close. The melody of the theme is more apparent in bars 3 and 4 than in 1 and 2, but the essential progression of the bass is clearly that of the theme.

Variation III might almost be called a variation of Variation I. It demands the same subtle care for its more remote excursions.

Variation IV is a melodic alteration of the theme. The eighth notes, B and D, stand for the second C-sharp; G-sharp is added before B in bar 2 to give a similar rhythmic curve to the A of the theme; and in bars 5–8, the melody is made to rise, instead of falling, to its major close. The legato of the melody must be maintained by the fingers, since the pedal must be taken (if at all) anew with each pair of sixteenths. If you cannot strike the tenths simultaneously, omit such notes as the second F-sharp in beat 1, rather than delay the motion by rolling both tenths.

Variation V departs, for the first time, from obvious correspondence with the thematic design. The rhythm is an intensification of that in Variation IV. We can see that the vigorous C-sharps in bars 1 and 2 proceed to B and A, and may take bars 3 and 4 to represent bar 3, and bars 5, 6, and 7 as the cadential bar 4. The next four bars must then represent bars 5–8, since the double bar marks the end of the section as in the theme. A similar and even more obscure relation to the theme can be found in what follows; but the variation has an independent rhythmic design, the cornerstones of which are the incisive octave figures of the beginning, and the harmonies do not closely follow the thematic pattern.

Variation 6 is again in the same dimension as the theme, with a new melodic pattern ingeniously suggesting, but seldom reproducing, the original. (The best fingering for the descending arpeggio seems to us 5321, 32. The thumb on the black key keeps the hand raised so that the 5th easily takes the following C-sharp and shapes the hand for the rest of the passage.)

Variation VII is a wonderful feat of suggestion. Only glimpses of the theme are given, in the fewest possible notes; but the intimation is compelling. Study carefully the rhythmic meaning of the fermata ( ⌢ ) over the chord on "three" of the last bar before the 3-4 time. Without this pause, the rhythmic shift sounds unbalanced. Intone the necessary accents for the suspensions (before and after the bar lines) softly but unmistakably. *Una corda* seems to us implied for the whole variation.

Variation VIII is a canon. The broken octaves of the left hand, entering at bar 3, give a virtually unaltered repetition of the melody in the right. The melody is unaltered except at bars 11-12, where of necessity (to avoid consecutive octaves in the canon) it is raised a third. The major key at the close is not a deviation in principle. In these alterations only is the canon "made." The rest of it is "discovered," as a musical possibility, in a theme which was doubtless never conceived as a canon. If the theme had not happened to be so shaped, Bach himself could not have performed this feat; but only a composer with an imagination would have perceived the possibility.

Variation IX is an additional tribute to Schumann. Its figuration is drawn from the *Albumblatt* which follows the chosen theme in Schumann's Op. 99. Perhaps because that piece is in B minor, Brahms has also changed the original key to correspond. The next two variations also depart from F-sharp minor. The two penultimate bars are very tricky to play, but the rest of the variation is less difficult than it looks.

Variation X, in D, is another contrapuntal feat. The theme is sketched in the middle voices; a quite new melody is provided above; and the bass, for eight bars, is the exact inversion of this melody. As in Variation IX, the first section of the theme, in its varied form, is repeated; but the inversion of the soprano is now in the alto, and enters canonically a bar later. In the following section, the separately stemmed bass notes are again the inversion of the highest voice, and this device, with new figuration in the accompaniment, is maintained to the end. (Brahms, according to Kalbeck, seems to have doubted, in later years, the artistic value of this one variation.)

Variation XI is a kind of Intermezzo in the whole sequence of variations. It hovers tentatively about the real tonic (G) without really coming to rest upon it. The delicacy of the character is so charming that a similar lightness is maintained in the next two variations.

Variation XII is easily related to the theme, the only departure being the staccato epilogue, in which groups of three notes persist against the 2–4 time.

Variation XIII, a miniature Toccata, not impossibly related to Schumann's wonderful Op. 8, is difficult only for the lightness of the twinkling figures and harmonies. Any failure in precision is fatal.

Variation XIV, again in F-sharp minor, returns also to the absorbing problem of canon. The melodic variant of the theme, beginning in the alto, is imitated from bar 3 in the soprano, but a tone higher in the scale. We have, that is, a canon in the second above. To complete the imitation it is necessary to extend the variant of four bars to six, and so on throughout. To differentiate the two melodies which are always in the same register is very difficult, and will be impossible if the staccato prescribed for the bass is not carefully observed.

Variation XV is still another canon. The soprano, which departs but little from the theme, is imitated by the bass, beginning at bar 2, at the interval of a sixth (plus two octaves). These imitations at other intervals than the octave or the unison were a favorite device of the learned composers, long before Bach's time. (In Bach's "Goldberg Variations," every interval from the unison to the ninth is exemplified.)

Variation XVI is another example of high poetic suggestion. The rhythm is all but motionless, and the melodic voice breaks silence only when the bass of the theme (maintained intact except for the major key) seems to compel a phrase of reluctant assent. Only the tensest concentration will yield a meaningful utterance of this pregnant thought.

These variations present matter which is so far from the habitual expectation of concert-goers that the piece is almost hidden from the public view. It is true that the "learned" experiments are beyond detection by any but highly experienced ears. But the interest of the composition lies hardly at all in the devices. The theme itself is a lyric poem of high rank, and the variations, without exception, either illuminate its sense or add totally unexpected interest to it. We shall meet with more imposing sets of variations, but with none more filled with nutrition for the musical spirit.

With Op. 10 we enter a very different field of expression. This is a collection of four *Ballades*—very unlike those romantic pieces which we found in Chopin under this title, and much more akin to the simple narratives in verse which go by that name in literature. The first is based on the gruesome border-ballad, "Edward." The other three have no relation to the narrative of the first, nor any acknowledged program, though the inventive-minded hearer will have little difficulty in contriving a story of his own, if he chooses.[6]

We noted that the *Andante* of Op. 5 opened with a melody rhythmed in precise accord with the verse chosen as motto for the movement. Correspondence with the verse of the ballad is here even closer. One cannot doubt that the phrases of bars 1–8 imply the words:

> Why dois your brand sae drap wi' bluid,
> Edward, Edward,
> Why dois your brand sae drap wi' bluid,
> And why sae sad gang ye, O?

[6] In the Peters edition of Brahms's piano music, edited by Emil von Sauer, and in the current reprint, the whole group of Ballades may seem, from the title, to be based on the "Edward" poem. This is not so in the original edition, which states that relation only as a kind of subtitle for the First.

even though the last notes fail slightly to correspond to the poetic meter. (Herder's German translation, Brahms's source, preserves intact the meter of the original.) But mere metrical identity would not of itself yield appropriate music for such a thought. The dreadful constraint with which the mother thus questions her son is felt in the sober melody with its bare, diatonic intervals, and in the mysterious fifths and the tentative harmonies with which her sentence ends. Edward's answer (*Poco più moto*) is not apparent as an evasion (you˙cannot literally tell a lie in music); but observe that, after the mother repeats her question, that which was the mere bass of Edward's first answer is now the melody of his second, while something very near the original melody is now in either tenor or bass. (Edward says, first, that he has killed his hawk; next, that he has killed his horse; but his mother says that such blood is not so red as this, and repeats her question.)

The music (*Allegro, ma non troppo*) now follows the implication rather than the letter of the text. Goaded by her insistent inquiry, Edward confesses that he has killed his father, and the mounting tension of his mind is depicted in the building up, in fragment after fragment, of the *second* melodic strain in Edward's answer. Already at bar 11, fortissimo is marked, but the build-up goes on, increased in volume and intensity by the towering harmonic sequences, until at the change back to D minor the theme of the *first* answer is shouted out, still fortissimo, for ten whole bars before it is allowed to diminish. The horror with which the music depicts the dreadful curse called down on the mother's head is as shattering as that with which we view the mental and physical agony of self-blinded Oedipus. The *sotto voce* return of the questioning theme is a commentative epilogue, appropriate in music where the emotion of the story has been set forth, but naturally without a counterpart in the poem, where it would be superfluous. Evidently, our maker of canonic variations is also capable of drama.

Except for the power it demands, which is prodigious, this piece
is not very difficult to play. Make the little finger, in the opening
theme, overtop the thumb. Thin tone is more in character. Play
legato, but keep the shading within very narrow bounds. In the *Poco
più moto,* play the bass rather louder than you would if it were not
presently to become melody, and maintain the same restraint in expression. In the *Allegro,* do not accentuate the first note of the triplets, else they will not build up to the following accent. The triplet
figure in the bass must be a little softer than that in the treble. Both
must of course be subordinated to the melodic phrase. As you approach the peak, and especially with the two B-flat chords, release the
pedal with the third eighth note of the triplet, and depress it with
the chord. The instant of silence will much intensify the terrible force
of the chord. Remember, also, that the great source of sonority in the
piano is the lower strings. You can get only tinny harshness by pound-
ing the treble above an insufficient bass. Three bars before the epilogue,
after the silence prescribed by the rests, bring out the progression E–F
both times, but in the second bar give the descending bass its due expressiveness. Play the epilogue *sotto voce* throughout (i.e., *una corda*)
with the least possible use of the damper pedal. The "dead-pan"
figures in bars 6 and 7 have high value for the implicit sense of
tragedy.

The Second Ballade begins with a phrase (here used for the
first time) which has a curious history. Joachim had adopted as
a kind of motto indicative of himself in relation to the world
of music the phrase, *"Frei aber einsam"* ("Free but lonely").
Brahms, who followed Joachim's more experienced lead in many
matters, in his correspondence with the great violinist applied to
himself the variant, *"Frei aber froh"* ("Free, yet joyous") or, as
some have it, *"Frei aber fern"* ("Free, but far away"). The notes
designated by the initial letters of the German words, F, A, E,
and F, A, F, appear in the compositions of each, and this sequence,
with Brahms, becomes what Weingartner once called a kind of
"Brahms leit-motiv." We have, in the Ballade, F-sharp for F, but
the sense, to the musical ear if not to the eye, is the same.

The mood of this Ballade is far removed from that of the

First. (There is no story, so we shall speak only of the evident character of the musical phrases.) The quiet motion, the effortless rise to the high F-sharp, which is in some degree aided by the similar motion of the bass, and the poising again on another F-sharp—all this is the very opposite of tragedy. The curve of the continuing phrase (bar 10) is in the opposite direction—downward. Its wider sweep seems to darken the feeling, but not to deny the first impression. The *Allegro non troppo,* since its mood is in no way forecast, enters with more of a shock than did the *Allegro* of the First Ballade; but its high energy is not tainted with tragedy. A characteristic of this energy is displayed in the unusual accent on the first of the four eighth notes. This should not, however, override that on the half note. The staccato triplets at the culmination are appropriately forceful; but the ensuing *piano* episode, although made in their pattern, seems to us a little irrelevant. The pedal, of course, cannot be used until the legato quarter notes appear. This Ballade is the least interesting of the four.

Brahms calls the Third Ballade an *Intermezzo.* It has the form of the Scherzo, and is both more humorous, in a very delicate way, and more imaginative than the earlier Scherzi. The tonal resource of the piano is also here more originally explored than in the earlier pieces. It is not very hard to play; but since its effect can easily be missed, we shall examine a few danger spots.

After the two staccato fifths, observe exactly the composer's pedal mark, releasing only with the F-sharp. Cut this note very short, and be sure that you give it no accent; else you will destroy the grace of the phrase, which is typical of the whole piece. The pedal from "six" in bar 6 to the E-sharp in bar 8 will produce a disagreeable jangle unless the sixteenths are struck piano. The indicated *f* will even so be realized by the blur, which must have been intended. Cut very short the ·A-sharp in bar 9; make the indicated accent on the G, but none on the "one" in bar 10, since the following A-sharp must be stressed. In bar 13, make the *dimin.* (after an unaccented "one") very lightly, and precisely in time. Observe again the typical pedal effect beginning at bar 14, which can yield an irresistible charm. Presumably the same pedal effect is intended in bars 23 and 35 as in 7. From bar 25, keep the F-sharps in the bass very light. You will find it hard to make the octave A-sharp (36) sound as the natural end of the passage. Play the repetition.

The first notes of the melody of the "Trio," as we may call it, are derived from the C-sharp, D, and F-sharp of the beginning of the "Scherzo," though the fact is perhaps of little import. The echo on D-sharp–A-sharp in bars 6 and 7 may seem to recall the phrases associated with the words, "Edward, Edward," in Ballade I; but this is surely mere coincidence. Although the pedal is to be used throughout the Trio, observe the sign for a change with the A-sharp in bar 37, sustaining from there to the end. This change gives a kind of ictus to the luminous tone of the many ringing minor ninths.

The Fourth Ballade, the most extended of all, is steeped in romanticism; yet to our ears it has not a sentimental note. The melodic curve of the first section is as beautiful—and as unconscious—as the winding of a river, but this is no mere landscape. It sweeps over two octaves without effort and without impediment, and loses itself on the very horizon of its register. The shorter phrases of the second portion are all but unbearable as they attain their climax; yet there is no hint of grief. The melody is quite untutored. It has, instead, the incredible skill of sheer inspiration—and only youth could be capable of it. Youthful also, in its entire self-absorption, is the sequel in D-sharp minor— perhaps the most intimate utterance in all Brahms's piano music. The dwindling of the former melody was intimation that something in this character was to come; but the wealth of the new substance is far greater than the prophecy implied. The first theme returns, in part, with its figure of accompaniment lightened; but a grave iambic motion follows, in thoughtful five-bar periods. This motion darkens, but does not obscure, the intenser portion of the main theme, and the conclusion is an appropriate reminiscence of the moment of intimacy.

Some of this piece is hard to read, and all of it is difficult to interpret; but the notes are not troublesome for the fingers. Do not drive the opening melody with a too-fast tempo, but keep the quiet flow of the accompanying figures smooth, and quite without rubato. Do not exaggerate by any definite punctuation the ends of the four-bar phrases, but give infinite care to the dynamics of the melodic line. The second section begins with two-bar groups which detach themselves; but the rest should be in breathless continuity.

The *Più lento,* in 6–4 time, must of course be read with great care. We are cautioned not to mark the melody too much; but we must not mark it too little, for the long curve of its line can easily be smothered in the accompaniment. We must hear, in its proper proportion to the melody, the descending tenor (bars 1–2) and bass (3–4). Warm the tone (i.e., swell a little, and intensify the high E-sharp of the accompaniment) from "six" in bar 4 to give value to the entering F-sharp major key. In bar 1 after the second ending, the rising contrapuntal line from "four" (i.e., E-sharp, F-sharp, G-sharp, A-sharp, B, A-sharp) must come in like an enriching 'cello against a violin; but this means that the long D-natural–C-sharp of the main melody must be fully intoned. A considerable crescendo seems inevitable in what follows, and is implied in the *dimin.* at the end of bar 4. A slight retardation at the end of bar 6 is similarly demanded, else the swell to the returning melody will sound pointless. At the end, the notation implies the fading of the reiterations of F-sharp–G-natural. Do not hasten the final unfigured bar.

The figure of accompaniment is now written portamento, which allows a very sparing use of the pedal. Until the first eighth note of the figure, however, pedal is indispensable; else the bass will sound only an empty thump. The phrasing in the grave continuation is so carefully marked that one can hardly misinterpret the sense, and the intimate 6–4 time will now be much easier to decipher. At bar 7 from the end, on "six," observe that the stemmed eighth note, B, is the concluding note of the preceding phrase (D-sharp, C-sharp, B), but the stemmed quarter-note, A-sharp, is the first note of the phrase (A-sharp, A-natural, G-sharp, F-sharp, and so on) which continues in the next bar. It is all but impossible to make the meaning of these two notes clear, and of course the A-sharp, more important than the B, must have the preference; but it is well to try even the impossible when it has important meaning.

As we have said, the two sets of variations, Op. 21, are earlier and less interesting than Op. 9. Although they are by no means negligible, we are obliged to dismiss them with little comment, in favor of more important works. The original theme, the basis of set No. 1, is more sonorous but less significant than Schumann's little *Albumblatt*. It seems to aim at exaltation, but to reach little beyond complacency. Skill is always in evidence, though there are fewer "learned" variations than in Op. 9. Variation V has a canon in contrary motion which is hard to hear, since the soprano begins with the inversion, while the original theme, figurated in triplets, is the following voice. The sonority of the piano is especially well explored in Variation VII, where the wide spacing of the single notes in each part, together with the pedal, produces a fascinatingly luminous tone. Variations IX and X interestingly disguise the theme; and the last, Variation XI, is much expanded, first by elaborating the repetition of each section, and then by adding a freer commentary on the whole thought. The adventures in pianistic technique are bolder than in the Schumann variations; but there is far less of poetry.

The theme of the second set is a Hungarian song—a vital, rhythmic tune, whose phrases each comprise seven rhythmic beats that Brahms writes as 3-4 + 4-4. This rhythmic peculiarity is retained for eight variations (most of which are very short), and Brahms shows much ingenuity in reshaping the melodic line (as in Variations III, V, and VI) or reducing the whole thought to its musical elements (as in Variation VII, but more conspicuously in the Schumann set). The effect, in this latter variation, of the pizzicato bass against the sustained upper voices we shall find frequently exploited in some of the later works. The last variation is again a kind of fantasia on the theme, freer and more extended than in the previous set, so that we are grateful for the restatement of the theme at the end.

This piece reflects not only the interest in folk music that Brahms felt, all his life, but also the particular affection for Hungarian rhythm and melody that prompted his familiar "arrangements" of Hungarian Dances. These Dances were originally written for four hands, in which form we recommend our readers to play them, since the arrangements for piano solo are by no means easy to play. Several of them, of course, are known to every newsboy, and thus need no comment; but you are likely to find that the unfamiliar ones are not less interesting.

Another set of variations, however, also for piano duet, and also on a theme of Schumann, appears as Op. 23. The theme is none other than that which Schumann, as the final disintegration of his mind approached, believed that he had received from the spirits of Schubert and Mendelssohn, with the command that he vary it. He was at work on the fourth variation when (on 27 February, 1854) he suddenly threw down his pen, ran out of the house onto the bridge over the Rhine, and threw himself into the river. Thereafter, he was cared for in an asylum at Endenich until his death. The theme had therefore somber associations for Brahms and Clara. The variations are addressed, not to those who may become admirers of Brahms, but to those who are already lovers of Schumann. The theme has indeed something of that unconscious melancholy which is never far from the surface in Schubert; but it is still unmistakably from the mind of Schumann. The variations are mostly rather free, and none, except the fourth (in canon, hushed and remote), speaks at all directly of the shadow of death which haunted the minds of Johannes and Clara even thus long after the fact. There is neither brilliance nor gaiety in this music; but it has a full measure of intimate poetry, and, being fairly easy to play, gives a large return for the effort it demands.

The *Handel Variations,* as they are familiarly called, are a decided contrast—a tour de force, not only as a feat of musical composition, but as an exhibit of pianistic brilliance and sonority. Except for the *Paganini Variations,* Op. 35, these variations are the most difficult of all Brahms's piano music. They are in every pianist's repertoire, and audiences find them imposing; but we cannot resist the conviction that their popularity rests rather on the astonishing fugue that concludes the piece than upon the variations themselves.

Our most unorthodox opinion arises from the theme itself— to our ears, a rather idle jingle, well suited to the harpsichord— on which Handel made five simple variations. (The set is one of a series of *Lessons for the Harpsichord*.) The tune is called an *Air;* but this implies neither an operatic aria nor a song, but rather one of those *Intermezzi* which, in the Dance Suite, were interpolated between the Sarabande and the Gigue. It displays, in the most compact shape possible, that two-part form which we described as the source of the sonata-allegro. The melody, which has indeed a kind of naïve charm, but no expressive character, is supported by the simplest of harmonies; neither is the bass in the least conspicuous as a polyphonic line.

The theme, then, although it has not the quality that either Bach or Beethoven would have chosen as a foundation upon which to build an imposing edifice, is chosen by Brahms for precisely that purpose; and it cannot be denied that his achievement is remarkable. Not "effects," which he hated as such, but solid, logical, self-sufficient musical structures, were his objective, and they do indeed exhibit powers that were possessed by none of those antagonists among the musicians of the future against whom Brahms had been pitted by Schumann's panegyric. They exhibit even more than one might expect, under the circumstances, of poetic imagination; but this quality could hardly predominate in this work, as it does in Op. 9.

This work is so difficult to play that it will probably be attempted by relatively few of our readers. Our comments, accordingly, will be less minute than in our study of Op. 9. The trills, in the theme (written as 〰 in the original) are probably best executed as

except in bar 4, where

seems indicated. Note that the melody, in the first three bars of each section, has two rising eighth notes on "four." This fact is often emphasized in the variations, and thus should be made apparent in playing the theme—but the unusual weight of the last eighth should not be exaggerated.

In Variation I, use firm fingers, absolute precision in tempo, and no pedal unless to color the first four notes of the passages in bars 4 and 8. In Variation II, where the triplets reshape the melodic line of Variation I, do not interpret too liberally the *animato*. The whole impression of the piece will be erratic unless a stable rhythmic beat is felt, continuing for a considerable time. In Variation III (as in the *Andante* of Op. 5) the upper notes of the left hand's two-note figures continue the melody of the right hand. The effect of antiphony, however, must not be obscured. In Variation IV, the sforzandi must be very conspicuous, but the weaker notes must all be sharp and clear. These accents derive from the rising eighths mentioned in the theme. The arch of the hand must be kept very firm, with the wrist hardly relaxed at all.

Variation V, the first of the four that are in minor, emphasizes the rising eighth of the theme by reiterating it immediately. Suavity here contrasts with the preceding energy. The dynamic shadings, marked by the composer, are intended to give that effect. Variation VI, likewise in minor, is in canon. Pedal, frequently changed, is necessary almost throughout to give subdued luminosity to the tone. The canon is fairly obvious, being hardly more than an arpeggio, so that the tone color becomes especially important. Variations VII and VIII, like I and II, and V and VI, have similarities of figure which group them in pairs. Variation VII is a little trumpet-piece, of course to be played with bright, detached tone and without pedal. Variation VIII has a persistent drumming on B-flat or F, and above this we may suppose the music to be played by the wood winds. Note that the upper parts are in "double counterpoint"—the soprano in bars 1 and 2 becoming alto in 3 and 4, and so on throughout.

Variation IX seems to us somewhat obscurely marked by the composer. The *sf* B-flat is to sound as a "pedal" for two bars, though it is struck five times in that space. Brahms marks no release of the damper pedal, but only a change at the end of bar 2. He marks no ⟩ until the middle of bar 2. To our ears, precise observance of these directions gives only obscurity and noise. We therefore take everything after the *sf* in piano, and make quick, discreet changes of the damper pedal during the chromatics of bar 2, and so on. Variation X persistently turns from major into minor, and would be almost banal if it were not for that very interesting change. Its threatening character is charmingly relieved in the two smiling little pieces which follow, both of which are almost naïve. The mark *soave*, in Variation XII, seems to us to justify a hint of rubato in the hesitant little phrases of bar 1, and similar passages.

Variation XIII, again in minor, is hard to make as sonorous as it seems intended to be unless we give a little fuller support to the sixths than is offered by the detached chords. To pedal through the rests, however, is fatal. Pedal with each eighth of the melody, and keep the dynamics of the melodic line vividly shaded. Think of long-swept bows on violas and 'celli, and try to equal the richness of their tone. (The curious qualification of the indication, *Largamente—ma non più*—really means "but not more," but probably intends to say, "but not too much.") Variation XIV is difficult to play as freely (*sciolto*) as the composer desires. The *sf* at the beginning does not imply forte throughout, as the two ensuing *f*'s prove; but we cannot descend to *p* anywhere but at the beginning of bar 6 without weakening the vigorous character of the whole variation. Variations XV and XVI offer an interesting contrast of dynamics in similar passages. Variation XV, being loud, is fairly easy; but in XVI, which has the previous figure in imitation, clearness and delicacy are hard to attain.

The *più mosso* of Variation XVII must not be exaggerated. This is proved in Variation XVIII, which is a variant of XVII, and should doubtless be in the same tempo. The figures of sixteenths must be very articulate, and should seem to descend from the right hand to the left in an unbroken line, against which the hint of the theme definitely changes its register from bar to bar. Too great a speed will make clarity in the sixteenths impossible. Variation XIX is a kind of Siciliano. The ornament ∿, shifting from melody to accompaniment, points up interestingly the change of register. It is hard to obey the imperative direction, *leggiero e vivace*. Variation XX is for Brahms an unwonted adventure in chromatics. Note how the rising eighths of the theme are built up, in the variation, by tense harmonies. Careless students generally misread some of the notes, forgetting that accidentals govern within the bar until they are contradicted.

Variation XXI, the fourth of those definitely in minor, is the only one to shift its tonic from the original B-flat. The direction, *dolce*, does not imply a smeary legato for the triplets. Both parts should be clearly articulated, the sixteenths smooth and quiet, and the triplets delicately detached. Variation XXII, with its droning B-flat bass and its jigging folk melody, is to the life a portrait of the bagpipe's skirl. The sixteenths between the regularly beating B-flats, if audibly inserted, lighten the motion, and are indispensable. In Variation XXIII, *vivace* cannot imply any great increase of speed, since its open pattern of triplet eighths is to be filled in with more active sixteenths in Variation XXIV. These two variations thus combine to effect a general increase of excitement up to the climax preceding the entrance of the fugue. In Variation XXV, the attacks of the "filling-in" left hand must be as precise as those of the leading right, else the incisive rhythm will become mushy. Pedal may be taken with each strong beat, and released with the third sixteenth.

The subject of the *Fugue* differs enough in design from the theme of the variations (though it is obviously derived from it) to give our attention a fresh start. The tempo is about the same as that of Variation XXV. The slurs can hardly imply any lazy smoothness, though they do forbid staccato. Note that the progression of energy is always toward the second and fourth beats, so that in spite of its long slur the second bar is divided into two exactly similar groups. The "answer" (the subject removed to the level of the dominant) is accompanied by the conventional "countersubject," whose most conspicuous feature is the rising scale. The countersubject appears again at bar 5, where the third voice (the bass) enters with the subject.[7] The fourth voice (tenor) now takes the subject, completing the exposition without the appearance of any episode (or *Codetta,* as an episode is often called when it appears in the exposition of a fugue). The countersubject (in the soprano instead of the tenor) is now inverted—i.e., the scale moves downward—and is doubled in thirds by the alto. It is somewhat unusual for the last entrance of the subject in the exposition to be in an inner voice. It makes the theme hard to play, and to hear, but is not unorthodox.

With bars 9–10, which form an episode (only a part—here the last half—of the subject is present), the middle section of the fugue begins. This consists of alternations between episodes (all of which are to be made of material already heard) and "middle entries" or "reper-

---

[7] It is again in the alto, whereas Bach would have put it in the soprano, continuing the answer; but in piano music the individual voices are not clearly discriminable, so that this would hardly be noted as a fault, even by a purist.

cussions" of the subject itself. Other keys than the tonic and dominant (which alone appear in the exposition) are reached by the episodes, and the subject thus gets new interest at each entry. Various devices are available to heighten this interest, as we shall see.

After the first middle entry (bar 11) a much longer episode (13–19), still on the latter half of the subject, but descending, leads to an "apparent" (because uncompleted) entrance of the subject, accompanied by the inverted countersubject. It rises to a culmination in two complete but slightly altered statements of the subject, in the bass (25–26) and soprano (27–28). After another entry in the bass (30), the soprano replies with the subject in inversion. It is accompanied, not by the countersubject but by a quiet figure of sixteenths derived from the alteration of the subject in bar 31. With this figure, and the immediate repetition of the inverted subject in the soprano, the music becomes momentarily "homophonic"—which is another valuable contrast, offering an admirable approach to the next new presentation of the theme.

At bar 49, against fragments of the subject and the inverted countersubject, the theme, augmented (i.e., in notes twice the length of the originals), thunders out in the bass, appears in its original dimension (53–54), and again in augmentation in the soprano (55). A long episode ensues, which makes expectant preparation for the entrance (75) of the subject (in soprano and alto) against its inversion (tenor and bass); and this, tremendously intensified within a few bars, leads to the final section of the fugue, at bar 82.

This is marked by a most original employment of the "pedal point": the dominant of the scale, continuously sounded, not on one bass note but on a succession of leaping, ringing F's, first in high register, then in low, while the first phrase of the subject, inverted or in its original contour, together with the scale passages of the countersubject, clang out in combination to yield one of the most jubilant passages in the literature of the piano.

This work is a convincing demonstration of the skill—amounting to virtuosity—which Brahms had now attained in the art of composition. If the contrapuntal ingenuities we noted in Op. 9 had been contrived upon a theme as lacking in expression as Handel's tune, they would rather have repelled than attracted us. The imagination which can make out of such material as Handel's so great a number of individual and meaningful character sketches is more mature than that which is required to perceive possibilities of canon where none were intended. The highest ingenuity, however, is not that which makes something out of nothing. It is that which brings into clear focus the core and the true substance of what we can sense as real, but have not the wit to focus for ourselves. Even with this work, Brahms has not yet reached his full stature.

Neither does he attain it in his next piano piece. The *Paganini Variations,* Op. 35, are a study in another aspect of virtuosity. They explore, with extraordinary insight, resources in the piano which remained untouched, even in an age of virtuosity, by those who were regarded as unrivalled in that field. The Études of Chopin are the product of an imagination seeking to give appropriate form to highly original musical images. Liszt's technical discoveries, in some respects more brilliant, are more derivative (since they had been suggested by Paganini) and less imaginative. But these two composers, together with Schumann, had apparently harvested the whole field of technique.

Brahms came as a gleaner after these reapers; nevertheless he found, unharvested, many precious kernels. The actual source of much of Liszt's technique seems unmistakably to lie in the twenty-four caprices for solo violin of Paganini. The theme of Brahms's variations is the last of those caprices; but the source of the technical devices displayed in the variations is the imagination of the composer, turned toward the piano for its realization. The variations are of hideous difficulty—so much so that we shall offer no comment on the problems they present—but they represent also (as many pious "Brahmins" seem to ignore) as fertile a ferment of the imagination as do the *Handel Variations.*

Brahms wrote them also to discipline his own fingers, even though they seem to have been stimulated by his new friend, Carl Tausig—a pupil of Liszt—who, at the age of twenty, had already mastered every known pianistic problem. (He confessed, however, that these variations "gave him a great deal of trouble.") They were written in the winter of 1862–63, and published in 1866. (Brahms himself played them, on a program of gigantic dimensions, at Vienna in March, 1867.) The title page announces them as "Studies for the Piano"; but he who has really mastered them must be able, as Kalbeck says, to submerge the étude in the variation. They seem to us, on the whole, the most difficult pieces extant in the literature of the piano.

Only one more composition for piano belongs to this general period—the *Waltzes,* Op. 39. These, in their original setting, were for piano duet, and they are recommended to our readers in that form; but our brief discussion can take account also of the solo version which Brahms made to satisfy the demand that arose for them. The duet is dedicated to Eduard Hanslick, the Viennese critic (a bitter opponent of Wagner, and an equally eager champion of Brahms), who was fond of duet-playing and seems to have been capable of more in that line than the average critic. In the letter announcing the dedication, Brahms confesses that the work came in part out of his affection for Vienna. (He had a hearty admiration for the waltzes of Johann Strauss, and for their composer.) The fabled mood of the town is reflected—not directly, as in Strauss, but prismatically, through his own more compendious imagination; but there is no sign of apology for the plebeian origin of the work.

Like Chopin's, these waltzes are idealizations of the dance; but the idealization is more in the spirit than in the form. Little comment is needed for most of them—if the composer's directions are obeyed. Unfortunately, they are often *not* obeyed, with the result that temperament obscures character. The initial tempo mark, *Tempo giusto,* means both "in strict time," and "in a suitable tempo"; and this sign seems to govern not only the first number, but at least the next two. Yet they are often taken, not only too fast, but with excited accelerandi and other rhythmic distortions.

Observe, in the first waltz, the staccato in the solo version at bar 3 (in the duet, the mark is *non legato*). If you pedal this passage, you will rob the similar figures in the second section of their contrast. The second number opposes quiet grace to the vigor of the first. Do not destroy this quietude by erratic valuation of the eighth notes, which must be of the same value in both parts. No. 3 is very naïve, and must hardly exceed, even at the indicated swells, the intensity of *p* which is prescribed at the beginning. The passion of No. 4 will then have room to declare itself. Do not misread the turn-figure in bars 2 and 4 as if it were identical with the opening up-beat. It is difficult to exhibit the distinction between this figure and that of four thirty-seconds in bar 10 of section 2. Bar 8 of that section may be slightly retarded to give point to the re-entrance of the main thought; but do not make a feeble diminuendo after the *f* in bar 15.

The inner voice in No. 5 is a quotation from the composer's Op. 31, No. 3, a quartet for voices entitled "The Moon Shines Down." The implication is obvious, but do not try to make it a honeymoon. Brahms's favorite device of cross-rhythm (here, a two-beat pattern in a three-beat measure) is piquantly exemplified in No. 6. The melody (G-sharp, E-sharp, C-sharp, G-sharp, A-sharp, F-sharp, D-sharp, and so on) is more visible in the duet than in the solo version, but these notes must come out against the leggiero of the rest of the fabric. Gradually sharpen the definition of the two-note groups in section 2 so that at bar 12 they will give an effective approach to the returning theme. The three bars of legato, near the end, are not a sentimental relaxation, but a swelling approach to the staccato conclusion.

Brahms uses his Italian terms somewhat vaguely. *Più andante* really means "going more"; Brahms undoubtedly means "going less," for No. 7 voices the first hint of desire thus far in the series. In contrast, No. 8 is smiling, and a little nonchalant. (Make very clear the high F's in bars 7–8 of section 2, so that the ensuing new harmonies will color these notes, not smother them.) No. 9 faintly suggests the final number in Schumann's *Davidsbündler,* and like that piece contains more than appears on the surface. Take pedal on "one," but release it with "two" so that the hesitant phrases of the melody will not drag and cling into a legato line. The direction, *espressivo,* permits dynamic gradations more extensive than those marked in the score. No. 10, into which No. 9 runs without a cadence, is marked *poco scherzando* in the solo version, but has no mark in the duet. This number is a kind of bridge from the reticence of No. 9 to the franker gaiety of No. 11. This, at the close of its first section, has a cadence which hints at a strain of Hungarian blood in the music. This racial character will appear more vividly in No. 14. There is no trace of the Hungarian idiom in No. 12; but in its pleading tone, so marked that at the end of each section it almost forgets to dance, there may perhaps be reflected a Magyar mood.

No. 13, in the duet form, is in C. The solo version transposes the dance to B major, and the transposition a half step down is made, in the solo version, for all the rest of the set. This is doubtless to give the solo performer more black keys to play; for if this number had been kept in its original key, it would have been all but impossible to play as a solo. It has such vital energy that it might almost be called angry. That, however, is not to be assumed. Rather, this piece forms a kind of introduction for the more definitely Hungarian dance which follows. In No. 14, the waltz character is almost wholly supplanted by that of the Czardas. In spite of the transposition from A minor in the duet to G-sharp minor in the solo version, the leaping figures in the left hand are very hard to play. (Hands with a considerable span can take the middle note of the figure—e.g., D-sharp, in bar 1—with the 4th or even the 3rd finger, and so establish a fairly stable pivot; short hands must just practice until they can make the difficult leaps.

No. 15 returns to the waltz character—almost ungratefully, for those who have long familiarity with the piece. Brahms can hardly have realized that the slight provocation to sentimentality which his music offers would be so eagerly seized by weak-minded players and arrangers. Strict time, not too slow, and quiet dynamic shading will take off most of the curse. The figures in sixths toward the end are not difficult if the hand begins with momentum enough to make the leap, which after all is only the transplantation to the higher octave. A second shift is needed, at the fifth bar from the end.

The final number is unpretentious in sound, but of high musical interest and considerable technical difficulty. Two melodies have to be played at once by the right hand, against a staccato bass that forbids the pedal. After eight bars, the two melodies change positions, the left hand now taking in the tenor what was before in the soprano, while the soprano takes the former alto. In the duet, the bass figure of the opening is kept throughout. In the solo, this would be unplayable, and is altered; but the staccato marks hint at the original design, and must be observed, else the combination of the two melodies will be obscured.

It is not strange that after having so fully demonstrated his mastery of the piano and of composition for it, a composer of high ambition should turn to other fields of expression. The Waltzes we have just studied were written in 1865. Not until twelve years later did Brahms publish any more pieces for piano solo. These (to which we shall turn in a moment) will show what his adventures in the fields of chamber, orchestral, and choral music had done to refine an already cultivated imagination.

We must go a little way off our path, however, to look at another set of Waltzes, the *Liebeslieder Walzer* ("Love-song Waltzes"), Op. 52. These are really for a quartet of mixed voices —or for duet or solo—with accompaniment for piano duet. (The title page says, for piano duet with voices *ad libitum;* but this was a publisher's notion, having in view the great question of salability, and was really against the desire of the composer.) The piano part, however, is so complete in itself that the lack of the voices—until they have once been heard—is nowhere noticeable. Here, almost for the first time, Brahms seems to write without consciousness of his high obligation to the Muses. Indeed, although it was written in 1868, it seems to us to be, in spirit, his most youthful work. The texts of the seventeen numbers set forth, somewhat fragmentarily, what is probably no more than a lively flirtation; but the sway of the rhythm raises the temperature of the affair to such heights that we are ourselves involved in it. The pieces, in the duet form, are not very hard to play (the arrangement for a single player is a different matter), and you will find their freshness quite inexhaustible. (In two of the numbers appears the now infrequent notation

$$\text{♩.} \; \text{♪♩} \; | \; \text{♩.} \; \text{♪♩.} \; \text{♪} |$$

which is the equivalent of

$$\text{♩.} \; \text{♪♩} \; | \; \text{♫} \; \text{♩.} \; \text{♪} \; |\text{etc.}$$

The picture of a succession of similar groups is really clearer in the old than in the modern notation.)

# 12

# JOHANNES BRAHMS —
# THE LATER WORKS

IF THE consciousness of method, discoverable in almost all the earlier works of
Brahms, disappears in the *Liebeslieder Walzer,* we may expect
it to be absent also in all the pieces we have still to consider. But
although these are almost excessively unpretentious in form and
dimension, they are more profound in implication than any of
the earlier works. They put forth their message in very few notes;
even in these, emphasis is mostly restrained; and it is easy, in
consequence, to overlook their significance. Indeed, unless they
are played with fine valuation, they seem stodgy and even meaningless.

To deal in words with such subtleties as are here so incessantly
present is a task difficult for both writer and reader. But to omit
such study would be to evade our problem. We have therefore
to warn the reader that our comment is not presented as a translation of the music into words. It is at best a sort of guidepost, attempting to point out what you may find for yourself in the
music. At worst, it may be seriously misleading. The writer has
chosen his words with care; but the reader must be on his guard,
both against the writer and himself.

Op. 76 is a collection of eight pieces—four with the title *Capriccio,* and four with the no more indicative title *Intermezzo.* The

*Capricci* are the more active pieces; the *Intermezzi* the more contemplative. They were mostly written in 1877, but at least the first number seems to have been sent to Clara Schumann as a birthday gift as early as 1871. She speaks of it as "fearfully difficult, but also so wonderful, so intimate, and so depressed in spirit that my heart is at once overjoyed and distressed as I play it." In spite of its difficulty (which is great, but hardly "fearful") we must examine the piece closely; for we have here the first example of a new manner of composition.

The German superscription, *unruhig bewegt* ("moving restlessly") is more meaningful than the Italian *un poco agitato,* given as an equivalent, and is almost a title and a sufficient "program" for the piece. Emerging out of a vague figure that reiterates three descending notes, a melodic phrase becomes tangible with the last three sixteenths and the "one" of the following bar. Brief and inconclusive, this phrase is nevertheless the whole foundation of the melodic pattern up to its climax in bar 9 (whence the music subsides in a long descent that still exhibits the three descending notes of the opening). A second melody, at bar 14—more self-conscious, but less agitated—is accompanied by another arrangement of the three descending notes; but as the melodic strain grows warmer, the accompaniment expands into wider sweeps of arpeggio. After an episode (bar 26) made of the first two bars, this theme is inverted, together with its three-note figure of accompaniment. The first theme then returns, but in the more sonorous tenor register, with the figure of arpeggio above; the second strain appears in the simplest melodic guise—with the three-note figure, augmented, for accompaniment—and an epilogue is made of that same regretful strain, with the figure of sixteenths above it.

The "manufacture" of this music is flawless; it is also, in one way, intellectual; but in its various guises the device of three descending notes is always so appropriate to the general thought that we are hardly conscious of it as a device. The mood of the music is not one of extreme tension. Indeed, it hardly protests at all, but minimizes, rather than stresses (as Tchaikovsky would have done), its painful aspect. This is highly civilized music.

The notation, for the first eight bars, prescribes an awkward entangling of the hands. It is much easier to take the second group of three descending notes, A, G-sharp, F-sharp, with the right hand, the low A, C-sharp, A, with the left, and the melodic motive, C-sharp, A, C-sharp, with the right. Continue similarly to bar 9. Brahms's fingering for the descending sweep cannot be bettered. Pedal the second strain, but only so much as will leave every note in the accompanying figures audible, and perfectly in time. The *sfp* C-sharp (26), and so on, cannot become *p* at once. It must therefore not be allowed to override the eighth notes of the ensuing melodic phrase. In bars 28–29, answer clearly in the bass the preceding strain, and sing the augmentation broadly from 38. In the last half of bar 44, the melodic F-sharp on "five" can be more easily taken with the left hand. (Similarly in 45–46.) Study the dynamics and the pedal attentively to distinguish the melodic phrases in the left hand from the surrounding figuration. Do not so accentuate the figures in 78f. that they sound like triplets. Observe that the two-note group, G-sharp–E-sharp, in the tenor, bar 78, is continued in the C-sharp–B and the D-sharp–C-sharp of the following bars to bring about the lingering conclusion. (The measure of bar 71 can be counted "one, two-*and*-three," and so on, with the second and fourth eighths of the right hand on the *and*.)

The *Capriccio in B minor* is one of Brahms's most popular pieces. It is also much harder to play than No. 1—if you respect the notation, which forbids the pedal almost throughout. Brahms did not actually write *senza pedale;* but he implied it in the very explicit staccato marks. Yet every edition more recent than the original puts in plentiful pedal marks where they have no business to be. The quaint melody—a curious mingling of gaucherie and grace—will have neither these qualities nor any others of interest if you ignore the staccato, or disobey the non troppo after the tempo mark *Allegretto*. The middle section is especially difficult, since the legato of the melody must be maintained without any help from the pedal.[1]

The off-beat accents in the left hand pose a considerable problem. (Note that they are absent against the legato groups in bars 2 and 4.) We find it necessary to place the melodic accent at the same point; but we find nothing in the shape of the phrase to forbid this. Note that there is no staccato dot on "one" of bar 5, in the melody. Against the staccato, the alto quarters, bars 7–10, must be legato. Make the staccato very short on the eighths, and do not extend the slur over the two sixteenths to include the following eighth (i.e., make the second sixteenth staccato).

At bar 13, the trace of awkwardness disappears, and the phrases become wholly graceful. (We—inconsistently?—take the pedal for those eighths which are not marked staccato.) Like the alto in bars 7–10, the tenor in 17–18 must be legato. The arpeggiation in bar 18 is a concession to short hands; but it also necessitates a touch of pedal; and a mere touch at "one" in 19–20 thus becomes allowable.

The middle section we find to be most manageable with the following fingering:

By analogy, you can work out the rest.

Counting from the *in tempo,* we find that the "one" in bar 2 lacks the staccato dot (compare bars 14 and 22, in section 1, which have it). This variant is doubtless because of the staccato bass. At "one" in bars 7, 9, 11, 12, and 13, a touch of pedal is allowable. You will find the *senza rit.* at the transition to the final section hard to obey, but it is authentic. The melody against the chords in the final section (bar 17f. from *a tempo*) comes out best with the following fingering:

[1] Brahms's obvious meaning is thwarted by even so accomplished a pianist-editor as Emil von Sauer, who has set pedal marks frequently throughout the section and elsewhere. Anyone who ever heard Ossip Gabrilowitsch play this piece would have been convinced that Brahms (and Gabrilowitsch!) knew what was what.

From bar 29, the fourth and eighth sixteenths are indicated to be played with the left hand. They can be more easily struck with the right; but if you adopt this method, be sure to realize the staccato and the grouping. which the indicated notation would give. From bar 35, the legato alto (and the later tenor) are best fingered with 2, 1, 2, 1, throughout. The unexpected modulation at bars 46–47 deserves the warmest possible tone, and a careful *una corda* imitation in 48–49. Brahms marked the pedal in the two final bars. If you can reach a tenth, however, it seems to us best to avoid it in bar 52.

No. 3 is a tiny Serenade. A couple of fiddles and a guitar (which has ultimately to be provided with some very low strings) play under Somebody's window—whose, you may decide for yourself; but she must be very charming. The legato of the melodic phrases is very hard to produce in the high register. It takes endless experiment to find the right dynamic shadings, since you have again, as in No. 2, a staccato accompaniment, but also a whole handful of legato voices. Again, the editors all spoil the piece by marking a frequent use of the pedal. It is particularly objectionable here, since Brahms himself marked the thicker substance of bars 11–13 to be pedaled, and it is obvious that bars 14–15 (and the similar passages at the end) are to be so treated.

When you have acquired an unconscious pedal technique, you will find that you can catch the last instant of a legato note with the foot, and release the pedal instantly with the next note, without spoiling a staccato accompaniment such as this. Note that the staccato of the left hand will have been silenced before the pedal is touched for the legato connection, and that the pedal will not affect the following melodic note. In the accompaniment to this piece, each group of two eighth notes lies within a single octave. Keep your hand at that span, and shift completely to a new position for the following two-note figure.

No. 4 sounds as if it might have been conceived by Schumann. Even the texture is reminiscent (e.g., of the *Arabeske in C*). But if there is any imitation, it may be taken merely as an act of homage. Technically, this is not a difficult piece. Its fluid melody is flavored by harmonies as elusive as its own line (the tonic chord of B-flat is not heard until near the end of the first section), and the whole fabric is imbued with a clean romanticism that even a modernist would hesitate to call decadent. Note how the elasticity of the melody is enhanced by the expansion of the period from four bars to six—partly by the repetition of the swifter figure in bar 3, partly by the sober "answer" in the bass, bars 5–6. The three-note motive

then builds another six-bar period; and even when this is finished, and the tonic chord appears, there is no more than a kind of restless stability. The "development," as we may call that which follows the double bar, intensifies but little the substance of the "exposition"; but it combines the main and the closing thoughts ingeniously, in similarly ungeometrical periods to those already built. The "recapitulation" is inconspicuously resumed at bar 11 of this section by the B-flat of the right hand and the A of bar 12. Fluidity is enhanced by the absence of any attack on "one" in both 12 and 13. The whole piece is what used to be called a "mood-picture" (*Stimmungsbild*) in the days before it was discovered that music consists of nothing but tone patterns.

No. 5, in C-sharp minor, is one of the most important of Brahms's piano pieces. It is very difficult to play, but is so highly characteristic of the composer that we must go into it at some length. Passion here overcomes the reticence that is always a component of Brahms's thought; but there is no mere noisy exuberance, nor is this, any more than the lighter pieces, to be taken as "intellectual" music. It does, indeed, exhibit the working of a powerful mind; but the "question" with which it deals—like all those questions which really matter—is one to which pure intellection can find no answer. You will not, however, be provoked by this music to the invention of an illustrative "program"; but you will find in it the indignation with which an impatient mind envisions a needlessly disordered world. There is triumph, too, if you will, at the end—no mere public celebration, but a moment of high and sweeping conviction: good stuff with which to endure a world too disordered for intellect to untangle. Make a story or not, as you please; but do not suppose that this music represents anything less than a high reality of complex experience.

The 6–8 time signature is the first fact to observe; for unless this rhythm imbues the music, nothing will appear in its right perspective. The melody appears to be in 3–4 time. It must never sound so. To prevent that is the task of the bass, and of the middle voice. If these have the right weight, they will establish the 6–8 sense. (Play the middle voice alone with the bass, and you will hear the true rhythm.) The melody, to accord with this, must yield something of the usual accentuation of the "one" to the emphasis of the second quarter note, which is both a syncopation and a suspension; and this, like any syncopated or suspended note, must have enough volume when it appears (*before* the beat) to pull audibly, *on* the beat, toward its resolution. The D-sharp in bar 1, that is, will be a little louder than either the C-sharp or the E. The bass, likewise, will be louder on the low C-sharp than on the "one." The melodic strain, however, continues for four bars, and its continuity must not be broken; so that a dynamic curve must be contrived to embrace the four similar bars in its single span. The rhythmic fact we have just discussed is emphasized in bars 5–6 by the eighth rest. Once you have made this rhythm live, you will have solved the hardest interpretative problem in the piece.

*Sostenuto,* in bar 19, obviously means *ritardando,* with strict time
ensuing. The huge climax at bar 35 must be prepared with its dimension in mind. The three bars of G-sharp in the right hand must
ring like a tocsin, and the left-hand octave must explode with the final
*sf* fifths. The directions *poco tranquillo* (53) and *più tranquillo* (61)
imply a slackened speed, but not an indifferent reading of the momentarily gentle melody. A slight rubato clinging on the high B and
A (61 and 63) seems allowable. The *agitato* (bar 71) after the *sostenuto*
seems to us to relate to the breathlessness of the brief phrases, and
thus to imply no accelerando. Observe that bar 77 is *not* marked
*sostenuto.* Bars 83–85 give an even more excited version of the ringing ·
G-sharps against the rising chromatic bass (derived, of course, from the
alto in bar 1) than do bars 33–35. Do not hasten the speed from bar
87, but keep the chromatic accompaniment very articulate and vigorous. Observe that the swells marked in the melody in 87f. are in accord with our reading of the melody in bar 1. You must bring out the
F-sharps and E in bars 91–93 against the accompanying octaves.
Strive for 'cello-like sonority at bars 95–96.

The epilogue (bar 111) was perhaps designed to suggest a certain
incoherence. Note that three groups of five eighth notes make up one
and a half bars of 6-8 time. These five-note groups must be articulated
as such; but in being played so they almost inevitably override the
6–8 sense. We find it well to put a slight stress on the real "one" of the
measure, while punctuating at the end of each five-note group. Against
the bass, the melodic lead is in those chromatically rising sixteenths
which coincide with the bass. From the middle of 113, the line is
given in broken octaves. The stringendo may be intensified by beginning bar 111 at somewhat less than the basic tempo.

The next Intermezzo (No. 6) is somewhat similar in mood to
No. 4. It is more troublesome to learn, but not to play after it is
learned. The rhythmic problem is easily solved by counting as
if the measure were 6-8, with the eighths of the bass then falling
on the "ands" between "two" and "three," and between "five"
and "six." The ⊳ bar 1f., if too literally interpreted, will up-
set the rhythmic flow. For the D on "one" must have the stress
of a "one," and must complete the phrase begun by the preceding
triplet; and to diminish this phrase will be to destroy its shape

and sense. Once this pattern is established, you have the key to most of the piece. (At bar 11f., you have essentially the rhythm of the opening of No. 5.) In the lighter middle section, which should offer no difficulty, note how the periods are extended so as to obviate the squareness of four-bar structure.

No. 7, underneath a quietly smiling exterior, conceals considerable bitterness. The motive

forming the crisis of the first phrase, is immediately twice reiterated with an evident sense of relinquishment, and later in the bass with a still darker quality. That same motive, at bar 8 (but with a new continuation), initiates and dominates the second strain of the piece. Compare this piece with the highly similar opening of Brahms's *D Minor Sonata for Piano and Violin,* Op. 108. What is here unobtrusive and almost hidden is there outspoken and grim; but the two thoughts are closely akin.

No. 8, in comparison to the others, is a kind of virtuoso piece, although its purpose is to charm rather than to overwhelm. It explores to the full the allurement of ringing strings which Chopin and Liszt had so abundantly revealed in the piano; yet there is not a phrase or a figure that can be traced to those masters. The piece—at least in the concert experience of the writer—has been much neglected; but since it is the virtuosi, and not the amateurs to whom this book is addressed, who must rescue it from obscurity, we shall offer no analysis of it.

The two *Rhapsodies,* Op. 79, were written, according to Kalbeck, in the summer of 1879—the third summer which Brahms spent at Pörtschach am See. The Wörthersee, a lake in the Austrian Alps on whose shore the village stands, is glowingly described by all the biographers, and by Brahms himself, who had never known such satisfaction in the whole routine of life as he found here. These pieces are among the most widely known of all his works. Neither of them—as we might expect—shows that wild abandon which is the first characteristic of the Rhapsodies of Liszt. Their form is very symmetrical, and it is perhaps because of this characteristic that they seem a little ill-defined by their title. Indeed, Brahms originally called the first of the two a Capriccio.

The *First Rhapsody,* in B minor, is much the more difficult. Its opening strain is almost tempestuous, and the contrasting theme in D minor, though more calm, has a sort of ache in it that is by no means out of character. The middle section of the piece is made from this second theme and—especially if the repeats are played—seems somewhat overlong; for the transformation and the B major key largely remove its pain. The return of the first section, complete, is a derogation from expected rhapsodic turmoil, and the Coda, instead of reawakening that state, subsides into somberness. But all this criticism makes sense only in the light of a pre-established definition of the title, *Rhapsody.* With this prejudice removed, the piece appears as the moving expression of a sturdy mind.

Do not spoil the theme by giving equal force to all the strong beats. The phrasing, as marked, is contrary to the sense of the theme. Surely, you must punctuate after the low F-sharp (bar 2), having put the main stress on the preceding A-sharp, and again after C-sharp (bar 4), with the obvious echo following. Articulate the triplet of sixteenths as clearly as possible, everywhere, and keep the eighths of the bass similarly audible. These notes contribute greatly to the rhythmic drive of the theme. The ensuing migrations of the theme from left hand to right, and so forth, are obvious. Diminish through bar 12, almost to *p,* so that the grim octaves may grow adequately to the forceful cadence. According to the notation, the right hand, from bar 16 to 21, plays only the syncopated F-sharps; but in bars 19 and 21 it is more convenient to take the E-sharps with the right thumb. Pedal generously the sonorous approach to the main theme in 22.

Bring out the F-sharp, G, A in 23 and A, A-sharp, and so on, in the right hand, together with the supporting bass. The augmentation of the theme in 26 then takes the lead. The *sostenuto sempre* seems to us to imply a slight but general slackening of the speed.

In the contrasting subject (30)—its suggestion of Grieg's *Åses Tod* was doubtless unconscious—shade the accompanying eighths as carefully as the theme itself. In 39, keep the high D in the staccato chords bright, and grow to an incisive attack on the theme. From 43 do not develop the *cresc.* too rapidly, or you will go bankrupt before the climax. In 50, take the high B-flat of the right hand chord with the left hand, along with its D-flat, and similarly in 52. Do not shorten or otherwise mismeasure the anticipatory tied eighths from bar 53; keep the little finger bright in the octaves, and give all possible value to the climactic climbing in the bass. Keep strict time with the rising scales in 62, together with the rests and the whole note. The final F-sharp (66), however strong your thumb-stroke, will be weak without pedal. From bar 81, the left hand has a very difficult task, but no facilitation is possible. The quarter notes, however, are more important than the eighths, since the thematic line is really in the right hand. Observe carefully the quarter rest in bar 86.

The middle section demands careful shading, but no other particular attention. Keep unvarying motion with the accompanying eighths. Rubato will make the whole section ridiculous. In the Coda, the countermelody is not separately stemmed for the first two bars, but may be appropriately brought out, to conform with the later notation.

The *Second Rhapsody,* when we consider its purport and effectiveness, is remarkably easy. Its opening theme might be compared to a vast, lowering sky with a portent of gales, rather than the more terrifying portent of lightning. But the mutter of its discontent is deep, and in its slow progress there is evidence of great force.

Unless you respect the *non troppo* in the superscription, you will make of this a stupid, tedious piece. (It is true that these words were added some time after the piece was composed—but they were added out of the composer's own conviction. The *First Rhapsody,* likewise, was first superscribed *Presto agitato,* but the *Presto,* for similar reasons, was deleted.) The triplet accompaniment offers the only alleviation of the square, quarter-note motion of the themes, and unless it is articulate, you will soon hear nothing but thumping and mumbling.

Mark the *rit.* in bar 8 by articulating the triplets still more clearly. The ⌒ is not over the notes—therefore it implies a breath-pause. The triplet motion from bar 9 to 13 must not be distorted by a mis-placed second eighth note in the left hand. Some *rit.* before the ⌒ in bar 13 seems to us imperative. Broaden the up-beat (A, B-flat, A) to give emphasis to the augmented sixth, G-sharp, in bar 14.

Mark the third quarter note, D, in bar 21, as the stress note in the phrase of three D's, keeping the triplets still articulate, though sub-ordinate. Contemporary taste usually rejects the repetition of the first section. The ensuing development offers no new problems. After the ⌒ at the return to the main theme, note that the D of the *f* chord is the real up-beat of the theme, and that the two following triplet eighths are weak. In the Coda, if you count two beats only to the measure and keep strict time you will make the *quasi rit.* sound as it was intended.

The two Rhapsodies were published in 1879. Not until 1892 did any new piano pieces appear. By this time, Brahms had come to feel that his work as a composer was really finished, and at-tempted no more works in large forms.

This, in so fertile and energetic a mind as his, is an attitude very different from that of Beethoven, who, at a similar period in his creative career, felt that he had only just learned how to compose, and was full of new purposes. There was, in Brahms's case, a certain bodily deterioration. Friends had remarked his whitening hair and waning strength. He no longer dared the higher reaches of the Alps. An unpredictable shortness of temper was beginning to perplex and momentarily to terrify his closest friends. The relatively cool reception of the double concerto (for violin and 'cello), which had followed the *Fourth Symphony* after a brief interval, seems to have discouraged an impulse (credibly reported by Kalbeck) to write another for the same in-struments; and the next works, accordingly, are all for smaller groups of players—trios, violin sonatas, and the like. But the piano, which had long seemed unequal to bearing the burden of his thought, becomes once more the vehicle of this mature but somewhat fatigued mind.

The last piano pieces, however, show but little of that reaching out into unexplored regions which is found in Beethoven's last piano sonatas and string quartets. But they are not on that account merely perfunctory utterances. He spoke of them in a metaphor that (although he is not often given to verbal explanations of his pieces) deserves some probing—if only to slough off the sentimentality that, at a superficial glance, seems to imbue his words. He called them *Wiegenlieder meiner Schmerzen*— "Cradle Songs of My Sorrows." Of sorrows in general, he was the last man to complain. He had never grasped at popularity, and had gained perhaps all of it that he had ever expected; and he knew that his work, now undervalued, had a good prospect of rising in the general esteem. Not mere personal peevishness at an inattentive world, then, but a deeper disillusionment—an awareness that the world could not learn to see by that light which, for him, illuminated the most obscure and significant corners of human experience—this was the source of his sorrows. They had tormented him all his life—had kept him a bachelor, and had at last made him into a crotchety, uncivil man. They could not be eliminated; but they could be put to sleep.

This, we think, is something like the sense of Brahms's metaphor. There is, indeed, one Cradle Song among these last pieces, but this is merely incidental. Many of them speak of far graver matters; some, on the other hand, have a kind of gaiety; but none of them—not even the *E-flat Rhapsody*—has the purposeful grip of the zealot, nor the rapt gaze of the prophet, such as we find in Beethoven's last works. These pieces look, not forward, nor very much upward. They look backward.

Yet they look backward with the gaze of one who has been, all his life, what Heine once called himself—*Ein Ritter von dem heil'gen Geist:* "a Knight of the Holy Spirit"—and they have that kind of understanding in them which is possible only to those who have fought successfully against easy self-deception.

The first piece in Op. 116 will seem to belie what we have just been saying. *Presto energico* is not the motion characteristic of a pensive, reminiscent mind. But see how the first four bars, in their springing, staccato gait, are followed by four more relatively dissonant descending phrases, whose weight burdens the whole buoyancy of the beginning. The descending phrases (e.g., in bars 25–36) in spite of the two exciting, syncopated accents, dominate the whole piece. They persist, against the descending octaves, throughout the ensuing passage; even in the more delicate staccato of bars 67–102 their shadow flickers; and although the excitement of the end is on the rising note of the beginning, the stress of the augmented triad has already acquired, in the earlier part, a character that maintains the darker tone.

This, of course, is not to be exaggerated or even especially emphasized in performance. It is only an undertone—but an important one—in a piece that is chiefly gay. The music is very hard to play. Keep the staccato very sharp, so that the short slurred groups may stand out in contrast. At bar 5f., do not too much subdue the E after the *sf,* since it must be felt as "one." Note that at bar 9, the bass has not only the rhythm of the opening phrases but also their notes—in a continually rising order. At 21, bring out the E, F, F-sharp, and so on, as well as the rising bass. At bar 26, the composer's swells alter the dynamic contour of the important three-note descending phrase, because of the syncopation in the accompaniment. Pedal with each right-hand quarter note. At bar 38f., the composer's fingering for the left hand proves that he did not wish the pedal to help out the legato. (Observe that the three-note phrase is here augmented.) At 67, do not ignore the theme and its continuation (C, B, A; D, C, B, and so on). The see-saw between higher and lower octaves, from bar 86, has a development of this phrase, but with the third note repeating the second, instead of descending.

The *Intermezzo in A minor* (No. 2) more immediately suggests Brahms's metaphor. Its grief is unobtrusive and without bitterness, but the experience implied is significant. Even the swifter section (whose melody is a variant of the main thought) moves its hand very gently over a very sensitive surface. There is a kind of resemblance—not in design but in character—between this piece and the slow movement of Schubert's little *Sonata in A,* Op. 120. That piece, like this, is not very difficult to play, and you will find the comparison illuminating.

In the opening bars, take pains to articulate (but very smoothly) the triplets against the melody. In this way, the triplet figuration from bar 10 will not too much detract from the character of the slight variant of the theme. Note that at bars 8–9 the melody is B–A, and do not ignore the rhythmic figure in the bass. In bars 14–15, the melody at "three" does *not* proceed to the next eighth, which note must be carefully subdued. Brahms wrote an alternative to the difficult right-hand part in the second section. It sounds pedestrian, however, by comparison with the preferred version. His fingering, designed for perfect legato, is good for those with a long reach, but smaller hands can take each group of four sixteenths with 1541 except at bar 3 and at similar passages, where 1451 is obviously preferable. Pedal was probably not intended, but we can see no harm in using it, very briefly, with any single eighth note. Observe that "two" in the left hand has a slight stress because of the quarter note. Kalbeck says that the little A major episode which prepares for the return of the theme is a Ländler from Upper Austria. The grace notes in bars 5–6 of this section are obviously short and before the beat, not on it, as are the sixteenths of bars 1–2.

No. 3 begins as if it were to be a Rhapsody, with a melody singularly angular and forceful. The irrationality of the Rhapsody, however, is no more evident here than in Op. 79, the A–B–A form being undisguised. This piece somehow lacks the distinction which almost invariably belongs to these last works.

No. 4, however, is one of the most perfect expressions of the mature poetic mind of the composer. For once it does look upward, and to a great height. James Huneker somewhere speaks of it as, in his estimation, the finest piano piece he knows. We shall differ with that opinion, but by no means vehemently.

The opening motive of three beats is carefully notated, with the low E to be played by the right hand, and the peak of the swell on the down-beat; but if you unimaginatively follow these markings you will still have nothing but three beats. In reality, it is pregnant with the suspense that belongs to the whole piece. The shape of this tiny phrase is all-important. You will make many experiments before you find the right softness for the beginning, and the right shading and motion to give the figure an impressive curve. It will sound, when you get it, as if it were being played rubato, though in reality it will be in perfect time. The two-note groups of the melody should be stressed, according to rule, on the first note; but the dots on C-sharp and A forbid too great a weakening of these notes. Stress the F-sharp and D-sharp in the left-hand figures, but do not ignore the E's which form the bass for six bars. The opening motive, reappearing in bar 4, may be stressed a little more, to make "atmosphere" for the longer leaps of the ensuing melodic phrases and the singularly moving cadence (bars 8–9). The descent of the bass from the long persistent E, the added triplets in bar 8, and the quiet rise of the even eighths in bar 9, all contribute to the impressiveness of this cadence.

Stress considerably the left-hand D-sharp (bars 10–11), which sounds as the initial melodic tone of the elastic triplet episode (10–14). This exquisite passage permits a slight rubato. (We lengthen slightly the two D-sharps, thus delaying the entrance of the high B's, and compensate by slightly hastening the third beat. This, recurring in bar 11, causes the two ensuing bars to be also slightly hastened, with compensation on the even eighths of 13 and the half note of 15.) Do not hasten the entrance of the returning motive—but the timing of its entrance is a subtle problem. The high two-note phrases, now elongated by the tied G-sharp and F-sharp, are hard to manage. The descending eighths against them must exhibit their pattern, but they must neither disguise nor distort the main melodic line. (We find these the most difficult notes in the piece.) The three descending notes (e.g., C-sharp, B, A, bar 16) which conclude this figure become very important in the sequel.

The opening motive could be uttered leisurely in bars 4–5; but in bars 18–19, the altered continuation of the melody compels unhesitating motion. The A-sharp, bar 20, may seem to be the equivalent of that in bar 6, but the more propulsive flow of the upper voice, as well as the notation, forbids that reading. Rather, the three-note groups just mentioned come to the surface in bars 22–24, and thus conclude an eleven-bar elaboration of the original nine-bar period. The triplet episode (bars 10–14) is similarly enriched in 26–32; but the rubato character of bars 26–7 now forms a prelude to a more definite melodic line. For this, from the G-sharp in bar 28, the composer indicates a general *cresc.;* but there is more than this to be done. The first two triplets in bar 29 are a figuration of the last two beats of bar 28; the third beat is in descending sequence with the second; and the first two beats of bar 30 are sequentially repeated on the following "three" and "one." With the preparatory triplet on "one" in bar 28, the stress on the next phrase falls on the E, and similarly in 29, with the third beat somewhat weaker. In bars 30–31, the sequential groups are slurred into one, but there must be stress points on the quarter notes E and D-sharp, with the swelled approach that will gently weight the first of the tied eighths in the lower voices. Soften notably the F-double sharp and E-sharp which follow the melodic stresses. The A-sharp of the melody must be slightly detached, to obey the composer's notation. Be sure to sustain the lower voices until the final active C-sharp is reached. The G-sharps are weighted more than the F-double sharps, to support the greater weight of the A-sharps in the fading melodic line. *Smorzando* seems justifiably to imply *ritardando*. The very sober cadence, beginning with the opening motive, needs space to attain its religious impressiveness.

The brief middle section releases the warmth that has been so far more implicit than expressed. Its stresses fall naturally on the long notes (in bar 39, D-sharp, C-sharp, and B are virtually melodic quarters). In bar 44f., though no phrasing is marked, analogy with the two-note figures in section I—and musical common sense as well—will bind the "three" to the "one." The arpeggio in 48–49 must retard a little if it is to vanish properly. Again, do not hasten the *tutte corde* phrase, which raises the tone of the utterance back to the high plane of contemplation that the warmer middle section somewhat forsook. Yet that warmth now shows its pervasive influence, for it colors almost the whole epilogue. In bar 62, it is easier to take the left hand's high E along with the chord in the right hand. In the last bar but one, we continue the descending line, A, G-sharp, F-sharp—slurred by the composer—to include the following E.

At a first reading, No. 5 seems harmonically obscure. The harmony of the up-beat is completely stated; that of the down-beat, although sometimes quite remote, is conveyed almost always by only two notes. The actual melodic line is not conspicuous, but the notation implies that the notes nearest the slurs i.e.:

B   | C  ꝛ  B   A♯ ꝛ B   | C  ꝛ  B   E, etc.

are melodic. Similarly, there is a counterpoint in the left hand

E   | D♯ ꝛ E   F♯ ꝛ E   | D♯ ꝛ E   G

which is almost an exact inversion of the melody, and which should similarly predominate over the merely harmonic notes. Section II, which is more sonorous in harmony, offers no particular problem. This piece is not very difficult to finger, and is both a valuable study in subtle tone relations and a delight in itself as a tiny "Moment Musical."

No. 6 is again quite in accord with Brahms's metaphor. Technically it is not hard to play. Musically, the two simultaneous lines of melody

seem to pose a problem as to which is predominant; but musical common sense is all that is needed for the solution. Kalbeck calls the melody of the middle section "reproachful"—a word more suggestive of the true character of the music than he usually finds. (The original edition, at bar 7 of this section, does not stem as a quarter note the C-sharp on "two." This is probably an error.)

If No. 6 is reproachful, No. 7, curt and impatient, is almost resentful—at least in its main subject. Note that the bass imitates (inexactly but meaningfully) the texture and the melodic structure of the upper voices. The delay of a sixteenth in the melodic entrance (bar 11f.) effectively intensifies the excitement. The rhythm of the next section is somewhat troublesome at first, but

s soon mastered. The dynamic problem—that of making the
ighth-note figures into a coherent background for the rhyth-
nically displaced melody—is harder. The song must be very
ull-throated. It has no real breath-pauses during the first part,
or the dark intensity of the line would be spoiled by them. In
he second part, with the melody in octaves shifting from hand
o hand, be sure that the upper note of the octave is always more
ntense than the lower, else the passionate development will be
nuddied. This section was intended to be played without pedal;
ut we cannot ourselves resist using it in the descending sixths
f the first and second endings, and the two final bars of this sec-
ion. The perky transition will be ruined if the sixteenths are in
he slightest degree out of time. Note that F–E in bar 2 is a tenta-
ive recall of the main theme, and that all the melodic phrases
ave this descending half step. In the ascending arpeggio just be-
ore the return of the main theme, make the accents conspicuous.
The quarter rest—exactly timed!—will then give energetic drive
o the theme. The first two bars of the 3–8 time conclude the
receding section and so introduce the Coda. The eighths in this
ection are of the same time value as those in the 2–4 time; but
n the final three bars, one bar of 2–4 equals one bar of the pre-
eding 3–8. We see no objection to a slight accelerando from bar
 of the 3–8 time.

The first piece in Op. 117 is an actual Cradle Song, to which
he text quoted as motto fits almost as satisfactorily as do the
vords of the "Edward" Ballad to Brahms's music.[2] There is little
n the quiet melody to suggest a tragic background until the last
our bars of the first section, where the hollow octaves, together
vith the sudden depression into the minor key, give the theme a
trange ominousness. The middle section, however, is not chilled
y this transition, save when the three notes of the main theme

[2] The song is called, in the original, "Lady Anne Bothwell's Lament," but
here is no connection with the dubious hero of the escape of Mary Stuart.
This is the song of a lady forsaken by her lover—precisely, a Cradle Song of her
orrow.

are recalled. It is, however, very unhappy. The enriched version of the beginning makes no mention, any more, of the darker middle section.

No unusual skill is required to differentiate the melody from the persistent pedal point, E-flat, which rules throughout most of the first part. In bars 5–6, the melody is in the octaves; in bar 7, in the bass; and in bar 8, in the upper voice, save for the high F, which is harmonic. Move quietly and without haste, and keep the longer descents that are made of the similar notes of the theme unperturbed by accentuation after the beginning. The cold minor version may well be colored by *una corda,* but do not dramatize this passage. The swells marked in bars 1–2 of the *Più adagio* of course govern all similar passages, differences of degree marking the points of greater or lesser intensity. Without pedal, the bass arpeggios are too "dry"; but they need not be prolonged into the rests, and the staccato marked for the nonmelodic eighths in the right hand can therefore be fairly well observed. *Un poco più Andante* means "going a little more"— than the *Adagio,* but not more than the *Andante moderato* of the beginning. To observe the imitation in bars 13–14 of this section, start it by intoning both the high E-flat on "one" and that for the thumb on "three."

No. 2 is more difficult—and more satisfying. The delicate melodic line indicated by the short slurs must of course come out; but every accompanying thirty-second, whether in right hand or left, must be audible and in its proper rhythmic place. Variation of tempo is as unendurable as any square, unshaded rattling of the thirty-seconds, save that a little freedom of motion may be taken at the end of arpeggiated interludes—e.g., bar 9. The melody—in itself by no means buoyant—receives from this persistent motion of its accompaniment a singular lightening of tone. In bar 22f., the theme appears in slower motion, but the major key dispels any hint of somberness until the chromatic sixteenths appear.

Detach and greatly soften the sixteenth which completes the feminine ending in bars 26 and 34, so that the ensuing repetition of this note, definitely louder, may be felt to begin the next phrase. Even a brief instant of time may be stolen to make this punctuation clear.

In the rhythmic displacement of the thirty-second-note figure in bar 43, give a perceptible stress to A-flat in the second figure, and to the following "one." Be sure that B-natural–C answers the high D-flat–C throughout bars 47–48. In 49–50, the higher notes of the right-hand figure have a distinct melodic line; but do not spoil the crystalline tone of the whole fabric by the least failure to synchronize the two hands. Make definite, but do not exaggerate, the pause in bar 51 before the resumption of the main melody. Emphasize somewhat the C-flats which give a new elasticity to the theme by hinting at a new tonality. That suggestion soon proves false, but it has much value in preparing for the rapid ascent to the climax. The simple form of the theme in the *Più Adagio* is more impressive than at its first appearance, its elegiac tone being enhanced by the recitational figures interpolated (bars 73 and 76) between the phrases of the theme. Delay, by slight expansion, the low E-natural–F of the bass, thus justifying the slight rubato without which the interpolations will be stiff. Their stress is on their highest notes (F and A-flat), and a slight pause is necessary before the thematic phrases are resumed.

No. 3 is the most somber, but is also the most meaningful, of the three pieces in Op. 117. We are here pretty close to a direct utterance of that grief which, in the works we have so far examined, is hardly more than implied. There is still no violence, no protest, nor any weakness of complaint; but the bleakness of the theme, announced without harmony until its cadence in bars 4–5, is ineluctable. In the repressed melodic line there are almost no skips (and those only of thirds), and the nearly unaltered repetition of the first phrase (bar 2) makes the ensuing slow ascent seem extraordinarily effortful. This sense is heightened by the more rapid descent and the inconclusive cadence. Even the repetition of the theme is provided with but the barest suggestion of harmony; nor does the raising of A to A-sharp in any marked degree brighten the tone. The ensuing phrase of contrast, beginning, not in A, but on the submediant of C-sharp minor, offers no relief, even though somewhat richer harmony is added.

When at bar 21 the first phrases return, they are extraordinarily warmed by the gently dissonant harmony. (The notation in bar

25 obscures the fact that the melody is D-sharp, C-sharp, B-sharp.)
Even the second strain, still unharmonized, sounds less hollow,
and the poco più lento, thus approached, becomes resigned, without bitterness.

The middle section is a grateful alleviation. The colorful device of leaping an octave for the completion of the phrase is
highly appropriate to the more urgent sense of the music. (Pedal
is indispensable. It may be taken with each preparatory sixteenth
—e.g., E, F-natural, and so on—of this section; but be sure to
give these notes such volume as will permit rhythmic propulsion
by the lower voice, on the beat.) The high F-natural (bar 1) is
stronger than the preceding E, and the high B still stronger, but
the ensuing longer phrase is weaker. The antiphonal strain in
bars 4–5 seems a little perfunctory, but it lengthens the period to
five bars. (The similar passages in 14–15, and 19–20, seem, however, quite appropriate.) The little interlude (Tempo I) before
the main theme returns is of a singular charm, and the two
repetitive phrases (bars 3 and 6) are made poignant by the
darkened harmony. Play the appoggiatura figures in sixteenths
very delicately against a finely shaded legato in the melodic—the
highest—notes. A new harmonization of the main theme now
follows, more than fulfilling the expectation aroused by the interlude. The quiet tragedy of the second strain of the main section
now becomes fully apparent, justifying the added emphasis which
the slight expansion gives to the più lento.

The two sets of pieces we have just studied were published in
1892. The next two (Op. 118 and Op. 119) appeared the following year. There is more diversity of title in this set (a Ballad, a
Romanze, and a Rhapsody being included with seven Intermezzi),
but there is little real difference in the general character. The implications are on the whole less dark, but you will hardly look
for youthful, untrammeled joy. And in one or two of them, the
familiar metaphor will clearly apply.

The first number in Op. 118 is a very immediate gust of passion, brief and tornadic, almost like one of the more imaginative Chopin *Préludes;* but this is the music of a stronger man. There is neither need nor space for more than one theme. Heine's poem, *Ich grolle nicht,* to which Schumann set one of his finest songs, comes to mind as an expression of the mood. You will find it a very unusual utterance for the staid and emotionally circumspect Brahms.

The notation, which carefully slurs the rising arpeggio from the left hand to the right, fails to indicate an equally significant fact— that the E (bar 2) in the left hand is the last note of the melodic phrase. Neither do we include the A against the D-sharp in bar 5 in the phrase in which the slur places it. The following B, if taken as up- beat to the D–C, seems the only proper analogue to the two preced- ing up-beats. The pedal marks permit and even prescribe a generous jangling. Though they appear only in the first three bars, they are implied throughout. In bar 12, detach definitely the last notes of the four-note groups, attacking each following note, to give vitality to the precipitous changes of harmony. Only so will the build-up to the climax be effective. Brahms marks only $f < >$ for the E and D in bar 22: but this D cannot be made too impassioned. Bring out the augmentation of the theme at the end to make a forceful and con- vincing epilogue.

No. 2 is much better known—indeed, it is one of the most popular of all Brahms's pieces. The songful melody is long- breathed and contented, and there are no interpretative obscurities. Neither is the music especially difficult to play. The note of tender- ness implied in the superscription is maintained throughout, with- out high contrast; but even so, there is no monotony. Only twice does any shadow fall upon the pleasant scene, and that is but momentary.

The tempo must be such as to avoid either languishing or impetu- ousness. (We think, about $\quad = 60.$) The melody phrases itself. The G-natural in the tenor at bar 4 can be unpleasant if the phrase end is too much detached so that a false relation with the preceding G-sharp in the melody appears. Think of the G-sharp (soprano), G-natural (tenor), and F-sharp (bass) as forming a chromatic slide, and the progression will be smooth. The intimacy of the second strain (bar 17) is beautifully appropriate, and its continuation, over the pedal E, rises to a hint of the opening phrases, which, just a little augmented, become singularly eloquent. The continuation has a tone as if of gratitude, so deep, indeed, as to be almost painful. (Observe, in bars 33–34, that same device of lowering the harmony from major to minor which was so significant in the interlude of Op. 117, No. 3.) The ensuing strains are inversions of the melody in bars 1 and 2; but they have a richer continuation, and the second strain is likewise vivified. The increase of speed marked at bar 38f. must be carefully studied. If it is too great, the significance of the descending bass from bar 42 will be lost. (Bring out, in this bass progression, only the essential notes of the descent—E–D and C-sharp–B.)

The second section (bar 49), although in minor and a little reproach-ful in tone, is almost at once raised to a tone of high serenity (bar 57). Note that the tenor here imitates the soprano. Make these two voices into a violin and a 'cello, and the *più lento* (which is also imitative) like the quiet richness of a full orchestra. At *tempo primo* the two voices of bar 49f. are inverted in double counterpoint, and should be made more eloquent than before. The fermata in bar 76 extends the C-sharp so long that it seems to us inadvisable to pause after the B that really completes the phrase. We therefore begin, with the B, the motion into the main theme. Note that in the last bar the high A completes the sense of the preceding C-sharp–B.

The *Ballade* was very possibly written in the same year as the *G minor Rhapsody*. It has not, certainly, the contemplative tone we have encountered, so far, in these later pieces. There is no authentic hint of the narrative (if there was one at all) which guided the musical discourse. Kalbeck has invented a sickly tale of an angry hero and a pleading sweetheart, which, if we play the rôle of Procrustes, we can force this music—or the Appas-sionata, or almost any other piece with a fairly vivid thematic contrast—to fit; but we suspect that Brahms would have repelled any such invitation to Hollywood. Neither the close nor any other feature of the piece seems to us to denote a dramatic con-cept such as we found in the "Edward" Ballad.

The staccato marked for the accompaniment of the theme forbids the pedal. The stern line of the melody, from its incisive beginning to the low D on which the five-bar period ends, will become banal if the eighth-note chords are not kept sharp and brittle, and if the accents on the strong notes are made too much alike. For the alternative phrase (bar 11f.), pedal is marked; and you will find, in this thicker tone, the reason for avoiding it at the beginning. The dominant seventh in C on which the transition ends is treated as the equivalent of a "German" sixth chord, and makes a colorful entrance for the songful second theme. The warm color of the B major key is appropriate to the mild but by no means tearful melody. The doubly stemmed eighth notes in the left hand (E, E, D-sharp, D-natural) may well be completed by a C-sharp in bar 4. At the end of bar 12, the main theme is interjected, but with a pedaled, not a staccato, accompaniment. The modulation back to G (momentarily, G major) is as effective as was that to B major. What follows is only a restatement, on a smaller scale, of the first part.

No. 4 is an actual Intermezzo—an Interlude—in the sequence of rather sober pieces so far included in this collection. The contriving of so delicate a fabric as this without descending to flimsiness or triviality is possible only by an artist who has already solved more serious imaginative problems. You can sense—indeed, to play the piece properly you must sense—this implication in the music; but to identify it verbally is beyond our power.

From the character of the music itself, we take the *agitato* in the superscription as implying speed rather than that disturbance of mind which we ordinarily call agitation. The motion is everywhere as light as a ballet dancer's step; yet this is no heedless or momentary gaiety. Such grace is too finished, too experienced, to be merely spontaneous. The music is therefore very difficult, not to finger, but to interpret. Observe that the figures in the left hand have the same general pattern as those in the right, and that their shading is as carefully marked. The relative weights of the right-hand up-beats and the left-hand down-beats therefore pose a problem. We must let the hearer know which figure is on "one" and which is on "two"; but if we thump the "ones" we shall awkwardly impede the motion of the higher figures. It seems to us best to swing into the tempo by way of a slight lengthening of the first A-flat in the up-beat and a corresponding hastening of the two following notes of the triplet. The left hand on "one," thereafter, can then assume the exact tempo without an awkward accent; and, the rhythm being thus established, the hearer will not be confused. The rightness of your rhythmic beginning will be tested at bar 7. If the two eighth notes feel like an up-beat, you began rightly. Do not ignore the tenor's imitation of the soprano from this point. The rubato of the beginning may be employed again in bar 11, with the slightest retarding of the two preceding beats.

What follows is easier. In bars 18–19, make the E-flat, G, B-flat, A-flat, G, legato—i.e., three against two. Bar 38 and half of bar 39 may again be very slightly retarded. The new section, from bar 52, is again strictly imitative, up to bar 98, but this passage offers little difficulty. The *più agitato* at bar 99 is again a direction for speed. From bar 111, and again from bar 118, bring out audibly the octave leaps on F. Keep the little finger bright in the final chords after the *fp*.

The somewhat bucolic *Romanze,* No. 5, is very unimpassioned, as if its inspiration had come from Thomas Hardy; but that novelist's pessimism is not reflected. Observe that the descending soprano voice, against a real melody which is sonorously doubled in the octave, will reappear in the alto from bar 9. (The melodic line at bar 4 is merely the three C's.) The *Allegretto grazioso* is made by figurating (rather than varying) its first eight-bar period. The difficulties of this piece are not great, but—to us—the reward is correspondingly small.

No. 6, on the other hand, is that piece which we referred to as the one we should put above Mr. Huneker's choice (Op. 116, No. 4) as the finest piano composition he knew. It is perhaps the most "subjective" of all Brahms's utterances. Indeed, a more immediate expression of an emotional attitude can hardly be found in the literature of the piano—that instrument which, as we have seen, became during the nineteenth century the most-favored vehicle for such expression. The piece is very dark, so that against this background the high lights count almost incredibly; yet there is no hint of mere "effect," which, above all, the composer hated.

The theme is remarkably confined—to the compass of a mere minor third. It insists on the third of the minor scale (G-flat), intoning that note at the beginning and returning to it four times with varying emphasis. These emphases must be carefully studied. Pedal the first note for richness of tone, and cling to it a shade too long, starting the motion again with the F. Make the next G-flat rather incidental, since the third, on "one," must have rhythmic stress; then, from a softer F, progress definitely to the F in bar 3, which is the crisis note of the theme. The accompanying arpeggio, against which this F is poignantly dissonant, must be perfectly spaced and the swell very slight, corresponding to the repressed contour of the theme. (Brahms marks these figures as sextolets, but we believe they are really two groups of triplets. A division of the six thirty-seconds into three groups of two—the true sense of the sextolet—is belied by the three detached thirty-seconds in bar 4, and by the general shape of the figures in bar 7.) These passages are extremely difficult to keep light and smooth. Mark slightly the left-hand sixteenths in bars 7–8, and intone the C in 9, which rhythmically propels the suspension of the warmer variant of the theme—harmonized in thirds and escaping its former narrow range—which now appears. Mark the G-flat on "three" in bar 10, which begins an imitation of the preceding upper phrase, keeping the left-hand arpeggios always smooth and quiet. Not to avoid the dissonance, but to mark more clearly the entrance of the imitations in bar 13f., we "stagger" very slightly the attack on the higher voice. Do not overdraw the quiet restatement of the main theme against the pedal F's in bars 17–20. It must seem no more than the reiteration of an inexorable fact.

There follows a repetition of what has gone before, save that the theme has a new figure of accompaniment—less swift, even more hushed, and moving stealthily in its own pattern over a vast space. We find this the most congenial fingering for bars 25–26:

The contrast of the ensuing section is high, and will be unnecessarily shocking unless the direction s. v. (sotto voce) is obeyed. (We use the soft pedal.) The tempo must not be hastened, else the tremendous emergence of the main theme (bars 53–54 and 59–61) will be distorted. The character is stern—the kinetic counterpart of the static contemplation that has so far ruled—and the growth from the *p* to the *ff* is fearsome. The pedal can be no more than touched, at the stronger instants, until bar 51, where it may give the legato phrases thick reinforcement. Against the theme in bar 53, make the low bass notes very solid. (Do not, as careless readers do, play A-flat instead of A-natural in the bass of the second eighth-note chord in bar 54.) The *più f* in bar 55 can hardly imply a greater force than the *ff* marked for the theme just played; but take care to make the *ff* in bar 60 bigger than that in 54. Bar 62 may well be retarded to give time for the full diminution of the tone.

Begin the returning theme as before, and in bar 65f. be sure that the descending sixteenths in the bass make a continuous line to the vitally important C-flat. This note gives a new and unbelievable warmth to the derivative of the theme which has already begun above it. (The tied E-flat must be audible against the C-flat of the bass.) If ever in your life you played legato, you must do it with this wonderful phrase. The glory recedes—as it should—and the more somber tone returns; but we have glimpsed an apocalypse.

As a greeting on his own birthday in 1893 (May 7), Brahms sent to Clara Schumann a composition that she describes as "a charming little piece, full of dissonances, but which one absorbs with pleasure. The piece is so sadly sweet!" Brahms, also, announcing his missive, speaks of the music as "extraordinarily melancholy, and [the superscription] *sehr langsam zu spielen* (to be played very slowly) doesn't say enough. Every note and every bar must sound as if *ritardando,* as if one were drawing melancholy from every note."

If it were not for the middle section of the *E-flat minor Intermezzo,* these words would fit it well enough—though one would hardly expect Clara to call it a "little" piece. Kalbeck thinks— rightly, as it seems to us—that it was of the *Intermezzo in B minor,* the first number in Op. 119, that she was speaking. This music fits the description much better, and is hardly less moving than the piece we have just studied.

Instead of *sehr langsam zu spielen* (a phrase often used by Schumann) the printed piece has the superscription *Adagio*. The melody, to us who are accustomed to more blatant expressions of grief, is more restrained than we might expect from the composer's words, but is also more "true." Note by note, the accompaniment develops beneath the sustained tones of the melody a "secondary" ninth chord[3]—decidedly a dissonance, in Brahms's harmonic vocabulary—which is absorbed into the melodic note and makes its tension accumulate. It is no mean problem to make these notes contribute to, instead of override, the thematic line. The fourth bar, with its up-beat, produces a figure (B | E D) which is at once imitated in the bass, and will soon become more conspicuous. In the melody, G, in bar 2, seems unmistakably the stress point, with the E of bar 4 secondary. F-sharp, in bar 5, is however secondary to A in bar 7. The ensuing recall of the beginning may well be less intense than before; but you must make room for a *decresc.* from bar 12. From here, detach carefully the second eighth note of each phrase, in both left hand and right, shading the imitations appropriately, so that the broad cadence (14–16) will be fully impressive.

The whole following passage, in the major key, has extraordinary warmth. The frequent marks of ⟩ from up-beat to down are at first confusing, since the most vital melodic notes are those which are thus weakened. To keep from smothering them, take the pedal (e.g., in bar 17) with the low D, which should be sonorous; take the third, D–F-sharp, on time, with the F-sharp a very little louder than the D; then delay a little the added A's, with the upper definitely brighter than the lower. The same dynamics will apply (with a slight general crescendo) up to the B in bar 18; but the rubato can be used only at the beginning. The next group is similar. Remember always to intone the bass notes so as to mark the beats against the syncopated right hand. The *cresc.* marked in bar 22 must be considerable, but the growth to the *f* in 24 must not be lumpy. Some diminuendo thereafter seems obligatory, but the G-sharp must grow toward the *fp* G-natural. This G must audibly proceed to E in bar 28. Therefore we take *una corda* from "two" in 27 to "two" in 28. Cling a little to the E-sharp in the lower repetition.

[3] One whose root is other than the dominant or the leading tone of the scale. The first, here, is a subdominant ninth; the second is built on the mediant and the third on the·tonic of B minor.

What follows is not a beginning over, but the beginning of a development. The enrichment offered by the descending chromatic line is most valuable, with C-natural the richest note. In the original edition, the quarter note D in bar 34, and that in 38, are not tied into the next bar, but slurred to the following G's. (Sauer, wrongly, adds the ties while keeping the slur.) In bars 35 and 36, some feel surer if they take the high G and B of the left hand with the right. Take much pains with the pointed echoing in bars 40–42. This passage naturally bears some retardation. Emphasize somewhat the F-sharp, B, E, and A in bars 43–44, but keep the tempo. The triplets in the accompaniment from 47·to 49 tempt one sorely to rubato; but except for a slight clinging to the initial F-sharp you will find the composer's *in tempo* the only possible means of avoiding an intolerable, fussy sentimentality. We can see no reason why the sixteenths, F-sharp–G, in bar 51, must now be taken with the left hand. Study carefully the fine dissonances in the upper voice of the left hand from bar 59 to the end. They are wholly appropriate to the renunciatory sense of the whole progression.

No. 2 makes far slighter demand upon the imagination. You will see that the melody of the second section is a transformation of that of the first; but it is probable that the beginning was worked out from the middle. The three different rhythmic figures vary interestingly the opening melodic idea, but the whole first section remains pretty much on a level. The middle, however, is a wonderful thing, as fluid as melody can be, and almost as un-self-conscious as if it had come from Schubert.

The two sixteenths in the opening figure should be "picked up" with a rather high wrist. The legato to the following eighth is then accomplished merely by dropping the wrist. The left hand is of course high and light throughout. The two variants are easier. Do not smear the legato sixteenths, seven bars from the end of the section. We do not detach the quarter note E from the D-sharp, in the final figure, but make a continuous line of the alto voice. Make the arpeggios in the middle section very legato, with pedal. Lighten always the "three" in the melody so that it may flow into the next "one"; but be careful to graduate the dynamics of these "ones." From bar 9, keep the upper notes in the octaves much brighter than the lower. At the end of the first part, accentuate the tied B so that the C-natural of the bass can be felt to pull strongly on the B. In bars 2 and 4 of the second part, keep the octave eighth notes light. In the second ending, intone a little the descending quarters in the left hand—G-sharp, E, and so on.

The humor implied in the superscription of No. 3 (*giocoso*— "humorously") is not very apparent. For us, it lies in the weighting of the quarter notes, which we intensify by a complete detachment of the preceding eighth in bars 1 and 2. The bass figure, with its low note on "one," prevents any misconception of the true rhythm. The speed must not be great. (The swift triplet sixteenths in bar 44, which must be articulate, will determine for you the proper speed of the whole piece.) The *sfp* C on "one" of bar 37 must be detached; otherwise the stress necessary to sustain audibly the D-flat cannot be developed. Keep the last five bars very leggiero and staccato. We both diminish and slightly accelerate the final rise—not, of course, ignoring the thematic hint.

The great *E-flat Rhapsody*—Brahms's last piano piece—is very difficult, but is a stimulating, and sometimes exasperating, study for those who have a fair measure of technical equipment. There is certainly no moaning of farewell, even though the composer was very possibly aware that he would write no more for his instrument. (The *51 Exercises for Pianoforte,* also published in 1893, had been written much earlier.) Instead, there is once more the energy and enthusiasm of youth; but it is hardly imaginable that even in his own younger days Brahms could have written this music.

Observe—as too many do not—that there is *no* accent on the "one" of bar 4. If you heedlessly put one here, you will quite spoil the drawing of the five-bar period. The high masculinity of the theme demands great strength and absolute simultaneity in the strokes of the two hands. But keep the highest notes brighter than the lower, in the right hand. The three accented E-flats in 4–5 must be very forceful, and about equal in loudness. This group of three notes often appears as a separate motive—e.g., in bars 24–5f., 57–8, and so on. Articulate clearly all the triplets from bar 65 (some may find their derivation in the three quarter notes just mentioned), but do not in the least alter the march of the rhythm.

In the A-flat section (93f.) we find another legato melody with a staccato accompaniment. (Sauer and other editors disregard the plain meaning of the notation here, putting in frequent pedal marks.) The legato is here much more difficult to maintain than in Op. 76, No. 2, since the right hand has also a good deal of harmony to play along with the melody. We find it easier, in bar 94 and similar passages, to bring out the melodic notes if the chords are rolled downward. This solution, however, is against the notation; moreover, the downward roll, when actually desired (as in 96f.), is indicated. Also, inconsistently with our advice, we take the pedal in bars 108–111 and 129–132.

Do not hasten the tempo at bar 159. The B and A in bar 157 and the D-sharp–D-natural in 162 must not be lost from sight. The rising tenor from bar 168 is slurred for only three bars, but the notation continues that line for two bars more. We can offer no help with the sprawling figures from bar 190. They must be perfectly articulate, with the boom, boom, boom of the bass threateningly heavy against them. (The rising left hand, 207–8, answers these passages, and must be similarly clear.) The single notes after the sixteenth-note octaves in bar 237f. may be taken either with the 2nd finger or the thumb. The aiming is easier with the 2nd, but with the hand already in motion for the sixteenth, a quick hop to the thumb is hardly more difficult, and has much more power. We do not think a slight retard in bars 215–16 too rhetorical. A slight hastening also seems natural from 252 to 258, with somewhat broadened emphasis thereafter.

The music of Brahms is the record of a very strong personality and a correspondingly vivid imagination—two characteristics which are indispensable to greatness in an artist. The direction which the energies possessed by such an artist are to take is not determined by their own momentum, but by other forces within, or by resistances without, the man himself. Almost always the highly artistic personality is egoistic to the point of ruthlessness— willing to overthrow, in the belief that he can himself rebuild and improve. The docility with which Brahms accepted what we may call the classical doctrine is a sign that egoism was in him far less rampant than, for example, in Beethoven. In the nature of things, an artist's faith in his own genius must be unshakeable, and Brahms was no exception. He learned, however, earlier than most, that genius needs not merely the discipline which yields competency, but that also which yields sound judgment of the value of artistic effort.

All of us make such judgments—and continue to remake them —out of little more than the whims of personal taste and the caprices of contemporary fashion. The lesser artists, although they often set our fashions for us, work upon a basis hardly sounder than our own—their resource being, first, that indisputable talent which makes them artists, and second, the same capriciousness of taste which make us followers of the fashions they set. Their talent being equal to the invention of fresh appeals to our taste, and our appetites being eager but inconsiderate, we are easily convinced that these are "great" artists—which is to say, providers of permanently nourishing food for the spirit. The frequent rectifications of judgment which this dependence on momentary taste forces upon us seldom teach us how unreliable taste is. But the problem of the "great" artist is harder, since he must make his decision as to what is worth doing before—or at least during—his creative act. Even so, he is taking a risk— either that of too great a trust in his own creative powers, or that of too great a faith in the already existent process of expression he chooses.

The latter alternative, very unusual, is the one Brahms chose. How much of spontaneity he lost through that decision can only be conjectured. The decision, no doubt, was reinforced by many circumstances, the chief of which seems to us to have been Schumann's laudatory article in the *Neue Zeitschrift*. We have seen that he turned from the sonata and the other freer forms to the process of variation—the most exigent of all, as he employed it —for the perfection of his method.

But we have also seen that from Op. 76 on there is at last

achieved a new and apparently easy mastery, not of intricacy of structure—for he considerably forsook that—but of simplicity in the expression of profound and subtle ideas. In the experience of very many, these things, once grasped, do not grow stale. Brahms, therefore, by the criteria we set up a moment ago, proves himself a "great" composer.

The impulses which Bach and Beethoven obeyed—the one, profoundly and unquestioningly religious, the other, similarly humanitarian—were impulses shared (especially in Beethoven's time) by the rest of their world. Protestantism was not new in Bach's day, but it was an abiding faith, and a guide to the elemental problems of living. Democratic sentiment was new in Beethoven's day—so new that its philosophy demanded exploration more extensive than even his vast energy could complete. During Brahms's life, however, the world seemed to be growing stable. (Two world wars have shown us how unstable it was; but Brahms never foresaw such catastrophes.) Even a stable world bears analysis—or, for the artist, interpretation—but such interpretation does not demand the frenzy of the reformer. Seldom, therefore, is Brahms incited to the thunderous invective of Beethoven—or to his prophetic dreaming. He often reasserts Beethoven's views. That is to say, the implications of his thought are similarly humanitarian; but, developed with a degree of contemplation which Beethoven's age hardly knew, they become humanistic.

Our two wars, and especially the last one, have shown the need for a pretty thorough revaluation of our humanism. Not having attained it, we do not know what, out of the old régime, will survive into the new. But the music of Brahms—which, according to older standards, was probably the most highly civilized music we possessed—seems likely to conform in many particulars to those standards upon which the conflicts of the present will at last come to rest.

# 13
# ACHILLE CLAUDE DEBUSSY

HOW unstable that world was which Brahms so stably portrayed was dimly revealed, in the last decade of the nineteenth century by many artists. The most provocative musicians of the day were Mahler, Richard Strauss, and Debussy. Neither Mahler nor Strauss left any piano music of consequence (except for Strauss's *Burleske* for piano and orchestra). Debussy, however, was himself a very capable pianist, and found that instrument the most congenial vehicle for his thought. No other composer, since his time, has loved the piano as he did, or has made through it any vital contributions to the new and often startling processes of composition which characterize our time. His "method," of course, no longer has novelty. His music, on the other hand, though also no longer novel, has attained by way of its former newness a very stable place in the world's affection.

Debussy was not marked, in infancy, for the career of a musician, but his talent, once discovered (by a certain Mme. de Fleurville, who had been a pupil of Chopin, and was the mother-in-law of Verlaine), was thereafter rapidly developed. At eleven (1873) he entered the Paris Conservatoire, where he was at once enrolled in two advanced piano classes. His work in solfège was especially notable—as were also his disconcerting questions about the supposedly indisputable rules of theory. His piano playing, already subtly colored, did not please his teacher, Marmontel;

yet he progressed rapidly for a time, and won various degrees of favorable mention in the annual competitions. In harmony his disposition to do the forbidden thing was duly frowned upon—but sometimes with a grudging admission that his work was very ingenious. His knowledge of his own tongue—sometimes said to be deficient—was at any rate equal to an extraordinarily perfect adjustment of his music to the verses to which it was set, and it was in this field of composition that the high originality of his mind was first unmistakably revealed.

There is no doubt that he was primarily a harmony-minded musician. His melody is generated from harmony—but that does not mean that he had no melodic invention. Neither does it imply that he was rhythmically uninventive. It does mean that the "subjects" about which he writes are those which imply a kind of static contemplation of feeling, such as may be "represented" by a strange and colorful series of harmonies, and that his rhythms and melodies are of a kind compatible with the harmony which embodies such visions. Much experiment is needed for such discoveries as these, and it was relatively a long time before his process of composition could be perfected.

Technical description of that process would hardly suit the purpose of this book; but one feature of it cannot be ignored. It is generally called a scale—the "whole-tone" or "six-tone" scale—but it seems to us that this device is itself more nearly a harmony than a scale.[1] It can be used, to any desired extent, as

[1] The essence of it is the augmented triad. The whole scale, indeed, consists of two interlocked augmented triads, a whole step apart (e.g., C–E–G-sharp and D–F-sharp–A-sharp); but these notes can also be seen as an amalgamation of the augmented triad with the ninth or the eleventh chord.

The familiar dominant ninth chord (e.g., C–E–G–B-flat–D) had long since been familiar with its fifth, G, raised to G-sharp, its dissonant pull being thereby considerably heightened. This chord, indeed, gives us five of the six notes of the whole-tone scale: C–D–E–G-sharp and B-flat (or A-sharp). The missing F-sharp may be construed as an augmented eleventh. The peculiar effect of this last addition you can demonstrate for yourself. Play, as an arpeggio, first the simple ninth chord; then, this same chord with the fifth augmented; then, the whole series of six notes, C–E–G-sharp–B-flat–D–F-sharp. You may at

melody, but even in this aspect it retains much of its peculiar fluidity.

Debussy did not actually "discover" the whole-tone scale, merely as a musical fact. It had already been used by Glinka (in the

---

first be reluctant to admit the F-sharp—because the other notes imply the orthodox tonality of the nineteenth century, and this F-sharp somewhat disturbs that implication. But if you repeat the experiment several times you will find: first, that it begins to sound like a natural combination; second, that the sense of key, clearly present without F-sharp, is supplanted by a peculiar—and very possibly agreeable—uncertainty of key. Now, having played these notes as an actual chord until they sound reasonable, you will find that you can also play them in their scale order (but with the pedal, so that they all sound at once) and still distinguish in this tone complex the sense of the chord which you heard before.

You can easily see that this "harmony" divides the octave into equal intervals of a whole step. That means that you cannot, by ear, discover in either the chord or the scale any root or fundamental tone. You know the keynote of the major scale because the intervals of that scale are of different sizes; you find that a triad is major or minor because the thirds of which each is composed are of different sizes. But with intervals all audibly of the same size, nobody can tell which is the fundamental tone. The division of the octave into equal minor thirds (one of them has to be written as an augmented second, but that is of no consequence to the ear) had long been familiar in the diminished seventh chord (e.g., C-sharp–E–G–B-flat–C-sharp). Its division into major thirds (e.g., C–E–G-sharp–C) is similarly accomplished with the augmented triad. The ear will readily take any one of the notes in either of these chords as a foundation tone. What was C-sharp–E–G–B-flat—the diminished seventh in D minor, which smoothly moved to that triad—may become, for example, A-sharp–C-sharp–E–G—the diminished seventh in B minor, and so, without turning a hair, may accomplish a modulation between those two keys (and, with similar manipulation, many others).

The obvious possibilities of modulation with the diminished seventh chord are greater than those with the augmented triad, because four notes, instead of three, are possible "roots." The possibilities with that "chord" which we take the six-tone scale to be are even greater—because there are six possible "roots" instead of four; and with that number, the very notion of a root, as we have seen by experiment, is likely to disappear altogether. There are of course two six-tone scales, and two only: the one here described, beginning on C; the other, a half step higher throughout. Like the other chords, they can be approached from any definite key and made to sound as if they belonged to that key, or may be so continued and quitted as to destroy the sense of key.

Overworked, any of these devices soon produces satiety, or worse. This has been unfortunately proved in many of Debussy's compositions; but you will also find that he discovers by its means a kind of fluidity which music never knew before.

*Overture* to *Russlan and Ludmilla*) twenty years before Debussy was born. What he discovered were the musical possibilities of this fact—virtually all of them. His discovery was gradual; his use of the device was excessive; but it was so completely suited to his imaginative needs that he may well be forgiven his overemphasis.

The earliest piano pieces are relatively unoriginal. Yet they have the charm that emanates from true musicalness, and some of them are still very popular. The first of any consequence are the two *Arabesques,* which are dated 1888. They are the work of a young man who had won the first *Grand Prix de Rome,* in 1884, with a Cantata, *L'Enfant Prodigue* ("The Prodigal Son"), which is far more indicative of genius than these two slight pieces. A few notes on their detail may help some readers to a first acquaintance with Debussy.

No. 1, in E. *Andantino con moto* does not mean *Presto leggiero.* Taken at their proper speed, the four chords at the beginning, flowing right over the tonic, have a delicate flavor that will be quite lost if they are taken brilliantly. The melody, when it does appear in bar 3, will then appear to have been invisibly present from the beginning. Do not disturb this easy motion, unless for a slight expansion of the last triplet under the tied A; but study the possibilities of dynamic shading. The ensuing trickle of notes is similarly fluid, and is quite self-sufficient without any pianistic cosmetics. The added high notes above the returning arpeggios of the opening prepare for the warmer melodic phrases which follow, and which may be given a considerable blush of color. The tied E at the beginning of the middle section becomes so nearly inaudible that we gently restrike it. Expand a little, and shade with great care the augmented triad with which return is made to the beginning.

No. 2 is more difficult. Clear articulation (with active fingers) must be assured for the triplet sixteenths before you can attain the considerable speed which this piece demands. A hint of hesitation at the end of bar 4 will give the entering theme its natural momentum. Take no pedal, except for the tenth chords, and strike these very lightly, else you will ruin all your careful preparation. The slurred eighth notes (bar 8), however, will not be harmed by the pedal. Accentuate the tied E in bar 15 to give propulsion to the new rising strain, and make the left-hand triplet figure chuckle (at bar 19) underneath the wavering of the high quarter notes. The gaiety of the climax (23f.) is very saucy. The little march which makes transition to the second theme must strut like a bellhop in a new uniform. Do not elongate the "four" in bar 33 into a quarter note. Make the rests very silent, and the conclusion (35-6) very naïve. The ensuing interlude is only a harmonic-rhythmic effect. Do not spoil it by ignoring the staccato of the rising figure against the sustained harmonies. You can hardly fail to make the sudden modulations colorful, but this effect can be enhanced by carefully contrasting your dynamics when new colors appear. At *meno mosso* the whole notes of course imply full pedal; and since its color is now characteristic, we hold it through bars 4 and 8 in spite of the staccato.

The *Petite Suite,* although originally written for four hands, is familiar in a solo arrangement. The pieces are of no great interest today, though they are pleasant, and occasionally exhibit, as in the passage in the barcarolle (*En Bateau*) marked *un peu retenu,* hints of the six-tone-scale feeling. The *Rêverie,* published in 1890, was republished in 1905, when the composer would have liked to repudiate it. From that year there is also a *Ballade,* a *Danse* (originally called *Tarantelle Styrienne*) which will demand some comment, a *Valse Romantique* and a *Nocturne,* in which there are again a few of Debussy's peculiar harmonies, but no matter of great interest.

The *Danse* was both edited as a piano piece and arranged for orchestra by Maurice Ravel. The main theme is vitally rhythmic. Note that its true measure is 6-8, with stress on the F-sharp, but also with the ictus on the following chord (the "four"). In the prescribed *pp,* these values can be conveyed by very slight dynamic forces; but they must be there, and appear frequently in the sequel. From bar 29 to 43, however, the 6-8 has been turned into 3-4 by the phrase designs. From 58, take no pedal, but bring out, like a strum on a mandolin, the rolled chords. (The legato phrase, 70-76, however, may be colored by pedal.) At bar 96f., be sure to maintain the 6-8 feeling. Pedal more generously the legato from 104. Stress the "one" in 107, with the E-flat much lighter, like a very high kick. In the *molto cresc.,* increase also the articulation, and end with a good thump on the B (131), perfectly in time. From 155, if you learn to make a smooth diminuendo, staccato, and perfectly in time, you will see what a high interest can inhere in notes almost meaningless in themselves. This vanishing rhythm is implied beneath the sustained chords with their melodic upper voice, and becomes audible again at bar 163. From bar 179, song takes precedence over dance. Take the pedal through such passages as that from 211 to 218, observing that E in 215 moves to the following F-sharp and C-sharp in the left hand. The figure from which the transition (239–270) is built is derived from bar 51. We take the pedal throughout the rebounding chords in 241–2, and so on. The speed of the 3–4 time can be seen from the quarters in 29f.

With the *Suite Bergamasque* (the verbal, but not especially the musical, allusion is to the town of Bergamo), which also dates from 1890, Debussy shows something of his future stature. Of its four pieces—*Prélude, Minuet, Clair de lune,* and *Passepied*— the third has far outshone the others. The *Prélude* toys amiably with the leaps and the running motion found in the first two bars, and in its avoidance of conventional cadences anticipates the works of later years. The *Minuet,* which has more notes within the beat than are usual in the classical examples, must be taken slowly enough so that the rhythm will exhibit real character. The stress at the beginning, and often thereafter, is on "two." The form is very free, the ancient designs of Trio and Da Capo being undiscoverable. The conventions of key are also interestingly defied.

No. 3 is the inexhaustible *Clair de lune*. Threadbare as it now is, the piece is exquisite, and very characteristic of the composer's sensitivity. The substance is hardly more substantial than vapor; yet the design is perfectly rounded and proportioned. And its popularity attests the vitality of those disturbances which moonlight evokes in even the most hardened antisentimentalists.

Beginning, you must somehow take an elastic spring from the eighth rest and reach the two eighth notes in one easy stride. Although the high A-flat is louder than the following F, that note must have enough tone so that your first audible rhythmic propulsion (the "one" in bar 2) can be felt. (That in bar 3 is still softer, and it is probably impossible to play the right-hand half notes so that the tied "one" is audible.) Thicken your tone at bar 9, but insert the chords in bar 10 so that they amalgamate with the melodic line. (Note how bars 9-14 revert to, but do not mechanically restate, the original thought.)

Not until it is marked should you allow tempo rubato. Leap, in time, from the E-flat to the high chord, but oversustain this chord so that a hastening in the descent may compensate—chiefly on "two" and "three" of the next bar. Retard a little the chords before *un poco mosso,* since this new tempo cannot be much faster than the original speed. Stress the C-flats in bars 1 and 2 of this section, and the corresponding notes in similar phrases. These few hints will suffice.

The *Passepied* makes a nearer approach than did the *Minuet* to the style of the day when these dances were alive. The time signature gives a 4-4 measure, but the notation compellingly suggests that it should be 2-2. There are no peculiarities which are not elucidated in the notation.

The next work which demands our attention—the Suite, *Pour le piano*—was published six years after the *Bergamasque* suite. It shows far more preoccupation with the problems of technique and sonority than the earlier, but it contains no parallel to *Clair de lune.* The first and last of the three pieces reveal a new delight in technique, and much more certainty in the choosing and arranging of notes for effect. The *Sarabande,* much more "modern" than the *Minuet* of the earlier suite, is also more in accord with the original character of the dance. It reveals a glimpse of the artist who later conceives the *Hommage à Rameau.*

The word *Assez* in the superscription is not the equivalent of the Italian *assai,* which means "very much." *Assez,* though from the same root, covers the ground from "somewhat" to "considerably." *Très rhythmé* ("very rhythmically"), indeed, almost of itself forbids speed which tries for a record. The slurs over the sixteenths seem to contradict the *non legato;* but those words certainly forbid any mere murmuring, and so, very largely, the pedal also. The low A's from bar 6 obviously cannot be held with the fingers; but from bar 9 the higher A—all that can be heard—can be reached. We allow the dynamics to exceed the prescribed *p* around bar 17. Do not disturb the tempo for the rest in bar 26, and do not begin a real crescendo until it is marked, in bar 40. You will be rewarded for your reticence. Take the chords (43) with very rigid fingers, simultaneously, beginning somewhat more softly after each "one." Play the glissando on the thumbnail, turning the hand as you approach the high C so that the 3rd finger can take that note. Begin it almost *p,* pedal throughout, and make the swell mostly at the end. In bar 57f. we find the first passage we have so far encountered that is wholly on the six-tone scale. From bar 59, try to murmur the sixteenths without blurring. From bar 71, the ringing A-flats must have full pedal. (The six-tone-scale version of the theme, from 75, may be taken as a chord, and pedaled quite thickly.) In the *tempo di cadenza,* play in free rhythm, but respect, nevertheless, the dimension of the sixteenths, thirty-seconds, and eighths. Make the scampering runs, from bar 3, fill approximately the "four" of the bar. The bar line in bar 7, which begins with a quarter note, is obviously an error. The following fifteen notes cannot make a "bar," even in such a cadenza as this. Pedal through the six sixteenths, *retenus.*

The *Sarabande* has the gravity and elegance claimed for it in the superscription, and is also largely in the ancient character of the dance, with frequent weight on "two." The parallel motion of the whole harmonic mass is characteristic of many a more sober strain in Debussy's later works. Roll no chords not so marked, and roll those that are as inconspicuously as possible. The rhythm must be very firm and stately, even though the dynamic curves of the melodic line are clearly shaded. Differentiate clearly the rhythms of the "three" in bars 1 and 5, and similar phrases.

The *Toccata* is more difficult than the *Prélude.* The slurs are again confusing, for a clear and almost brittle tone is essential for all that recalls the first eight bars. From bar 9, however, the simultaneous sixteenths only need be articulate, so that you may pedal from "two" to the next "one." From bar 26, also, more fluid motion makes judicious pedal possible. At bar 46 (contrary to bar 9) we pedal the first half of the bar and not the second; but from bar 50, the sustained bass is itself a pedal mark. (This, however, appears in the rising, not in the descending, passages. From bar 78 we begin all the right-hand figures with the fingering 231, so that the rest of the notes always lie within the octave from the thumb. The figures from bar 67, like those in bar 9, do not come out in this pattern. We find it most convenient to take these with 12412532). The double sharps in the final development are hard to read, but are not hard to play once they have been conceived in terms of mere black and white keys.

From 1892, when Maeterlinck's *Pelléas et Mélisande* appeared in book form, until 1902, when the extraordinary music he set to that play was at last finished, Debussy was chiefly occupied with that work. The piano, during that time, was a secondary interest, as is shown by the small number of piano pieces written or published. The Suite we have just studied reflects only slightly the subtle musical processes of which *Pelléas* shows new command. But the next publication (1903)—a set of three pieces called, collectively, *Estampes* ("Prints")—gives ample proof of the novelty of his thought and the perfection of his skill. Individually, the pieces are called *Pagodes, La soirée dans Grenade,* and *Jardins sous la pluie.* Although the pictorial suggestion of the titles is obvious, this is no mere program music. Not the detail of the scene but the value of it as an awakener of the imagination is the burden of the tones; and although "illustration" is in some measure inevitable in such presentations, to stop with a mere recognition of the object illustrated is to lose all sight of the greater value.

*Pagodas,* which is musically Chinese only to the extent that its theme is on a pentatonic (five-note) scale, is even less suggestive of the style of architecture called to mind by the title. But there is nevertheless a hint of ringing bells and of a kind of formalized behavior, repeating set patterns meticulously but without passion, which awakens something of the impression we get on a visit to Chinatown.

There are three thematic phrases: the pentatonic pattern, pursued for the first ten bars; a slower, stiffer phrase, combined with a variant of the first at bar 11, and one in the whole-tone idiom at bar 33 (*sans lenteur*). The polyphony is not of the learned variety, but has a spontaneity that such learned devices often lack. The whole picture is remote and cool, though it seems presented in full sunlight. We suspect that there is some sort of religious observance going on which is strangely impressive, even though we are without a clue to its meaning. The dissonant close startled the contemporary ear, but has no longer even any strangeness.

Debussy never went to China. Neither did he ever visit the scene of the next piece. But *The Evening in Granada,* even to the ears of the Spanish composer, de Falla, seemed "nothing short of miraculous when we consider that this music was written by a foreigner, guided almost entirely by his own insight and genius." There is the rhythm of the Habañera, almost incessant; hints of languor, of passion, and of the franker ecstasy of the dance, come and go in the darkness—no other music ever enacted darkness as this does—and on this magic carpet of tone, you and I, who have never seen Granada either, are transported into the living heart of the place.

The rhythm of the dance begins at once. C-sharps climb up above its muffled throb and almost vanish in the higher air. An oriental strain, a minor second on either side of this C-sharp, wails out from some forlorn oboist, far below. A gayer rhythm supervenes and grows and disappears; a misty air wafts up intoxicating odors. Now that rhythm, returning, brings almost in sight its troupe of dancers. They, like songs and odors, pass. The scent comes back; and there—beneath that one dim light—a figure dances, lithe and swift, to hidden fiddles; then, both sounds and steps are veiled in that same odor. Revellers shake castanets and stamp; once more we glimpse the dancer; then the oboe, harmonized as if by night itself and that strange odor, departs and leaves a silence all constrained.

In spite of the superscription, it seems best not to relax too much the habañera rhythm at the outset. Fade the C-sharps in bars 5 and 6 into the entrance of the oboe phrase, which must be very flexible though the rhythm remains precise. Retard a little and fade the triplet before the *retenu*. *Tempo giusto* is here both "appropriate" and "strict" time. Keep the hands very firm, for precision, but exceed the *pp* only slightly, even at the end of the swells. The odorous rubato phrase (bar 23f.) will not be intoxicating if you spoil the triplets' fluidity by making the dashes all alike. Cling a little to the first note, gently hasten the next two, and fade the tied G-natural into the A, keeping the rhythm in the left hand always audible. (The sharp for A in the second and last chords in bar 33 is so faintly printed in many copies that it may escape your attention.) Respect the two-note phrasing, but keep the triplets fluid, nevertheless. (This is a feature of Spanish rhythm.)

Take the pedal at "one" in bar 38f., releasing on the very short staccato A; and pedal again on the last eighth note. Maintain a solid crescendo up to the *ff*. The new strain demands pedal, but if you have made the rhythm vivid in 38–41, its throb will not be too much obscured by that thickening. The long diminuendo is very hard to manage. Let the higher C-sharp on "one" of bars 62, 64, and 66 ring out a little (omission of the roll in 62 is probably an error), fading and retarding considerably to prepare for the wonderful phrases in 67f. The lilt of this strain is irresistible. The persistent G-double sharp–A-sharp must color the leaping line, but must not impede its motion. (In bar 69f., we take 4324 for F-sharp, E-sharp, D-sharp, F-sharp, and at "two" in 70, 322 for E-sharp, D-sharp, C-sharp, omitting the low F-sharp which is in the left hand.) The rhythmic C-sharps from 78 must be studied in the left hand alone. Swing freely into the octave melody, bars 97–8, and keep the little finger bright in the right hand. The low E's are bothersome. You can leave the preceding notes in plenty of time, but to leap back to the melody with the proper weight is very difficult. In the 3–4 time, observe that only the first three sixteenths form a triplet. Space the others precisely and make them very brittle. (In the first printing, the bass clef was omitted for bar 1.) The prescribed tempo is so fast that articulation of the sixteenths is very hard. We try for the articulation rather than the speed. Bring out the fading melodic line, G-sharp–F-sharp from bar 130.

*Gardens in the Rain* is a far less poetic subject; yet Debussy's impression is vivid and memorable. The themes are two French folk songs, *Nous n'irons plus au bois* ("We shall go no more to the wood") and *Do, do, Bébé, Do,* a lullaby. Fortunately, our American ears are unperplexed by their importation into the scene. We see only that the rain spatters bravely, and the sun shines out at the end.

The first melodic note being a quarter, pedal is necessary; but the clear articulation of the sixteenths (which you will find is no mean problem) is not much disturbed thereby. Pedal a little also for the swelled D's in bars 4 and 5. Begin a new period with bar 7. "Click in" the E, the last sixteenth of "two" in bar 10, and similar notes, so that they form a part of the melodic progression. From bar 16, the swells above the right hand imply that A–D, D-flat–F, and the like, are melodic. (It would have been clearer to double-stem these notes.) Pursue this melodic line to the high C-sharp. Pedal is indispensable up to the climax, but not thereafter. Take only a touch of it on "one" of bar 27f. From 37, the right hand is melodic to 43, and from 52 to 71.

From bar 75, make the tone very limpid, with dynamic differentiation of the bass and treble, but almost no shading, and murmur the triplets unchangingly. Pedal is essential. At bar 100, be sure to reach a low dynamic level, so that the long ensuing climb may be stirring. Note that at 103, 105, and so on the separately stemmed eighth note is to be taken with the left hand—the right then continuing with the easy pattern of quintolets to the climax. Accelerate bars 116–17 into the cadenza, and note that the right hand, bar 125, is *not* in the treble.

The direction at bar 176—hastening until the end—must be more implied than literally executed. In bar 133, teach the right hand alone to do its easy octave shift, counting only two beats to the bar. Teach the left hand its more difficult part, counting the same two beats. The two will soon go together quite easily. From bar 151, a definite accelerando is possible. Pedal right through to 155, where the arpeggiation must be taken very quickly. Give the melodic notes, against a new and sustained pedal, a sunny brightness.

Two separate pieces, *D'un cahier d'esquisses* ("From a sketch book") and *Masques*—the first a rather colloid substance, the second somewhat reminiscent of the *Danse* and of other things —were published in 1903 and 1904. They doubtless satisfied financial need far more than the composer's artistic instinct. Both are evidently earlier works.

In 1904, however, comes a thoroughly contemporary piece— which is to say, one considerably in advance of its time—the *Isle joyeuse.* It is very brilliant, yet thoroughly coherent and to the point in every note. "Heavens! How difficult it is to play," Debussy said of it. " . . . This piece seems to embrace every possible manner of treating the piano, combining as it does strength and grace . . . if I may presume to say so." After Debussy's death, it was orchestrated by Bernardino Molinari; but to our ears the pianistic character of the piece is too distinctive to be transferred to any other medium. It is indeed very difficult, but is so important in the whole body of the composer's work that we must examine it closely.

In the opening, *Quasi una cadenza,* the fermate on the C-sharps provide all the available freedom of rhythm, since the thirty-second-note figures, if unrhythmic, become mere slithers. Continue the trills as long as you like (remembering that they represent three beats), but play the thirty-seconds in time. (Careless readers forget that the last D is sharped.) Give rhythm enough to bar 3 so that the left-hand triplet is intelligible as such. Give the ictus to the trills in bars 6 with the *sfz* eighth note, in strict time.

In the bass figures in bar 1 of *Tempo* (from which we count) differentiate the more articulate thirty-seconds from the swifter grace notes. Keep the two E's staccato, pedaling only with the thirty-seconds, but letting the chord on "three" ring a shade beyond its notated time. Make the rest, however, to give aplomb to the "four," which can be pedaled. Preserve this character, of course, against the theme. In the gay little theme, maintain the contrast between the shorter thirty-seconds and the triplet sixteenths. The sustained A's are now secondary, but will emerge into countermelody. In bar 6, stress the F-natural in the left hand more than the preceding F-sharp, leading it to the E in the ensuing right-hand figure, and similarly through the ascent. Take the *retenu* freely enough to make the last thirty-seconds comfortable (from F-double sharp finger 541231). The impossible-looking leaps in bars 9 and 10 can be made in time if you play the lower grace note, D-sharp, simultaneously with the C-sharp. In bar 11, play the eighths in the right hand all with the thumb, fingering the triplets 354, 354, 353, 234. In bar 12, play the eighths and quarters all with the 5th, and finger the sixteenths 131, 213, 213, 234.

The new motive entering at bar 15 will grow into the most

stimulating figure in the whole piece. Its entrance, therefore, must
not be obscure—yet to overdo it now will be fatal. Pedal is available
for each whole bar. Observe precisely the rest in bar 19. Accentuate
the high F-sharp but not the lower, and keep the upward swoops
thick. In contrast, tinkle the scintillant figures of bar 20 very clearly,
but with pedal throughout, as the fifths in the bass demand.

In the 3–8 section, the main melody is in the tenor, but the alto is
nearly as important, and the other notes of the triplets contribute to
the harmony. Study the sound values in the first bars until you find
them flowing suavely, with a warmer harmonic glow than has previously been heard. In bars 9–24, the eighth-note melody of the right
hand is doubled by the "off-beat" sixteenths of the left; and unless this
doubling is kept pretty bright, the passage will sound thick and dull.
In bars 25–27, accentuate the trills at each beginning, along with the
marcato chords. In bar 28, the figure from the opening cadenza, harmonized, demands even greater clarity. Mark the descending progression, B, B-flat, A, A-flat, G. We lead the B-natural–B-flat in the last of
the three bars of 4–4 time over into the A of the new theme.

The quintolets which accompany this exuberant new song were
made for the left hand, and if you learn them as having but one beat
to the bar they will soon be easy. In bars 9–10 of this section, bring out
G-sharp, F-sharp, E, against the melody. In bar 33f., the triplet thirty-
seconds are for fingering convenience, and should not be especially
marked; but the broad melodic line for the four bars (E, C-sharp, E,
C-sharp, D, F-sharp) should be well to the fore. See that the color
grows richer; stamp energetically in bars 75–78; and lose none of the
aliveness you have gained when the motive from bar 15 reappears.

From bar 94 of this section, do not try to fit the two-beat rhythm
into the triple-time scheme so that triple time will be heard. The
mixtures and alternations of duple and triple rhythm are perfectly
suited to the swirling that is now becoming giddy. The combination
of two motives (from bar 155, *un peu cédé*) is less difficult than it
seems to the eye. Do not waste the fine pull of G-natural into G-sharp
in bar 162. The culminant jangle (187–188) is so ill-balanced between
the two hands that it will not give the ringing effect which is indispensable. We play a C-sharp between the A and E of the left hand,
and in place of the C-sharp in the right hand (now taken by the left)
we play a D-sharp with the right thumb. It is hard to get the swoop
to the last low A in time. Lean to the right to reach the preceding

high notes, shaping the fingers for the grupetto in advance; then, just as you strike, begin to lean to the left, so that your bodily momentum may carry your right hand over to the bottom of the keyboard.

Having achieved his ambition to devise a new piano technique, Debussy now turns his mind frequently to this kind of writing. The first publications after the *Isle joyeuse* are a set of three pieces called *Images,* comprising *Reflets dans l'eau, Hommage à Rameau,* and *Mouvement.* Of these, only the first has gained general favor. Reverence for the great French master of the eighteenth century is not very high in America, although we are beginning to be aware of him as something more than a name in a history book. Neither is the *Sarabande*—in a considerably modern guise—a vehicle through which we can grasp his greatness. The "Movement" is something like a perpetual motion, extremely clever, but too evidently designed for momentary excitement to probe far beneath the surface of our thought.

The *Reflections in the Water,* however, are marvelously painted. There is rich suggestion also outside the visual field—of the kind which the spectacle itself of the tremulous mirroring of sky and tree must always evoke—but seldom, again, shall we encounter the obsession that we found in *The Evening in Granada.* Naturally, the piece is pretty hard to play; but it yields surprisingly to earnest persuasion.

*Andantino molto* is not a very definite direction for speed. We can best determine the tempo by studying bar 35, where the sense of the beginning recurs, with the A-flat, F, E-flat surrounded by a definite figuration. (We suggest $\flat = 72$–$76$.) *Tempo rubato,* to our mind, implies no erratic motion for the whole piece, but only flexibility within the phrases.

Keep the fingers firm, so that the opening chords will sound as ringing units, like the clear luminosity of calm water, not like ripples. Intone the motive A-flat, F, E-flat over a fairly sonorous bass. Make the swells in bars 9 and 10 considerable, so that the antiphonal figures may be luminous. Do not hasten bar 12f., else bars 16–17 will seem unrelated; and keep exact time in 18–19. The stringendo in the cadenza, if it emerges out of a slower beginning, is more convincing than if it is allowed greatly to exceed the normal speed, which will make the sixty-fourths in bar 24 seem to drag. Shape the new melody here so that the E-double flat will be audible for its whole length, keeping the (pedaled) sixty-fourths above it as clear as possible. Count accurately the left-hand part in the last half of bars 30–33, and note that even the mere eighth notes in 34 are to be retarded. Make the trickle of triplets from bar 35 crystalline (with high, precisely timed fingerstrokes), while intoning the three quarter notes richly. If bar 50 is to be in tempo, as prescribed—observe that there are thirty-seconds, not sixty-fourths, in the left hand—the preceding accelerando (*en animant*) is likely to cause a jolt as the tempo is resumed. We therefore make a tiny ritardando in bar 49, and take a tempo slightly faster than the original from 50 to 56, where we resume the basic motion. (The sweep of the figures in bars 52–53, we think, has also to be somewhat hastened over the speed of bars 50–51, and 54–55—but not so much as to destroy the sense of two beats in the bar.) From bar 59, submerge the articulation of the triplet sixteenths, but not that of the thirty-seconds. The *plus lent* at bar 65 need be but slightly slower than the main tempo. From bar 81, count six to each bar, playing the even quarters on "one" and "four," and the triplet quarters on "one," "three," and "four."

A "second series" of *Images* appeared in 1907. Public favor—guided, we think, by sound instinct—has been but meagerly accorded to these pieces, most of whose virtues will be found more satisfyingly embodied in one or another of the *Préludes*. The first of these, *Bells through the Leaves,* so persistently clings to the six-tone scale as to become wearisome to ears long accustomed to that novelty. The second, *And the Moonlight Falls on the Temple That Was,* employs the device of large blocks of parallel-moving chords which is more tellingly exhibited in *The Sunken Cathedral.* And the *Goldfish,* although the cavortings have in reality little resemblance to pyrotechnics, are represented in a manner sufficiently like that of *Fireworks* so that we are attracted rather to the more brilliant spectacle. All these pieces are very hard to play, so that we feel that on that ground—if on no other

—we are justified in foregoing their study in a book not meant for virtuosi.

Much more appealing is the little collection which was published in 1908 under the English title, *The Children's Corner.* It is dedicated "to my dearest Chou-chou, with her father's affectionate apology for what is to follow." (Chou-chou was Debussy's little daughter, Claude-Emma.) There is here set forth a much less intimate companionship of spirit between child and grownup than we found in Schumann's *Kinderscenen.* But one is more than pleased to find, in a mind so remote from most of the world's interests, so much of imagination for the things of childhood. Chou-chou had piano lessons very early, so that the first piece of the set is appropriately called *Dr. Gradus ad Parnassum.* This is a really witty parody on Clementi, though like many another joke on a distasteful subject, its humor remains largely unappreciated. You can recapture it, however, if you forget—as you are intended to do—the virtues of Clementi, and pursue the prettier phrases, from which, occasionally, as from a bad conscience, you return to the drier task.

*Jimbo's Lullaby* is for a toy elephant, as much beloved of Chou-chou as the Teddy bear is by American children. He had to be put to sleep before she herself would consent to be there transported. The music is indeed elephantine—in a suitably childish dimension. The toy is also reluctant to go to bed. You can hear him yawn (in the six-tone scale) and can see how, after his droning theme has been transplanted to the highest voice (probably Chou-Chou's), he lazily drops off.

The *Serenade for the Doll,* although it had been published separately two years before, was appropriately included in the Suite. Played with the soft pedal throughout (as the composer directs), and with the dainty rhythm delicately marked, the piece has immediate and lasting charm. (Only the highbrows deplore the reminiscences of Lalo or Massenet.)

*The Snow is Dancing* is really difficult. The sixteenths must fall as do the snow flakes on windowpanes, weightlessly and—in spite of their rhythmic measure, which must be undeviating—capriciously. The composer has found, somewhere in their antics, a melody which gives them an apparent purpose. It should not, however, override them.

*The Little Shepherd* pipes away, quite self-centered, amid the gambolings of his sheep—upon which his thought is quite evidently not turned. Although half their paint is doubtless sucked off, the shepherd and his sheep both come alive.

*The Golliwog's Cake-walk* is of course the most familiar (but not necessarily the best) of the pieces. The Golliwog, a hideous toy which looked like a frog assuming the rôle of Buddha, has long been superseded by other even more repulsive grotesques. In the days of this piece, it was to be seen everywhere—at least in France and England—as a mantel ornament. Its dance steps (of which a creature with such anatomy was incapable) were drawn from that American antecedent of jazz which was called ragtime. But the phrase marked *Cédéz* and "with a great emotion" is a parody of the opening of the Prelude to *Tristan and Isolde.* (Debussy, once a violent Wagnerian, was now an implacable opponent.)

Two more incidental pieces, the *Hommage à Haydn* and an ironically sentimental waltz, *La plus que lente* ("The More than Slow"), intervened between *The Children's Corner* and his last important piano works, the two books of *Préludes.* Brief indulgence in the waltz is not unpleasant—which is doubtless why Debussy orchestrated it.

The first book of twelve *Préludes,* which appeared in 1910, in many respects represents the summit of the composer's achievements in piano composition. In others, it seems to represent a decline. Those subtleties which we found in *The Evening in Granada* and *Reflections in the Water* are abundantly in evidence; but the poetic concept is often very remote, and is set forth in a manner that makes us read the title (which appears at the end of the piece) with a certain wonder that so simple a subject could evoke such abstruse imagery. Yet, the more we ponder these images the richer their interest becomes. We return, it is true, to the world of every day with an uneasy sense of having been in a place where such ordinary mortals as ourselves hardly belong. But it is perhaps well to be jolted, sometimes, into a question of our title to the place in which we think we belong.

The first piece, *The Delphic Dancers,* is at any rate a wonderful thing. The dancers, absorbed in their rite to the point of hypnosis, are celebrating some ineffable idea, whose impact on us is so portentous that we cannot doubt its significance, even though we do not grasp its substance. Technically, the piece is easy. We must try to get at its musical implications.

The "pull" of the first phrases falls on the "two," which must flow elastically out of the "one" and into the active "three." The upper line, F, G, A, is predominant, but the B-natural of the middle voice contributes the pull. If you begin with too solid a tone, the whole design will be unmanageable. The sixteenth note, F, in bar 2 is up-beat to the undulation in bar 3. The composer's swells are significant— and hard to realize, for the weighted sixteenths can hardly be actually detached. To give them weight, it is obvious that you must under-weight the dotted eighths. At the end of the undulation, in bar 4, one may imagine that the principal dancers take an attitude, while the subordinate weave a pattern about them. The next five bars, which repeat this whole evolution more sonorously, are really easier to play.

At bars 11 and 13, the slow legato descents are the relaxation from the high spiritual tension reached in what we called the "attitudes." (The D of the melody is hard to realize against the rising phrase, which is now more important. Sacrifice it, if you must.) Hasten not at all the grave motion from bar 15 to the *f* in 16, and be sure not to curtail the second beat in the 4-4 bar. The syncopated chord (its high note is A, not G) adds to the tension with which the high note is sustained over the unmarked "three." Subside with the echoing phrase in bar 17, keeping the measure absolutely precise over the tied "one" in 18, and beyond to the cessation in 20. (The two rises on D–F will have a compelling curve if you give a slight stress to the D's.) The fermata over the comma implies silence, not prolongation of the sound.

The tableau represented by the comma dissolves only tentatively in bars 21–22. Break off the G, therefore, with another instant of silence before you depict the more exalted pose represented by 23–24, and pause, similarly, to allow the brief epilogue (25–31) to have a definite beginning. Delay nothing, however, and shorten nothing, throughout. The *f* chord (29) will be shocking if hammer noise is audible. Strike it in the midst of an extended, wholly flexible descent and without too much firmness of the fingers, which may also slide somewhat along the keys as they descend. Even the final B-flat is the last step in a dance that has been tensely rhythmic to the end.

*Voiles* means either "veils" or "sails" in French. The latter is reported to be the accepted meaning of this title, but the music, with its almost unrelieved insistence on the six-tone scale, and the by no means wavelike rhythm, seems to us more in accord with the former sense. The fluidity of the one harmonic device is altered only briefly (in the pentatonic episode marked *en animant*) so that the promising poetic suggestion of the beginning, to our ears, loses its imaginative compulsion before the end is reached.

*The Wind in the Plain* blows gently (but with singular speed, considering its mild force) and indulges only now and then in gusts. The sense of sunshine permeates its airs, and it departs, at the end—as all winds do—without telling us whither it is bound. The piece is more difficult than valuable. The long stretches on rapid figures fatigue the fingers; but they give them good exercise.

*The Sounds and the Perfumes Swirl in the Evening Air,* the title of No. 4, is a phrase from Baudelaire. The air is less fragrant and less warm with sensibility than that which we breathed with difficulty in *The Evening in Granada.* Our more sensuous pleasure can be taken with repose, but it is nevertheless a delight. The direction for harmonious and supple rendering, thoughtfully followed, will give a sufficient clue to the relatively easy problem.

*The Hills of Anacapri* is much more mundane, but here we breathe, not merely sniff, the air. Six little bells ring. Out of their vibration springs a strain from a tarantella, which, after another chime, reveals itself completely. There is then a frank, very Italian tune, with an almost overwarm refrain. Whether purposefully or not, the notes of the "verse" of the song are those of the bells, in a different order.

Blend the bell tones, of course, with the pedal. Bring in the dance step when you like, with stress on the C-sharp. Accelerate the chords from bar 7, bringing out the inner thirds against the bright F-sharp. Keep the triplet sixteenths from bar 11 clear (not murmured), taking pedal only at points of dynamic interest. *Cédéz,* in bar 31, if applied only to the up-beat, hardly has time to count as a preparation. We begin it a little earlier. At the *tempo,* give the ictus with the right hand also—more emphatically, of course, where the bass is tied. In bar 43, since the accented B does not belong to the theme, we "shove off" with that note, but hesitate an instant before the two following sixteenths to attach them to the D-sharp up-beat. In the baritone solo, short hands may double the F-sharps in the right thumb, playing the melody with the left hand in octaves. At bar 66, finger the figure 131235. Rush the speed a little from bar 90. Give time for the final arpeggios to develop their "luminous" sound, and play the much retarded final sixteenths against the pedaled ringing of the last swoop.

No. 5 is called *Steps in the Snow.* The stealthy rhythm, Debussy says, "ought to have the sonorous value of a sad and frozen landscape." We have probably never seen such a landscape in terms of sonority, but we shall find that his vision is keener than ours. (Note that the figure 3 denotes a triplet composed of the sixteenth and the following eighth—not of the whole beat.) Until you are directed (*En animant,* and so forth), do not make the melody too dolorous, else you will quite remove the chill from the landscape. It suffices to have the human element take precedence over the natural only toward the end.

*What the West Wind Saw* was evidently something much more exciting than that which was passed over by the *Wind in the*

*Plain.* It is probably the many-sounding sea. This piece is somewhat less difficult than it looks, since most of the figures lie well in the fingers, and the pedal is almost incessantly in use. It is nevertheless very hard to play well—and yields, to our notion, little beyond the satisfaction of a task well performed.

*The Girl with the Flaxen Hair* is the most familiar of all—which is in a way an offense to this very self-satisfied blonde. She has no desire to know, or to be known by, everybody. But she does love to be seen. Whether moving or standing, she is happily condemned to exhibit the very epitome of grace. How long she maintains the easy pose she takes on the D-flat of bar 3; and how undisturbedly she goes on to others—always giving us time to admire, yet never appearing to be conscious of our gaze! Her flaxen hair is the crown of her beauty, no doubt, but there is a faint pink glow under her cheek. Even a hint of haste (*un peu animé*) throws nothing out of drawing, but only makes her gait more cloudlike. It took a very imaginative artist to draw this amazing portrait. But you can evoke it, merely out of black and white keys, if you have learned fine dynamic discrimination, and have discovered that rhythm is motion.

*The Interrupted Serenade.* Practical jokes on serenaders have been the substance of many prankish tales—perhaps, for the most part, envious—at least since the days of the troubadours. This serenader seeks his delectable object somewhere in Spain (as de Falla gladly recognizes). Just what physical disturbance ruins his effects—and perfects Debussy's—is not revealed; but his adventure is absorbing to its hard-won happy end. The piece is hard to play as delicately as it must be, to be vivid, but the requirements are all set forth in the text.

*The Sunken Cathedral* seems to be that same legendary edifice whose history is involved in the plot of Lalo's opera, *Le roi d'Ys*. There is no plot here, but there is magic which is more compelling than any action according to reason. At uncertain times, and for unknown causes, the old cathedral rises bodily from the depths, the organ playing, the choir chanting; and at its own moment it sinks again to its bed. The music really makes us believe.

The 6–4—3–2 time signature is not meaningless. The notation itself tells us what rhythm to imagine. The beginning is in 6–4 (else the two tied quarters would be a half note); bar 7 is clearly in 3–2—always, of course, with unaltered time value for the quarter. The "sweetly sonorous fog" into which the church is rising is first depicted. You hear at bar 7 something like an old Gregorian chant (this time, against a pedal E; later, against G-sharp). The waves swell, bearing the cathedral higher; against a solemn chanting, bells ring out; then the chant is sung by a choir of many voices, harmonizing it in plain triads, with what is known as the organum of the fourth between bass and soprano. After a quietly ringing pause, the organ takes up the chant somewhat faster, and with slightly more diverse harmonies. A rumbling as of many waters now surrounds the dwindling theme, and the cathedral sinks to its unmarked foundation.

Do not disturb the calm amazement of the spectator by any looseness of rhythm or any rolling of the solid chords. Judicious pedal and dynamics as marked will draw the picture. The directions in French mean: Bar 1—Profoundly calm, in a sweetly sonorous fog; bar 7—sweet and fluid; bar 14—without gradations; bar 16—little by little emerging from the fog; bar 17—marked; bar 20—increase continuously (i.e., in tone) without hastening; bar 47—a little less slow (with expression intensifying as it continues); bar 72—in the (original) tempo, like an echo of the phrase just heard; bar 84—with the sonority of the opening.

*The Dance of Puck* reputedly originated out of the *Midsummer Night's Dream*. That antic figure, however, was known to the world of the imagination long before Shakespeare's time; and to Anglo-Saxon eyes Debussy's portrait bears too many Gallic traits to be readily associated with Shakespeare's mischief-maker. That, however, does not prevent this from being an engaging and lifelike sketch.

The task, both of the fingers and of the musical imagination, is difficult. Observe that the impudence of the melody is most marked with the leap of the fourth. Note, also, that the thirty-seconds are *not* slurred forward to the dotted sixteenths, but forward from the sixteenths, and are staccato. There is no time for silence after so short a note, but if you play the thirty-seconds very lightly, after heavier sixteenths—first in your imagination, then with your fingers—you will at least approximate the indicated effect. (Note also that sometimes, as in bars 3 and 4, the motion is legato.) Count only two to the bar; the triplet of sixteenths in bar 6 will then give no trouble—unless you stupidly read it in the bass clef. The *grupetti* in bar 8f., unless played like rolled chords, take unallowable time. The grace notes in bar 18f. are best if struck simultaneously with the principal note, the fingers releasing them instantaneously (in bar 22f., *before* the pedal is depressed). From bar 30, note again the slurs *to* the thirty-seconds. From 49, the half notes imply pedal, even against the staccato; but it seems wise to release it at least with the last eighth. At bar 55 and similar phrases, motion is more necessary than articulation. We play these runs a little too fast, and alike in time, ascending and descending, quitting each an instant before its proper time. The attack on the trilled C-sharps is thus rhythmically more vivid. Against the sustained alto from bar 63, the left hand can hardly articulate the thirty-seconds. We let them murmur, since in any case the low B-flat implies pedal. Yield a good deal in 71–72, and resume the rhythm with a decided ictus. The thirty-seconds from 79 must not murmur indistinctly, else the *retenu* will sound disrelated. The *retenu* after the new signature extends so far that it must be very slight at the beginning. Let the triplets in 91 and 93 increase in breadth, ringing little bells with the high figure. Note the tie from 94 to 95. Make no accent anywhere in the final scale, but try, in spite of the speed and the ⟩—to increase its articulateness as you ascend. Make the high G a mere click, and the low E-flat the light thud of a padded heel.

*Minstrels* is the last Prélude in this series. Our grandfathers applied this name to Negro entertainers in general. Debussy took it as applying to the dance bands which were already beginning to attract the attention of Europe. After an expectant introduction, the rhythm becomes that of very action toes and heels. Soon the "hot" trumpet interjects its raucous note, a characteristic half step too low. Muted brasses squawk on slithering augmented triads; the drums have a moment of solo; and then comes a tune that, if there had been a Hit Parade in those days, would have been a topper. The end is appropriately saucy.

Begin a little deliberately, yielding generously where that is prescribed. (The *grupetti* are like chords rolled downward.) Start bar 9 with a bump, and rattle the sixteenths in very brittle staccato, up to the accented chord and thereafter. In bar 29f., the first of the slurred sixteenths, after the staccato, must be practically *sf* to make their point. (But the eighths are marked ◁.) Take the last eighths in bar 39 a little staccato, landing rather heavily on the next chord. Pedal through this chord to a much lighter "one" in bar 40, and observe the heavy "twos" and the lighter "ones" thereafter. Lead the G and B in bar 43 to G-sharp–B-sharp in 44, holding this while you snap the right-hand thirty-seconds off sharply. This B-sharp, propelled by the A, is satisfied only at the C-sharp in 45. (We make the fermata into a whole silent bar.) Do not anticipate the ◁'s in bars 46 and 48, but make them vigorous when they do come. Keep the little finger bright, with all the rest softer and very staccato, in 51–52, and similar phrases. Play the drums *una corda,* even though they are forte, and do not let the C-sharp drown out the D. Attempt no retard as you approach the swaying tune (63). The eighth-note groups in this tune are more vivid if really staccato. Do not misread—or fear—the discords in bar 72.

In the second book of *Préludes,* which appeared in 1913, it seems to us that Debussy's imaginative power shows signs of exhaustion. Like Chopin, he had hardly realized that the artist who makes a world of his own must ultimately live in it, and must progressively abandon communication with the commonplace world from which he has fled. Nor does he realize that that world also shies away from him. A few gaunt spirits, enamored of beauty as he sees it but incapable of creating it for themselves, gaze hungrily in at the windows of his ivory tower, and are even, on occasion, admitted. But even these are often, and in their most eager moments, ignominiously repelled. They, and the artist with them, are like poor Ophelia, incapable of their own distress. In the commonplace world, this spectacle often inspires a rather uncomplimentary pity.

This is a harsh opinion to express with reference to the second book of *Préludes*. But although we recognize, as in the later works of Chopin, the extraordinary technical finish of these pieces, we can find in the book but one example in which imaginative "drive" seems to be the real source of the music. That is No. 3, *La Puerta del Vino*—another Spanish scene like that we witnessed in Granada, and similarly obsessed with the rhythm of the Habañera. The other pieces are either repetitive, like *La Puerta* (is *General Lavine* as interesting as the *Minstrels*, or *Brouillards*—Mists—as seductive as *Voiles?* and are the *Fairies* as *Exquisite Dancers* as *Puck?*)—or they are fancies on inconsequential themes, poetized beyond their proper degree. The spectacle of decline is melancholy. Complete critical study—which would point out contributions to the future of musical composition that we must here ignore—would be more cheerful, but more tedious. We shall only hope that our efforts thus far has made the reader who wishes to do so, able to study the second book for himself.

A few more pieces for piano were composed, laboriously but with great perfection of detail, while the spiritual bleakness incident to the war and fatal disease was arresting his musical effort. In 1913, there was a Ballet, *The Toy-box*, set down for piano only by Debussy, but orchestrated after his death. In 1914 appeared *Six Epigraphes*—invocations *To Pan; To a Nameless Tomb; To Night, That It Be Propitious; To the Dancer with the Drums; To an Egyptienne;* and *To Give Thanks for Rain*. These are more esoteric than the *Préludes*.

From 1915 there are also twelve *Études,* dedicated to the memory of Chopin, which exhibit with great brilliancy the resources of the piano as Debussy employed them. But these, too, are specialties, inappropriate to the purpose of this book. We shall therefore assume that our task is finished.

# Appendix
# FIRST ESSENTIALS
# OF PIANO TECHNIQUE

~~~~~~~~~~~~~~~~~~~~~~~~~~~~~~~~~~~~~~~~~~~~~~~~~~~~~~~~~~~~~~~~~~~

THE statements that follow are all made in the light of the fact—discussed in Chapter 1—that the problem of touch is essentially a problem of applying exquisitely graduated forces to piano keys. The problem of technique is primarily one of selection—of striking the right key; but unless that stroke can also be adapted to the precise tonal intensity required by the player's image of the musical phrase, mere accuracy will be of little value. We have tried, therefore, to describe the behavior of the playing mechanism as adapted to both these ends. Since this brief account may have to serve some students in lieu of a teacher, we have tried to give a reasoned account of the main features of the playing process. For the sake of clarity, it has been necessary to take the factors of the mechanism (fingers, hand, wrist, arm, and so forth) separately, even though the actual process of playing involves their simultaneous action. But some attempt will be made at describing the whole co-ordinated effort.

### The Fingers

The fingers, in delivering their forces to the keys, act in one of two ways: either (1) as individual units, or (2) as portions of a larger unit (the hand). We shall study first the action of the finger as an individual bearer of force.

For certainty that the intended force will be delivered, the curved or "rounded" finger is essential.[1] Only in this position will the "flexor" muscles (those which contract the fingers) give sufficient firmness to the finger to transmit the whole energy of the stroke to the key. Nor is the mere curved position enough. At the instant of contact with the key, the two finger joints must be kept firm. The tip joint is often very hard to control in this way; but every effort must be made to control it. For if this joint is weak enough to "cave in" under the stroke, only that part of the whole striking energy which is enough to make the joint collapse will be delivered to the hammer. For the hammer rises to the string slightly *before* the key reaches its bed, whereas the full energy of a finger stroke, delivered through a yielding joint, will be exerted only *after* the key has reached its bed—too late to be transmitted to the hammer.[2]

The finger thus moves, as if all in one piece, from the knuckle joint. How high its tip must be above the key before the stroke depends on many factors that cannot now be mentioned in our discussion. It may be said, however, that the maximum height to which the finger should rise is that at which the first joint of the finger is in a straight line with the back of the hand. For most hands, this is nearly a natural limit. Some have such loose knuckle joints that the finger can be pulled far above the natural level by the "extensor" muscles alone (those which extend or

[1] Since the thumb is used as a finger, the hand must be held in such a position that the thumb can always reach its key. This of itself compels the use of the arched finger; but the action described in the text is a more cogent reason.

[2] It must be understood that this firmness of the finger is not maintained while the finger is out of contact with the key. Such an effort would exhaust the hand in a few moments. The firmness is assumed, instantaneously, as the finger comes in contact with the key. To maintain it, along with the whole force of the stroke, as a continuous pressure on the key after the tone has been struck, can have no effect whatever on the tone, and is often roundly condemned as a waste of energy. It may, however, have a more than compensating value, as we shall see.

lift the fingers). But this is a weakness to be overcome, not in any sense an advantage. This brings us to a study of

## The Position of the Hand

Obviously, the hand must be held in such relation to the keyboard that the raised finger may deliver its stroke without waste of effort. It would appear that the best hand position would be that in which the back of the hand is level, and at such a height that the finger stroke will be a direct thrust downward. Actually, however, this high position involves the expenditure of much unnecessary effort. This can be made clear by a simple experiment.

Holding the back of the hand level, with the first phalanx of the fingers extended in line with the back of the hand, strike forcefully with the third finger any white key, and maintain both the position of the hand and the pressure of the finger (for observation) after the key has been struck. You will find that you are *pushing* the key—because, from this high position of the hand, you can exert this pressure in no other way. You will also find that your wrist is stiff; for you cannot push, with a finger tip, unless the wrist is stiff. Your finger stroke, therefore, was an effort not only of the finger but of the wrist—not merely of the particular muscles that actuate the one member you desired to use, but of much larger muscles as well. For stiffness, in any movable joint, must be accomplished by the working against each other of the opposed sets of muscles that can move the member (here, the hand) in opposite directions (here, up and down).

To measure the effort you were making with the wrist, lift the whole arm so that the finger is no longer in contact with the key, but keep the wrist stiffness exactly as it was. Your wrist, if you keep this up, will soon get very tired. It is clear that you could not strike with finger after finger, in rapid succession, without incurring this fatigue. Also, if you move the fingers as if they were striking keys in rapid succession while at the same time you hold the wrist stiff, you can perceive a certain impediment to their motion which is removed when the wrist is relaxed. If, then, you hold your hand so high that your finger strokes must be made by pushing, you will be working against two troublesome obstacles, neither of which can be removed by practice. For you cannot push unless your wrist is stiff.

To push, however, is not the only way to exert a force with the fingers. You can also pull. And it is easily possible to pull without stiffening the wrist. Supporting the hand only by the 3rd finger, either from the key or from some object a foot or so higher, relax the wrist, elbow, and shoulder until your whole arm will swing like a rope between finger tip and shoulder joint. Your finger muscles only will now be perceptibly tensed; but you will probably find that the pressure on the supporting surface is as great as it was when your effort was a push. The actual finger effort, also, is hardly greater than before. This is certainly a better condition for the playing mechanism than was the stiffness. It is also a workable condition.

With the arched 3rd finger thus planted on the key, and the arm relaxed, you will find the most comfortable position of the arm to be that at which the underside of the forearm is about on a level with the finger tip. (It is about the same as if the forearm and the finger tips lay on a table, with the knuckle joints forming the highest part of the hand, while the hand is shaped about as if it were holding a ball.) It may take some time to acquire the ropelike condition of wrist and arm. You can test for the condition by sideways motion of the elbow or a rotation of the wrist in a circle. When you can do this without materially altering the pressure you feel on the finger tip, you have got it.

You will now find that you are pulling on your key, not pushing it; that the impeding stiffness has disappeared; and that the weight of your arm (or such portion of that weight as you care to release—the rest is supported by large muscles in the shoulder and forearm) is about equal to the force you formerly exerted by pushing. Your finger, arched and tensed, bears the burden; but its total effort is little if any greater than before, and it can easily assume the preparatory position for another stroke by rising, at the knuckle joint, to that same even line with the back of the hand which it assumed when the hand was held level.

To be able to use the fingers while maintaining this condition of hand and arm is the first step in the acquisition of a dependable technique. You may well begin with the 3rd finger, as already suggested. Raise the other fingers to striking position (not straining them to effortful height); test for the flexibility of wrist and elbow; then, strike with the 4th finger on the adjacent white key by transferring the weight you have been supporting with the 3rd finger to the 4th without any intermediate lifting of the weight at the shoulder or elbow. Test the arch of the 4th finger and the whole condition of wrist and arm as before, and be sure that at the instant of the new stroke no stiffness appeared which was thereafter removed. Go on to the 5th finger, then back, in order, to the thumb, all on adjacent white keys. The thumb stroke, although made by a somewhat different sort of muscular effort, should *feel* essentially like the finger strokes. When you have gained such command over the motions and conditions you are studying that you no longer need to scrutinize every detail, you can relieve the tedium of striking the same five notes by playing the following patterns:

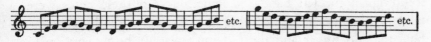

which may of course ascend or descend indefinitely, and which may also profitably be varied by placing the skip of a third between the 2nd and 3rd fingers, or the 3rd and 4th, or the 4th and 5th.

Remember, as you practice, that relatively little attention is needed for the act of striking. Your chief concern is for the prepa-

ration of the stroke, and the maintenance of the proper condition of hand and arm. Above all, until this condition and position
are perfectly easy to maintain, give no attention to the question
of speed. For if you are preparing correctly the aim and the
proper arching of your finger, you are already doing everything
that is requisite for speed. For speed is only the more rapid succession of the motions you are now making, and "is as easy as
lying" if once the preparation has been properly made.

Unfortunately, however, only a small proportion of the passages that the pianist must execute lies within the compass of five
consecutive fingers, however widely they may be extended. More
extended scales and arpeggios (which, in various combinations,
compose most of the figures of single notes appearing in piano
music) cannot be played smoothly unless the thumb substitutes
for one of the fingers (usually the 3rd or 4th), or the fingers pass
over the thumb as if they lay on the other side of it. These "thumb-
crossings," as we may call them, thus present a problem as fundamental as that of the primary finger strokes.

Let us first study the problem of passing the thumb under the
fingers. The simplest pattern requiring this passage is the diatonic scale. In all such scales, in each octave of notes, the thumb
will strike once in place of the 4th and once in place of the 5th
finger. In the C scale, and many others, the succession is 123,-
1234,123, and so on. In the C scale, we have to strike the F and
the C (ascending, in the right hand) or the G and the C (descending, in the left hand) as smoothly as if these notes were
taken by the next adjacent finger; and having made this substitution, the 2nd finger and the rest must already be in position to
strike their proper notes.

The first thing to do, once the thumb has released its note,
is to bring the thumb as nearly as possible into position for striking its next key. The thumb, that is, must be tucked under the
hand the instant it is free. Even while the 2nd finger is striking
its note, the thumb should be well on its way to its next note.

Here, however, if we maintain the "five-finger" position we have just studied, we encounter a difficulty. The thumb can manage to pass under the fingers, but it cannot, with the low position of the wrist, make any proper preparation for its stroke, for it cannot get far enough above its key to be able to strike it with that motion which it used in its free position outside the hand. The equivalent of a finger stroke is impossible, unless the wrist is raised. If it is kept raised, you will find that the downward stroke will inevitably be accompanied by a tension of the wrist. And since, as the speed of the scale increases, the time between these tensions will lessen, we shall at last reach a point where the instants of tension will be so close together that intervening relaxation will be useless. It would have been of little value to study so carefully the relaxed condition for the five-finger position if that condition had to be abandoned in scales and arpeggios.

Several solutions of this problem have been found, two of which have many advocates. One is to avoid the actual passing under of the thumb by slanting the fingers away from the thumb far enough to permit it to use the equivalent of a finger stroke. The fingers, in this case, strike diagonally, not vertically, on their keys; and, according to the mechanical principle of the composition of forces, must suffer some loss of energy in so doing. (A given force, applied diagonally to an object, will impart less energy to that object—here, the key—than the same force applied vertically—here, the direction in which the key *must* descend.) This is nevertheless a practical method, as is proved in a great number of instances.

It seems to us, however, that the vertical attack is preferable, and that it can be accomplished with no more effort than the other. Passing the thumb instantly under the hand, as already described, let the wrist rise enough to leave a certain space (less than that between the tip of a prepared finger and its key) between the thumb and its key. This lift need never be so high that the finger strokes preceding that of the thumb will be pushed, instead of pulled, nor need the motion of the wrist, which is slightly lateral, impair the verticality of the finger strokes. The great advantage of this process is that the thumb, which is now poised above its key, can strike with no muscular effort whatever. For the wrist, from its raised position, now merely falls to its original level, so that the poised thumb *falls with it,* and thus effortlessly performs its stroke. The fall of the wrist is of course controlled by the muscles that raise and lower the hand from the wrist, and since the general condition of weight (which, as in the five-finger position, is still transferred from finger to finger) is maintained during the lifting of the wrist, the thumb stroke is again the product of another transference of that weight. Moreover, the constant motion of the wrist is an aid toward maintaining that flexibility of arm and wrist which is really what the pianist means when he speaks of "relaxation." [3]

The passing of the thumb under the 4th finger requires a slightly greater oscillation of the wrist than that under the 3rd finger. Executed very slowly, this is a rather uncomfortable act. But as even very moderate speed is acquired, this discomfort disappears. For with that speed there comes a certain momentum of

[3] To move any member of the body, some muscles *must* be tensed. Complete relaxation, which is complete muscular inertness, would make impossible not only the striking of the keys but the upright posture of the body. We have already seen that rigidity of the two finger joints is essential for the transmission to the key of the force generated in the finger muscles. But this rigidity, required and assumed only at the instant of the stroke, is not very fatiguing, and unlike rigidity of the wrist, impairs no other playing acts. It is true, however, that the fingers, acting together with the flexible wrist, are sometimes unable to generate sufficient force for a fortissimo tone. In that case, the wrist must be stiffened. But you need have no fear that that stiffening will of itself produce a harsh tone. For harsh tones are not necessarily very loud. A harsh tone is an unbalanced, ill-related tone, protruding disagreeably from the surrounding tone-mass; and such a tone may easily occur even during what is called "relaxed" playing. That technical process is best which will give the most effortless control over the loudness of any and every individual tone; but the fingers, by any method whatever, cannot of themselves acquire that control. It comes from the imagination and from no other source; and the fingers merely learn to obey the imagination.

the hand which itself accomplishes the last stage of the thumb-crossing, smoothly enough so that no break in the continuity of the tones is perceptible, nor any cramping of thumb or wrist.

To pass the hand over the thumb (as with the right hand, descending) is much easier than to pass the thumb under the hand. For in this direction an actual thumb stroke can be given, without any aid from the falling wrist. There is thus no need for the wrist to descend lower than to that level at which pushing strokes are avoided. Nor is any oscillation of the wrist, even laterally, necessary or desirable. The thumb, at the instant of its stroke, becomes the carrier of the hand, which rides over the thumb into such position that the next finger to be used is poised above—or nearly above—the adjacent key. (The 4th finger, it is true, cannot reach its key without a lateral bending of the wrist; but this bending, as soon as even a moderate speed is acquired, is obviated—exactly as in the passing of the thumb under the hand—by the momentum of the hand.)

## The Fingering of the Scales

The competent pianist is as familiar with every other scale as he is with the C scale. That familiarity is a vast aid in sight-reading; for the pattern of any key is a revealing clue to almost any sort of music in that key. Not only the scales, therefore, but the chords and their arpeggios, should be a part of the pianist's mental and physical "background," and the time spent in mastering this knowledge yields a richer return than almost any other effort.

The fingering of the scales, as usually presented in the books, seems to us needlessly complicated to learn, and in some cases needlessly difficult to perform. The most suitable fingering for any scale can be stated in a single, comprehensive principle.

In diatonic (seven-note) scales the finger-succession is invariably in the general pattern, 1 2 3, 1 2 3 4 (1); but the playing cannot always begin with 1. It is obvious that the thumb, in a scale, should not have to strike a black key. (It is hard enough to make the crossing onto a white key.) It is also harder to pass the thumb under the 4th finger than under the 3rd, and it is easier to pass the thumb under a finger that has just struck a black key than under one that has struck a white key. Now, the 4th finger strikes but once in each octave. That finger, therefore, ought if possible to strike a black key, and the next note—that for the thumb—should be a white key. (If the 3rd finger, when it is followed by the thumb, can also play a black key, the thumb-crossing is similarly easier.) These simple facts dictate the best fingering for all diatonic scales; and a simple rule may be formulated thus: if possible, give the 4th finger a black key that is followed by a white key; and make the same selection, secondarily, for the 3rd finger.

The "sharp" scales, in the right hand, all fall naturally into this pattern; and all, up to B major, fall into the 1 2 3, 1 2 3 4 sequence. The B major scale (which Chopin, quite rationally, used to teach first) is the easiest of all, in the right hand, since the white key for the thumb is only a half step beyond the black key played by the 3rd or 4th finger. In the left hand, however, the sharp scales do not lie so congenially. Take, for example, the D major scale, descending. All the usual scale-books give the fingering 1 2 3, 1 2 3 4—since the thumb still falls on a white key both times. But so also do the 3rd and 4th fingers, each of which is required to make a deep stroke, since the 2nd (on C-sharp) is followed by the 3rd on B, and the 4th (on E) has to strike after the 3rd has been lifted up by striking F-sharp. To pass the thumb under after these deep strokes is not a little awkward. You have only to play the scale of D, four octaves, descending, to be pretty conscious of this discomfort.

Now play the same scale with the fingering 2 3, 1 2 3 4, 1 (2) and you will see at once that your hand is much relieved. The same is true of A major; but here you will take 2 3 4, 1 2 3, 1 (2), until the lowest notes of the four octaves, which may well be played with 4 and 5. Whether, in G major, with only one sharp, it is better to put the 4th finger on the F-sharp or to use the C-scale fingering, you may decide for yourself.

The "flat" scales fall into our recommended pattern automatically. In the right hand, the 4th finger always falls on B-flat; and in the left (except for F major, which is analogous to G major in the right hand), you will hardly be tempted to discard our common-sense principle.

The harmonic minor scales (those which have the augmented second—the step-and-a-half—between the 6th and 7th notes) are more difficult, but not less necessary to know. The augmented second, a rather long interval for adjacent fingers, mostly involves both a black and a white key (as F–G-sharp, in A minor), but may involve two black keys (as B-flat–C-sharp in D minor) or two white keys (as D–E-sharp in F-sharp minor). The thumb and 2nd finger are obviously best suited to this longer interval, but they can take it only when the progression is from white to black, or from white to white. When the progression is from black to white, or from black to black, there is for most hands little difference whether the augmented second is taken by 2nd–3rd, or by 3rd–4th.

The following table will show that our general principle of fingering will apply, in most cases, in the minor scales, although the patterns are necessarily more uncomfortable. The table shows but one octave, and indicates the 8th note only where, for convenience, that note is taken by a different finger from that with which the scale began. (In that case, both the 1st and the 8th notes are indicated by a figure in parentheses.) The passing of the thumb is indicated by a comma; the augmented second is indicated by a space; and the black keys are indicated by bold-faced figures. Both right-hand and left-hand fingerings, read from left to right, indicate ascending progression. The descending progression is of course the reverse of the ascending.

| MINOR KEY | LEFT HAND | RIGHT HAND |
|---|---|---|
| A | (5)4321,3  2(1) | 123,123  4 |
| E | (5)4321,3  2(1) | *34,123,1  2 |
| B | (4)321,43  2(1) | 34,123,1  2 |
| F-sharp | 4321,32  1 | 34,123,1  2 |
| C-sharp | 321,432  1 | 34,123,1  2 |
| G-sharp | 321,432  1 | 34,123,1  2 |
| D-sharp or E-flat | 21,4321,  3 | 3,1234,1  2 |
| B-flat | 21,321,4  3 | (2),123,123  (4) |
| F | *21,321,4  3 | 1234,12  3 |
| C | (5)4321,3  2(1) | *234,123  1 |
| G | *21,321,4  3 | 123123  4 |
| D | (5)4321,3  2(1) | 123,123  4 |

* Also possible with the conventional fingerings, (5)4321,321 (left) and 123,1234 (right); but the 4th finger is less comfortable.

## *Arpeggios*

A ready execution of all forms of arpeggios is as fundamental to a competent technique as is command of the scales. Arpeggios are merely "broken" chords, and are extended beyond the limit of the octave exactly as are the scales—by substituting the thumb for the 5th finger. The process of thumb-crossing is essentially the same; but the distance from the 3rd or 4th finger to the thumb-note being greater, the shift is more dependent on the momentum of the hand. The arpeggio of a triad is fingered like the triad itself, and the only question is whether to use the 3rd finger or the 4th after the 1st and 2nd. The accepted principle is this: If there is one white note only between that which, in striking the whole octave, is taken by the 5th finger and the note next to it, that adjacent note is taken with the 4th finger; but if there are two white notes between, use the 3rd. Two triads (those of G-flat major and E-flat minor) have black keys only, so that the thumb must here pass to a black key; but since the hand is elevated throughout by the black keys, this passage is less difficult than might be expected. The principle of the thumb-crossing which we described for the scales is possible also for arpeggios, and when it is available gives the easiest execution. Often, however, the passage to be played "lies" so that this resource is not available. The succession of chords given below, arpeggiated through four octaves, gives most of the positions in which arpeggios appear, and is probably sufficient to prepare for any others. It will be seen that the fingering is not always the most congenial, but it is well to practice the uncomfortable ones since they are sure to occur in music.

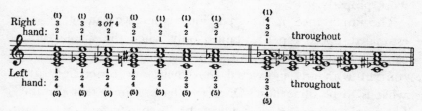

Play the triad-arpeggios in rhythmic groups of four notes

and the seventh chords in groups of three

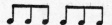

This will place the slight rhythmic accents (which should always be felt, although they need not be forceful) successively on different fingers, and will thus avoid that disposition to accentuate the thumb-stroke which appears so often in amateurish arpeggio-playing. The action of the wrist, in arpeggios, is exactly of the pattern used in scales, save that the oscillation is here more extended.[4]

The accurate measurement of the intervals, in arpeggio-playing, is something of a problem, since the pattern assumed by the fingers, in any one octave, is necessarily disturbed by the long

[4] The series of chords given above may of course be transposed to any desired degree; but the number of actually new patterns will not be great, nor their difference sufficient to present essentially new problems.

thumb-crossing. That pattern should be clearly imaged, as the shift is made, and should be resumed as soon as possible thereafter. Even so, errors are here harder to avoid than in scales. You will probably find, however, that one finger is more inaccurate than the others. Discover, if you can, which finger this is; then, as you shift, *look in advance at the note which that finger is to play,* and let the others take care of themselves. You will almost certainly find that this will correct your trouble—unless you are trying to play so fast that you cannot trust any finger to do its work properly.

The importance of slow, considered practice cannot be over-estimated. Speed can be attained only when the whole pattern can be executed slowly with such ease that there is neither discomfort with any individual movement nor uncertainty as to what is to be done next. Once you have gained that certainty, however,—once your hand, which has been reluctant or hesitant, seems to say, "There! Now I can do it!"—you will be surprised at the rapidity with which you can play these carefully prepared passages. Remember that your hands do only that which you teach them to do, and that they will as readily learn the wrong notes, and the wrong motions, as the right. If, then, you persistently make the same mistake, your hand will require to unlearn what it has thus been taught, before it can learn the correct behavior; and if you are mentally erratic as you learn, you can never expect your hands to behave accurately.

The learning process cannot be more clearly seen, nor more profitably studied, than in the practicing of scales and arpeggios. These patterns are so easy to memorize that the behavior of the hand can soon receive your undivided attention. Nor, if your attention is really alert, will the task become a bore. Surely, only a very stupid person would expect to find profound musical pleasure in the sound of a scale or an arpeggio. But only a very insensitive mind could get musical pleasure out of great compositions whose sense was continually distorted by wrong notes and wrong rhythms; and no one who is incapable of smooth and accurate scales and arpeggios can play otherwise.

## Varieties of Touch—Legato and Staccato

The word *legato* means "bound together"; and the legato touch is that in which one tone flows into the next in unbroken continuity. Physically, this continuity will occur if the damper causes the first tone to cease only at the instant at which the next tone begins. That is to say, a proper legato touch is that in which every note is held down by the finger for its full duration as prescribed in the score. It is true that after Bach's time, as the pedal or its equivalent began to be applied to keyboard instruments, composers increasingly demanded legato in passages that could not be played legato without the use of the pedal; but the foundation of a legato touch nevertheless lies in the sustaining and connecting of notes and chords, according to the notation, by the fingers themselves. Bach's music is invaluable for this study.

It is also true, however, as we saw in Chapter 1, that the mere continuity of progression from one tone to another will not of itself give the sense of flow which is implied in the word legato. That sense cannot be conveyed unless there is an almost continuous gradation from soft to loud or from loud to soft; and that gradation will be felt as legato only when it is in accord with the implied sense of a musical idea. It is evident, therefore, that beyond that sustaining of the notes which we have just described, there can be no general manner of attack that will produce the legato effect. Legato is a matter of dynamics as well as of unbroken continuity of tone.

We spoke, above, of the possible usefulness of continuing, after a key has reached its bed, the pressure with which that key was struck. That usefulness appears conspicuously in legato playing. In such a melody as that with which we illustrated the importance of dynamic shading (in Chapter 1), it is of considerable value to continue to feel, for the duration of a given note, the intensity with which that note was struck. You know, from the mental image of the melody that you have formed, that the next note must be a certain degree louder or softer than the one you are now playing. Feeling in your finger tip the intensity of this present note, you have a guide to the intensity of the next. The whole dynamic succession that well-played melody must present, if conceived in terms of the sensations of the playing act itself, is more likely to come off successfully when you are thus guided than if you have to "calculate" the attack for each note anew. To relax (as many advocate) the pressure of your stroke as soon as the key reaches its bed is to lose this guidance. To press the keys after they are struck has of course no effect whatever on their tone. But if such pressure can help to insure the right intensity for the *next* tone, the physical waste of energy (which is obvious) may after all amount to a high economy of expression.

The word *staccato* means "detached." It is thus the opposite of legato. This implies that staccato notes are short; and it is true that the duration of their sound is shorter than the exact time length indicated in their notation. How much shorter, however, can be determined only by musical common sense.

Physically, the fact of staccato is produced by releasing the key soon after the note is struck. Only in successions of staccato notes does this release present any serious difficulty; but in rapid successions of staccato notes the fingers are confronted with their most difficult problem. Two conditions arise which demand different modes of staccato attack: that of the same note repeated, and that of different notes in succession. The second is the more frequent condition, and demands a more severe effort. We shall study this problem first.

Two types of staccato stroke are needed in fast passages: one executed wholly by the fingers, the other by a combined motion of finger and wrist. Pure finger staccato is necessary in very rapid passages, since the hand is too heavy to move up and down at such a rate. The stroke, in finger staccato, is made by the same downward impulse of the finger as in legato; but that impulse must be instantly followed by the lifting of the finger, and it is this lifting—not the down-stroke—which is difficult.[5] To see the difficulty, play a fairly rapid scale, legato. Each finger remains on its key for a very short time, but you will hardly feel the lifting effort. Now, without the aid of any other than the finger muscles, try to play the scale at the same speed, staccato. To shorten the already short time between stroke and lift requires a considerable effort; and you will soon begin to feel rather acute pain in the upper side of your forearm, for it is here that the extensor muscles for the fingers are located.

The value of staccato practice should be evident. For if the finger is prepared for its stroke, the stroke itself is not hard; and we have just seen that a great part of the necessary preparation is made precisely by those finger impulses which are conspicuously *the* problem in finger staccato. But again, it is not necessary to play the notes of an exercise in finger staccato with any great speed. It is much easier both to see and to feel (as a kind of discomfort in the hand) the errors of behavior when one is playing slowly than when one is trying for speed; and it is all but impossible to correct them fully if the mind is filled with the excitement of speed.

In wrist staccato, the greater part of the effort is made by a throwing of the hand from the wrist, similar to the throwing of the finger from the knuckle in finger strokes. The striking finger, however, must be somewhat more contracted than the others, and this protrusion is a finger act. Thus the *stroke,* in wrist staccato, is a combined action of finger and wrist; but the with-

---

[5] There are two reasons why this is so. In order to follow a downward impulse by an upward, the innervation of the flexor muscle must cease completely, almost as soon as it is begun—else the upward movement will be retarded. Moreover, the extensor muscles (the lifters) are small and weak, compared to the flexors. Their ordinary task is merely to "let go," and we almost never make any effort, except that of playing, which taxes the extensor muscles.

drawal is made almost wholly from the wrist. The muscles which lift the hand at the wrist are of approximately the same strength as those which depress the hand. Wrist staccato is thus less acutely fatiguing than finger staccato. It is of the utmost importance, however, that the elbow, during this stroke, be free of tension. For just as finger strokes are less tiring with a relaxed than with a tensed wrist, so wrist strokes are easier with a relaxed than with a tensed elbow.[6] There is of necessity a *reaction* to the *action* of your stroke—a force that travels backward through the finger and is absorbed into the hand, arm, and perhaps into the body. Tensed muscles increase the area over which the force of reaction is distributed; relaxed muscles help to limit both this area and the effort that enlarges the area.

Two strokes on the same key, and even three or four, can be given in rapid succession by the same finger. The action is difficult to describe, but not to perform. Very slight strokes of the

---

[6] A downward thrust of the hand will generally be attended, as the fingers strike, by a slight upward motion of the wrist. This upward motion is an absorption of the *re*action to the delivered force. (Action and reaction are equal and opposite in direction.) If the elbow is relaxed, the downward pull of the weight of the arm helps to absorb the energy of reaction. But if it is tensed, the reaction travels through the whole arm into the shoulder and so into the body, where it can be distributed over a larger mass. This fact is hard to illustrate, but it can probably be seen in this experiment:

Raise the hand and arm as for a wrist staccato stroke. *Tense the elbow only.* Maintaining this tension, move the hand rapidly up and down, as if for successive strokes, but without striking anything. You will feel a distinct effort of resistance in your shoulder; and even your chair may shake with the energy transmitted from your moving hand, through your rigid arm and tensing shoulder, into your body.

Now, with the same conditions of hand and elbow, strike something—the key or the table. The absorption by your body is less because the direct *action* of your effort is absorbed by the object you struck, while you are now absorbing only the *reaction*. Yet, with a stiff elbow, your shoulder has to exert an effort.

Now relax your elbow and make the same strokes. Unless they are pretty heavy, the relaxed arm will absorb the reaction without perceptible effort at the shoulder. "Dead weight" is working for you.

Up to a certain degree, the saving of effort with a loose elbow is significant. If greater energy is needed for the strokes themselves, greater absorption of the reaction must be provided, and this exists in the shoulder and the body. But to use it needlessly is waste.

hand from the wrist are possible in rapid succession—too slight, however, for any sizable tone. A combination of finger and hand action is therefore necessary in most cases. To execute

forte, strike with the finger, from a rather low wrist, elevating the wrist slightly as you strike. This elevation contributes also to your finger's energy. The second note is made by the same actions, but from the higher level reached by the wrist during the first stroke. The final stroke, if we assume that it is to be more forceful, will be made by a proportionately greater elevation of the wrist, and a proportional stiffening. The two lighter strokes can be very fast; but you will see that the speed must decrease with the number of strokes, and with their force. A single light stroke, followed by a heavy, can be made with great speed; but if the whole mass of the hand has to move both upward and downward, it is obvious that more time will be required than for finger action alone, and the larger apparatus will soon be tired out.

Such a figure as

piano, especially if continued, demands another treatment. Only finger strokes, with a minimum of motion in wrist or hand, are available; and since a single finger cannot rise, after a stroke, in time to repeat its effort at the speed we are here considering, an adjacent finger—normally that which lies toward the heavier (thumb) side of the hand—will take the next note. The 5th finger is little adapted to such shifts, but 321, or 4321 (according to the number of notes to be played, and their rhythm) can easily be trained to the motion. Because the thumb passes naturally under the hand, and the hand over the thumb, this is the best finger with which to end the pattern, since either 4th or 3rd can now easily be poised to attack the same note. Speed is attainable with this pattern, since any finger, after its stroke, has ample time to resume its striking position. But that removal is not here a lifting, but instead a sliding off the key, by contracting the finger after the stroke—really, a continuation of the stroke itself. The lift follows the "scratch." Because the lift is delayed, this scratch is not a proper stroke in finger staccato, except for a single note.

### Octaves, Double Notes, Chords

All that is needed for a single octave stroke is a firm arch between the thumb and the striking finger. The force exerted by thumb and finger may be equal or unequal, according to the requirement of the musical idea. Very often, the higher note needs to be louder than the lower, else dull tone will result. To exert this effort, however, requires strength rather than any peculiar skill.

Octave passages, however, demand a particular attack. There are several varieties of attack, of which the following are probably the most important:

(1) The hand may be thrown from the wrist, essentially as in wrist staccato. The elbow must not be tensed. The downward thrust of the hand should slightly elevate the wrist; and with a stiff elbow this elevation is prevented. But do not allow the relaxation of wrist and elbow to weaken the arch of thumb and finger. This stroke is suitable for repeated notes and for passages requiring considerable speed. The elevation of the hand for each stroke need be but slight, since the weight of the hand, falling through even a narrow arc, will give enough tone. When greater power is needed, however, a different stroke will be required.

(2) This may be a stroke from the elbow, with the wrist tensed proportionately to the required force. The weight of forearm and hand together being greater than that of the hand alone, this stroke can attain less speed than (1). Note also that a vertical stroke with the forearm is impossible if the upper arm is much extended outward from the body. The elbow has only

a simple hinge joint, which compels the forearm to move in one plane only with respect to the upper arm. Vertical motion of the hand with the upper arm extended is produced from the shoulder, which has a "universal" joint. In proportion as you extend the upper arm to reach the ends of the keyboard, strokes of the arm will become whole-arm strokes, made from the shoulder. It follows that forearm strokes are available only for passages of rather narrow compass. Those in the middle region of the reach of each arm are the easiest; those at the extremes can be executed by the forearm stroke only if you lean toward that region far enough to make vertical motion of the forearm possible.[7]

(3) The whole-arm stroke is needed when the upper arm must be extended from the body, and when still greater power is needed than the forearm stroke can give. With great force demanded, the wrist will be tensed, and the elbow will rise as the hand descends, the extent of the rise depending on the force of the stroke. Obviously, this stroke is not adapted for speed. But note that if the wrist is relaxed, the motion of the whole arm, from the shoulder, may to a considerable extent be substituted for the motion of the forearm from the elbow. This substitution is gradual and often imperceptible.

The problem of passages in double notes (thirds, sixths, and so on) is, first, to be sure that both notes strike simultaneously,

---

[7] In passages such as the reiterated octave figure in the A-flat *Polonaise* of Chopin, the oscillating arm stroke described under (2) is most useful. Within the narrow compass of this figure, and in its rather low register, the hand can attack most naturally with the elbow somewhat protruded from the body, and with very little lateral motion of the hand. The wrist may remain quite stiff (increasing its tension as the crescendo grows), and the whole elevation necessary for the hand may thus be obtained by a very slight rotary motion of the arm at the shoulder joint. The process is hard to describe, and hard to "catch on to"; but once grasped, it is easy to execute, even at very considerable speed. It is not a good stroke, however, for extended scales or erratically spaced intervals; for the forearm must be somewhat protruded before the leverage from the shoulder can operate. Also, with a stiff wrist, the measurement of the intervals must be made at the shoulder, where a very slight muscular contraction produces a great deal of lateral motion in the hand. Accuracy is thus difficult, except in passages like that under discussion.

and then to find a suitable fingering for the passage. Satisfactory fingerings are very often indicated in modern editions, but the problem of the finger strokes can be solved only by rigorous attention.

Chords might seem to require even more study, since more fingers must strike simultaneously. But the finger problem is here ordinarily much easier, for the whole hand, shaped to strike the chord, can be made into a single unit, with as many "prongs" (fingers) as there are notes, and all arched into one unyielding agent. Seldom, however, will the forces exerted by the several fingers be equal. One of the notes of the chord will probably be a melody note, or at any rate, a note of especial harmonic significance, and therefore one that must be brought out more prominently than the others. Greater weight must therefore be applied to this one finger. Whether this is done by protruding this finger slightly beyond the others, or by concentrating greater weight in this region of the hand, is a question difficult to answer. In either case, the marcato note will doubtless sound an instant before the lighter notes—for even if the fingers strike the keys simultaneously, the key struck with the greater energy will descend more rapidly—but the discrepancy will hardly be perceptible. Whether or not the wrist is relaxed after, or even during, the stroke is of import only in so far as the manner of the attack seems to the player appropriate to the musical sense he is trying to convey. Stiffness, it is true, will often yield harsh tone— because it prevents that fine dynamic discrimination which is essential to beautiful tone. But what produces the beautiful tone is neither the relaxation nor the stiffness, but the execution— through appropriate dynamic intensities—of a musical purpose appropriate to the composer's intention.

# INDEX

## A

Action, pianoforte:
  Diagrams of, 2, 3
  Behavior of, 4f
"Active" notes, 12
Agogic accent, 13
Appoggiatura, long, 42

## B

Beethoven, Ludwig van, Sonatas:
  Op. 2, No. 1, 25f
  Op. 2, No. 2, 39
  Op. 2, No. 3, 40
  Op. 7, 40f
  Op. 10, No. 1, 41
  Op. 10, No. 2, 41
  Op. 10, No. 3, 41f
  Op. 13 (Pathétique), 48f
  Op. 14, No. 1, 59
  Op. 14, No. 2, 59
  Op. 22, 60
  Op. 26, 60f
  Op. 27, No. 1, 75
  Op. 27, No. 2 (Moonlight), 76f
  Op. 28, 79f
  Op. 31, No. 2, 87f
  Op. 31, No. 3, 92f
  Op. 49, Nos. 1 and 2, 94
  Op. 53 (Waldstein), 28, 94f
  Op. 54, 100, 104

  Op. 57 (Appassionata), 28, 100f
  Op. 78, 109
  Op. 79, 110
  Op. 81a, 110f
  Op. 90, 112f
  Op. 101, 118f
Brahms, Johannes:
  Ballades:
    Op. 10, No. 1 (Edward), 267f
    Op. 10, No. 2, 269
    Op. 10, No. 3, 270
    Op. 10, No. 4, 271f
    Op. 118, No. 3, 308f
  Capriccios:
    Op. 76, No. 1 (F-sharp minor), 286
    Op. 76, No. 2 (B minor), 287f
    Op. 76, No. 5 (C-sharp minor), 290f
    Op. 76, No. 8 (C major), 293
    Op. 116, No. 1 (D minor), 297f
    Op. 116, No. 3 (G minor), 299
    Op. 116, No. 7 (D minor), 302f
  Intermezzos:
    Op. 76, No. 3 (A-flat major), 289
    Op. 76, No. 4 (B-flat major), 290
    Op. 76, No. 6 (A major), 292

367